SMALL WARS

THEIR PRINCIPLES AND PRACTICE

COLONEL C. E. CALLWELL

THIRD EDITION

Introduction to the Bison Books Edition
by Douglas Porch

University of Nebraska Press
Lincoln and London

⊝ The paper in this book meets the minimum requirements
of American National Standard for Information Sciences—
Permanence of Paper for Printed Library Mateials,
ANSI Z39.48-1984.

First Bison Books printing: 1996

Library of Congress Cataloging-in-Publication Data
Callwell, C. E. (Charles Edward), Sir, 1859–1928.
Small wars: their principles and practice / by Colonel C. E.
Callwell; introduction to the Bison Books edition by Douglas
Porch.—3rd ed.
p.   cm.
Originally published: 3rd ed. London: H.M.S.O., 1906. With
new introd.
Includes index.
ISBN 0-8032-6366-X (alk. paper)
1. Low intensity conflicts (Military science)   2. Tactics.
3. Military history, Modern—19th century.   I. Title.
U240.C32   1996
355.02—dc20
95-25837   CIP

Originally published in 1896. Third edition published in 1906
by His Majesty's Stationery Office, London.

INTRODUCTION TO THE BISON BOOKS EDITION

DOUGLAS PORCH

In its day, Major General Sir Charles Edward Callwell's *Small Wars* came to be regarded as a minor classic of military writing. Callwell was one of those colonial soldiers who knew instinctively what modern historians by dint of diligent research took some time to conclude—that trade did not follow the flag, that scant interest in the commercial exploitation or political advantages of imperial expansion existed in Europe. Imperialism moved forward, not as the result of commercial or political pressure from London, Paris, Berlin, St. Petersburg, or even Washington, but mainly because men on the periphery, many of whom were soldiers, pressed to enlarge the boundaries of empire, often without orders, even against orders. Imperialism, therefore, was essentially a military phenomenon. To grasp its dynamic, one must understand the central component of imperial expansion—imperial warfare. And no author in his century commanded a more sweeping knowledge of that subject, or was more able to distill and compress information from such a staggering variety of campaigns, than C. E. Callwell.

Callwell's work retains its vitality and usefulness in our own era. Nowhere else will the historian or military specialist discover an analysis of what today would be called "low-intensity conflict" that reposes on such a command of irregular warfare experiences ranging from Hoche's suppression of the Vendée revolt during the French Revolution, to the British wars against semi-organized armies of Marathas and Sikhs in mid–nineteenth century India, to the Boer War of 1899–1902.

Callwell's background was a common one for British imperial officers of his era. Of Anglo-Irish extraction, schooled at Haileybury, which specialized in educating sons of colonial soldiers and civil servants, and the Royal Military College, he was commissioned into the Royal Artillery in 1878. He fought in the Afghan War of 1880, and the first Boer War the following year. After passing through the Staff College in 1886, he served five years in the intelligence branch of the War Office. It may have been in these years that Callwell began collecting his notes for *Small Wars,* the first edition of which appeared in 1896. Callwell served with Greek forces in the Turko-Greek War of 1897, and joined the staff of Sir Redvers Buller on the outbreak of the South African War in 1899, the year in which a second edition of *Small Wars* appeared. He fought in several of the major actions of that war, including the relief of Ladysmith, and in 1901–2 commanded a mobile column against Boer guerrillas. Promoted to colonel in 1904, Callwell published two years later a third edition of *Small Wars* that incorporated the experiences of the South African War. Callwell retired in 1909, but was recalled on the outbreak of the Great War, promoted to major general, and made Director of Military Operations at the War Office, in which position he attempted to dissuade Churchill from undertaking an assault on the Gallipoli peninsula.[1] He occupied this post until 1916, after which he was appointed to various Allied liaison missions. After the war, he continued his writing career with a book on the Dardanelles campaign and a life of Field-Marshal Sir Henry Wilson.

An indication of how much the world of *Small Wars* was altered by the Great War is apparent in the 1929 edition of the *Encyclopedia Britannica,* published in the year following Callwell's death. Although General Callwell had contributed articles to the *Britannica,* the author chosen for the entry on "Guerrilla Warfare" was not Callwell, but T. E. Lawrence. In a mere four pages, the hero of the "Arab Revolt" offered a vision of insurgency that appeared to consign the 559 pages of Callwell's text to obsolescence. Lawrence wrote: "Here is the thesis: granted mobility, security (in the form of denying targets to the enemy), time, and doctrine (the idea to convert every subject to friendliness), victory will rest with the insurgents, for the algebraical factors are in the end decisive, and against them the perfections of means and spirit struggle quite in vain."[2]

This suggests that *Small Wars* is distinctly a period piece, artifact of an era for which few monuments remain. But to draw such conclusions in haste would only offer the opportunity to repent at leisure. Certainly, Callwell, even more than Sun Tzu and Clausewitz, was a man of his time. Perhaps it is more useful to compare Callwell to two of his illustrious contemporaries, both theorists of naval warfare—A. T. Mahan and Julien Corbett. Like Mahan and Corbett, Callwell was writing about his world, but from an optic that transcends the narrow boundaries of a historical epoch. Callwell is still read because he possessed a profound knowledge of the unconventional conflict of his day, he offered interesting ways of thinking about that conflict, and, finally, because the conditions in which "small wars" proliferate are multiplying, not decreasing. In other words, although Callwell writes about the past, he also presents, some argue, a vision of future combat.

Although *Small Wars* reflects the era in which Callwell wrote, the High Renaissance of imperialism, it is more than a quaint anachronism. By the end of the nineteenth century, the advantage in "small wars," so long as the commander followed Callwell's advice, had swung definitively in the invader's favor. Yet, it had not always been so, as Callwell was well aware. From its earliest period, imperial warfare was considered a hazardous and difficult enterprise. Although, in the Western Hemisphere, Europeans advanced inland almost from the beginning, their conquest was facilitated as much, if not more, by an *avant garde* of disease as by military superiority *per se*. In the East and in Africa, Europeans lacked the numbers, the technology, or the incentive to advance inland. They remained sea-bound, clutching a tenuous lifeline to the homeland, content to export spices, gold, and slaves from coastal "factories."

Three things caused this to change over the course of the nineteenth century: political instability in Asia and Africa, European rivalries played out in the wider world, and officers and officials driven by patriotism and personal ambition, eager to claim vast stretches of territory for the Fatherland. As a result, imperial soldiers faced operational challenges of the sort that had confronted Cortés from the moment he had fired his boats at Veracruz—how was a relative handful of Europeans with limited technological means to traverse an inaccessible country, conquer a numerically superior enemy, and pacify a new empire? While these challenges remained difficult, over time European soldiers mastered them to the point that imperial conquest came to be regarded as hardly more than a technical problem to be solved. *Small Wars* is simply the best known of a number of works, like French Lieutenant Colonel A. Ditte's *Observations sur les guerres dans les colonies,* and any number of smaller studies of individual colonial campaigns that could adopt an essentially prescriptive approach to colonial warfare.

What had happened? As in all warfare, European expansion had kindled a competition between European and indigenous forces, a process in which each attempted to respond to the challenges of new foes and conditions, a competition which, over the course of the nineteenth century, the Europeans clearly won. This had not been an automatic process, however, but involved much trial and error. One value of *Small Wars* as a historical document is that Callwell chronicles that process, one which gradually accelerated as the nineteenth century drew to a close. However, to understand why *Small Wars* was considered such an important document in its own day, and why it remains relevant in today's world, one must ask three questions: First, what were the constraints—political, technological and organizational—that shaped the adaptive response of Europeans in the imperial context? Next, as war is an interactive process, European adaptation was conditioned in part by the native response to these invasions. Therefore, one must also ask: why, in most cases, did indigenous societies fail to organize a successful resistance? Finally, what were the forces unleashed by the Great War that appeared to consign *Small Wars* to oblivion in the twentieth century?

A first point one must realize about *Small Wars* is that Callwell was writing during a period in which imperial expansion met indifference, even hostility, at home. The late nineteenth century may have been the High Renaissance of imperialism, but as a movement, imperialism moved forward on a very narrow base of popular support. The benefits of distant conquests were not altogether apparent to Europeans. The brutality of colonial wars that could be exploited by the opposition, the political risks of military reversal in far-flung wars, and the demands of home defense combined to make European politicians in the nineteenth century reluctant to commit forces to expensive imperial expeditions. Popular support might be mobilized for a significant imperial expedition if a convincing case could be made that national interests were clearly at stake, and the expedition could deliver quick, decisive results. Otherwise, colonies could be conquered and policed only if the magnitude of the investment was kept low.

Nowhere in *Small Wars* does Callwell acknowledge that the marginal popularity of imperial warfare placed constraints on commanders. However, the requirement to maintain garrisons for home defense, and the reluctance of the imperial powers to commit their sons to wars of seemingly marginal national interest, meant that up to two-thirds of French and British expeditions were composed of troops recruited in the colonies. Specialized European units like the Foreign Legion or marines were also raised for colonial service.[3] Modern experience suggests that little has changed in this regard. The political leader must gain a quick, decisive victory in these conflicts as did the United States in Haiti, Grenada, and Panama. A second tactic is to keep the level of magnitude low enough, such as British intervention in Northern Ireland or United States counterinsurgency efforts in Latin America, so it will not impinge on the public consciousness. A third is to hire client armies or United Nations contingents. Leaders who commit large numbers of troops but who are unable to achieve quick, decisive results condemn themselves to an agony similar to that of the United States in Vietnam.

Another constraint on imperial conquest was technology. At first glance, this seems contradictory as technology should have supplied the invaders with a decisive advantage, especially with the introduction of breach loading rifles, machine guns, and light artillery in the second half of the nineteenth century. But although Hillaire Belloc could write, "Whatever happens we have got / The Maxim gun and they have not," truth was that firepower gave Europeans an important, but by no means decisive, advantage, as Callwell was well aware. The native resistance could also acquire modern weapons, sometimes through "gifts" from European rivals, which might give them fire superiority, as the Ethiopians enjoyed at Adowa in 1896 and the Boers did in the early phase of the South African War. Machine guns did give Europeans firepower advantages in defensive situations, especially when the enemy charged with reckless abandon, as in the Matabele War of 1893. But early versions were so unreliable that, for instance, Custer left his Gatling behind when he departed for the Little Big Horn in 1876. Maxims, which began to appear in the 1890s, were more reliable but never prominent items in the inventories of European expedition—Kitchener had only six at Omdurman. Artillery was useful to attack forts, walled villages, or defensive enclosures. But the remoteness of imperial battlefields could make artillery a liability. An artilleryman, Callwell argued that his arm was of only marginal use in colonial warfare—for instance, artillery employed in a European manner of an opening barrage only forfeited surprise. A clever enemy could negate the European technological advantage by dispersal, working around the flanks as did the Zulus at Isandlwhana, or by resorting to guerrilla warfare.

Historians looking for causes of the awful carnage of World War I may fault Callwell for displaying in full measure the fatal prejudice of the soldiers of his era when he argued that technology is never decisive. Rather, success in battle relied on the superior discipline, tactics, and morale of European troops. When these were absent, as with the Italians at Adowa, firepower alone might not save them. No doubt, those who ignored the effects of technology desperately underestimated the importance of firepower in 1914. On the other hand, Callwell simply foreshadowed the contemporary debate between proponents of technological solutions, and those who, like Callwell, argue that, in low-intensity conflict especially, technology is no substitute for strategy; that the insurgent will always evolve an operational or tactical counter to a technological advantage.

In the 1860s and 1870s, Europeans mastered the final constraint when organizational ability allied with technology combined to give them a potentially decisive advantage. The turning point came, perhaps, with the Abyssinian expedition of 1868, when the British imported a complete railway to support the advance into the interior. However, it was General Sir Garnet Wolseley who probably first realized the marriage of technology and organization during the Ashanti campaign of 1873–74. Successful commanders like American General George Crook in the Sierra Madre campaign against Geronimo in 1883, or French General Alfred Dodds in Dahomey in 1894, took care to imitate Wolseley. They reduced the size of the expedition to a minimum, took care to provide roads, way stations, porterage, pack animals, tinned food, potable water and quinine. From then on, battle became almost incidental to the success of a campaign.

In Callwell's day, as in our own, technology and organization were only adjuncts to, not substitutes for, inventive operational solutions. Callwell believed that an ability to adapt to terrain and climate, to match the enemy in mobility and inventiveness, to collect intelligence were all ingredients which helped to determine success or failure in imperial warfare. But above all, the nature of a war was determined, as far as it lay within the power of the counterinsurgent force to dictate the nature of the war, by what the commander wished to achieve.

It requires only a modest stretching of credulity to call Callwell the Clausewitz of colonial warfare, for he applies a rational Clausewitzian paradigm: set clear goals, and do a thorough assessment of the enemy's and your own capabilities before devising strategies to achieve those goals. Callwell identified three classes of campaigns—those of conquest and annexation; those to suppress insurrection; and, finally, those devised to wipe out an insult—although he was careful to note that these categories were not watertight. In Callwell's view, it was especially important that the goals of a campaign be clear, and the operational and tactical capabilities of the invaders must be exceptional. This was because, while tactics favored the European, strategy favored the resistance. By controlling the pace of the war, refusing battle, drawing the invader deep into hostile country where he became overextended and vulnerable, an intelligent enemy might negate European technological, operational, and tactical superiority. The goal of the invader, therefore, must be to achieve the collapse of enemy resistance as quickly as possible.

A strategy that promised quick, decisive victory was not always obvious. Callwell invoked Wolseley who counseled the commander to "seize what the enemy prizes most." "From the days of Clive down to the present time," insisted Callwell, "victory has been achieved by vigor and dash rather than by force of numbers." One advantage of the "one blow" approach was that it was favored by governments over more patient strategies which prolonged a conflict. Still, Callwell recognized that decisive results might be made difficult by the remoteness of the battlefield, the lack of "capital" or critical objective which will cause the enemy to give up, or by a clever enemy like Abd el-Kader in Algeria, Shamil in the Caucasus, Samori in West Africa, or the Boer commanders who resorted to guerrilla warfare. Callwell's preference clearly lay with small expeditions of mounted men: "The most brilliant exploits," he wrote, "were carried out by mounted troops along. . . .

Savages, Asiatics and adversaries of that character have a great dread of the mounted man." By "mounted men," he meant mounted infantry rather than classic cavalry, a trend accelerated by warfare in the colonies. Yet he recognized that this was not invariably a formula for success. The size of the objective might require large forces and even larger logistical efforts—for instance, it was far easier for Wolseley to punish the Ashanti by burning their "capital" as a prelude to strategic withdrawal, than for the Russians to conquer the Caucasus or the French to extend their control over Tonkin against a conventional Chinese army and its local allies. The dilemma for colonial commanders was to disembark with a force with sufficient mobility and firepower to protect itself from the fate of Jean Danjou, surrounded with his Foreign Legionnaires and forced to fight to the death at the Mexican village of Camaron (Camerone) in 1863, Custer at the Little Big Horn, Chelmsford at Isandlwhana, or Hicks Pasha on the Nile in 1883. On the other hand, the force must not become so large that it might collapse under the weight of its own logistics (as nearly did the 1868 British expedition to Abyssinia and the French invasion of Madagascar in 1895) or simply be stung to fury by more mobile indigenous forces, as were early French expeditions in Algeria. All of these observations strike home with students of the French wars in Indochina and Algeria, and the American war in Vietnam.

Because decisive victory—that is, a single battle or quick series of battles which brings about the total surrender of the enemy—is always difficult to deliver in any theater, especially in a colonial environment, even the best commanders fell back on attrition warfare to bring the enemy to heel. The problem was that an attack on the indigenous economic base made imperial expansion a very destructive process. To modern eyes, Callwell does not show himself at his best on this point. While he concedes that Hoche achieved some success by adopting a conciliatory attitude toward the Vendée insurgents of the French Revolution, he believed forbearance a gesture wasted on "uncivilized races [who] attribute leniency to timidity. Fanatics and savages must be thoroughly brought to book and cowed or they will rise again." Unfortunately, arrogance and racism were attitudes typical of his era as they are too common in our own. French General Thomas Bugeaud raised the *razzia* or raid to a strategic concept in Algeria in the 1840s, the Russians systematically destroyed the Caucasus and evicted its inhabitants to "pacify" it, and Sherman believed that Amerindian troubles would cease only with "the ringleaders . . . hung, their ponies killed, and such destruction of their property as will make them very poor."[4] Kitchener followed similar policies against Boer insurgents, as did the Germans against the Herrero rebellion in Southwest Africa.

That said, however, Callwell, like Bugeaud, recognized that colonial commanders forced into "committing havoc which the laws of regular warfare do not sanction" ran the risk of making the reconciliation of the conquered peoples with the imperium more difficult. A second drawback of harsh measures was that their application "shocks humanitarians." Although commanders in Callwell's day did not have to deal with televised images of the battlefield transmitted home, plenty of journalists and war protesters were prepared to recount the brutality of colonial warfare, which made small wars a periodic source of criticism and even scandal in Europe and America during the decades prior to World War I. For this reason, European adaptive response was increasingly shaped by attitudes at home as much as, if not more than, by what went on in the colonies. Although Callwell does not mention them, the *tâche d'huile* or "oil spot" methods of pacification developed by French generals Gallieni and Lyautey in Tonkin, Madagascar, and Morocco, which combined the carrots of trade and security with the stick of military retaliation, aimed primarily to convince French people that French imperialism advanced by "peaceful penetration" rather than by brute force.[5]

The second question, to which *Small Wars* offers only a partial reply, is: why was the indigenous response to European invasion generally so inadequate? The answer is that few of the indigenous societies were cohesive enough to survive a military *débâcle*. Divided by geography, by rivalries of caste, tribe, clan, or family, their bonds of common culture weak, they found it difficult to devise a unified response based on a shared sense of self-interest. Callwell does admonish commanders to understand the "nature of the enemy." He recognized that resistance to the European advance was seldom absolute, that "irregular armies always count many waverers . . . mere lookers-on." The way to deal with this, Callwell opines with substantial justification, is a "vigorous offensive [which] has the effect of keeping at home those who hesitate to take up arms and thereby diminishing the fighting strength of the enemy."

Callwell was correct, at least up to a point. A primary weakness of *Small Wars* as a useful contemporary text is its over-reliance on operational solutions to political problems, unfortunately a failing characteristic both of the French experience in Indochina and Algeria, and that of the United States in Vietnam. Indigenous societies were viewed by Callwell not as complex organizations, but as "inferior races" destined to be smashed into submission. Callwell should—indeed, he must—have known better, both from scholarship and practical experience. Though he devotes several pages to the importance of intelligence in colonial campaigns, he views it exclusively as an operational tool, rather than as a way to lend a political dimension to strategy. Despite his almost encyclopedic knowledge of nineteenth-century colonial campaigns, Callwell nowhere acknowledges that clever commanders with a fine sense of politics, like Wellesley in India or Lyautey in Morocco, were able to exploit these differences to fragment the opposition. Campaigns were frequently preceded, and operational victories followed, by agents who would bribe, suborn, or coopt native elites into acceptance of the imperial mandate. In North Africa, the French developed the "Arab bureau," later renamed the "intelligence service," whose officers became experts in local tribal poli-

tics, and who operated on the principle of "divide and rule."
Native states were hard-pressed to resist European en-
croachment. Those that attempted to modernize to meet
the European challenge like the Sikhs, Egyptians, or Mo-
roccans, discovered that the process stimulated social and
political disintegration, pushed the rulers into debt and
drove them into the arms of the very Europeans they were
trying to resist. This aroused the discontent of tradition-
alist and nationalist elements. In less centralized societies, minor chiefs with private access to arms merchants
challenged central authority. Furthermore, indigenous
rulers seldom succeeded in altering a semifeudal social
structure to accommodate a modern army. These armies,
though superficially modernized, lacked a coherent officer
corps and administrative structure to support them. In
most cases, indigenous forces simply incorporated modern weapons into familiar tactical systems, rather than
evolve methods that allowed them to be used to advantage. Many of these armies were designed for raiding
rather than for total war, a concept in itself alien to most
indigenous societies. The prospect of fighting a series of
bloody battles against a relentless European invader
caused empires to shatter, subject groups to rebel, and
isolated villages or tribes to make their own peace with
the invader.

Within a decade of the publication of its final edition,
events made *Small Wars* seem obsolete, because, as T. E.
Lawrence believed, advantage had shifted irrevocably to
the insurgency. As far as this was true, it was because in
large measure European success in Callwell's era contained
the seeds of its ultimate demise, for at least three reasons.
In the pre-1914 era, native resistance usually failed because it lacked a common ideology or sense of self-interest. This would change as imperialism produced from
within its own ranks a leadership capable of articulating
a coherent vision for resistance. Nationalism, Marxism,
or Islam supplied ideologies that rationalized and focused
discontent. Theorists of revolution, Mao Tse-tung prominent among them, supplied blueprints that showed indig-

enous societies how to anchor their resistance in a social organization able to resist the pressures of European operational methods of the sort laid out by Callwell.

Second, Western societies were poorly placed to respond to these changes. Imperialism had never been popular in Britain and America in any case. Even in France and Germany, it had been a minority movement. With confidence in Western values undermined by the destructive bloodletting of World War I, Britain, Holland, and the United States, and to a lesser extent France and Portugal, began to distance themselves from empires that seemed ever more marginal to their economic or geopolitical interests, but increasingly dangerous to the moral integrity of Western nations.

Finally, after the experience of two World Wars, together with a Cold War stalemate in Europe, most Western armies viewed small wars as missions to be avoided. Most proved unwilling to alter force structure designed for conventional conflict in Europe to face the challenges of unconventional warfare in distant lands. None of these factors made an indigenous resistance unbeatable. It simply meant that small wars remained very much a minority interest in military establishments.

More's the pity, because Callwell might have been read with profit by those tasked with confronting post–World War II insurgency movements in Greece, the Philippines, Malaya, Indochina/Vietnam, Algeria, and Latin America. Nor did Callwell's usefulness decline with the end of the Cold War—some modern military analysts argue that the dominance of Western technology, combined with breakdown of the state in many of those same areas of the world where Callwell's soldiers campaigned, will make "small wars" the weapon of choice for those who, in the future, wish to challenge the status quo.

In these conditions, Callwell offers a reminder that insurgency movements are neither a modern phenomenon, nor, T. E. Lawrence and Mao to the contrary, are they unbeatable. Commanders in Callwell's time, like those in our own day, must realize that every insurgency assumes a different complexion given the circumstances—political, ideological, cultural, and geographic—which shape it. It remains to the commanders to define what they wish to achieve, to determine "what the enemy prizes most," and to remember that technological superiority in no way relieves them of the obligation to craft a viable strategy based, at least in part, on a range of operational methods documented by Callwell.

NOTES

1. Winston Churchill, *The World Crisis, 1911–1914* (London: Thornton Butterworth Ltd., 1923), 488. One of the unfortunate consequences of Callwell's pointing out to Churchill that sixty-thousand troops would be needed to force the straits, was that the First Lord attempted the operation with the navy alone, which alerted the Turks that landings were probable.

2. T. E. Lawrence, "Guerrilla Warfare," *Encyclopedia Britannica*, (London, 1929), 953.

3. Because the recruitment, training, discipline, and morale, not to mention the loyalty, of indigenous forces were a constant preoccupation of colonial soldiers, it is somewhat remarkable that Callwell fails to discuss their strengths and weaknesses. He simply treats indigenous forces as interchangeable parts of a colonial juggernaut. On this subject, see Douglas Porch, *The French Foreign Legion: A Complete History of the Legendary Fighting Force* (New York: Harper Collins, 1991).

4. Robert Utley, *Frontier Regulars: The United States Army and the Indian* (New York: Macmillan, 1973), 144.

5. Douglas Porch, *The Conquest of Morocco* (New York: Knopf, 1982), 184.

PREFACE TO THE SECOND EDITION.

In preparing this new edition for the press, advantage has been taken of experiences gained in campaigns which have taken place since the book was originally compiled. These include the French advance to Antananarivo and their later operations in Madagascar, the guerilla warfare in Cuba previous to the American intervention, the suppression of the rebellions in Rhodesia, the operations beyond the Panjab frontier in 1897–98, the re-conquest of the Sudan, the operations of the United States troops against the Filipinos, and many minor campaigns in East and West Africa.

Some of the later chapters have been re-arranged and in part re-written, and new chapters have been added on hill warfare and bush warfare. Useful hints have been obtained from the notes which Lieut.-Colonel Septans, French Marine Infantry, has incorporated in his translation of the first edition. An index has been added.

My acknowledgments are due to the many officers who have afforded valuable information, and who have aided in revising the proofs.

CHAS. E. CALLWELL,
Major, R.A.

July, 1899.

PREFACE TO THE THIRD EDITION, 1906.

THIS book has now been revised and brought up to date by the author, Colonel C. E. Callwell. It is recommended to officer as a valuable contribution on the subject of the conduct of small wars. It is full of useful facts and information on all the details which must be considered in the management of those minor expeditions in which the British Army is so frequently engaged. But it is not to be regarded as laying down inflexible rules for guidance, or as an expression of official opinion on the subjects of which it treats.

N. G. LYTTELTON,
Chief of the General Staff.

TABLE OF CONTENTS

CHAPTER I.

INTRODUCTION.

CHAPTER II.

CAUSES OF SMALL WARS AS AFFECTING THEIR CONDITIONS. THE VARIOUS KINDS OF ADVERSARIES MET WITH.

CHAPTER III.

THE OBJECTIVE IN SMALL WARS.

CHAPTER IV.

DIFFICULTIES UNDER WHICH THE REGULAR FORCES LABOUR AS REGARDS INTELLIGENCE. THE ADVANTAGE IS USUALLY ENJOYED BY THE ENEMY IN THIS RESPECT, BUT THIS CIRCUMSTANCE CAN SOMETIMES BE TURNED TO ACCOUNT.

CHAPTER V.

THE INFLUENCE OF THE QUESTION OF SUPPLY UPON SMALL WARS AND THE EXTENT TO WHICH IT MUST GOVERN THE PLAN OF OPERATIONS.

CHAPTER VI.

BOLDNESS AND VIGOUR THE ESSENCE OF EFFECTIVELY CONDUCTING SUCH OPERATIONS.

CHAPTER VII.

TACTICS FAVOUR THE REGULAR ARMY WHILE STRATEGY FAVOURS THE ENEMY—THEREFORE THE OBJECT IS TO FIGHT, NOT TO MANŒUVRE.

CHAPTER VIII.

TO AVOID DESULTORY WARFARE THE ENEMY MUST BE BROUGHT TO BATTLE, AND IN SUCH MANNER AS TO MAKE HIS DEFEAT DECISIVE.

CHAPTER IX.

DIVISION OF FORCE, OFTEN NECESSITATED BY THE CIRCUMSTANCES, IS LESS OBJECTIONABLE IN THESE CAMPAIGNS THAN IN REGULAR WARFARE.

CHAPTER X.

LINES OF COMMUNICATIONS, THEIR LIABILITY TO ATTACK, THE DRAIN THEY ARE UPON THE ARMY, AND THE CIRCUMSTANCES UNDER WHICH THEY CAN BE DISPENSED WITH.

CHAPTER XI.

GUERILLA WARFARE IN GENERAL.

8

CHAPTER XII.

TACTICS OF ATTACK.

9

CHAPTER XIII.

TACTICS OF DEFENCE.

CHAPTER XIV.

PURSUITS AND RETREATS.

CHAPTER XV.

The employment of feints to tempt the enemy into action and to conceal designs upon the battlefield.

CHAPTER XVI.

Surprises, raids and ambuscades.

CHAPTER XVII.

SQUARES IN ACTION ON THE MARCH AND IN BIVOUAC.

CHAPTER XVIII.

PRINCIPLES OF LAAGER AND ZERIBA WARFARE.

CHAPTER XIX.

HILL WARFARE.

13

CHAPTER XX.

BUSH WARFARE.

CHAPTER XXI.

INFANTRY TACTICS.

CHAPTER XXII.

CAVALRY AND MOUNTED TROOPS GENERALLY.

CHAPTER XXIII.

CAMEL CORPS.

CHAPTER XXIV.

ARTILLERY TACTICS.

CHAPTER XXV.

MACHINE GUNS.

CHAPTER XXVI.

THE SERVICE OF SECURITY.

CHAPTER XXVII.

NIGHT OPERATIONS.

INDEX.

PLANS.

SMALL WARS.

SMALL WARS.

CHAPTER I.

INTRODUCTION.

SMALL war is a term which has come largely into use of late years, and which is admittedly somewhat difficult to define. Practically it may be said to include all campaigns other than those where both the opposing sides consist of regular troops. It comprises the expeditions against savages and semi-civilised races by disciplined soldiers, it comprises campaigns undertaken to suppress rebellions and guerilla warfare in all parts of the world where organized armies are struggling against opponents who will not meet them in the open field, and it thus obviously covers operations very varying in their scope and in their conditions.

The expression "small war" has in reality no particular connection with the scale on which any campaign may be carried out ; it is simply used to denote, in default of a better, operations of regular armies against irregular, or comparatively speaking irregular, forces. For instance, the struggle in 1894–95 between Japan and China might, although very large forces were placed in the field on both sides, from the purely military point of view almost be described as a small war ; for the operations on land were conducted between a highly trained, armed, organized, and disciplined army on one side, and by forces on the other side which, though numerically formidable, could not possibly be described as regular

troops in the proper sense of the word. Small wars include
the partisan warfare which usually arises when trained
soldiers are employed in the quelling of sedition and of
insurrections in civilised countries ; they include campaigns
of conquest when a Great Power adds the territory of barbarous races to its possessions ; and they include punitive
expeditions against tribes bordering upon distant colonies.
The suppression of the Indian Mutiny and the Anglo-French
campaign on the Peiho, the British operations against the
Egyptian army in 1882, and the desultory warfare of the
United States troops against the nomad Red Indians, the
Spanish invasion of Morocco in 1859, and the pacification of
Upper Burma, can all alike be classed under the category of
small wars. Whenever a regular army finds itself engaged
upon hostilities against irregular forces, or forces which in
their armament, their organization, and their discipline are
palpably inferior to it, the conditions of the campaign become
distinct from the conditions of modern regular warfare, and
it is with hostilities of this nature that this volume proposes
to deal.

General scope of the work. Upon the organization of armies for irregular warfare
valuable information is to be found in many instructive mili-
tary works, official and non-official. The peculiar arrangements as to transport, the system of supply, the lines of
communications, all these subjects are dealt with exhaustively
and in detail. In this volume, therefore, questions of organization will be as far as possible avoided. It is intended merely
to give a sketch of the principles and practice of small wars
as regards strategy and tactics, and of the broad rules which
govern the conduct of operations in hostilities against adversaries of whom modern works on the military art seldom take
account.

Arrangement adopted. The earlier chapters will deal with the general principles
of strategy, the later chapters with tactics. In a treatise
which necessarily covers a great deal of ground it is difficult

to avoid a certain amount of repetition, but it has been thought better to incur this than to interpolate constant references from one part of the book to the other. The subject will throughout be discussed merely from the point of view of the regular troops. The forces opposing these, whether guerillas, savages, or quasi-organized armies, will be regarded as the enemy. A comparison will be to a certain extent established between the conduct of campaigns of this special character and the accepted principles of strategy and tactics.

The teachings of great masters of the art of war, and the experience gained from campaigns of modern date in America and on the continent of Europe, have established certain principles and precedents which form the groundwork of the system of regular warfare of to-day. Certain rules of conduct exist which are universally accepted. Strategy and tactics alike are in great campaigns governed, in most respects, by a code from which it is perilous to depart. But the conditions of small wars are so diversified, the enemy's mode of fighting is often so peculiar, and the theatres of operations present such singular features, that irregular warfare must generally be carried out on a method totally different from the stereotyped system. The art of war, as generally understood, must be modified to suit the circumstances of each particular case. The conduct of small wars is in fact in certain respects an art by itself, diverging widely from what is adapted to the conditions of regular warfare, but not so widely that there are not in all its branches points which permit comparisons to be established.

In dealing with tactical questions arising in small wars General the more recent campaigns are chiefly taken into consideration, treatment. owing to the advances in the science of manufacturing war material. Tactics necessarily depend largely on armament, and while the weapons which regular troops take into the field have vastly improved in the last 40 years, it must be remembered that the arms of the enemy have also improved. Even savages, who a few years ago would have defended themselves with bows and arrows, are often found now-a-days with breech-loading rifles—the constant smuggling of arms into their territories, which the various Powers concerned seem wholly unable to suppress, promises that small wars of the future may involve very difficult operations.

On the other hand the strategical problems presented by operations of this nature have not altered to at all the same extent. Therefore there is much belonging to this branch of the military art still to be learnt from campaigns dating as far back as the conquest of Algeria and as the terrible Indian struggle of 1857-58. And the great principle which regular troops must always act upon in small wars—that of overawing the enemy by bold initiative and by resolute action whether on the battlefield or as part of the general plan of campaign—can be learnt from the military history of early times just as well as it can be learnt from the more voluminously chronicled struggles of the present epoch.

CHAPTER II.

CAUSES OF SMALL WARS AS AFFECTING THEIR CONDITIONS.
THE VARIOUS KINDS OF ADVERSARIES MET WITH.

SMALL wars may broadly be divided into three classes— *Classes into which these campaigns may be divided.* campaigns of conquest or annexation, campaigns for the suppression of insurrections or lawlessness or for the settlement of conquered or annexed territory, and campaigns undertaken to wipe out an insult, to avenge a wrong, or to overthrow a dangerous enemy. Each class of campaign will generally be found to have certain characteristics affecting the whole course of the military operations which it involves.

Campaigns of conquest or annexation are of necessity *Campaigns of conquest and annexation and their characteristics.* directed against enemies on foreign soil, they mean external not internal war, and they will generally be directed against foemen under control of some potentate or chief. Few countries are so barbarous as not to have some form of government and some sort of military system. So it comes about that campaigns of conquest and annexation mean for the most part campaigns against forces which, however irregular they may be in their composition, are nevertheless tangible and defined. Glancing back over the small wars of the century the truth of this is manifest. The conquest of Scinde and the *Examples.* Punjab involved hostilities with military forces of some organization and of undoubted fighting capacity. The French expedition to Algeria overthrew a despotic military power. The Russians in their gradual extension of territory beyond the Caspian have often had to deal with armies—ill armed and organized, of course, but nevertheless armies. To oppose the annexation of his dominions, King Thebaw of Burma had collected bodies of troops having at least a semblance of system and cohesion, although they showed but little fight. The regular troops detailed for such campaigns enjoy the obvious advantage of knowing whom they are fighting with ; they have a distinct task to perform, and skilful leadership, backed by sufficient force, should ensure a speedy termination of the conflict.

The suppression of insurrections and lawlessness, and its features.

But campaigns for the subjugation of insurrections, for the repression of lawlessness, or for the pacification of territories conquered or annexed stand on a very different footing. They are necessarily internal not external campaigns. They involve struggles against guerillas and banditti. The regular army has to cope not with determinate but with indeterminate forces. The crushing of a populace in arms and the stamping out of widespread disaffection by military methods, is a harassing form of warfare even in a civilised country with a settled social system ; in remote regions peopled by half-civilized races or wholly savage tribes, such campaigns are most difficult to bring to a satisfactory conclusion, and are always most trying to the troops.

This, a frequent sequel to conquest and annexation.

It should be noted that campaigns of conquest and annexation not infrequently pass through two distinct stages. In the first stage the forces of civilization overthrow the armies and levies which the rulers and chieftains in the invaded country gather for its defence, a few engagements generally sufficing for this ; in the second stage organized resistance has ceased, and is replaced by the war of ambushes and surprises, of murdered stragglers and of stern reprisals. The French conquest of Algeria is a remarkable illustration of this. To crush the armies of the Dey and to wrest the pirate stronghold which had been so long a scourge of neighbouring seas from his grasp, proved easy of accomplishment ; but it took years and years of desultory warfare to establish French rule firmly in the vast regions which had been won. The same was the case in Upper Burma ; the huge country was nominally annexed, practically without a struggle, but several years of typical guerilla warfare followed before British power was thoroughly consolidated in the great province which had been added to the Indian Empire.

Insurrections and revolts in districts difficult of access Examples. where communications are bad and information cannot readily be obtained involve most troublesome military operations. In Europe the Carlist wars and early wars of Balkan liberation are examples of this. In the United States, the periodical risings and raids of the Red Indians led to protracted indecisive hostilities of many years' duration. The Kaffir and Matabili rebellions in South Africa have always proved most difficult to suppress. The case of the Indian Mutiny is somewhat different at least in its early stages for here the rebels owing to the peculiar circumstances of the case were in a position to put armies in the field, and this led to field operations of most definite and stirring character ; but, as the supremacy of British military power in India became re-established, and as the organized muti- neer forces melted away, the campaign degenerated in many localities into purely guerilla warfare, which took months to bring to a conclusion. As a general rule the quelling of rebellion in distant colonies means protracted, thankless, invertebrate war.

Campaigns of the third class have characteristics analo- Campaigns to gous to the conditions ordinarily governing wars of conquest an insult or and of annexation. Hostilities entered upon to punish an avenge a wrong. insult or to chastise a people who have inflicted some injury, will generally be on foreign soil. The destruction of a for- midable alien military power will necessarily involve external war. Under this heading, moreover, may be included expedi- tions undertaken for some ulterior political purpose, or to establish order in some foreign land—wars of expediency, in fact. Campaigns of this class when they do not (as is so frequently the case) develop into campaigns of conquest, differ from them chiefly in that the defeat of the enemy need not be so complete and crushing to attain the objects sought for.

Examples.

The Abyssinian expedition of 1868 is a typical example of a campaign to avenge a wrong; it was undertaken to compel the release of prisoners seized by King Theodore. The China War of 1860, and the Spanish invasion of Morocco in 1859, were of the same nature. The Ashanti imbroglio of 1874 and the French operations against the Hovas in 1883 and the following year may be similarly classed. Most of the punitive expeditions on the Indian frontier may be included in this category; but many of these latter have resulted in annexation of the offending district, and the French campaigns in Annam in 1861 and recently in Dahomey ended in like fashion.

Campaigns for the overthrow of a dangerous power.

Wars entered upon to overthrow a menacing military power likewise often terminate in annexation. The Zulu war was a campaign of this nature—the disciplined armies of Ketchwayo were a standing danger to Natal, and the crushing of the Zulu power was indispensable for the peace of South Africa; the war, however, ended in the incorporation of the kingdom in the British Empire. The Russian expeditions against the Tekke Turkomans were partly punitive; but they were undertaken mainly to suppress this formidable fighting nomad race, and the final campaign became a campaign of conquest. The short and brilliant operations of the French against the Moors in 1844 afford a remarkable instance of a small war having for its object the overthrow of the dangerous forces of a threatening state, and of its complete fulfilment; but in this case there was no subsequent annexation.

Campaigns of expediency.

Wars of expediency undertaken for some political purpose, necessarily differ in their conditions from campaigns of conquest, punitive expeditions, or military repression of rebellious disorders. The two Afghan wars, and especially the first, may be included in this category. The Egyptian war of 1882 is another example. Such campaigns are necessarily carried out on foreign soil, but in other respects they may have few features in common.

To a certain extent then the origin and cause of a small war gives a clue to the nature of the operations which will follow, quite apart from the plan of campaign which the commander of the regular forces may decide upon. But when conflicts of this nature are in prospect, the strength and the fighting methods of the enemy must always be most carefully considered before any decision as to the form of operations to be adopted is arrived at; the tactics of such opponents differ so greatly in various cases that it is essential that these be taken fully into consideration. The armament of the enemy is also a point of extreme importance. In regular warfare each side knows perfectly well what is to be expected from the adversary, and either adversary is to a certain extent governed by certain rules common to both. But in small wars all manner of opponents are met with, in no two campaigns does the enemy fight in the same fashion, and this divergence of method may be briefly illustrated from various campaigns of the past century.

The great variety in the natures of enemy to be dealt with.

Some small wars of late years have been against antago- nists with the form and organization of regular troops. The hostile armies have been broken up into battalions, squadrons, and batteries, and in addition to this the weapons of the enemy have been fairly efficient. This was the case in Egypt in 1882, to a certain extent in Tonkin as far as the Chinese were concerned, and also in a measure in the Indian Mutiny. In such struggles the enemy follows as far as he is able the system adopted in regular warfare. In the campaigns above-mentioned, the hostile forces had enjoyed the advantage of possessing instructors with a knowledge of European methods. In cases such as these the warfare will somewhat resemble the struggles between modern armies, and the principles of modern strategy and tactics are largely if not wholly applicable.

Opponents with a form of regular organization.

At the outset of the last Afghan war the hostile forces had a form of regular organization; this could, however, scarcely claim to be more than a travesty, and the Afghan armament was, moreover, most inferior. The Russians in their campaigns against Khokand and Bokhara had to deal with armies standing on a somewhat similar footing as regards organization and weapons. Somewhat lower in the scale, but still with some pretence to organization and efficient armament, were the Dey of Algiers' troops which confronted the French invasion in 1830. There is, of course, a great variety in the extent to which the hostile forces approximate to regular armies in various small wars ; but there is a clear distinction between troops such as Arabi Pasha commanded in 1882, and mere gatherings of savages such as the British and French have at times to cope with in Western Africa.

Highly disciplined but badly armed opponents.   The Zulu impis, again, presented totally different characteristics. Here was a well disciplined army with a definite organization of its own, capable of carrying out manœuvres on the battlefield with order and precision ; but the Zulu weapons were those of savages. The Matabili were organized on the Zulu model, but their system was less perfect. Zulus and Matabili fought in a fashion totally different from the Chinese, the Afghans, and Arabi Pasha's forces, but they were none the less formidable on that account.

Fanatics.   The Hadendowa of the Red Sea Littoral, the Afghan Ghazis, and the fanatics who occasionally gave the French such trouble in Algeria, had not the discipline of the Zulu or of the Matabili, nor yet their organization ; but they fought on the same lines. Such warriors depend on spears and knives and not on firearms. They are brave and even reckless on the battlefield. Tactics which serve well against forces armed with rifles and supported by artillery, are out of place confronted with such foes as this. Face to face with Sudanese and Zulus old orders of battle, discarded in face of the breech-loader and of shrapnel shell, are resumed again. The hostile tactics are essentially aggressive, and inasmuch as they involve substitution of shock action for fire action, the regular forces are compelled, whether they like it or not, to conform to the savage method of battle.

In the Boer war of 1881 the British troops had a different *The Boers.* sort of enemy to deal with altogether. The Boers were armed with excellent firearms, were educated and were led by men of knowledge and repute, but they at that time had no real organization. They were merely bodies of determined men, acknowledging certain leaders, drawn together to confront a common danger. The Boers presented all the features of rebels in a civilized country except in that they were inured from youth to hardship, and that they were all mounted. As a rule adversaries of this nature prefer guerilla warfare, for which their weapons and their habits especially adapt them, to fighting in the open. The Boers, however, accepted battle readily and worked together in comparatively speaking large bodies even in 1881. The incidents of that campaign, although the later and greater war has rather overshadowed them and deprived them of interest, were very singular, and they afford most useful lessons with regard to the best way of operating against adversaries of this peculiar class. In 1901 and 1902, after the overthrow of the organized Boer armies had driven those still in the field to adopt guerilla tactics, the operations partook of the character of irregular warfare against a daring and well armed enemy gifted with unusual mobility and exceptional cunning.

The Turks in Montenegro, the Austrians in Bosnia, and *Guerillas,* the Canadian forces when hunting down Riel, had to deal *civilized and savage.* with well armed and civilized opponents ; but these preferred guerilla methods of warfare, and shirked engagements in the open. Organization they had little or none ; but in their own fashion they resisted obstinately in spite of this, and the campaigns against them gave the regular troops much trouble. These operations afford good illustrations of guerilla warfare of one kind. Guerilla warfare of a totally different kind is exemplified by the Maori and the Kaffir wars, in which the enemy, deficient in courage and provided with poor weapons, by taking advantage of the cover in districts overgrown with bush and jungle managed to prove most difficult to subdue. To regular troops such antagonists are very troublesome, they shun decisive action and their tactics almost of necessity bring about a protracted, toilsome war. The operations on the North-West Frontier of India in 1897 afford admirable examples of another form of guerilla warfare—that against the well armed fanatical cut-throat of the hills, fighting in a terrain peculiarly well adapted to his method of making war.

Armies of savages in the bush. Savages dwelling in territories where thick tropical vegetation abounds, do not, however, always rely on this desultory form of war. In Dahomey the French encountered most determined opposition from forces with a certain organization which accepted battle constantly. The Dutch in Achin, where the jungle was in places almost impenetrable, found an enemy ready enough to fight and who fought under skilful guidance. The Ashantis during the campaign of 1874 on several occasions assembled in large bodies; they did not hesitate to risk a general engagement when their leaders thought an opportunity offered.

Enemies who fight mounted. Another and altogether different kind of enemy has been met with at times in Morocco, in Algeria, and in Central Asia. In the Barbary States are to be found excellent horsemen with hardy mounts. The fighting forces of the Arabs, Moors, and Tartars have always largely consisted of irregular cavalry, and the regular troops campaigning in these countries have been exposed to sudden onslaught by great hordes of mounted men. The whole course of operations has been largely influenced by this fact.

The importance of studying the hostile mode of war. Military records prove that in different small wars the hostile mode of conducting hostilities varies to a surprising extent. Strategy and tactics assume all manner of forms. It is difficult to conceive methods of combat more dissimilar than those employed respectively by the Transkei Kaffirs, by the Zulus, and by the Boers, opponents with whom British troops successively came in conflict within a period of three years and in one single quarter of the African continent. From this striking fact there is to be deduced a most important military lesson. It is that in small wars the habits, the customs, and the mode of action on the battlefield of the enemy should be studied in advance. This is not imperative only on the commander and his staff—all officers should know what nature of opposition they must expect, and should understand how best to overcome it. One of the worst disasters which has befallen British troops of recent years, Isandlwhana, was directly attributable to a total misconception of the tactics of the enemy. The French troubles in Algeria after its conquest were due to a failure to appreciate for many years the class of warfare upon which they were engaged. The reverses in the first Boer war arose from entering upon a campaign without cavalry, the one arm of the service essential to cope with the hostile method of conducting warfare. In great campaigns the opponent's system is understood; he is guided by like precedents, and is governed by the same code; it is only when some great reformer of the art of war springs up that it is otherwise. But each small war presents new features, and these features must if possible be foreseen or the regular troops will assuredly find themselves in difficulties and may meet with grievous misfortune.

CHAPTER III.

THE OBJECTIVE IN SMALL WARS.

Selection of objective in the first place governed by the cause of the campaign. THE selection of the objective in a small war will usually be governed in the first place by the circumstances which have led up to the campaign. Military operations are always undertaken with some end in view, and are shaped for its achievement. If the conquest of the hostile territory be aimed at, the objective takes a different form from that which it would assume were the expedition dispatched with merely punitive intent. A commander bent on extorting terms from some savage potentate will frame his plans on different lines from the leader sent to crush the military power of a menacing tribe. But in all cases there are in warfare of this nature certain points which will, apart from the cause of the campaign, influence the choice of the objective, and which depend mainly on the class of enemy to be dealt with.

Cases where the hostile country has a definite form of government. The enemy is often represented by a people with comparatively speaking settled institutions, with a central form of government, and with military forces regulated and commanded by a central authority. Monarchical institutions are to be found in many semi-civilized and savage lands, amounting often to forms of despotism which are particularly well calculated to ensure a judicious management of available military forces when at war. The savage Zulu warriors fought in organized armies controlled by the supreme authority of the king. Runjeet Singh was a respected ruler who could dispose of organized forces completely at his command; the Amir of Bokhara stood on a similar footing during the campaigns which ended in the annexation of his khanate to the Russian Empire. The Ashantis and Dahomeyans were nationalities which although uncivilized were completely dominated by their sovereigns. In cases such as these the objective will generally be clear and well defined. There are armies the overthrow of which will generally bring the head of the hostile state to reason. There are centres of government the capture of which will paralyse the forces of resistance of the country. To a certain extent the destruction of the military forces of the enemy under such conditions almost necessarily involves the fall of the capital, because the military forces gather for the protection of the capital and the fall of the capital follows upon their defeat almost as a matter of course. The conditions approximate to those of regular warfare in the very important particular that from the outset of the campaign a determinate scheme of operations can be contemplated and can be put in force.

In great campaigns of modern history it has come to be considered as the usual objective that the capital of the hostile nation should be threatened, and that it should if possible be actually captured. In a civilized country the metropolis is not only the seat of government and of the legislature, but it is also generally the centre of communications and the main emporium of the nation's commerce. Its occupation by an enemy means a complete dislocation of the executive system, it brings about a collapse of trade, and, if the occupation be long continued, it causes financial ruin. But the capitals of countries which become the theatres of small war are rarely of the same importance. In such territories there is little commercial organization, the chief town generally derives its sole importance from being the residence of the sovereign and his council, and its capture by a hostile army is in itself damaging rather to the prestige of the government than injurious to the people at large.

The question of the importance of the capital as an objective.

In the last Afghan war Kabul was occupied early in the campaign, after the overthrow of the troops of Yakoub Khan. But its capture by no

(10830)   c 2

means brought about the downfall of the Afghans as a fighting power, on the contrary it proved to be merely the commencement of the campaign. The country was in a state of suppressed anarchy, the tribes scarcely acknowledged the Amir to be their King, and when Kabul fell and the government such as it was, ceased to exist, the people generally cared little; but they bitterly resented the insult to their nation and to their faith which the presence of British troops in the heart of the country offered.

But, although the relations of Kabul to the Afghan race may be taken as typical, there are often exceptions, and cases have often occurred in these wars where the capital of the country has proved the core of its resistance. In the case of a petty chieftain the capital means his stronghold. Sekukuni's and Morosi's mountains are examples of this, and their capture put an immediate end to the campaign in each case. When the object of the war is to extort certain conditions or to exact reparation from some half-civilized or savage potentate, the capture of his capital will generally have the desired effect. It was so in the Chinese war of 1860, when all efforts at negotiation failed till the allied forces were at the gates of Pekin.

When the capital is a place of real importance in the country its capture generally disposes of regular opposition.
　　　　When the capital is really the focus and centre of a State, however barbarous, any approach to organized resistance under the direct control of the head of the State, will almost always cease when the capital falls ; but it does not by any means follow that the conflict is at an end. The capture of Algiers in 1830 closed the campaign as one against armies including troops of all arms ; it proved, however, to be only the prelude to years of desultory warfare. It was the same in Dahomey, where the fighting power of Benanzin's forces was utterly broken in trying to bar the advance of the invaders to Abomey, but there were troublesome hostilities with guerillas subsequently. On the other hand, the fighting after the occupation of Ulundi in the Zulu war and of Buluwayo in the Matabili campaign, was only of a desultory description. The amount of resistance offered to the regular troops after they have overthrown the more or less organized forces of the

enemy and seized the chief town varies in different cases. But the French experiences in Algeria, and the British experiences in Afghanistan, show that these irregular, protracted, indefinite operations offer often far greater difficulties to the regular armies than the attainment of the original military objective.

The advantage of having a well defined objective even for a time can, however, scarcely be over-rated, and the Central Asian campaigns of Russia illustrate this vividly. Turkestan was territory inhabited largely by nomads, but its rolling plains and steppes were studded with historic cities many of which had been for ages the marts of oriental commerce. The invaders went to work with marked deliberation. They compassed the downfall of the khanates by gradually absorbing these cities, capturing them in many cases by very brilliant feats of arms. The conquests were not achieved by any display of mighty force, the actual Russian armies in these operations were rarely large, but the objectives were always clear and determinate ; the capture of one city was generally held sufficient for a year, but it thereupon became a Russian city. The troops had always an unmistakable goal in front of them, they went deliberately to work to attain that goal, and when it was attained they rested on their laurels till ready for another coup. Such is the military history of the conquest of Central Asia. It is a record of war in which desultory operations were throughout conspicuous by their absence. Such conditions are, however, very seldom found in small wars ; important towns and centres of trade, moreover, are not the sole conditions offering distinct objectives.

Sometimes the circumstances of the case will cause the enemy to muster in full strength, and will permit of a decisive victory being gained which concludes the war, and it is most fortunate when the operations take this form. The enormous importance of moral effect in these campaigns will be dealt with in a later chapter, suffice it to say here

The great advantage of having a clear and well-defined objective.

that it is a factor which enters into all their phases ; a defeat inflicted upon a large force of irregular warriors terrifies not only those engaged, but also all their kind. It is the difficulty of bringing the foe to action which, as a rule, forms the most unpleasant characteristic of these wars ; but when such opponents can be thoroughly beaten in the open field at the commencement of hostilities, their powers of further serious resistance often cease. And so, when by force of circumstances the enemy is compelled to accept battle to defend some point of great importance to him or to safeguard some venerated shrine, thus offering a well-defined objective, the regular troops greatly benefit. Many examples of this might be quoted. Denghil Tepe, for instance, became the stronghold in which practically the whole military power of the Tekke Turkomans concentrated itself in 1879 and 1880, although the Turkomans are, in the main, a nomad race ; the Russians failed in their first campaign through mismanagement, but the objective never was in doubt, and in their second venture the formidable nomad race, which might have taken years to subdue, was crushed for good and all when the fortress fell. The experience of the French in Annam in 1861 is another case in point. They had formed a small settlement at Saigon, and this the Annamese, profiting by the inability of the French to detach troops thither during the China war, blockaded in great force, forming a regular entrenched camp close by. Thus it came about that when the French were at last able to land a large force at Saigon, they found a formidable hostile army before them in a highly defensible position, which was just what they wanted. By bold and skilful dispositions they signally defeated the Annamese drawn up to meet them, and the effect of the blow was so great that they were able to overrun the country afterwards almost unhindered.

Tirah, a peculiar case.   The Tirah campaign of 1897 affords a singular example of the advantages of a definite objective. It was the just boast of the Afridis and Orukzais that the remarkable upland valleys which constitute their summer home, and which were practically unknown to the British, had defied the efforts of all invaders. The duty of Sir W. Lockhart's army, therefore, was to overrun these valleys, and to prove to the formidable tribesmen that whatever might have been their experience in the past, they had now to do with a foe capable of bursting through the great mountain barriers in which they put their trust, and of violating the integrity of territory which they believe to be incapable of access by organized troops. The army performed its task of penetrating into Tirah, and of leaving its mark in the usual manner by the demolition of buildings and destruction of crops. Nor did its subsequent retirement, harassed by the mountaineers in defiles where they could act to the very best advantage, appreciably detract from the success of the operation as a whole. For the enemy had learnt that an Anglo-Indian army could force its way into these fastnesses, could seize their crops, destroy their defences, burn their villages, and could, after making its presence felt in every ravine and nook, get out again ; and that settled the matter. The conditions here were peculiar, but they illustrate well the broad principle that in warfare of this nature it is half the battle to have a distinct task to perform.

Sometimes when the war is undertaken, as in the case of Zululand, to overthrow a dangerous military power, the objective is the army of the enemy wherever it may be. The very fact of this being a formidable force will generally cause it to accept battle readily to confront an invader. The objective becomes primarily some point in hostile territory which the hostile army will certainly endeavour to protect—the capital or some stronghold involving the military prestige of the enemy, and an advance on this leads to a pitched battle, which is what the regular troops want. Thus in the Spanish campaign of 1859 against the Moors the town of Tetuan was made the goal of the invaders, and in endeavouring to bar the road the forces of the Sultan suffered several severe defeats. On

Objective when the purpose of hostilities is the overthrow of a dangerous military power.

the Red Sea littoral, in the days when Mahdism was a power in those parts, the very fact of any Anglo-Egyptian advance always ensured great gatherings of dervishes eager for the fray. In the Matabili war the advance of the small British force on Buluwayo forced the impis of Lobengula to assemble and to fight.

Objective when there is no capital and no army.

But when there is no king to conquer, no capital to seize, no organized army to overthrow, and when there are no celebrated strongholds to capture, and no great centres of population to occupy, the objective is not so easy to select. It is then that the regular troops are forced to resort to cattle lifting and village burning and that the war assumes an aspect which may shock the humanitarian. "In planning a war against an uncivilized nation who has, perhaps, no capital," says Lord Wolseley, "your first object should be the capture of whatever they prize most, and the destruction or deprivation of which will probably bring the war most rapidly to a conclusion." This goes to the root of the whole matter. If the enemy cannot be touched in his patriotism or his honour, he can be touched through his pocket.

Raids on live stock.

Fighting the Kirghiz and other nomads of the steppes the Russians have always trusted largely to carrying off the camels and flocks of the enemy as a means of bringing their antagonists to reason. In Algeria the French, adopting the methods of Abd-el-Kader and his followers, made sudden raids or "razzias"—dealt with later in the chapters on guerilla warfare and raids—carrying off the live stock and property of their wandering opponents. In the Kaffir wars, especially in 1852, this mode of procedure has been very common, adapted with success, and it is the usual plan of action in the small punitive expeditions in East and West Africa. The United States troops used to retaliate upon the Red Indians in similar fashion.

Destruction of crops, etc.

The destruction of the crops and stores of grain of the enemy is another way of carrying on hostilities. This method

of warfare is more exasperating to the adversary than carrying off live stock; for while they appreciate the principle
that the victor is entitled to the spoils, wanton damage tends
to embitter their feeling of enmity. The same applies to the
destruction of villages so often resorted to in punitive expeditions, but it hardly does so to the same extent, since the dwellings of these races can be reconstructed easily while their
food supplies, if destroyed, cannot be replaced. It is so often
the case that the power which undertakes a small war desires
to acquire the friendship of the people which its armies are
chastising, that the system of what is called " military execution " is ill adapted to the end in view. The most satisfactory
way of bringing such foes to reason is by the rifle and sword,
for they understand this mode of warfare and respect it.
Sometimes, however, the circumstances do not admit of it,
and then their villages must be demolished and their crops and
granaries destroyed; still it is unfortunate when this is the
case.

When, however, the campaign takes the form of quelling Suppression
of rebellions.
an insurrection, the object is not only to prove to the oppos-
ing force unmistakably which is the stronger, but also to inflict
punishment on those who have taken up arms. In this case
it is often necessary to injure property. " A war," wrote
Sir G. Cathcart from Kaffirland in 1852, " may be terminated
by the surrender or capitulation of the hostile sovereign or
chief, who answers for his people; but in the suppression of
a rebellion the refractory subjects of the ruling power must
all be chastised and subdued." Still there is a limit to the
amount of licence in destruction which is expedient. Hoche,
whose conduct of the campaign against the Chouans and insurgents from La Vendée will ever remain a model of operations of
this kind, achieved success as much by his happy combination
of clemency with firmness, as by his masterly dispositions in
the theatre of war. Expeditions to put down revolt are not
put in motion merely to bring about a temporary cessation of

hostility. Their purpose is to ensure a lasting peace. Therefore, in choosing the objective, the overawing and not the exasperation of the enemy is the end to keep in view.

Special objectives.

In some small wars the conditions have imposed certain objectives on the regular forces of necessity. For instance, the Nile Expedition was undertaken for the relief of Khartum, and it was only when the beleaguered city fell that any doubt with regard to its objective arose. The Chitral campaign was analogous. Such cases are, however, peculiar.

Conclusion.

The subject of the selection of the objective does not lend itself to exhaustive treatment, and is certainly not one with regard to which rules of conduct could with advantage be drawn up. Each case must be decided on its merits. The main points of difference between small wars and regular campaigns in this respect are that, in the former, the beating of the hostile armies is not necessarily the main object even if such armies exist, that moral effect is often far more important than material success, and that the operations are sometimes limited to committing havoc which the laws of regular warfare do not sanction. The conditions of a campaign undertaken against a savage race swayed by a despotic sovereign differ so fundamentally from hostilities against gatherings of independent clans, that principles which govern the operations from the very outset in the one case are wholly inapplicable to the other. The crushing of an insurrectionary movement or the settlement of a conquered country, are undertakings so distinct from enterprises entered upon to overawe a semi-civilized state, that what may present itself as the obvious objective under the former set of circumstances may be non-existent in the latter. It is this extraordinary diversity of conditions which makes the consideration of small wars so complex and so difficult to discuss as one general object.

CHAPTER IV.

DIFFICULTIES UNDER WHICH THE REGULAR FORCES LABOUR AS REGARDS INTELLIGENCE. THE ADVANTAGE IS USUALLY ENJOYED BY THE ENEMY IN THIS RESPECT, BUT THIS CIRCUMSTANCE CAN SOMETIMES BE TURNED TO ACCOUNT.

OF late years it has become the practice at the head-quarters of all regular armies to study the strength and organization of other countries in view of possible eventualities, and to collect information as to, and to prepare plans of, theatres of war which may some day take place. Accurate information as to the organized military forces of other leading nations is not difficult to obtain ; the topographical features, the communications and the military resources of civilized countries are well known. But it is a very important feature in the preparation for, and the carrying out of, small wars that the regular forces are often working very much in the dark from the outset.

Absence of trustworthy information frequent in small wars.

The reasons for this are obvious enough. Small wars break out unexpectedly and in unexpected places. The operations take place in countries often only partially explored if not wholly unexplored. The nature of the enemy, his strength, his weapons, and his fighting qualities can be only very imperfectly gauged. The routes which the troops will have to follow are little known. The resources of the districts to be traversed cannot be estimated with any certainty. What is known technically as " intelligence " is defective, and unavoidably so.

The difficulties which arise from this ignorance of the conditions under which the regular army will be operating really divide themselves into two main headings ; difficulties

Want of knowledge may be as to the theatre of war or as to the enemy.

arising from want of knowledge of the theatre of war, and difficulties consequent upon the doubt that exists as to the strength, the organization, and the fighting qualities of the enemy. Of these the former may be said upon the whole to be the most important as a rule. For it is perhaps the most distinguishing characteristic of small wars as compared with regular hostilities conducted between modern armies, that they are in the main campaigns against nature.

Illustrations of effect of uncertainty as to routes;
The evil effects which will from time to time result from ignorance of the theatre of war can perhaps best be demonstrated by a few examples. One fruitful source of trouble, for instance, is that the route to be followed may not be accurately known.

This is well illustrated by Hicks Pasha's disastrous attempt to march from the Nile to El Obeid in 1883. The staff were not familiar with the position of the wells, the distances, and the difficulties to be encountered. The guides were treacherous. The force lost its way, lost time, and lost heart, and when at last the Mahdists attacked it, the troops, worn out and despairing, made no fight of it, and were annihilated.

In the Ambela campaign of 1863, the route over the Sukhawai Pass leading to Chamla had been reported to be easy in the extreme, but it turned out to be quite the reverse, and this disarranged the plans.

Sir H. Stewart's force on its march from the Abu Klea wells to the Nile in 1885 was taken, unnecessarily as was subsequently discovered, through some thick bush at night. The movement being conducted in the dark great confusion occurred amongst the transport; and the force was so seriously delayed that it failed to reach the river before daylight and was forced to fight at a great disadvantage in consequence.

General Dodds in writing of his campaign in Dahomey remarks, " Le manque complet de renseignements sérieux a été la plus grosse difficulté qu'ait rencontrée la conduite des opérations."

The French expedition despatched to effect the capture of the Madagascar capital and the subjugation of the Hovas in 1895, is a good illustration of the unfortunate consequences of defective information as to a theatre of prospective war. After studying available sources of intelligence, the Paris War Office decided to make a carriageable road from the point selected for disembarkation, and to trust almost entirely to wheeled transport. It was not known that there were extraordinary engineering difficulties to be overcome and that the work involved an inordinate amount of manual labour. The construction of this road caused much serious delay, and kept the troops hard at work in unhealthy districts for months, which resulted in a deplorable mortality. In the end General Duchesne threw the paper scheme to the winds, and, pushing on with a fraction of his army equipped with pack transport, made short work of the Hovas before Antananarivo.

Again, the resources of the theatre of war in supplies, in water, and in transport may not be properly estimated. It is a most serious thing if an operation has been undertaken in the belief that supplies will be found in a certain locality and if this belief is, when too late, discovered to be unfounded. On the other hand, an under-estimate of the resources of a district may lead to the troops being encumbered with a mass of transport which might have been dispensed with, and which hampers them in their operations. *as to resources of theatre;*

In both the Russian campaign against Khiva in 1873, and in the French expedition into Dahomey in 1893, great inconvenience arose from water not being found where it was expected. One of the Russian columns against Khiva was indeed obliged to turn back and suffered considerably from privations.

Inconvenience and even disaster may be caused by doubt as to the exact position of some topographical feature or locality, or by an error in a map in which the commander of the troops is trusting. Ignorance as to the nature of a place which it has been determined to capture may also cause much trouble. *as to exact position of localities.*

(1) A remarkable example of this is afforded by an incident in the first Dutch expedition against the Sultan of Achin in 1873. The primary object of this expedition was the capture of the Sultan's capital and stronghold Kota Raja. Only the approximate position of this was known. But the force fought its way to its immediate vicinity, the country being for the most part overgrown with thick tropical vegetation in which were scattered numbers of fortified villages.

The troops had gained a place of some importance known to be close to Kota Raja. A fortified village crowded with warriors was found a few hundred yards off, and as a preliminary it was decided to capture this. A part of the force was detached for the purpose which after severe fighting succeeded in gaining a footing within the defences ; but it soon became manifest that the troops detailed were insufficient to clear the place, artillery especially being wanting. The officer in command thought it better not to ask for support. He decided to retreat, and the enterprise therefore miscarried. Largely owing to this reverse it was resolved to retire to the coast, and as a consequence the expedition completely failed in achieving the object for which it had been sent, and it re-embarked.

It was afterwards discovered that the village, some of the defences of which had been carried by a portion of the Dutch force as above described, was Kota Raja itself. Had this been known at the time of attack, and had all available troops been launched against it, it is quite possible that the place would have fallen and that a most important success would have been achieved.

(2) A somewhat analogous episode, but attended by no bad consequences, occurred when General Bourmont was preparing to attack the fortress of Algiers in 1830. A heavy mist hung over a plain near the city, and this was mistaken for the sea. The general had no great confidence in his maps which, however, turned out to be perfectly correct. He assumed from the position of what he took to be the sea, that the point he was making for lay quite differently from that what was shown on the map, and he started his columns in an altogether false direction. The mistake was only rectified when, riding, forward on to some high ground, he was startled by finding Algiers lying immediately below him, and close, at hand.

(3) During the first part of the Bhutan war in 1864, a column of 2,000 men with a transport train including 150 elephants was sent over 40 miles of most difficult country, hilly and overgrown with jungle, to capture the hill fort of the Bhutias known as Bishensing. After a toilsome march of some days the place was reached, and was found to consist of a single stone house occupied by an old Lama priest. No fort existed, and the place was destitute of any importance whatever, military or other.

(4) The disastrous battle of Adowa seems to have been brought on by a mistake as regards a certain locality, or rather by the fact that there were two localities of the same name a few miles apart. Owing to this, one of the three separate Italian columns advanced towards Adowa by night, moved considerably further than was intended by General Baratieri, and its advanced guard came unexpectedly on the Abyssinian host early in the morning. The consequence was that the column was soon enveloped and almost annihilated, and that the whole of the arrangements designed by the Italian commander-in-chief were thrown out of gear.

Uncertainty in the mind of commander reacts upon his plan of operations.

These few examples give actual instances of mistakes occurring through ignorance of the theatre of war. But it is not only mistakes and miscalculations of this kind which may prove a source of inconvenience and possibly of danger. There is also the uncertainty in the mind of the commander to be taken into account. The effect of this uncertainty cannot be illustrated by instances selected from history, although it will often be a powerful factor in influencing his course of conduct. Nothing more tends to hinder the framing of a decisive and assured plan of campaign and to delay the execution of the plan when it has been resolved upon, than this feeling of doubt, the fear that something unexpected will mar the combination and upset the calculations upon which it was based.

But while many small wars—the Indian Mutiny for instance, some of the campaigns of the United States troops against the Red Indians, the first Boer war, &c.—take place in theatres of operations which are well known, where the uncertainty above spoken of as regards communications, supplies, and so forth, does not then exist, there is almost always doubt as to the fighting strength of the enemy. Information as to this is invariably defective. The intelligence department finds great difficulty in organising an efficient service of espionage for obvious reasons—the spy captured by civilized troops does not have a very good time, in the hands of barbarians his lot is even more unenviable. Even where the opposing force has an organization which has been studied in peace time, it is not known how far it will work when put to the test of war against a civilized power. Even more important than the fighting strength of such antagonists, moreover, are their fighting qualities; although these can at times be fairly well estimated it is surprising how often the estimate turns out to be quite incorrect—as in the case of the South African war of 1899–1902.

A few examples may be given to show the uncertainty on these points which is such a feature of small wars. It may, however, be accepted as a general rule—and the reason why this is so needs no demonstration—that the less organized the forces of the enemy are, the more difficult is it to form any estimate of their strength or their quality.

Effect of doubt as to strength and fighting qualities of enemy.

Twice over during the last Afghan war the strength of the Afghans was *Examples.* altogether under-estimated, and on both occasions with somewhat unfortunate results. The first occasion was in the winter of 1879, when the great uprising of the tribes took place which ended in the siege of Sherpur ; serious losses were suffered in endeavouring to hold an extended line round Kabul, owing to the great numerical strength of the enemy not becoming for some time known. The second occasion was, later on, when Ayoub Khan advanced from Herat to the neighbourhood of Kandahar with a large force well supplied with artillery ; owing to a failure to appreciate the importance of this movement only a brigade very weak in British troops was sent to confront it, and this was disastrously defeated at Maiwand.

The unfortunate reverse suffered by the Italian troops at Dogali near Massawa arose almost entirely from ignorance of the hostile strength. A small force was left isolated, and the reinforcements sent to its assistance were overwhelmed by vastly superior numbers.

The French in Dahomey were not prepared to find the enemy in possession of guns ; and as they operated in compact formation the hostile artillery proved somewhat inconvenient on one or two occasions. Similarly the United States troops had not at first expected to find the Filipinos with artillery ; but these brought up two guns to defend Kalumpit.

At the outbreak of hostilities between the British and the Boers in 1881, the prevailing opinion in Natal, and in South Africa generally, was that the Boers would fight with little spirit and would easily be dispersed by the slender force under Sir G. Colley. But the event proved that the general estimate of their capabilities and courage was wrong, that the campaign had been undertaken with an altogether insufficient number of troops, and that the quelling of the revolt must have proved a difficult and costly undertaking had it been persisted in.

The Dutch in their first expedition to Achin were altogether unprepared for the warlike qualities displayed by the Achinese and for their skill in constructing works of defence. The consequence was that the campaign was entered upon with an insufficient force, and that unnecessary loss was on several occasions incurred in attacking fortified localities without proper preparation.

The Italians appear to have altogether under-estimated the fighting capacity and the numerical strength of King Menelek's army before the battle of Adowa. This was the chief cause of the very serious reverse which befel their arms. Neither the commander-in-chief nor his brigadiers seem to have had any idea that they were within a few miles of an army five-fold superior to their own, and consisting of formidable warriors effectively armed and full of fight, when the unfortunate nocturnal advance was made which brought on the battle.

The French, on the other hand, entered upon their final campaign against the Malagasies with an exaggerated notion of the opposition they were likely to meet with. Visitors to the country came away with the idea that the Queen's army was a fairly efficient force which would give a good account of itself under the circumstances. In previous campaigns, moreover, the Malagasies had given the French a good deal of trouble. The consequence

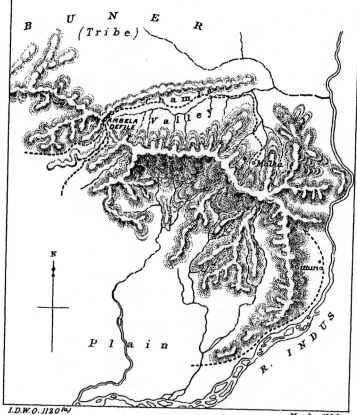

PLAN I.

THE
AMBELA CAMPAIGN

Scale of Miles

5 4 3 2 1 0   5   10 MILES

Routes of Expedition......

B   U   N   E   R
(Tribe)

Chamla
AMBELA
DEFILE   Valley

Malka

N

Sittana

Plain

R. INDUS

I.D.W.O. 1120 (a)

March, 1896.

was that it was very properly decided at Paris to send a large expeditionary force, to make the road already referred to, and to take the campaign very seriously. The resistance proved, however, beneath contempt, and there seems now to be little doubt that the invading army was unnecessarily large and that its size proved an incubus to its commander, who eventually concluded the campaign in brilliant fashion with a small flying column.

In irregular campaigns it is always doubtful how far the people of the hostile country, or in minor operations the hostile tribe, will put forth their entire strength. The attitude, moreover, of neighbouring peoples and tribes is at times a subject of great uncertainty. The very serious inconvenience which may arise when a neighbouring tribe unexpectedly assumes an unfriendly demeanour is singularly well illustrated by the Ambela campaign.

Uncertainty as to extent to which the hostile population itself, and the neighbouring tribes, etc., will take part in the campaign.

The operations were undertaken with a view of attacking and dispersing a settlement of Hindustani fanatics at a place called Malka, north of the Peshawur valley (see plan opposite). The plan decided upon was to fall upon the place from the north by a sudden march through the Ambela defile in the Chamla valley, so as to drive the enemy towards the Indian plains and into the arms of troops advancing from about Sitana.

Example of Ambela.

The expeditionary force under Sir N. Chamberlain was advancing slowly into the Ambela defile, a long and difficult pass through the hills, when the Buner tribe, a warlike mountain race dwelling in the hill country north of the Chamla valley, suddenly assumed a threatening attitude. For a march from Ambela to Malka with so formidable an enemy on the flank, a far larger army than that told off would have been necessary, and the consequence was that Sir N. Chamberlain found himself obliged to halt in the defile. The Hindustanis who were blocking the exit were supported actively by some small Mahommedan tribes, and were supported passively by the Buners. The inaction of the British force tended to encourage the enemy. For nearly a month it was in close contact with a resolute and enterprising foe, and severe fighting took place in which considerable loss was suffered. In the end the Buners were conciliated and, the hostile gathering in the defile being dispersed, the column marched to Malka and carried out the programme decided upon at the outset.

The difficulty of dealing with Orientals and savages, whether as informers or spies, is referred to in many textbooks and works of reference on reconnaissance and intelligence duties. The ordinary native found in theatres of war peopled by coloured races lies simply for the love of the thing

Difficulty of eliciting correct information from natives.

and his ideas of time, numbers, and distance are of the vaguest, even when he is trying to speak the truth. Most officers have experienced this during the ordinary course of foreign service. In small wars the field intelligence department is often greatly hampered by this difficulty in eliciting correct information from the people of the country—more so than would generally be the case in civilized countries. But that this difficulty is one which can be overcome has often been proved in actual campaigns, and notably in the remarkable set of operations which carried the Anglo-Egyptian troops by successive stages from Wadi Halfa to Omdurman in the years 1895–1898, and which afford a signal illustration of what can be achieved by a thoroughly efficient intelligence department. Even then, however, the incapacity of appreciating numbers which Orientals habitually display, was evidenced by the fact that the Khalifa mustered for his last stand a considerably larger army than the native reports had given him credit for.

Treachery.
One other difficulty which the regular army has sometimes to contend with in small wars is treachery on the part of ostensibly neutral bodies or tribes, while in civilized warfare such a thing is almost unknown. The Indian Mutiny furnishes the ever memorable case of Cawnpore, and in the campaigns against the Red Indians the United States troops had constantly to be on the watch against hostile perfidy. The standard of honour varies greatly among different uncivilized or semi-civilized races ; but it is not by any means the case that those lowest in the human scale are the least to be trusted. When operating in certain parts of the world or in contact with certain people a commander has always to be on his guard, and the following incidents are worth citing as showing what has at times to be expected :—

In 1884 the French concluded a treaty of peace relative to Tonkin with the Chinese, in virtue of which Tonkin was acknowledged to be a French acquisition. Shortly afterwards, however, a column of troops marching through the country was suddenly attacked by the Chinese near Bac Lé; a regular ambush had been formed, and the column was very roughly handled. Hostilities were therefore resumed.

During the march of the Anglo-French expeditionary force from the Taku Forts towards Pekin in 1860, the Chinese had consented in the course of negotiations that the allies might advance to Tang Chow, ten miles short of the capital; but the hostile army was found barring the road and, in consequence of the enemy's threatening demeanour, it was found necessary to attack this army and to drive it off.

The Boer war of 1881 commenced with the ncident of Bronker's Spruit—an incident that would never occur in regular warfare. Part of a British regiment was marching through the Transvaal, no hostilities having occurred. An ambush for it was prepared, and it was suddenly ordered to halt. The commanding officer naturally declined. The troops were fired upon when practically unprepared, and so many were killed and wounded that the force was obliged to surrender.

In every class of warfare uncertainty must exist as to the movements, intentions, and whereabouts of the enemy. Unless there is some special reason for acting to the contrary, a commander always endeavours to keep his antagonist in doubt upon these points. To correctly interpret the auguries derived from reconnaissances, from information brought in by spies, and from the various forms of circumstantial evidence provided by the theatre of war, is often one of the most difficult of military problems. But the causes which tend to bring about this uncertainty differ considerably in irregular warfare from those prevailing in great campaigns.

Uncertainty as to movements and intentions of enemy prevails in all classes of warfare.

Regular armies are governed by certain strategical laws —elastic laws no doubt, but none the less laws—a complete disregard of which will lead to disaster. They conceal their movements and concentrations behind screens of outposts. They control as far as practicable the telegraph lines, the postal system, the press, and the other channels for disseminating news, and by these methods they can for a time keep their adversaries in perplexity as to when and where the blow will fall, and can conceal combinations by which they propose to parry the adversary's attack. But this concealment can only be kept up for a certain time and till the opposing forces

Difference in this respect between regular warfare and small wars; reasons for it.

come in contact. Once the two armies really confront each other, and the veil which has hidden one from the other is rent asunder, each can guess not only the position and strength but also the intentions of the other, and each can infer how the other will act in the various contingencies that may arise. Both are governed by the same laws, and are as it were playing the same game.

But in a small war it is not so. The more irregular and the less organized the forces of the enemy are, the more independent do they become of strategical rules. An army which disperses if it is beaten, cannot be treated in the same way as an army which under such circumstances retreats in as compact and regular formation as the case admits of towards its base. It is far more difficult to infer from the indications which come to hand what such an enemy means to do, and to foresee what will happen under any conditions which the regular army may be able to bring about.

There is, moreover, another peculiarity which is very generally found in the antagonists with whom the organized forces in small wars have to cope. This is the extreme rapidity with which the enemy conducts his movements and operations. This mobility, which as will be seen in later chapters greatly influences the strategical and tactical conditions, is attributable to various causes—actual marching power, freedom of impedimenta, knowledge of the theatre of war, and so forth. But one important consequence of this mobility on the part of the enemy undoubtedly is to increase the perplexity and uncertainty in which the regular army is plunged. In the Red Indian campaigns the great difficulty was generally to find the camps of these nomad marauders, who travelled huge distances in a few hours after one of their devastating forays. In Algeria the French were incessantly despatching expeditions against the Kabyles which could effect nothing because the enemy disappeared. The mobility of the Zulu impis kept the British in constant bewilderment as to their approximate positions, in the earlier stages of the war. As a consequence of the rapidity of the enemy's movements, large hostile forces were on more than one occasion met with quite unexpectedly in the Afghan and Sudan campaigns.

It may be taken, then, to be a feature of small wars that the regular army labours under grave embarrassments due to want of accurate intelligence as to the theatre of war, and as to the movements, the strength and the fighting value of the bodies opposed to it. The extent to which this is so varies of course greatly in different campaigns. But in operations of this nature there is always an amount of uncertainty which ought seldom to exist in regular warfare between two modern armies maintaining efficient staffs in peace time. This doubt reflects itself in the movements of the regular forces ; it dogs them in their advance, cramping their liberty of action to such an extent that it not unfrequently brings them to a complete standstill, to the great encouragement of the enemy and to the detriment of a decisive campaign.

On the other hand, the enemy enjoys many advantages in the matter of " intelligence." It is of course the case that semi-civilized or barbarian nations, that tribes on the borders of the foreign possessions of Great Powers or insurgents within their borders, that the class of people, in fact, who form the enemy in small wars, are very ignorant as to the resources, the military strength, and the, comparatively speaking, perfect army organization of the country with which they engage in hostilities. Were it not so small wars would be of far rarer occurrence. But from the very nature of such campaigns the enemy is generally operating in a theatre of war with which he is familiar. He knows the tracks over the hills, the paths through the jungle, the passages over the rivers, the points where he can be sure of replenishing his few requirements.

Advantages enjoyed by the enemy as regards intelligence.

Knowledge of theatre of war.

More than this. The enemy, however little he may understand the fighting system of the regular troops, or appreciate the value of their weapons, or grasp what they are aiming at,

The enemy seems always to know the movements of the regular army.

is generally aware of every movement which they make as soon as it is completed, and often before it has begun. This arises from the social system in such theatres of war and from the manner in which the inhabitants live. News spreads in a most mysterious fashion. The people are far more observant than the dwellers in civilized lands. By a kind of instinct they interpret military portents even when totally deficient of courage or fighting capacity. Camp gossip is heard by those who are attracted by the ready payment which supplies brought to a civilized army always meet with, and it flies from mouth to mouth till it reaches the ears of the hostile leaders. The regular army is being watched in all its operations and cannot prevent it. The enemy has no organized intelligence department, no regular corps of spies, no telegraphs—and yet he knows perfectly well what is going on. He sees his opponent's hand. And it may be added that the press is apt to favour the enemy, for the war correspondents are generally all on the side of the regular army, and may, even with the best intentions not to prejudice the course of operations and in spite of censorships, give information to the foe.

To take a recent example of the difficulty of concealing movements and intentions from the enemy. In the campaign against the Hunza-Nagar tribes north of Kashmir in 1891, the British force was, after the storming of the fort of Nilt, brought to a standstill for several days by a formidable line of defence works covering an extensive mountain position of great natural strength. Attempts were on more than one occasion made to gain a lodgment in these lines by a night attack but the enemy seemed always to know what was intended beforehand. One night an attack had been intended; but it did not actually take place because the enemy suddenly opened a heavy fire before the storming parties approached, evidently knowing that an assault was impending.

This can be turned to account by publishing false information as to intentions.

Inconvenient as it is that the enemy seems always to be so well informed as to what the regular army does or is going to do, this circumstance can sometimes be turned to account. By spreading fictitious information as to proposed movements, or by publishing it abroad that some imaginary enterprise is impending, the hostile leaders can be put on a false scent. The news is sure to reach them. And although the troops in small wars find their opponents as a rule skilled in the arrangement of ambushes and the carrying out of surprises, masters in the art of military deception, crafty and cunning, they find them on the other hand to be by no means so wary in avoiding snares as they are artful in setting them. This fact—the ease with which such warriors can often be deceived, surprised, lured into ambushes, and so forth—will be referred to again in another chapter. Suffice it to say here that when the plan is adopted of propagating misleading intelligence as to prospective operations, the enemy generally falls into the trap readily enough.

During the war in Tonkin in 1884, an advance was about to be made from Hanoi to Bacninh by the French. The Chinese and Black Flags had constructed a series of fortified positions blocking the direct road, and were prepared to contest the passage. The French general therefore spread the report that he meant to fight his way through ; then he suddenly marched off to a flank, and, moving across country, reached Bacninh from another side. The enemy, completely deceived, was unprepared to bar the way to the French force, which gained its destination with little trouble.

The transfer by sea of the British expeditionary force from Alexandria to Ismailia, in 1882, was carried out under the cover of a pretended attack on Aboukir. It was of the utmost importance that a secure footing should be gained in the Suez Canal before Arabi Pasha should guess that this was the real point of attack. Rolling stock, which it was foreseen would be required on the railway from Ismailia to the Nile Delta, was embarked at Alexandria on the pretence of being sent to Cyprus. Orders were drawn up for a combined attack by land and sea upon the Aboukir forts. The fleet and the transports on their way from Alexandria to Ismailia actually steamed into Aboukir Bay, and on the same day 3,000 Egyptian troops were sent thither from Cairo. It is said that Arabi Pasha first heard of the great transfer of force from one side of Egypt to the other a year later when a prisoner in Ceylon.

Previously to the second attack on Dargai in the Tirah campaign, information had been allowed to leak out that it was contemplated to conduct the operation on the same lines as on the previous occasions—to advance direct on the position with one column and to turn the right with another. The consequence was that large bodies of the enemy remained on the hostile right flank awaiting this expected turning movement, a turning movement which was never really intended to take place. This division of the tribal forces reduced, at any rate during the earlier part of the day, the numbers available to hold the formidable position against which the assault was eventually delivered. On hearing that the Dargai heights were likely to be held in strength, Sir W. Lockhart had ordered the tribesmen's attention to be occupied in front, while a force was to proceed as rapidly as possible past the front of Dargai so as to threaten their line of retreat; this turning movement was not, however, carried out, the result being that great difficulty was experienced in capturing a position which would probably have been evacuated by the enemy the moment our troops had established themselves in rear of it. But the storming of the heights, if it was attended with serious loss, exerted great moral effect on the tribesmen and gave the enemy the severest losses of the whole campaign.

The evening before the battle of Khartum information reached Sir H. Kitchener that the Khalifa contemplated a night attack. Such an eventuality was most undesirable, and so villagers were sent out to reconnoitre the hostile position and to convey the idea that the Anglo-Egyptian army intended a night attack upon the Mahdists. The consequence was that the enemy's host remained in its position, and that the battle was deferred till the morning.

Conclusions arrived at in chapter only to be considered as generally applicable.

But all that has been said in this chapter with regard to the peculiar conditions as to intelligence which prevail in small wars must be understood to be applicable only generally. In many cases they hold good only partially. In some cases they do not hold good at all. The operations may take place in districts to the full as well known to the regular army as they are to the enemy, perfect acquaintance with the organization and strength of the hostile force will at times be enjoyed, the inhabitants of the theatre of war may be strongly in favour of the regular army and may avoid giving information of any kind to the other side. All this depends upon the circumstances of the case. The conditions vary so greatly in small wars that the principles which govern them, as a whole, are in the highest degree elastic. It can therefore only be laid down as a usual condition in warfare of this nature that the regular army is at a disadvantage as compared to the enemy as regards what we call military intelligence, but it is by no means an invariable rule.

CHAPTER V.

The influence of the question of supply upon small wars and the extent to which it must govern the plan of operations.

The fact that small wars are, generally speaking, campaigns rather against nature than against hostile armies has been already referred to. It constitutes one of the most distinctive characteristics of this class of warfare. It affects the course of operations to an extent varying greatly according to circumstances, but so vitally at times as to govern the whole course of the campaign from start to finish. It arises almost entirely out of the difficulties as regards supply which the theatres of small wars generally present. *Small wars are campaigns against nature mainly so owing to supply.*

Climate affects the health of troops, absence of communications retards the movements of soldiers, the jungle and the bush embarrass a commander; but if it were not for the difficulty as regards food for man and beast which roadless and inhospitable tracts oppose to the operations of a regular army, good troops well led would make light of such obstacles in their path. It is not the question of pushing forward the man, or the horse, or the gun, that has to be taken into account, so much as that of the provision of the necessaries of life for the troops when they have been pushed forward.

The less fertile and productive the theatre of war, the more elaborate have to be the arrangements for the commissariat. The worse are the tracks, the more difficult is it to ensure an efficient transport service to carry the supplies which do not exist on the spot. The larger the columns of transport are, the greater force do they require for their protection from hostile raids. This all-important question of *Reasons for this.*

supply is in fact at the root of most of the difficulties, and has been the cause of some of the disasters, to which regular troops engaged in small wars seem ever to be prone.

Connection between supply and transport. Supply and transport are intimately bound up in all military operations. On the Continent of Europe where roads, railways, and canals generally abound, where the districts which may at some future period become scenes of war can be foreseen in times of peace, and where contending armies can live largely if not wholly upon the country they traverse, an organized supply service comes into existence as armies change from the peace to the war footing. Unless railways make it unnecessary, arrangements are generally made for ensuring that with, and immediately in rear of, the troops, shall move great trains of wagons carrying rations for the force to last for several days; and, as the army advances on a broad front, it covers these trains from hostile attacks, and their protection is not therefore a source of great anxiety to the leader. Then, as the supplies carried in these trains are consumed, they are made good, partly from what can be obtained from the theatre of war, and partly by the empty transport moving back to fixed supply magazines for replenishment. As long as the army does not move forward with great rapidity and does not outstrip its supply train, or does not suddenly change its course as a result of defeat or of some unforeseen event, there is no reason why all should not work smoothly.

Supply trains in small wars In small wars the circumstances are, however, wholly different. The absence of communications makes the transport of a given quantity of food a matter of far graver difficulty than it is in the average European theatre of war. Animals can draw a considerably greater weight than they can carry, and therefore the substitution of pack transport for wagons at once greatly increases the size of the train—a British battalion on the Indian scale requires for its 1st and 2nd line transport a little over a mile of track, if from its nature the mules have to move in single file. Moreover, the worse the route is, the slower does the transport move. Supply in fact is largely dependent upon the nature of the route which the force is following, and if the route is very bad or very narrow the commissariat service is apt to suffer in proportion.

If no supplies can be obtained from the theatre of war, as is so often the case in these operations, everything in the way of food for man or beast has to be carried. It must be remembered that the transport animals themselves have to be fed, and that if no forage is obtainable they have to carry their own food. It may be taken as a rough rule that a transport animal cannot under the most favourable circumstances carry food for itself for more than a month; this, moreover, takes no account of the return journey. A little consideration of these points makes clear what difficulties the question of supply is apt to raise.

Experience shows that in small wars very great distances have often to be traversed through barren arid districts, where the soil is not cultivated, where no sheep or cattle are to be found, where a scanty population subsists on food unsuited for European soldiery, and where no forage for horses or mules exists. Supplies have then to be carried sufficient to subsist the force while it traverses the whole distance, and the consequence of this is that supply trains grow to an enormous size and become very troublesome to control and difficult to protect. The army in fact becomes a mere escort for its food, and it often has to establish some form of entrenched camp to leave its food in under the guardianship of part of the force, before it can fight a battle. A few examples of these great unwieldy moveable magazines may be cited here in illustration.

In the British expedition to Abyssinia in 1868, the moveable magazine for a force of 10,000 fighting men amounted to 26,000 animals and 12,000 followers. When the Russians conquered Khiva in 1874, the column from Tashkend, consisting of 5,500 men, was accompanied by a supply column of

8,800 camels. When during the last Afghan war Sir D. Stewart marched from Kandahar to Kabul, his force of 7,000 had 6,000 transport animals, and later on, on Sir F. Roberts's return march to Kandahar, his army of 10,000 had with it over 8,000 transport animals. The French expeditionary force of 15,000 men despatched to capture Antananarivo started with 5,000 two-wheeled wagons; eventually the flying column which captured the place, and which was 4,000 strong, moved off with 2,800 pack animals.

Into the question of how best to protect these great supply columns, it is not proposed in this chapter to enter. But it is obvious that their convoy through a country occupied by a hostile population is a formidable problem; and as a consequence it may be accepted as a general principle that in small wars supply presents not only great difficulties in the way of organization, but exerts also a powerful influence over actual tactics when the regular troops meet their antagonists in conflict.

Difficulties as to supply tend to limit the force employed.   So great indeed are the difficulties that arise in many small wars from supply, that it becomes necessary to cut down the forces engaged to the lowest possible strength consistent with safety, and that campaigns have to be embarked upon with armies barely capable numerically of performing the work which they may have in hand. A condition of things is evolved, in fact, such as called from Henry IV of France the remark with regard to campaigns against Spain in his day :—" Invade with a large force and you are destroyed by starvation ; invade with a small one and you are overwhelmed by a hostile population." General Skobelef, when engaged upon his campaign against the Turkomans in 1880, which will be referred to later, was constantly in fear that the Russian Government would take alarm at the slowness of his progress and would send reinforcements across the Caspian ; weakness of force to him was under the circumstances a source of strength.

The question of water.   An element moreover enters into the question of supply in many small wars which seldom need to be taken into consideration except transitorily in a Continental campaign.

This is the question of water. When the theatre of war is a desert with only a few scattered wells, water becomes a matter of supply, and has to be carried with the force. Its transport is exceptionally troublesome. The transport animals themselves require it as well as troops and horses. From its nature much of it is apt to be lost in transit. It requires special arrangements for its storage as well as for its carriage. A failure of the water supply means disaster if not annihilation. During the protracted operations of the German military forces against the Herreros and other tribes of Damaraland and Namaqualand, this question was constantly a source of difficulty and a cause of delay.

(1) During the Russian campaign against Khiva one of the three invading columns, that based on the Caspian Sea at Krasnovodsk, after suffering terrible privations from want of water, was in the end obliged to turn back, and never reached the Khivan oasis. In 1866, a Russian column under General Tchernaieff attempted to march from Tashkend to capture Samarcand ; but after proceeding a considerable distance it was obliged to turn back owing to difficulties as to supply, principally water.

(2) In 1840, a small British force holding Kahan in the Marri country which flanked the Bolan route to Kandahar, was hemmed in by hostile tribesmen ; a detachment sent back from it had met with disaster ; the garrison was known to be in grave jeopardy from lack of good water and sufficient food ; so a force was organised to succour it.

The relieving troops had been assured of water at the foot of an important pass ; but on reaching the spot designated none was found : the Marris were holding the heights, the water supply with the troops was exhausted, there was nothing for it but to storm the position and get to Kahan. But the assault miscarried. The waverers among the hostile tribesmen lurking among the hills to watch the issue, then rushed down eager to participate in the fray, and only by dint of resolute fighting was this counter-attack repelled. The force was now in desperate straits from want of water and had to retire to seek it, abandoning everything. When the stricken remnant reached water the supply train had been lost and there was no food left, so the force had to march back 50 miles to its original starting point, where it arrived in piteous plight. Kahan had to be left to its fate and the disaster was at the time irretrievable. This misfortune appears to have been entirely caused by the failure to find water where its existence had been calculated upon.

It may be mentioned that the Kahan garrison, after a most gallant defence, was granted a safe conduct, and eventually reached the frontier post, " emaciated, ragged, hungry and destitute, yet bringing with them their gun and their honour."

(3) During Admiral Rawson's advance on Benin in 1897, it had been expected that water would be found in a place called Agagi, 12 miles from the capital, but on reaching the locality the wells were found to be dry. It was decided therefore to push on as a flying column, carrying three days' water supply as well as provisions and ammunition.

The position of the wells fixes the lines of military operations in a desert, just as it fixes the caravan routes and the highways of commerce. They become points of supreme strategical importance, a fact of which the enemy is well aware. The Mahdists made a desperate attempt to prevent Sir H. Stewart's forces from reaching the Abu Klea wells; and it is said that during Hicks Pasha's ill-fated attempt to march to El Obeid from the Nile, they closed up the wells in rear of his force as it advanced, so as to make its retreat impossible. The enemy is generally fully alive to the importance of destroying the water supply, which can easily be done in the case of scattered wells; in the Mohmund campaign of 1897, the hill men broached their tanks, and this was one of the chief difficulties General Elles had to contend with. It is clear then that the question of water exerts at times a dominant influence over the course of these campaigns. In almost all tropical campaigns the subject of water is a source of anxiety and it is constantly in the mind of the commander as he shapes his plan of operations.

Supply a matter of calculation, but there is always great risk of this being upset by something unforeseen.

Supply both of food and of water is in reality merely a matter of calculation. For a given force proceeding a given distance at a given rate, the amount that will be required is a question of figures, and, in a theatre of war possessing good communication, problems of this kind can be worked out with considerable probability of the results arrived at in practice corresponding to those arrived at in theory. But in uncivilized countries it is almost impossible to predict the rate at which the force will advance. Trustworthy information as to the country to be traversed is often lacking; unexpected obstacles spring up, quite apart from the endeavours of the enemy to check progress ; the extent to which the theatre of war itself may assist as regards providing supplies is undetermined ; doubts and perplexity on this score are constantly arising and thwarting the regular army. A good example of a wholly unforeseen difficulty arising as regards supply, and falsifying predictions based on a most careful review of the situation with reference to available food, occurred during the Nile expedition of 1884–85.

The River Column, starting from Hamdab beyond Korti carried with it 100 days' supplies, which was believed to be sufficient to take it to Berber. It was discovered, however, after the force had proceeded some distance that one-third of the biscuits were unserviceable, which reduced the time that the column could operate independently by more than one month. This unfortunate *contretemps*, which could not of course be foreseen, completely upset the calculations upon which the general plan of campaign had been based.

In countries where small wars take place, communications are generally most indifferent. Railways there are none. Proper roads admitting of the passage of wheeled transport are seldom existent. The inhabitants of the theatre of war are generally satisfied with rugged tracks available only for pack transport. But navigable rivers are often to be found, and these, even if they are not used for the actual movement of troops, are of incalculable assistance at times as channels for forwarding supplies, especially if steamers can be put on them. *Rivers as affecting supply in small wars.*

The rivers in Cochin China and Tonkin proved in this manner of great service to the French in their campaigns in 1861 and 1884-85. The Achin river similarly aided the Dutch in their second expedition against the Achin Sultanate.

But this is especially well illustrated by the French campaign against Dahomey in 1892-93. The Wémé river leading into the heart of this jungle-grown theatre of war, enabled General Dodds to advance with assured steps more than half way from the coast to Abomey the capital, in spite of determined action on the part of the enemy, for supply and water were during that stage a matter of little difficulty. As soon as the French column was obliged to strike off from the river the difficulty of protecting the transport train began to manifest itself, and progress became deliberate and dangerous.

The boat
expeditions
to the Red
River and up
the Nile.
The use of steamers may, however, be denied by circumstances. It may be impossible to tow barges from the bank.
Sailing is generally impracticable. And from the nature of
these wars it is generally the case that the regular forces are
advancing from the sea, and that the current is therefore
against them. But two notable British campaigns have shown
how rivers can be used for forwarding supplies even under
such unfavourable circumstances. In both the Red River
Expedition and the Nile Expedition of 1884–85, row-boats were
used, by which at once the force itself and the supplies for
the force advanced. The troops rowed the boats themselves
and carried their supplies with them, thus forming their own
transport—a transport which from its nature needed no
forage to be carried for it. The Red River Expedition moved
through a country wholly destitute of supplies, the entire
force going by boat. The Nile Expedition moved through a
country where some supplies were obtainable ; part of the
force—the mounted portion—marched, some steamers and
barges were available, and the force was assisted by some
transport on its line of advance. But both these campaigns
show how rivers can be made use of as channels of supply,
the troops themselves forming the transport.

Principle of
holding back
the troops
and pushing
on supplies
ahead of
them.
Earlier in this chapter the enormous amount of transport
required for a force penetrating far into a territory destitute
of supplies has been pointed out. The fact that this transport has to be fed itself and that it may have to carry its
own food has been commented upon. It is clear that the
longer the troops are operating in a resourceless country the
more supplies will they want, and the larger will be the
transport columns. Obviously, therefore, it is often of vital
importance in the conduct of such operations that the army
should be as short a time as possible away from its base,
and that the troops should be kept back while the supplies
are pushed ahead under the escort of the smallest force which
can safely be entrusted with the duty.

It often occurred in the later days of the South African War of 1899–1902, when the struggle had degenerated into guerilla warfare that, at the cost of vast trouble and accompanied by an imposing escort, a convoy would be sent out into the heart of some district far from the railway. But then the supplies which it carried would be consumed by troops which were not engaged on active operation at the moment because there happened to be no enemy at hand—by troops which could have been fed without the slightest difficulty on the railway. Sometimes the very column which had escorted a convoy far afield would bivouac by the convoy till its contents were consumed, and would then escort the empty wagons back. That this occurred so often can only be attributed to a failure to realize the interdependence which exists between the administration of supply and the strategy of the campaign. The commander who does not realize this interdependence, and who does not frame his general plans of operations with it in view, will assuredly not make the most of that aggregate of fighting men and animals and non-combatants and transport and stores which make up his command, under the conditions usually prevailing in small wars.

But on the other hand the principle of holding back the bulk of the troops and pushing supplies on ahead, must not be carried too far. The supplies must move under adequate escort and must be guarded by a sufficient force when they have reached their destination. As the escorts and guards consume supplies, the great object is to reduce them to a minimum, and the best means of doing this is to create fortified depôts in the enemy's country, where the supplies are collected and stored ready for the army to use when it advances in force. Or it may be necessary, as suggested above, to push out a portion of the army to fight its way into the theatre of war and to hold its ground, while supplies are moved forward in rear of it and collected under its protection, the rest of the force remaining at the base waiting till all is ready. But however the

(10830)   E operation is carried out, the broad principle is to advance with the smallest force consistent with safety under the given circumstances, and to store sufficient food for the whole army to be enabled to perform its allotted task. The Russian campaigns in 1879 and 1880 against the Turkomans, and the advance of the British troops form the Suez Canal to the Nile delta in 1882, afford fine examples of this great principle of conducting a small war in a desert country.

Examples
illustrating
this.

(1) In 1879 a Russian army of some 16,000 men under General Lomakin was detailed to move from the Caspian Sea into the Turkoman country and subdue its people. A place called Ch.'kislar, in somewhat unhealthy surroundings near the southern end of the sea, was made the base, and there elaborate preparations of all kinds was made for the campaign. But the enterprise failed disastrously, mainly owing to a disregard of the principle enunciated above.

The country between Chikislar and the Tekke oases is not a desert, but it is not on the other hand a district which a large army could live upon. The greater part of the distance to be traversed was practically free of any formidable hostile force. But instead of keeping the bulk of his army west of the Caspian Sea while supplies were collecting, General Lomakin assembled his troops immediately at Chikislar, they ate up the supplies as fast as they were disembarked, and, as a consequence, the large force was for months detained in an unhealthy locality. Depôts of supplies were not formed in advance along the line to be followed, and when the army eventually moved forward it was followed by a gigantic but nevertheless insufficient transport train. The difficulty of feeding the troops grew from day to day. Nothing could, indeed, more clearly show the fatal effects of a failure to grasp the essential principles of supplying an army operating in a desert country, and of a defective organization of the commissariat and transport services, than the fact that only 1,400 fighting men out of the original force of over 16,000 could be assembled for the one battle of the campaign—the disastrous assault on Denghil Tepe.

(2) General Skobelef the following year conducted the campaign on altogether different lines. He did not assemble his main body at Chikislar till the last moment. He pushed out small bodies and formed defensive posts on the intended line of operations, where he stored provisions for the army he was about to lead to Denghil Tepe. He recognised that the campaign he was undertaking hinged upon supply, and with this constantly in view, everything was arranged for deliberately and in advance. His system was slow, but it was absolutely sure. It is indeed a remarkable illustration of the great influence which the question of supply exerts over the conduct and course of small wars, that a leader like Skobelef, whose daring and

resolution had been so signally conspicuous two years before in the campaign in Bulgaria against the formidable Turkish troops, should, while operating against the feeble military forces of the Tekke Turkomans, be found spending months in organizing his commissariat and in forming advanced food depôts, while he must from his intrepid disposition have been even more anxious than were the Russian army and the Russian people to wipe out promptly the disgrace of the previous year's disaster. In the end organization and calculation triumphed, and the campaign concluded with a brilliant success.

(3) The Egyptian campaign of 1882 differed from those against the Turkomans above referred to in that the distance was short, and that the line of advance from Ismailia was through country held strongly by the enemy. To ensure the water supply it was of vital importance to secure the Kassassin lock on the sweet water canal, which marked the course of the proposed line of operations, and owing to the difficulty of forwarding supplies up to this point it was necessary to send the smallest possible force to seize it, and to hold it. Therefore a mere fraction of the expeditionary force was pushed to the front and bore the brunt of the Egyptian attacks, while the bulk of it remained idle at Ismailia and was only moved forward when sufficient food had been collected for it to operate with rapidity and decision. The operations lasting up to the fight of Tel el Kebir serve as a model of how a campaign should be conducted in a country where the transport of supplies is a main difficulty.

The difficulty of supplying an army in warfare of this class may arise from the nature of the country as in Tirah and in the district about Ismailia, or from the great distances to be traversed as in the Turkoman campaigns and in South Africa, or from both, as was the case in Lord Wolseley's Nile Expedition and the later campaigns which broke up the Mahdist power. But the principle remains the same.

Before finishing this chapter on supply as affecting the course of small wars, an example may be cited of a campaign where this question decided the selection of the actual theatre of war. The Nile Expedition of 1884–85, serves this purpose well. Apart from the exigencies of supply, the shortest route by far to Khartum was that from Suakin *viâ* Berber : but between Suakin and Berber, water is only to be found in a few wells scattered far apart, so it would have been necessary to carry water ; and as a great part of the Egyptian Sudan north of Khartum is practically a desert, a force advancing

Example of a theatre of war being selected owing to reasons of supply.

through it needs a vast transport train to carry its food unless it follows the line of the great natural highway of the Nile. But an army following the course of the great river was free of all anxiety as to water, and was able, by using boats as shown in an earlier paragraph, to dispense with the huge trains of transport animals which usually form so essential a feature of a desert campaign. Thus it was that the supply question almost necessarily made the Nile valley the theatre of the campaign for the relief of Khartum, instead of the desert between Suakin and Berber.

The Nile Expedition a remarkable illustration of the subject of this chapter. This Nile Expedition has been frequently referred to throughout this chapter. Like many of the Russian campaigns in Asia, like the French Madagascar expedition of 1895, and like many other small wars, it was essentially a campaign against nature, a struggle against the difficulties arising from supplying the wants of troops traversing great stretches of desert country. But it had this peculiarity—it was a campaign not only against nature but also against time, because it was undertaken to relieve a beleagured city. For this reason, and also because of the remarkable manner in which its phases demonstrate the influence which the question of food and water may exert over a small war, an outline account of it from the point of view of supply will not be out of place in closing the subject.

Sketch of this campaign from the point of view of supply. From Lower Egypt to the second cataract at Wadi Halfa, the railways along its course and the numerous steamers upon its waters make the Nile and its valley an excellent line of operations for a small army. For this reason the Nile Expedition may be taken as having had its base at Wadi Halfa.

Above Wadi Halfa up to the Third Cataract (see the plan facing next page) the Nile, at the season when the despatch of the force really commenced, and for several months afterwards, forms a series of rapids most difficult to navigate. From the Third Cataract to Hamdab the river offers no difficulty to small steamers; but only two were available on this stretch. Armed opposition was not to be expected north of Korti, therefore between Wadi Halfa and that point the transport of the troops and their food, and the arrangement of supplies for feeding them *en route*, were practically the only points to be thought of. The campaign proper would only begin after passing Korti.

Lord Wolseley's plan was to start his force from Korti with 100 days' supplies, which, supplemented by supplies which would be conveyed across the desert from Korosko to Abu Hamed as soon as that point had been reached, it was hoped would carry the army from Korti to Khartum. The force was to row itself from Wadi Halfa to Korti in the boats specially sent out for the purpose, carrying its 100 days' supplies with it and fed by the way from depôts established in advance along the route. A small mounted detachment and the specially organized camel corps, however, marched the whole way.

The first thing, therefore, was to push on supplies by every available means so that the whole force should be fed on its way to Korti, and so that there should be sufficient supplies at the front for the mounted troops (who had not the boat supplies to depend upon) to be able to carry out such operations as might prove necessary. In the meantime most of the troops were held back below Wadi Halfa up to the last possible moment, although a small force had to be pushed on to protect the supply depôts and secure the line to Korti.

In spite of the most strenuous exertions, the difficulty of collecting the necessary supplies along the route and at Korti gave rise to delay. The force took longer to assemble at its advanced base than had been anticipated, because food for its consumption took longer to collect than had been expected. Time was throughout of the most momentous importance. And so it came about that when the troops eventually began to reach Korti, the situation had become so critical at Khartum that Lord Wolseley decided to at once send the camel corps across the desert from Korti to Metemma, to open up communications with General Gordon. The camel corps had been organized with the possibility of this contingency in view, although the original plan of campaign had been that the whole force should move by river. The difficulty of calculating the time within which supplies can be stored along a line of communications, even when the enemy has not to be taken into account, was thus demonstrated before the actual campaign began.

The force detailed to march to Metemma reached Gubat close to that point and 180 miles from Korti; but it took 21 days to do so. The delay was entirely due to supply difficulties, for instead of marching straight across, it was found necessary to form a depot at Jakdul about half way where there were good wells, and to send the transport back from there to Korti to bring up more food, before the rest of the distance could be covered. The fight at Abu Klea, which will be referred to in other chapters, had a most unfortunate effect as regards supply, for the transport suffered considerably in the action; and the transport being throughout heavily worked and getting little rest was seriously crippled by the time that the force had reached its destination near Metemma.

Khartum having fallen immediately after this and a complete change having thus occurred in the strategical situation, the desert force after a time withdrew to Abu Klea. Lord Wolseley had for a time hoped before closing operations for the season to capture Berber by a combined movement of the desert force and of the River Column which was in the meantime following the Nile, and thus to establish an advanced post at an important strategical point in anticipation of a campaign against Khartum some months later. But it was found that the transport of the desert force had completely collapsed under the strain thrown upon it, and that the necessary food for the force intended for this enterprise could not have been carried. Owing to the supply question the desert force had thus become inoperative.

But the River Column had also become practically inoperative, likewise on account of supply. This advanced by boat with its 100 days' ration as originally intended, but, owing to an exceptionally low Nile, the rapids to be ascended proved to be more difficult than had been anticipated, and the progress of the column was unexpectedly slow. A convoy had been organized to move from Korosko to Abu Hamed and replenish supplies ; but before the column reached that point it became clear that, even allowing for this assistance, the supplies would not suffice to carry it to Berber and back— the already referred to loss of a month's biscuits very seriously affecting the question. So it became necessary to recall the column to Korti, and the operations came to an end.

It may seem strange that the conveyance of a large store of food from Korosko to Abu Hamed should have offered no serious difficulties, consider- ing the great distance, 230 miles—two-thirds of that from Wadi Halfa to Korti and across an almost waterless desert. But in this case the camels, starting fresh, would have made, as it were, a forced march in a very few days, so that their own food was not a serious item. As long, moreover, as they reached Abu Hamed with their loads, the operation was successful even if they then collapsed. Such conditions seldom occur. As the force did not reach Abu Hamed this notable item in the programme was not actually carried out ; but it is practically certain that it would have been, had not the River Column been recalled.

From beginning to end the question of food governed the movements of the expeditionary force. The question of water also greatly influenced the operations of the desert force, and introduced this important element of supply into the problem. It was not the impossibility of getting the troops themselves to Khartum, with or without fighting, in the short space of time available which brought about the failure of the campaign, but the impossi- bility of arranging for their supply within that time. And it must be added that the supply difficulties were enormously increased by the lateness of the start, by the unfortunate postponement in deciding on the despatch of the expedition. A few weeks sufficed to convert the Nile between the second and third cataracts from a great waterway up which the steamers from below Wadi Halfa could have steamed with ease, into a succession of tortuous rapids passable only with difficulty by small boats.

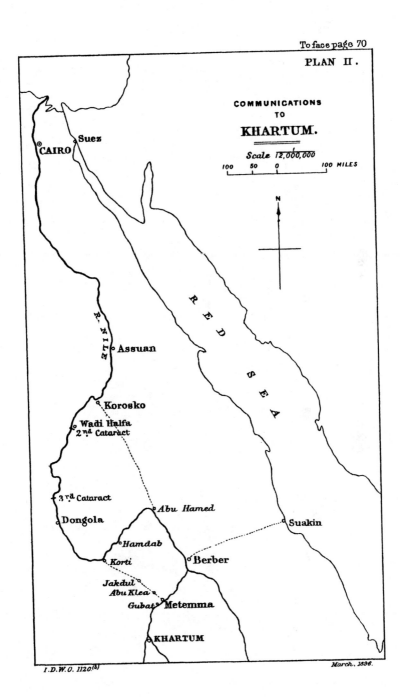

PLAN II.

COMMUNICATIONS
TO
KHARTUM.

Scale 12,000,000

100   50   0   100 MILES

N

CAIRO   Suez

R. NILE

Assuan

RED SEA

Korosko

Wadi Halfa
2ⁿᵈ Cataract

3ʳᵈ Cataract

Abu Hamed

Dongola

Suakin

Hamdab

Korti   Berber

Jakdul
Abu Klea
Gubat   Metemma

KHARTUM

CHAPTER VI.

BOLDNESS AND VIGOUR THE ESSENCE OF EFFECTIVELY CONDUCTING SUCH OPERATIONS.

IT is an established canon of the art of war that the seizure of the initiative at the outset and its maintenance thenceforward, is one of the best assured means of commanding success. To dominate the course of operations, to hold the lead and compel the antagonist to follow suit, is the way to achieve the victory.

The initiative.

In an earlier chapter it has been pointed out that the conditions which bring about small wars are such as generally to throw upon the regular troops the responsibility of acting. Whether the object with which it enters upon hostilities be to wipe out an insult, to repress a rebellion, or to consolidate a conquest, the onus of opening the campaign will rest usually with the trained and organized army. It follows therefore from their very nature, that the initiative in small wars at the start belongs to the regular force, and that the question of seizing it does not in consequence arise.

Forced upon the regular army to start with.

Under certain circumstances the enemy will sometimes make the first move. In an insurrection this is indeed generally the case—it was so in the Indian Mutiny. But rebels, unless the disaffection has been carefully concealed and unless the movement is organized and controlled by very capable leaders, rarely open proceedings by an effective operation of war. The massacre of a few settlers, the capture of some small defensive post, the banding together of a few parties of armed and angry men, does not constitute a seizure of the initiative in its military sense. The campaign only commences when troops are put in motion to put down the disturbance by force.

In regular warfare between two nations possessing highly organized military systems, this taking the lead at the outset is an object which both seek to obtain. Each has its plan of campaign. The one that gets the start can thereby dislocate the whole scheme of operations which has been elaborated, in theory, by the other. But in small wars, although promptitude in opening hostilities is more or less incumbent on the regular army, there are not the same reasons for precipitating events. The opponents have no intricate mobilization system which a sudden blow may throw out of gear. It is not a case of seizing the initiative, for that is not in the early stages, except in a few rare cases, in dispute. The great point to aim at is not so much that there should be no delay in getting into motion, as that when once in motion there should be no check. An ephemeral triumph is dearly purchased at the cost of a subsequent period of discreditable inaction.

For it is a cardinal principle in the conduct of warfare of this nature that the initiative must be maintained, that the regular army must lead while its adversaries follow, and that the enemy must be made to feel a moral inferiority throughout. The lower races are impressionable. They are greatly influenced by a resolute bearing and by a determined course of action. "A la guerre," wrote Napoleon, "le moral et l'opinion sont la moitié de la réalité"—a maxim which is especially applicable to small wars. "Do not forget that in Asia he is the master who seizes the people pitilessly by the throat and imposes upon their imagination" was Skobelef's view. The spectacle of an organized body of troops sweeping forward slowly but surely into their territory unnerves them. There must be no doubt as to which side is in the ascendant, no question as to who controls the general course of the war; delays must not occur, they cause the enemy to pluck up courage; every pause is interpreted as weakness, every halt gives new life to the foe. That being so, it is essential that the campaign should not be commenced till there are sufficient forces on the spot to prosecute the work with vigour, and till these are thoroughly organized and equipped for the task which they have in hand, whatever it may be. " If you have at any period of the operations to halt for some time in order to bring up provisions," says Lord Wolseley, " you give the enemy such renewed courage as to make him often forget the success you had perhaps already achieved ; he imagines you halt from fear."

The Ambela campaign, already referred to on p. 49, is an excellent example of embarking on an expedition insufficiently prepared. The Indian Government ordered this undertaking against the advice of Sir H. Rose, the Commander-in-Chief, who pointed out that an adequate transport service did not exist and that one could not be got ready for a considerable time, and who wished the campaign to be deferred. As soon as the force moved off into the hills the transport broke down to such an extent that it was impossible to deliver a blow at the tribesmen who were preparing to bar the way, and a halt ensued. This decided the Bunerwals who were wavering, to throw in their lot against the British force ; and although they eventually held aloof their attitude compelled Sir N. Chamberlain to await reinforcements. In consequence his army was, as previously related, for a considerable time acting on the defensive and it felt to the full all the disadvantages of that situation.

Small wars for the most part take place in distant lands. If they are entered upon without a correct estimation of the strength and organization of the army necessary to achieve the end in view, and if it is found out when the die is cast that more men are required to ensure a triumph, it is sometimes by no means easy to get reinforcements within a reasonable time. For instance, in 1884 the French undertook operations in Formosa with a quite inadequate force, and, being unable to afford it any assistance after its insufficiency had become apparent, they were obliged to withdraw it after it had gained some ground and had made the French army respected in that part of the Chinese dominions.

Once the war has commenced, a delay has the effect of

giving the enemy an opportunity of organizing his fighting strength, and this he will not be slow to take advantage of. Previous to the opening of hostilities such people often do not recognize what is impending, and they are in consequence apt not to avail themselves of the chance which the respite affords them ; so that at that stage a pause on the part of the regular troops does little harm. On the other hand the history of small wars offers many striking examples of the evil which results when a miscalculation of supply and transport requirements brings the operations of the regular army to a standstill in the middle of a campaign, or when circumstances arise in the course of military events which demand action on its part for which it was not organized.

Examples of the evil consequences which arise from insufficient organization when the campaign is in progress. When in 1880 the British disaster at Maiwand led to the investment of Kandahar by Ayoub Khan's forces, there were considerable bodies of troops on the line of communications from Kandahar to India. These, had their transport service been in effective condition, could have rapidly concentrated and moved forward for the relief of the threatened city. But, as it was, the Afghan army was for a time permitted to hold a complete mastery in this part of the theatre of war, a condition of things which might have led to very serious results but for the despatch of Sir F. Roberts's force from Kabul.

Owing to the circumstances attending the outbreak of the Indian mutiny the rebels for a time secured the initiative. It was due to no want of vigour, and it was certainly in no way the result of want of foresight, that the force organised at Allahabad by Sir H. Havelock and Colonel Neill was unable to move on Cawnpore till the small British force holding out there in grievous straits had been induced to surrender. But the delay—a delay arising chiefly from transport difficulties to start with—had disastrous consequences quite apart from the terrible massacre with which the name of Cawnpore will be associated for all time. It enabled the rebels to gather strength and for a time to hold a complete ascendancy in the Doab and Oudh. It left them with the upper hand at that most critical stage of a small war, its opening phase after hostilities have actually taken place.

Examples of decisive results being obtained by promptitude at the outset. But, on the other hand, occasions will arise when prompt action at the outset may crush the enemy before he becomes formidable, and may stave off a troublesome campaign. The effect of a heavy blow struck without hestitation is always very great when uncivilized races or guerillas have to be dealt with. Obviously circumstances may sometimes attend the outbreak of a small war when vigour and promptitude may achieve brilliant results, and when it behoves the commander to strike at once even with inferior forces. This course is, of course, the best to pursue if the circumstances promise decisive results in case of the operation succeeding, and when the conditions will not require the success to be followed up.

The campaigns of the United States troops against the Red Indians furnish frequent examples of this. But there the detachments in the territory subject to the hostile raids were kept constantly on the alert and ready for action. The nature of the warfare, moreover, was not such as to call for a great development of force demanding elaborate organization. The Indian forays which gave rise to the punitive expeditions were very sudden, and they could only be met by prompt and vigorous action.

The affair at Sarras near Wadi Halfa, in 1887, is an excellent specimen of an operation of this class. A force of Mahdists, the advanced guard of more formidable bodies, had occupied this point, 33 miles from the Egyptian outposts. No sooner was news of this brought to Wadi Halfa than Colonel Chermside, who was in command, arranged for a night march of mounted troops, so as to surprise the enemy in the morning and to occupy his attention till the infantry should come up. The Mahdist force was completely defeated and Sarras remained free of hostile bodies for some months afterwards. The risk of news of the impending attack of the Egyptian troops reaching the enemy was averted by the promptitude with which the operation was carried out.

It cannot be insisted upon too strongly that in a small war the only possible attitude to assume is, speaking strategically, the offensive. The regular army must force its way into the enemy's country and seek him out. It must be ready to fight him wherever he may be found. It must play to win and not for safety. It was his thorough grasp of this great principle and his insistence on its being kept constantly in view which, rather than any transcendent display of tactical genius or powers of organization on his part, has made the name of General John Nicholson so illustrious. It is not a question of merely maintaining the initiative, but of compelling the enemy to see at every turn that he has lost it and to recognize that the forces of civilization are dominant and not to be

Strategical offensive essential.

denied. And it must be remembered that the strategical offensive is not incompatible with acting on the defensive

This not incompatible with tactical defensive.

on the battle-field. In many recent campaigns the regular forces have, as a rule, when it came to actual fighting allowed themselves to be attacked. The Zulu war illustrates this principle very well; Colonel Wood's force at Kambula and Lord Chelmsford's force moving to relieve Ekowe were both on Zulu ground, they compelled the Zulus to fight or to acknowledge inferiority; but both at Ginghilovo and at Kambula it was the Zulus who assumed the offensive not the British, and it was the same at Ulundi.

Effect of decisive action upon waverers in the hostile ranks and upon those hesitating to throw in their lot with the enemy.

There is one very important point in which the hostile forces met with in small wars differ from those met with in great campaigns. They swell and contract according to the moral effect which is produced, and quite apart from losses in action or from the exigencies of the conflict. Irregular armies always count many waverers, there are always crowds of warriors ready to flock to the standard in case of victory, even on the battle-field a large proportion of the opposing force consists generally of mere lookers-on. But these lookers-on will be the foremost in pursuit should the regular army meet with disaster, and will probably join in the next engagement should it meet with a reverse. A vigorous offensive has the effect of keeping at home those who hesitate to take up arms and of thereby diminishing the fighting strength of the enemy. A bold plan of campaign tends to reduce the hostile forces to the lowest limits and to disincline those who are uncompromised from joining in.

The effect of a victory in this respect is well illustrated by the fight at Ibeka in Kaffirland in 1877. The affair was in itself of little importance; but the colonial troops gained a distinct success over the Galekas who made a concerted attack upon them, and this occurred just as the Gaikas were about to rise. The consequence was that this latter tribe deferred commencing hostilities for some months, by which time the forces in the colony had been augmented and were far better prepared to deal with them.

Sir F. Roberts's action when advancing on Kabul in 1879, in attacking at Charasia with only the part of his force available at the time, so as to prevent threatening gatherings of tribesmen from joining the Afghan troops in their resistance to the British advance, illustrates the effect which vigorous action will have in preventing waverers from taking up arms. A part of the Amir's army had occupied a strong position barring the way to Kabul, and the advanced British brigade found its further progress arrested. On the hills on the flanks were to be seen parties of hill-men evidently meditating mischief, and reports gave grounds for expecting that their numbers would rapidly swell. It was decided to attack without waiting till the other brigade, which was a march in rear, should come up, and the attack completely succeeded, the Afghan troops being driven in confusion off the ground. The tribesmen, as soon as they saw which way the issue was decided, dispersed to their homes and offered no molestation to the British army, which occupied Kabul without further opposition. Although, later on, a great uprising of the tribes round the city took place, there can be no doubt that the prompt action at Charasia, for the time being, prevented a national movement against the invaders at a juncture when these were in a position full of danger.

It must, of course, happen sometimes in small wars that the regular troops are for a time compelled by the existing conditions in the theatre of war to adopt a defensive attitude strategically. It is most unfortunate when this occurs, because it puts the disciplined army in a thoroughly false position. The enemy gathers courage, many who have held aloof flock to join the hostile standards, the longer the situation lasts, the more formidable will be the forces which must eventually be overthrown. But under these undesirable circumstances the great tactical principle that a passive defensive is inadmissible must be kept in view. It may not be possible to act decisively, to carry out great operations of war, or to seize the initiative in the theatre of conflict as a whole ; but it will rarely happen that isolated enterprises cannot be undertaken which will prevent the troops from becoming disheartened and which will ensure that the enemy maintains his respect for the forces of civilization.

Even when the regular army is obliged to act strategically on the defensive, this must not be a passive defensive.

The army before Delhi, in spite of the tremendous difficulties of the situation, never permitted the mutineers to dominate the surrounding country. On the other hand the disasters of the first Afghan war are mainly traceable to the want of boldness and vigour shown at Kabul when the situation began to grow grave. And it is worthy of note that during the

Boer war of 1881, at a time when the troops on the Natal frontier were acting strategically on the defensive, waiting for reinforcements, a cavalry reconnaissance under Sir E. Wood to Utrecht in the Transvaal assumed an importance out of all proportion to. its military significance, from the impression which the news of it created among the Boers who were daily growing bolder, and from the satisfaction which it caused in the British camps and throughout Natal.

When such conditions prevail it is, of course, essential that any offensive movement by the regular army should not meet with reverse. Any chance of such a contretemps must be avoided. But it will often happen that the situation admits of some sudden stroke being delivered, not necessarily on a great scale, which will prove to the enemy that the regular army is only biding its time to regain the upper hand, and which will exert a great moral effect within the force itself. Opportunities of this kind must not be allowed to slip away.

Great impression made upon the enemy by bold, resolute action.

The records of small wars show unmistakably how great is the impression made upon semi-civilized races and upon savages by a bold and resolute procedure. The military history of our Indian Empire affords proof of this on every page. From the days of Clive down to the present time victory has been achieved by vigour and by dash rather than by force of numbers. The spirit of attack inspiring leaders and subordinates alike has won the day for us. Arcot, Plassey, and Meani may be cited as examples; their story is familiar to all. And in no campaign has this spirit been more constantly evinced, and has its influence been demonstrated with such irresistible force, as in that where the enemy was from strength of numbers and from the peculiar conditions which prevailed the most formidable—the Indian Mutiny.

During this great struggle the operations in the field consisted, almost to a monotonous extent, of a succession of combats in which small British columns always attacked the very superior forces of the enemy, and always beat them.

Blow upon blow was delivered, and the rebels were never allowed to strike back. It was not that there was no resistance—far from it ; the mutineers in the earlier stages always fought with courage, at times they fought with desperation. Nor was it that the enemy was crushed by force of armament ; relatively to the British troops the rebels were supplied with efficient weapons. It was the spirit of the offensive animating the British leaders and their men throughout the vicissitudes of a singularly active campaign, which led to their long succession of victories. Conspicuous for the unflinching courage and the restless energy with which the operations were conducted was Sir H. Rose's memorable struggle in the Central Provinces. The rebels were given no rest and no breathing space. Every success was instantly followed up. The campaign of Gwalior was not merely a triumph of strategy and tactics but also of resolution. Asiatics do not understand such vigour and are cowed by it. The records of the Mutiny teach us the art of conducting small wars with unmistakable clearness, and they cannot be too carefully studied as examples of leadership. In the field after the first few gloomy weeks the issue never was in doubt, it was only where, as at Delhi, attack was impracticable, that the enemy was for a time enabled to hold his ground.

In the Russian campaigns in Central Asia it has generally been the same. Energy and resolution have been the watchword. The procedure has been rather to overawe the enemy by a vigorous offensive, than to bring against him a mighty force, and the results achieved by comparatively speaking small forces in that vast territory speak for themselves. Prestige is everything in such warfare. It is the commander who recognizes this and who acts upon it, who conquers inferior races absolutely and for good.

The secret of overcoming such adversaries does not, however, lie only in bold attack. In all warfare a victory to be complete must be followed up. In small wars a single blow

The importance of following up successes with vigour.

will often achieve important results, but a succession of blows paralyses the enemy. Irregular warriors do not understand the importance of following up a success at once; if they defeat their opponents they are satisfied for the time being, and they pause to glory in their triumph and to divide the spoils which they have won. When they find themselves struggling against a foe who is not content to rest on his laurels after a victory but who presses vehemently on and gives them no rest, their hearts fail them and they collapse. Vigour in pursuit is as important in small wars as is intrepidity in attack.

This was well illustrated in a recent campaign. Colonel Kelly in his daring advance from Gilgit to Chitral acted upon the principle of giving the enemy no breathing space to recover from his reverses. After driving the hillmen from their formidable position at Chokalwat, as a result of some hours of fighting, he pushed on and completed his day's march as if nothing had happened. This sort of thing bewildered the Chitralis. They did not understand it. It was the same principle as had been adopted in the Indian Mutiny, where the rebels were always pursued relentlessly, no victory was held to be complete enough, every success being followed up as long as man or horse could march. This method is sound on tactical grounds in all wars; but in campaigns against savages and guerillas the, procedure is not merely sound on tactical grounds but also as part and parcel of the system of overawing and terrifying the enemy, which is the great object always to be kept in view, and it can be employed with far less risk against irregular forces than it could against a regular army, inasmuch as irregulars have so little rallying power.

Small forces can at times perform exploits of great subsequent importance by means of bluff.

The alarm which this sort of resolute offensive creates in the ranks of the enemy in small wars can scarcely be exaggerated. A masterful military policy bewilders such antagonists. Moral force is even more potent than physical force in compassing their downfall. All history shows that this is so, and before concluding this chapter it will not be out of place to point out how, in campaigns of this class, a happy appreciation of this great principle has from time to time enabled soldiers of decision and resource· to achieve most signal results, and has led to their gaining startling triumphs with relatively insignificant forces. Dash and audacity displayed at the right moment have given rise to episodes flavouring the tedious operations which are characteristic of, and inevitable in, warfare of this nature, with a spice of romance. Handfuls of men have overawed a host. Mere detachments have wrested historic strongholds from the grasp of potentates with warlike races at their beck and call. For such episodes great campaigns offer no opportunity and grand combinations of war afford no precedent.

(1) The capture of the great walled city of Tashkend by General Tcher- Examples. naieff in 1865, is a case in point. The place contained more than 100,000 inhabitants, and it was defended by 30,000 fighting men. It was one of the great commercial centres of the East, its name was known from Stambul to the Yellow Sea. Its perimeter was about 16 miles, its ramparts were of stout design, and its battlements sheltered a respectable artillery.

The Russian General arrived before it with 2,000 men and 12 guns, and determined upon a *coup de main*. An entrance was surprised at dawn of day at two points by storming parties, and these opened the gates. The guns upon the battlements on one side were seized and spiked. So great was the effect produced within the city by this daring feat of arms, that its notables surrendered at once, this in spite of the fact that in street fighting the Russian troops could not have successfully coped with the great numerical superiority of their adversaries. Tashkend fell and was incorporated in the Tsar's dominions from that time forward.

From a number of examples which the Indian Mutiny affords two may be given.

(2) A handful of civilians were holding out in a bungalow in Arrah against the mutineers of several regiments from the neighbouring garrison of Dinapore, who were aided by the inhabitants of the district. It was one of the opening scenes of the outbreak, the rebel cause was in the ascendant still, and the besiegers of Arrah had heavily defeated a relieving column from Dinapore under circumstances which will be referred to in another chapter. But Major Eyre, who was proceeding by water up the Ganges with his battery, heard of the peril in which the little band was placed, and he determined to make one effort for its succour. He formed a little flying

column, consisting of a company of infantry borrowed from a small cantonment close by, of two of his own guns, and of a party of mounted volunteers. He landed this insignificant detachment at a point a few miles from Arrah, and marched against the enemy. The rebels gathered in great force to bar the way, but the petty British force attacked them without hesitation. The struggle was severe, the odds desperate. The determined attitude of the small British force, however, daunted the mutineers, and by resolute fighting it forced its way through the middle of their line of battle. So great was the effect of the intrepid bearing of the assailants upon the hostile array, that all resistance to the British ceased when the column was still some miles from Arrah, and that the garrison was relieved without further conflict. It was a brilliant exploit, not so much in its execution, skilful as this was, as in its conception. This is the way to deal with Asiatics—to go for them and to cow them by sheer force of will.

(3) The other instance from the Indian Mutiny is of a somewhat different kind, an episode which involved no fighting. The story is a familiar one, and the sequel to it, which does not here concern us, has excited keen controversy. Just as the British troops after the storming of Delhi had finally gained the mastery in the city, but while parts of it and many of the villages around were still infested with armed rebels, a report came to hand that the King of Delhi, the descendant of the Moguls who had been set up by the insurrectionary forces as a kind of puppet figure-head upon the throne of his ancestors, had taken refuge at a tomb a few miles distant. Major Hodson with only 50 troopers rode out to bring him in. The road was thronged with sullen angry crowds retiring from Delhi. Around the tomb the followers of the king were mustered in great force. Their demeanour was so grim and ominous that it was clear that the least indecision would change their attitude from one of passive hostility into one of active resistance, but Hodson's iron will and hardihood fairly daunted the mob. Not one of the vast multitude dared to lift his hand when, arrived at the tomb, he rode up to it alone and ordered the fallen monarch to surrender. No one ventured to intervene when the king was brought back a prisoner to Delhi. On the following day Hodson under very similar circumstances, but supported by a somewhat stronger detachment, captured the king's two sons at the same place.

(4) A fine example of a great military achievement by a force insignificant as compared with that opposed to it, is afforded by the Duc D'Aumale's attack on Abd el Kader's " smala " in 1843. " Smala," is the name given in Algeria to a nomad settlement—an assemblage of families or clans, or even at times of whole tribes which moves from place to place in search of sustenance or safety ; with it go its camels and its herds which form its principal wealth. The general-in-chief had ascertained the approximate position of the smala, far beyond the chain of defensive posts which at that time marked the limits of French sway, and he resolved upon a combined movement to attack it. The Duc D'Aumale's column consisted of 600 cavalry and 300 foot soldiers. The mounted portion, pushing on ahead of the less

mobile infantry, came suddenly upon the great gathering, just as it was taking up new camping ground after one of its periodic changes in position ; Abd el Kader himself happened not to be present, but 5,000 of the Emir's regular troops were on the spot. The Duc resolved upon a bold stroke. Without waiting for his infantry, without heeding the vast superiority of the hostile force, he attacked with his squadrons, profiting by the confusion in the smala and by the circumstance that his appearance on the scene was wholly unexpected. His success was complete. The enemy was utterly dispersed. Numbers of prisoners were taken. An immense booty in camels, sheep, and cattle was secured, and the banners and the treasure of the great nomad chieftain fell into the hands of the insignificant body of French cavalry. The most decisive reverse suffered by Abd el Kader throughout his years of struggle with the conquerors of Algeria was inflicted upon him in what was almost an accidental encounter with a few troops of horse.

(5) Another cavalry exploit of later date deserves a mention here. This was the capture of Cairo after the British victory at Tel-el-Kebir. The circumstances are so well known that they need not be detailed. ·Suffice it to say, that a few squadrons succeeded, without firing a shot and by mere exercise of moral force, in compelling the surrender of a great Oriental city, crowded with armed soldiery and containing all the needful means for driving such a force in confusion from its gates.

(6) Only one more instance need be given—Lieutenant Grant's memorable feat of arms at Thobal in Manipur.

Lieutenant Grant commanded a detachment of 84 men in Tamu, one of the nearest posts to the town of Manipur when the outbreak occurred there. On the news reaching Tamu he volunteered to advance and to try to succour the prisoners believed to be in the Manipuris hands, and he obtained the necessary sanction. He advanced for three days, gaining about 30 miles, driving the enemy before him ⸱and marching chiefly at night. Advancing again on the third night, the party came early in the morning of the fourth day upon the enemy in force on a stream, the bridge over which the Manipuris were destroying.

Grant attacked at once, forced the passage and then formed a defensive post beyond. This the enemy, who had guns, attacked for two days. Then three days were spent in negotiations in which Grant throughout adopted a peremptory demeanour and impressed the enemy with the belief that his force was far larger than it was in reality. The negotiations having fallen through, the Manipuris attacked again, but they were beaten off and the following day they withdrew. Grant then received orders to retire. With this insignificant detachment he had been 14 days in the enemy's country unsupported, had defeated far superior hostile forces again and again, and had created an impression among the Manipuris which went a long way towards re-establishing British prestige in the country.

These numerous illustrations of remarkable results attained Conclusion. by, relatively to the hostile strength, feeble forces have been quoted not merely to demonstrate what small bodies of regular troops can achieve in warfare of this class. They serve also to point the moral which it has been the object of this chapter to enforce, to teach the great principle that vigour and decision are at the root of effective conduct of such operations. To attempt to lay down rules for guidance in such enterprises, to suggest the conditions under which such exploits may or may not be safely ventured on, would be wholly out of place. The military instinct of the responsible authority on the spot must point the way and must hold the balance.

To the commander thrown upon his own resources in a distant land, hedged round by dangers and perplexity, outnumbered and perhaps at bay, who sees a great chance open should he risk all on one single throw, the accepted code of strategy and tactics is of no avail and the maxims of the academic school of military thought have small significance. A reverse means not defeat alone, it means destruction. If he decides to venture there is no going back. It is in cases such as this that genius triumphs over theory, and that the leader endowed with the gift of command knows instinctively how to act and to create for himself his own rules of conduct.

CHAPTER VII.

TACTICS FAVOUR THE REGULAR ARMY WHILE STRATEGY
FAVOURS THE ENEMY—THEREFORE THE OBJECT IS TO
FIGHT, NOT TO MANŒUVRE.

IT is a singular feature of small wars that from the point of view of strategy the regular forces are upon the whole at a distinct disadvantage as compared to their antagonists. *The regular forces are at a disadvantage from the point of view of strategy.*

In spite of sea power, in spite of the initiative, in spite of science, and in spite of the wealth, of the reserve of fighting strength and of the resources at their back, the trained and organized armies of the civilized country have undoubtedly the worst of it as regards strategical conditions, and that it is so is actually in a large degree directly traceable to the very causes which establish their tactical superiority, and which eventually lead as a rule to the triumph of the forces of civilization. For it is the elaborate organization of the regular troops which cramps their freedom in the theatre of war, and it is the excellence of their armament and the completeness of their equipment which overburdens them with non-combatant services and helps to tie them to their base.

The bonds which fetter a modern army to its starting point result partly from the supply question dealt with in a former chapter, partly from the necessity of replenishing ammunition and military stores, and partly from the obligations of sending sick and wounded to the rear. They enforce the establishment of a line of communications and its maintenance and defence. They hamper the commander's liberty of action at every turn. In a special chapter dealing with lines of communications later on it will be shown what a terrible drain in men they are, and how they reduce the *Communications a main cause of this.*

fighting force with which it is hoped to decide the issue. As it presses forwards the regular army drags after it a lengthening chain which increases in burden at every step.

Moreover, communications are not required on account of the replenishment of food and war material alone. They may also be required to afford a line of retreat should a reverse be met with. An organized force must from its nature maintain its cohesion, come what may, and it must if beaten hold together as best it can and fall back on its base ; to enable it to do so it should be linked to this base. Lines of communications are in fact a necessary consequence of elaborate and systematic organization, of modern armament, of the extensive requirements of the soldier of to-day, and of the conditions under which a regular army operates. The enemy, on the other hand, in most small wars works upon an altogether different system.

Enemy has little anxiety as to communications, and operations cannot be directed against them. The adversaries with whom the regular troops in these campaigns have to cope depend on no base and have no fixed system of supply. They are operating in their own country. Their food requirements are small—what they need they carry with them. Each man takes with him all the ammunition that he wants. The wounded in battle have to shift for themselves as best they can. The enemy lives in fact from hand to mouth, and it follows from this that he does not need communications as a channel for replenishing food or warlike stores, nor does he need lines of communications to retreat by if defeated. Warriors such as form the enemy in small wars simply disperse when they are worsted. They disappear in all directions, but unless awed by their experience into submission they are ready to collect again should an opportunity offer at a later period.

So it comes about that the enemy is untrammelled by the shackles which so limit the regular army's liberty of action, a fact which is of great strategical importance ; for while the organized forces are dependent upon communications which their antagonists may attack and even cut, they cannot retaliate. And as operations directed against an opponent's communications represent the most effective weapon in the armoury of strategy, the regular army is clearly at a disadvantage.

(1) The extent to which the enemy disregards the safety of his communications in this sort of warfare is well exemplified by the campaign of 1889 on the Nile, which terminated in the fight of Toski. Wad en Nejumi, the Mahdist emir, was sent to invade the territories effectively occupied by Egyptian troops. He directed his advance by the left or west bank of the river. The frontier post Wadi Halfa, a formidable fortress to warriors such as formed Nejumi's following, lies on the right bank. Below it the Egyptian forces had armed steamers at their command, which empowered them to cross the river from side to side at pleasure. Therefore from the moment that he passed Wadi Halfa making northwards, Nejumi was making a flank march along an obstacle of which his opponents held the passages, he was leaving his communications at the mercy of his adversary, and he was judged by the experience of regular warfare, placing himself in an impossible strategical position. *Examples of this.*

Nejumi nevertheless resolutely pressed on. Soon after passing Wadi Halfa he was attacked in flank and roughly handled by the Egyptian frontier forces, under Colonel Wodehouse, but he moved on undismayed. He was eventually brought to a standstill and defeated, not by the severance of his exposed communications, not by the attacks upon his rear which his antagonists could deliver where and when they liked, but by an enemy who confronted him and beat him on the battlefield in a fair stand-up fight.

(2) Another example from Nile warfare is afforded by the situation previous to the battle of the Atbara. The capture of Shendi cut the Dervish communications with Omdurman. No European army would under such circumstances have maintained its ground and accepted battle.

But it is not alone from the fact that the regular forces are hampered by communications while the enemy is not, that the strategical advantage rests with the latter. The rapidity of the hostile movements, which arises partly from the freedom from impedimenta and partly from the singular marching power which are characteristics of irregular warriors, prejudices the course of the campaign to their great benefit. If defeated they disperse, so that the victory cannot be followed up. The regular army finds that some mysterious influence *The enemy's mobility benefits him strategically.*

will on occasions draw down great hosts of angry foemen to give it battle, but those hosts melt away and vanish when their design miscarries. Restricted by no precedents, governed by no strategic code, embarrassed by no encumbrances, they come and go at will.

The doubts and perplexities which such unconventional procedure causes the commander of the regular forces, has been referred to in an earlier chapter. He is moving as it were in a groove, chained to a fixed line of operations and to a fixed line of conduct, while the enemy enjoys an independence amounting at times almost to absolute freedom of action, and this freedom of action is a direct consequence of the conditions under which the irregular warriors assemble for a conflict. In the hostile ranks there is no solid cohesion and no mutual reliance. No man fully trusts his comrade or his leader. As long as all goes well, irregular forces hold together and obey their chiefs, but in the hour of trial the bonds which keep the mass intact are apt to snap, and then the whole dissolves and disappears. This is not only the case with mere guerilla bands ; even when the hostile forces have a military organization, even when they comprise battalions, batteries and squadrons it often is the same.

His power of sudden concentration and dispersion. In the Afghan wars and in most Indian hill campaigns these sudden gatherings and prompt dispersions have been a feature of the enemy's mode of levying war ; after a fight Afghans and hill-men hide their arms at home and then come out and welcome troops who are pursuing them. In Spain's campaign against Morocco in 1859 the bulk of the Moorish array similarly disappeared after each fight before pursuit could be organized, but it always collected again a litttle further back ready for another trial of strength. The French operations against Abd el Kader drifted on for years ; the Kabyle chieftain would appear with his following where least expected and inflict much damage, but he always vanished when an organized body of troops was put upon his track. Although the enemy was of quite a different character, these same conditions prevailed in the later stages of the South African war, it was the difficulty in inflicting serious injury on the nomad Boer commandos which was the main cause of the operations being so protracted. Dealing with adversaries who operate in this capricious fashion, regular troops are, in so far as strategy is concerned, clearly at a serious disadvantage.

While emphasising the fact that in small wars the enemy almost always possesses far greater mobility than the regular troops, and that strategically this mobility favours the side of the irregular warriors, it is well to point out that the leaders of the hostile ·forces are apt to under-rate the mobility of the disciplined army. They see what a cumbrous machine it is, how long it takes to get ready for its advance, how tied and bound it seems to be to its communications, and they persuade themselves that it is incapable of rapid, deft, and sudden strokes. No greater mistake can be made than to suppose that because the enemy enjoys the singular power of sudden concentration and dispersion, and of rapid transfer of force from one part of the theatre of war to another, it is impossible to carry out a strategical surprise upon such adversaries. Indeed such enterprises are to a certain extent favoured by the contempt which irregular opponents entertain for the marching powers of the regulars. It appears that the Khalifa meant to confront Sir H. Kitchener's army in a favourable position for defence two marches short of Omdurman, but that he was not prepared for the rapid advance of the Anglo-Egyptian forces. An earlier incident in the reconquest of the Sudan—the surprise of Abu Hamed by General Hunter after a rapid march of several days from near Hamdab—affords another remarkable illustration of strategical surprise by a disciplined force in a campaign against adversaries noted for their powers of movement. Still these examples and others which might be quoted, in no wise disprove the fact that in small wars the enemy is

Note that the mobility of the enemy does not necessarily prevent strategical surprises by the regulars.

as regards mobility the superior of the regular army and gains thereby from the strategical point of view.

The better organized the enemy, the less does he enjoy the strategical advantage.

While laying down the principle that the strategical conditions in small wars favour the enemy, it is necessary to point out that the extent to which this is the case varies greatly with the nature of the hostile forces. For, as already shown in Chapter II, these differ widely in their composition, in their organization, and in the circumstances under which they take the field in different cases. Sometimes the regular army has to cope with a military system not unlike its own —the forces of Arabi Pasha in 1882 had, in appearance at least, a modern organization, and the Chinese troops who opposed the French in 1884–85 were on the same footing. It is an undoubted fact indeed that the more nearly the enemy approximates in system to the European model, the less marked is the strategical advantage he enjoys.

On the battle-field the advantage passes over to the regular forces.

Strategy is not, however, the final arbiter in war. The battle-field decides, and on the battle-field the advantage passes over to the regular army. Superior armament, the force of discipline, a definite and acknowledged chain of responsibility, esprit de corps, the moral force of civilization, all these work together to give the trained and organized army an incontestable advantage from the point of view of tactics.

Reasons for the tactical superiority of the organized army.

The tactical superiority of the regular troops is somewhat discounted, it is true, by the enemy's rapidity of movement when in action, by his power of getting over difficult ground and by the physical endurance of warriors of this class. But nothing can compensate for the difference in weapons, in training, in cohesion and in method, between regular troops and the forces of an uncivilized adversary. Preponderance of numbers may at times give victory to the other side, some local feature on the battle-field may turn the scale against the regular army, the impulse of a ghazi rush may break the line and smother the efficacy of its overwhelming ascendancy in armament. In the hills and in the jungle the activity and knowledge of the terrain of the enemy tend to minimize the benefits which disciplined troops enjoy owing to their weapons. No rule in war is absolute. But under the ordinary circumstances under which small wars take place, and as a general rule during their progress, the tactical conditions are all in favour of the trained and organized force. Man for man, the fanatic or cut-throat, the hardy nomad or the reckless savage, may match or be more than a match for the European soldier ; in the aggregate irregular warriors fail.

And so we arrive at a great broad principle which stands out clear and well defined amid the vague uncertainties which enshroud all operations of this class. Since tactics favour the regular troops while strategy favours the enemy, the object to be sought for clearly is to fight, not to manœuvre, to meet the hostile forces in open battle, not to compel them to give way by having recourse to strategy. Of course exceptions to this rule will arise at times. They are rare, however, and it cannot be too strongly insisted upon that, to beat irregular opponents and savages, the most efficacious plan is to engage them on every possible occasion.

Since tactical conditions are favourable, while strategical conditions are the reverse, the object is to bring matters to a tactical issue.

It will sometimes happen that the adversary takes up ground eminently favourable to his mode of combat, thus minimising tactical inferiority, and in such a case it may be better to dislodge him by some manœuvre not involving battle. Such conditions must, however, be understood to be exceptional. In the majority of cases which present themselves, the boldest will be found to be the wisest course, and an assault upon the enemy—it may be on his flank, it may be on his rear—will prove at once a safer and a more efficacious procedure than some profound strategical combination designed to drive him from his ground without a fight. It constantly occurs that the opponents of the regular troops have occupied a position from which it is imperative that they should be dislodged. Rarely will it occur in such

Usually better to fight the enemy than to manœuvre him out of his position.

a contingency that the officer in command does not find presented to him two alternatives—one of driving the enemy out by force, the other of demonstrating against his line of retreat in such a manner that he will make his escape. But there should rarely be any doubt as to which alternative to follow. When there is a chance of a fight it should not be allowed to slip by.

One single example may be cited in support of this, an example which illustrates with exceptional vividness and force the principle enunciated above.

Example of Tel-el-Kebir.

The Egyptian forces in 1882 had strongly entrenched themselves in the important strategical position of Tel-el-Kebir, covering the point where the railway from Cairo to Ismailia and the fresh water canal quit the Nile delta and enter the shallow depression in the desert by which they reached the Suez Canal. This depression formed the line of advance selected by Sir G. Wolseley. The British expeditionary force having advanced to within striking distance of the Egyptian lines, it was necessary either to carry them by assault or to pass them by a flank march through the desert. The latter course would have compelled the enemy to evacuate their entrenchments and to fall back into the delta, and it would in all probability have brought the British army on to well watered and highly cultivated ground without a serious action. But Sir G. Wolseley's great object was to fight a decisive battle in the desert; for in the intersected ground beyond, Arabi Pasha could probably have avoided a general engagement, and could have carried on a harassing resistance for some time. It was also foreseen that, if the hostile leader and his troops found themselves being worsted and were given time for mischief, great damage might be done to Cairo and elsewhere. The surest means of averting this danger was to inflict a crushing defeat on the enemy, which would paralyse his further action and which would enable Cairo to be occupied by a sudden coup.

But the works thrown up at Tel-el-Kebir were evidently formidable, and to storm them in broad daylight would have incurred most serious loss. Therefore it was decided to attack the lines at dawn of day after a night march in line of battle. The complete success which attended the execution of this plan is a matter of history. The issue which might have been decided, though less promptly and less absolutely, by a strategical manoeuvre, was left to tactics to decide, and the result was a prompt and brilliant termination to the war.

Objection to elaborate manoeuvres as compared

Then, again, there may sometimes be a choice between attacking the enemy, and embarking on an elaborate strategical combination which, should it succeed, will achieve a brilliant and far reaching success, but the execution of _{to direct action.} which bristles with difficulties. Profound plans carefully worked out on paper in advance are very apt to miscarry when they come to be put in practice in irregular warfare, which is so often carried on in a difficult and not very well known terrain. In Chapter IX it will be shown how difficult it is to ensure co-operation between separate columns and forces in this class of warfare, and any elaborate plan almost necessarily means the attempt to manœuvre a number of separate columns and forces with some definite object in view. There will often be temptation to attempt some far-reaching combination, but in nine cases out of ten it will probably be better to fall upon the enemy with whatever forces are to hand and thereby to make sure of a fight, even if there be no hope of annihilating the foe.

A good example of this has recently been provided in the attempt of the Germans to surround the main body of the Herreros in the Waterberg in 1904. There were only about 2,500 troops with 30 guns actually engaged in this operation, but, broken up into small columns, they moved very slowly owing to transport difficulties, and they had to operate over a wide extent of country before anything like a ring round the Waterberg was completed. While this ring was closing in the enemy was, however, breaking out through the intervals, and although there was some desultory fighting the result was that the Herreros with their wives, children, and herds, practically all escaped. They withdrew, it is true, into a district of sand-veld where they appear to have suffered severely.

A rapid movement of the Germans more or less concentrated and a sudden attack, would almost certainly have produced a greater moral effect, and it would have permitted of an energetic and obstinate pursuit by forces not already exhausted by long marches in a difficult country.

In the latter days of the South African War of 1899–1902 it came to be fully recognised that it was not elaborate manœuvres, but rapid movement and attack wherever the enemy could be found, which paid. The "drives" it is true involved careful and deliberate planning. But that was a special phase of the campaign, and one which was only rendered possible by exceptional conditions as regards blockhouses, and by the circumstances of the case permitting of great developments of force.

Circumstances will, no doubt, sometimes arise where it is desirable to resort to strategy. If the enemy has taken up a position so formidable as to make its attack a risky operation, it may become unavoidable to manœuvre him out of it; or he may be covering some point the occupation of which with promptitude is essential, and it may be possible to reach this by a turning movement; or the immediate objective may be the succour of some beleaguered garrison which may be best effected without fighting. In such cases engagements are to be avoided, and the general principle above laid down does not hold good. The following instances where commanders of regular troops have to a certain extent shirked actual combat and have gained their object by manœuvres, and where their action appears to have been quite justified, may be quoted before concluding the chapter.

Circumstances when this principle does not hold good.

(1) The case of the French march from Hanoi to Bacninh in 1884, already referred to on p. 55, is a good illustration. The occupation of Bacninh was most desirable in view of the moral effect which it must nevitably have in Tonkin, where the general situation gave rise to anxiety. The enemy was in great force, and had thrown up elaborate earthworks on the direct line. The French troops would, no doubt, have fought their way through successfully if called upon, but the losses must have been severe. By marching round the hostile flank Bacninh, fell into the French hands almost without fighting, and the Chinese in consequence withdrew out of this part of the theatre of war in haste.

(2) Colonel Kelly in his advance for the relief of Chitral, while never hesitating to attack the hostile forces if these attempted to bar his way, managed by detours over the hills to avoid conflicts in some positions exceptionally favourable to the enemy. His object was to reach a hard-pressed garrison with all possible despatch; the overthrow of the enemy was subsidiary to the relief of Chitral, and in this case the judicious course clearly was to fight when necessary, but not to court battle. The mountainous tracts between Gilgit and Mastuj were eminently favourable for an obstinate defence, and the Chitralis showed considerable aptitude in selecting formidable positions to bar the road to Colonel Kelly's column. In the two actions which were fought the British commander turned the enemy out of their positions by pushing detachments round their flanks. With a small force

having a difficult and dangerous task to achieve, direct frontal attacks would have been quite out of place. Under such circumstances the broad principle that an irregular opponent should be attacked and not manœuvred out of his ground, cannot be said to apply.

The object in this chapter has been to explain that since irregular warriors have generally the advantage strategically over disciplined forces, these latter enjoy a tactical superiority in virtue of their arms. Before closing it, however, a word may be said about one especial difficulty under which the regular army labours in this class of warfare—care of the wounded. Alike in their movements to and fro about the theatre of war, and when in the presence of the enemy on the battle-field, the wounded are almost always a special cause of anxiety to the regular troops. Strategically as well as tactically the disciplined army is at a very serious disadvantage in this respect.

The question of the wounded.

Fighting against savages, Asiatics, Red Indians, and foes of that class, the responsibility for safeguarding the troops who may happen to be placed *hors de combat* is a perpetual source of worry to the commander. Nor does this difficulty arise only when campaigning against uncivilized races. In guerilla warfare in civilized countries the wounded can seldom be left to the tender mercies of the peasants in arms. Civil strife is demoralising and leads to pitiless reprisals on the part of soldiery and insurgents ; the partisan warfare in La Vendée, in the Peninsula, and in Cuba was marked by the utmost ferocity on the part of the guerillas. It was, on the other hand, a most gratifying feature of the prolonged struggle against the Boers in 1901-1902 that, even at a time when the British troops were sweeping the whole country bare and were burning farms and collecting the Boer women and children into concentration camps whether they would or no, when the contest had lost all semblance of regular warfare, and when the roaming bands of the enemy were suffering great privations in what had degenerated into a hopeless resistance to overwhelming forces, the Boers almost invariably treated British wounded who fell into their hands with the utmost consideration.

How this may hamper the regular troops strategically. In later chapters the influence of this question of wounded on the tactical dispositions will appear. But quite apart from their being one of the many causes which necessitate the maintenance of communications by regular troops in the field, the presence of wounded—and often of sick—will sometimes seriously hamper the strategical freedom of an army in this class of warfare, and of this the following episode is a good example :—

During the advance of Sir B. Blood's division against the Mohmunds from Malakand, in 1897, his rear brigade was attacked one night in its camp by the Mamund clan, inhabiting a district on the flank of the general line of march. This clan was not concerned in the campaign, but its un-called-for hostility had to be dealt with and the brigade at once undertook punitive measures. The operations in the first instance led to heavy fighting, which will be referred to in other chapters, and they resulted in serious loss to the brigade—so long, indeed, was the list of casualties that the brigade was brought to a standstill. The wounded could not be sent away, and to have left them behind under adequate guard would have weakened General Jeffreys' small force to such an extent that it could not safely have resumed the coercion of the recalcitrant clan.

Other impediments, such as supply columns and spare stores, an army can take with it when it goes to fight, and if the worst comes to the worst they can be abandoned ; but the wounded cannot be moved about like this, and they cannot be left in the lurch. Transport for the supplies and stores exists, but it may not be available if the number of the wounded grows very large. The question of the wounded constitutes a difficulty quite apart, and at times this will endanger the safety of the entire force.

CHAPTER VIII.

To avoid desultory warfare the enemy must be brought to battle, and in such manner as to make his defeat decisive.

In the last two chapters have been pointed out the import- *Prolonged campaigns to be avoided.* ance of a vigorous and masterful conduct of operations in these campaigns, and how their nature tends to render trial by battle preferable to out-manœuvring the enemy in the theatre of war. In this chapter the object will be to show how essential it is to prevent the struggle from degenerating into desultory warfare, to regular troops the most tedious and harassing form which hostilities can assume.

In campaigns of this class a main object to be aimed at *Reasons for this.* is to shorten their duration. They take place as a rule in territories and in climates which do not suit the trained soldier. Even where this is not the case, as for instance in some of the campaigns in South Africa, in Morocco, or in North America, the very fact of being on active service necessarily entails hardships on the troops, which in time causes wastage and leads to loss. The enemy fighting in his own country suffers far less; and even if he suffers as much or suffers more, this does not justify the exposure of the troops to the risks of disease longer than is absolutely neces- sary. The experiences of small wars of the past all go to *Troops suffer from disease.* prove that the losses in men which the regular army sustains are due far more to sickness than to fire and sword—accurate statistics have in many cases been compiled, and they place this beyond question. There are exceptions, of course, to this as to every other rule in war—as for instance

(10830)   G in the case of the Zulu campaign where the disaster at Isandl-whana brought the wastage due to battle up to a figure rather higher than that arising from disease—but in most operations of which details upon this point exist, and especially where the struggle has been prolonged as in Afghanistan, in the Russian expeditions against the Tekkes and in the case of Burma, it is sickness and not the loss involved by actual conflict which saps the strength of the regular army. The hostilities, moreover, often take place in unhealthy, and even deadly, climates, in torrid, fever-stricken theatres of war such as Dahomey and Benin, as Tonkin and Achin; when this is so the troops are decimated by ill-health even when the war is of short duration. In the French operations against the Hovas, in 1895, they lost 3,400 out of a force of 15,000; of these losses only a very few occurred in the battle-field.

Supply difficulties render protracted operations undesirable. Another reason why protracted operations are to be avoided has been already dealt with incidentally in a former chapter. This is the difficulty of supply. The pro-vision of food for man and beast being so very serious a con-sideration in this class of warfare, it is obvious that, as a rule, every day's delay means a waste of power. Just as the supply question tends to cut down the force detailed for the campaign, so it also tends to cut down the time that is avail-able. In the case of the Nile Expedition, sketched from the point of view of supply on pp. 68–70, it was essential that the task allotted to the River Column should be completed within a given period. In all campaigns in unproductive districts, time must be a very important matter.

Enemy gains time to organize his forces. And there is yet another reason for hastening the issue of such campaigns. As already pointed out in Chapter VI, the enemy is generally far more energetic in organizing his strength once the operations have commenced, than he is when they are merely impending. If allowed time the hostile forces are apt to become much more formidable than they would have been had the war been prosecuted with greater rapidity at the outset.

This is illustrated by the French operations against Madagascar in 1883-85. The proceedings were, as far as hostilities on land were concerned, carried out in a very half-hearted manner and they drifted on over many months. The Malagasies were at the outset unprepared and without organization ; but during the war the condition of their forces steadily improved under the guidance of Europeans, and they were far more formidable at its conclusion than at its commencement. The French obtained satisfactory terms of peace as a consequence of their blockade of the island ; but the campaign on land was little better than a failure.

Protracted campaigns are then to be avoided as far as possible, and the question how to accelerate their progress is one which the commander and staff must ever keep in view. To ascertain the surest method of shortening their duration it is best to consider what are the causes of these delays which are so mischievous. These causes are often preventible causes. Dilatory proceedings may arise from bad organization or they may follow from insufficient preparation, questions with which we are not concerned here. They may arise from lack of zeal among subordinates, or they may be due to want of energy in high places. But one of the commonest causes of operations being unduly prolonged, is to be found in their having been allowed to drift into a desultory form of warfare, and this is a question of strategy and tactics.

Desultory operations tend to prolong a campaign.

It may be accepted as a general rule that guerilla warfare is the most unfavourable shape which a campaign can take for the regular troops. At surprises and ambushes, at petty skirmishes, at attacks on detached parties and at cutting off stragglers, the enemy is usually an adept. Intimate acquaintance with the terrain, natural agility, cunning, and the warlike instinct which is natural in races where security of life and property does not exist, all combine to make antagonists of this kind most formidable if the hostilities are confined to operations of a guerilla character. In most small wars the enemy inclines to this mode of carrying on the

Guerilla warfare very unfavourable to regular troops.

(10830) G 2

campaign, and shirks more regular engagements, and it becomes necessary when this is the case to force him into decisive action. During the French campaigns against Abd el Kader it was found almost impossible to get the wary emir to fight. The Spanish armies were confronted by the same problem, as were the American forces in the Philippines. British troops have experienced the same difficulty in recent times in Burma, in the South African wars, and in the Tirah campaign. It is a feature of most insurrectionary wars on a small scale, as for instance in Montenegro in 1876-77. The great Circassian leader, Schamyl, kept the Russians at bay for years with guerilla tactics ; it was when he formed his followers into armies and weighed them down with guns that his cause declined. The Poles in 1863 committed the fatal error of assembling in formed bodies ; had they confined themselves to desultory warfare, their overthrow would have proved a far more difficult task for the Russian armies. Still circumstances often are such that the enemy cannot be tempted into battle, and adheres entirely to the guerilla form of making war, and in Chapter XI this contingency is especially dealt with.

Indecisive conduct of campaign tends to desultory warfare.

Invertebrate, undecided leadership of the regular troops induces desultory operations, and guerilla warfare is merely the most aggravated form of desultory operations. Marches with no particular object in view or marches with no object apparent to the enemy, advances followed by retirements, attacks on hostile positions and the abandonment of the ground after it has been won—it is operations such as these which raise the spirits of the hostile forces and which may lead to a prolonged, costly and ineffective campaign, disastrous to the health of the troops and damaging to the prestige of the civilized power which has put them in the field. Every undertaking should have a definite and distinct purpose, and once entered upon should be carried out to the end unless some insuperable objection unexpectedly arises. The enemy must be forced to understand that business is meant, that the regular army intends to accomplish whatever enterprise it engages in. Half measures are fatal.

(1) The Russian failures in the Caucasus were mainly due to the objectless character of their campaigns. They would assemble a great force and march through the forest and over the hills to capture some stronghold, which they often would find abandoned. Then they would march solemnly back again, harassed all the way by the warlike Circassians, Georgians, and Chechens, and would settle down into cantonments till the spirit moved them to undertake some similar spasmodic enterprise.

(2) During the campaign in Morocco in 1859, the Spanish forces allowed themselves on several occasions to be drawn by the Moors into purposeless engagements. Although they generally gained a certain measure of success in these during the actual fighting, they were obliged at its termination to relinquish what ground they had won ; and the Moors interpreted this into a victory for themselves. Unpremeditated actions of this kind are to be deprecated ; they lead to loss for no advantage. On the occasions on which the Spanish troops deliberately and with a definite object in view attacked the forces of the Sultan, they were almost always rewarded with signal success.

(3) The small Russian columns sent against the Tekke Turkomans in 1876–77, afford illustration of the evil of desultory, indecisive operations, although the Asiatic wars carried out by the military forces of the Tsar against inferior races have generally been conducted in a very different spirit. Detachments too weak to effect any good purpose were sent out with no very clear object in view, pottered about and after a time were driven back, the result being merely to damage Russian prestige and to confirm the Turkomans in their hostile attitude.

(4) The campaign against the Mahdists about Suakin in 1885 was opened by the action of Hashin, consisting of the capture of some hills a few miles north-west of the town. One of these hills, the furthest off and by far the largest and most important, was stormed in fine style ; but the bush about its base was thick, and at this point the action was indecisive. When after a short time the large hill was abandoned the enemy at once reoccupied it ; and as the British force, after leaving a garrison in zeribas constructed some distance to the rear, thereupon retired back to Suakin, the Dervishes were justified in concluding that, if not victorious, they at least had not been beaten. Two days later the British force commenced an advance south-westwards, and the insignificant moral effect which the slight success at Hashin had exerted over the enemy, was shown by the determined onslaught made upon it at Tofrek.

(5) In the Dutch campaigns in Achin their troops were on more than one occasion sent to capture a fortified village which, when captured, was promptly abandoned. A minor episode in 1874, may be narrated as an

instance of the objectless fighting which was rather a feature of the operations. A patrol of one non-commissioned officer and six men with a native drummer went out further than was intended, and was attacked and driven back, the drummer being mortally wounded and being left behind. Several small detachments moved out to the place from different points, till some 200 men were engaged, and in the end the enemy drew off. But the Dutch lost an officer and 3 men killed and 11 men wounded, having gained nothing whatever, for the patrol was merely reconnoitring in advance of the Dutch lines and the enemy was not in force and was making no attack or even demonstration.

Skirmishes should be avoided.

As a general rule it appears to be desirable to avoid skirmishes unless the enemy compels the regular troops to engage in them. Skirmishes mean desultory war. "Ne faites jamais de petits paquets à la guerre," was a saying of Skobelef's. The tendency of skirmishes is merely to temporarily frighten the enemy, not to inflict lasting injury. Petty annoyance is the favourite weapon of the guerilla, and regular troops are sorely tempted to retaliate in the same coin, to haggle as it were with the hostile gatherings instead of enduring worry and molestation for a season, biding their time till they can strike home. For instance, using artillery to drive off insignificant bands will seldom be desirable, they merely disappear to come again; it is far better to tempt them into some rash action, to let them gather strength and courage and then fall upon them and give them a lesson which they will not forget. And it must be remembered that the smaller the scale of a conflict the less does the tactical superiority of the regular troops tell, for it gives the enemy a better chance of utilising to the full his skill in ambushes and in profiting by accidents of ground; the larger the detachment the less liable is it, generally speaking, to be overwhelmed by a sudden rush.

Sometimes desirable to conceal strength so as to encourage enemy to fight.

To lay down as an arbitrary rule that it is better to conceal than to parade the strength of the regular army would be improper, for the moral effect upon the adversary of a show of force is often great. But at times it will be advisable to impress the hostile forces with the belief that they are confronted by a less formidable opponent than is in fact the case, otherwise it may be impossible to get them to fight. Whether concealment of strength is, or is not, expedient depends entirely on the nature of the enemy and of the war. Brave and determined warriors like the Black Flags of Tonkin, the Zulus or the Achinese, fanatics like the Mahdists or the Afghan ghazis, rebels who have no alternative but to fight like the defenders of Delhi, will acept battle in any case. In the later French campaigns in Algeria on the other hand, in the Russian operations against Schamyl, in wars against the Kaffirs, the Maoris and the Burmese, the great difficulty has generally been to bring on a decisive struggle—most unfortunately for the regular forces.

For general engagements are the object to be aimed at. Some losses may be suffered at the moment, but loss is saved in the end. There can be no doubt that pitched battles take the fight out of adversaries such as have to be dealt with in these wars. The severer the conflict, the more the superiority of the regular troops is brought home to the enemy. It sometimes happens that, even when the enemy gains the upper hand, the havoc caused by arms of precision convinces him that the cause is hopeless. Isandlwhana, so terribly disastrous to the British troops, opened the eyes of the Zulus to the nature of the antagonists they had to deal with and shook their confidence in their own invincibility. The heavy losses suffered by the followers of the Mullah in the fight at Gumburu in Somaliland, where Colonel Plunkett's force was annihilated, counteracted the effects of their victory.

General engagements the object to be aimed at.

In 1864, in the early days of the Russian operations against Khokand, a detached sotnia of cavalry with a gun was surrounded by an immensely superior force of Khokandians at Ikan. For two days the Russians defended themselves against overwhelming odds; they inflicted great loss upon the enemy, and finally managed to escape. The moral effect inspired by the fight made by this detachment was very great; although it was almost the only conflict of the year it appears to have so gravely impressed the Khokandians as to have materially assisted the Russians next year in their successful attack upon Tashkend, mentioned on p. 81.

Examples.

The British victory at Ahmed Khel over a formidable force of Afghans who, attacking with great determination suffered very heavy losses, had an excellent effect over the tribes round Ghazni. When Sir F. Roberts's force some months later traversed the same district on the march from Kabul to Kandahar, no opposition was offered.

In the second attack upon Dargai in the Tirah campaign the British troops suffered serious losses and only gained the day with great difficulty. But their victory seems to have enormously impressed the tribesmen, and, indeed, to have had the somewhat unfortunate result of impelling them to adopt guerilla tactics during the future operations.

Examples of this might be multiplied. The enemy seldom fights so well again after having had a taste of the arms and methods of a regular farce, and this is a powerful argument for bringing matters to a fighting issue. The records of small wars prove beyond the possibility of doubt that the campaigns marked by a few general actions are those which are the most decisive and the most satisfactory. The Zulu war, in spite of its unfortunate commencement, is a case in point. The military power of the Matabili was broken by their attacks upon the laagers at Imbembesi and Shangani during the first campaign in that country. The Indian Mutiny was remarkable for the readiness displayed by the enemy in accepting battle ; had it been otherwise its final suppression would have been far more arduous.

The Russians in Central Asia have been very fortunate in finding their opponents, as a rule, inclined for decisive conflicts. At Yedshar in 1866, a very large army from Bokhara marching in Tashkend in the hope of recovering that city, was confronted by a far inferior Russian force. A severely contested action ensued in which the latter was completely victorious. Two years later a decisive engagement was fought under the walls of Samarcand. These two battles decided the fate of Turkestan, the capture of Tashkend havⁱng given the Russians a firm footing in the country to start with. Minor engagements have been conspicuous by their absence in Central Asia. Almost every episode in the campaigns which brought the Cossacks to Bokhara and the sources of the Sir

Daria was an important operation or war, and to this may be attributed the extraordinary success which the Russians have achieved.

The conditions of the struggle may of course compel the enemy to commit himself to decided action, and it is a most fortunate circumstance when this is so. In the Abyssinian campaign, for instance, in 1868, King Theodore had no choice except to trust to the natural strength of his position at Magdala with its defences and its guns, and to stand his ground when the British troops arrived. The first phase of the French invasion of Algeria—the overthrow of the power of the Dey and seizure of his capital—gave the regular forces little trouble, for there was a distinct objective and one which the enemy was bound to cover ; as soon as General Bourmont effected his landing, the forces of the Dey were concentrated so as to bar the French line of advance to Algiers and they were of course utterly defeated. The seizure of Delhi by the mutineers in 1857 was not without a certain advantage to the British troops, for it led to this point becoming the focus of the rebel movement, it raised the city into being a strategical centre of supreme importance, it bound the enemy firmly to that centre, and it enabled our forces by the capture of that centre, to strike a blow at the insurrectionary movement which utterly shattered the hostile chances of achieving ultimate success. In the Ashanti and Dahomey wars the British and French columns in each case aimed at the Royal capitals ; Kings Koffee and Benanzin were forced to bar the way as best they could and to thus expose their armies to the risk of general actions in which the regular troops could bring their superiority in armament, in discipline, and in leadership decisively to bear. During the prolonged hostilities on the Red Sea Littoral near Suakin, Osman Digna's forces were always based upon the fertile district of Tokar ; a natural disinclination to engage in military enterprises long deterred the Cairo authorities from occupying the locality ; but when at last in 1891, a

Campaigns where circumstances oblige the enemy to adopt a decisive course of action are the most satisfactory.

force was sent to seize and hold it, the sagacious Dervish chief recognized how far-reaching would be the consequences, and he made a resolute attempt to stop the Egyptian advance from Trinkitat ; this led to the decisive engagement at the ruins of Tokar which finally broke up the Mahdist power in that theatre of protracted and desultory operations.

Owing to difficulty of getting enemy to accept battle, it is expedient to ensure a decisive victory when he does so.

Battles, then, are the objects to be sought for by the regular troops, and since the enemy as a general rule shirks engagement in the open field, the strongest grounds exist for tempting him to fight, for drawing him on by skilful dispositions, and for inducing him to enter eagerly upon the conflict if he shows symptoms of inclination for a battle. Where it is so difficult to bring matters to a tactical issue, it is clear that when efforts in this direction prove successful the fight should be decisive. The question of luring such adversaries on to action will be dealt with in a later tactical chapter, as will also that of flank attacks and turning movements aiming at the hostile line of retreat—forms of operation rendered very necessary by the importance of beating the enemy thoroughly when he is brought to action. Battles being so desirable and so difficult to bring about, it stands to reason that when a conflict does occur the opportunity should be taken full advantage of. It must be fully realised that mere defeat of the adversary is not enough, the opposing forces should be beaten so thoroughly that they will not offer further opposition. They must if possible be in a military sense destroyed. Decisive victory is to be sought for and not merely success.

In the Egyptian campaign of 1882, already referred to on p. 92, the recognition to its full extent of this important principle was a distinctive feature. Some days before the battle of Tel-el-Kebir, the Egyptian army came out in force from its entrenchments and attacked the British troops at Kassassin, where they were then rapidly concentrating. The enemy was repulsed with little difficulty, and was followed up to within a short distance of Tel-el-Kebir. The Egyptian works might possibly have been carried by assault then and there without serious resistance being encountered. But the British forces available on the spot at the time were not sufficient to achieve an absolutely decisive victory, the cavalry were not ready to follow up a success at once, and in any case attack by day on the hostile fortifications must have entailed heavy loss. The troops were therefore recalled, the attack was delayed till everything was prepared, and the brilliant result which followed on this temporary postponement of decisive action justified it conclusively.

The experience gained in small wars of the past seems then to point unmistakably to the need of so conducting operations as to bring about general actions, and if possible decisive actions, and the reasons for this are readily deducible from the peculiar characteristics of such warfare. But, as pointed out in the last chapter, cases may arise—if a beleaguered garrison has to be relieved for instance—when it may be wiser to avoid a battle, if that be possible without too great a show of weakness. And when a small force has some important task to fulfil, the carrying out of which will tax its strength, it may be undesirable to incur heavy loss in conflicts not absolutely necessary. When Sir H. Havelock first advanced from Cawnpore for the relief of the Residency at Lucknow he lost so heavily in three engagements—unavoidable engagements in which the enemy was signally defeated—that he was compelled to return to Cawnpore and await reinforcements, because with his diminished force he could not have accomplished what he had undertaken. It is the same when a convoy has to be protected; an irreducible minimum of force will be necessary as escort and if this minimum becomes diminished through losses suffered by the way in battle, the escort is no longer equal to its task and the convoy may be placed in great peril. The inconvenience which will sometimes follow from a fight even if the regular force is victorious, is well illustrated by what occurred in the Bayuda desert in 1885; the heavy losses suffered by the column at Abu Klea and about Gubat, although the hostile attacks were beaten off with great slaughter, so seriously reduced its fighting strength that, till reinforced from Korti, it was barely strong enough to guard the great transport columns under its protection.

[Marginal note:] Battles sometimes to be avoided if losses cannot be risked.

CHAPTER IX.

**DIVISION OF FORCE, OFTEN NECESSITATED BY THE CIRCUM-
STANCES, IS LESS OBJECTIONABLE IN THESE CAMPAIGNS
THAN IN REGULAR WARFARE.**

Usual
objections to
division of
force.

DIVISION of force in the theatre of war is generally held
to be bad strategy, and with good reason. An army broken
up into fragments runs risk of being beaten in detail, because
it may afford the enemy an opportunity of throwing his whole
available strength into the scale at some particular point
against a mere fraction of the total army which has been
put into the field. "L'art de la guerre se réduit pour ainsi
dire à un seul principe : réunir en un point donné une plus
grande masse que l'ennemi," wrote Napoleon. Strategy
and tactics alike are held to hinge upon the principle of
securing superiority at the point of contact, and division
of force tends to place the enemy in the position of putting this
principle in practice.

But even in regular war this rule is far from absolute. As
long as the separated portions of an army are strong enough
to hold their own against any hostile bodies likely to be
brought against them, they run no risk. Circumstances will
often render it impossible or undesirable to move the whole
army as one compact force.

Conditions of
campaign
often render
it unavoidable
in small wars.

In small wars separation in the field is often a necessary
consequence of the conditions of the campaign. In the first
place there frequently is more than one objective in struggles
of this nature. Thus in the Afghan wars the cities of Kabul
and Kandahar have always been in the first instance aimed at,
necessitating at least two entirely different lines of advance.
During the Indian Mutiny, Delhi and Lucknow became two

distinct gathering points of the rebel forces. In guerilla warfare the regular army of necessity becomes split up into many fractions—as will be seen in Chapter XI, separation of force is the basis of conducting operations against opponents who adopt this method of making war.

Then again, the peculiar circumstances attending the conduct of small wars often render a separation of force desirable even when it is not dictated by the conditions of the case. The importance of rapid decisive combinations has been referred to in former chapters. In roadless inhospitable districts, however, quick movements of large armies are impossible, and in such theatres of operations the mobility of a body of troops is in inverse proportion to its size. Supply is a great difficulty, and only a certain amount of supplies can be moved along a particular route within a given time. Operations take place in broken intersected country where there is little room to deploy, and where only a limited force can be drawn up in line of battle. All this tends often to make it preferable, even if not absolutely necessary, to move in several columns instead of moving concentrated.

Moreover, moral effect has to be taken into consideration. The importance of impressing the enemy with a sense of his inferiority to the forces brought into the field against him, has been already dwelt upon. There can be no doubt that the spectacle of several well appointed columns of regular troops pouring into their territory, alarms the semi-civilized races and savages more than does a single army, and for this reason division of force is often expedient. A skilful commander with well organized forces under his control welcomes an opponent who moves against him in several separate detachments, for, working on interior lines, he hopes to beat these one by one; but the chiefs, to whom races such as form the enemy in most small wars look for guidance, possess neither the knowledge nor the skill requisite for turning to good account the division of the regular forces into groups. To

Moral effect of numerous columns.

beat in detail an army separated into fractions, a better military system is needed than tribesmen, savages, or rebels can lay claim to, or than even fairly organized forces like the Chinese, or like the Egyptian troops as they existed in the campaign of 1882, generally can boast of. Therefore, because invasion by several lines tends to impress the adversary without as a rule involving serious risk, this plan of action is often adopted in operations against irregulars, even when the circumstances of the case do not in themselves dictate a division of force.

The French operating against Tunis in 1885 invaded the beylik from several points, and the feeble resistance offered by the Tunisian people can largely be attributed to the alarm caused by this procedure of the invaders. The invasion of Manipur in 1891 was carried out by three converging columns. In many Indian frontier campaigns, the Black Mountain operations in 1888 for instance, several columns have entered the hostile territory and have exercised a great moral effect upon the enemy, as was the case when two separate divisions, one invading their territory from the side of Peshawur and the other from Malakand, and meeting in the heart of it, caused the complete submission of the Mohmunds in 1897.

Enemy unable to profit by the situation, and confused by several invading forces.

The appearance of numerous distinct invading forces not only terrifies an antagonist who possesses neither the dexterity nor the power to deal with them in the most effective manner, but it perplexes him and confuses his plans. In attempting to cover all points he covers none. In endeavouring to arrest the advance of each of the several invading columns he fails to utilise his fighting strength to the best advantage. One of the greatest difficulties which the leader of a tumultuary assemblage labours under is to bow the whole to his will, and when irregular forces see their territory invaded from several points their chief must possess an exceptional personality, and must enjoy unusual authority, if he is to keep them concentrated for decisive action.

Many instances can be adduced from small wars to show how true this is, of which the following may suffice.

In the Zulu war, although Ketchwayo's impis possessed a rude organiza- Examples. tion, were highly disciplined, and enjoyed extraordinary mobility, the fact that his territory was invaded at three different points seems to have so greatly disconcerted the monarch that, although the British operations for some months were singularly ineffective, he made no attempt to carry the war into Natal.

It appears that during the Russian expedition against Khiva, part of the Khivan forces sent to check the column from Turkestan was withdrawn just as this reached the oasis, being moved northwards to reinforce the detachments confronting the column coming from the other side. In consequence the Turkestan column was almost unopposed.

The Ashanti war of 1874 illustrates this particularly well. The real line of attack ran northwards by the shortest road leading from Cape Coast Castle to Kumasi. But three detached forces of limited fighting value worked independently in support on the flanks. One of these forces, operating on the left, never penetrated into Ashanti territory at all, but in spite of this it appears to have contained a large hostile force. Another, on the right, moved forward parallel to the main attack a considerable distance, eventually retiring without fighting, but it likewise occupied the attention of considerable Ashanti detachments. The third, which advanced by a line a long way to the right, possessed some fighting value and, penetrating far into the hostile territory, had to overcome some resistance. This column eventually reaching Kumasi from the right after the place had been destroyed by Sir G. Wolseley's main body and evacuated, retired by the same line as the main body had followed in its advance to, and withdrawal from, the capital. The Ashantis thus having four forces to deal with, detached large bodies to arrest the progress of two of them, neither of which were entitled to much respect, and by doing so they weakened themselves at the decisive point for no purpose.

There is another reason for invading the opponents' terri- Several columns have advantage that, even if some fail to make way, the others succeed. tory in several distinct bodies which will in some of these campaigns render such procedure desirable. This is that occasionally when great difficulties of terrain have to be overcome or when accurate information of the theatre of war is unobtainable, it may be doubtful if the objective can be reached at all by any particular line. In such a case it is clearly a wise precaution to move by several different lines if possible, since it is fair to assume that all of the routes will not prove impracticable. Such conditions are no doubt unusual, but history shows that they will sometimes be found to exist. In the Russian campaign against Khiva it will be remembered that the Krasnovodsk column had to turn back on account of want of water, and that the oasis was subjugated by the other two. The Chitral campaign of 1897 also illustrates this ; had Colonel Kelly's column failed to reach the beleagured fort, it is doubtful if the army advancing from the south would have been in time to save the garrison.

Separation only permissible if each portion can stand by itself. Difficulty of judging requisite strength.

It is the case, then, that division of force is at times dictated by circumstances, and is at other times rendered desirable by the conditions in spite of the well known strategical objections to separation in the field. Splitting up the available forces is, however, only justifiable when each fraction is strong enough to stand by itself and to hold its own against any force which the enemy will be able to bring against it. This is where the difficulty arises in planning the campaign, because it is so often impossible to foresee how far the opposing forces may be able to assemble in any particular part of the theatre of war. When it is so hard to estimate the total hostile strength, it naturally is often quite impracticable to calculate the amount of fighting power which may have to be dealt with along one of the several lines of operations. The great mobility which the enemy enjoys, the suddenness of hostile concentrations, and the complete disintegration of the opposing forces after a reverse, all tend to complicate the problem. Moreover, there is always a chance that the antagonists may possess a chief who will know how to profit by the separation of regular armies in the field. At one crisis of the campaign in the Indian Mutiny the rebel leaders displayed sufficient grasp of the art of war to gravely imperil the safety of the British armies ; this was when they launched a formidable force against Cawnpore while Sir Colin Campbell was carrying out his first relief of Lucknow—had they been a little prompter, the Cawnpore garrison might have been destroyed before the Lucknow force could get back to its assistance.

But it must always be remembered that separation in the Separation dangerous when superiority is not established. field is very dangerous to an army if there is any doubt as to its superiority over the forces opposed to it. The disastrous termination to the first occupation of Kabul in 1841–42 was in the first instance largely due to the detachment of small forces far away towards the Hindu Kush. The vacillation of those in high command soon became apparent to the Afghans, to whom it seemed as though the invaders feared to take any energetic action. The forces of the enemy grew apace, they began operations by swallowing up the isolated fractions, and these small successes encouraged the hostile swarms which were gathering so ominously in proportion as they disheartened the central body of troops at Kabul. The first Afghan war was, of course, a somewhat exceptional case, for at the very root of the art of the effective conduct of operations against irregular antagonists are the assumption and the maintenance of a dominant bearing in the theatre of war. Still, circumstances sometimes arise which, for a time at least, impose upon the regular troops a cautious attitude, and when this is the case a splitting up of the army is wholly inadmissible unless each detached portion can be trusted to act decisively in case of trouble. The disasters suffered by the Republican troops in La Vendée prior to the arrival of Hoche upon the scene, were largely due to their being scattered about in small bodies, which from their organization and nature were quite incapable of striking effective blows against the insurgents.

It is obvious that, the longer the divided portions of an Difficulty of calculating upon exact co-operation between two separated forces, intended to unite for some particular object. army are kept apart and the further the distance they have to march before uniting, the greater is the risk of failure. When the French were advancing to occupy Bacninh in Tonkin they moved for some days in two distinct forces, the idea being that these should meet at the stronghold and attack it from two sides, but one of the two columns came late upon the scene. The same thing

(10830)   H

occurred shortly afterwards in the attack on Hung Hua, where the plan of cooping up the Chinese was well conceived but where it failed in execution. To ensure the simultaneous arrival of the separate bodies demands very careful calculation of times and distances, even under the most favourable circumstances. But in theatres of war of which no accurate maps exist, and of which the topographical features and communications are imperfectly known, it is almost impossible to make a correct forecast of the length of time which troops will take to reach some spot at several marches distance. Operations of this character are dangerous in regular warfare owing to the fact that an alert opponent may bring his whole army to attack one of the fractions on the march. In small wars, on the other hand, the fear is rather that one of the fractions will, owing to unforeseen difficulties of terrain checking the other, arrive prematurely, and that the plan of operations will miscarry in consequence.

CHAPTER X.

LINES OF COMMUNICATIONS, THEIR LIABILITY TO ATTACK, THE DRAIN THEY ARE UPON THE ARMY, AND THE CIRCUMSTANCES UNDER WHICH THEY CAN BE DISPENSED WITH.

IT is not proposed in this chapter to discuss the proper organization of a line of communications, a subject which is somewhat outside of the scope of this work. Suffice it to say that an elaborate arrangement of posts and depôts, a well regulated chain of command, and a sound system of decentralization under which local commanders are given great powers, are the essential features of the system. Many military works exist, official and unofficial, which explain the organization. In this chapter the object will rather be to draw attention to the drain which, owing to the hostile methods of fighting, the protection of lines of communications makes upon an army operating in such districts as usually form the theatre of small wars, and to consider the circumstances under which communications can be dispensed with altogether. *Organization of lines of communications need not be considered in detail.*

The necessity as a rule of maintaining communications with the base, and the freedom which the enemy enjoys in this respect, have been already referred to as showing how, strategically, the regular troops are in these wars at a disadvantage. Communications cramp the operations of the regular army, they act as a drag on its mobility and they tend to tie it down. But there is another respect in which lines of communications in warfare of this character prove a very serious difficulty—they are often of immense length and are generally much exposed to hostile enterprises. The consequence of this is that their protection absorbs a large proportion of the forces in the theatre of war.

H 2

　　Lines of communications may lead through districts where
the temper of the population is intensely hostile, and when
this is the case the posts and depôts along the line, and the
convoys and detachments passing between them, are so constantly exposed to attack that special troops have to be told
off to provide against it. Not only may operations be directed
against the line by the military forces of the enemy, but the
depredations of the local population are a constant source of
anxiety. Moreover, experience shows that in small wars lines
of communications through an enemy's country are often of
great length, and this obviously adds to the difficulties of their
efficient protection. The distance from Peshawur to Kabul was
160 miles, nearly the whole of which ran through rugged tracts,
infested with turbulent marauders and inhabited by unfriendly tribes. The distance from Zula, the base on the Red
Sea, to Magdala was 380 miles. From Majunga on the coast
to Antananarivo the distance traversed by the French was
about 230 miles, and for about 130 miles of this they maintained a regular line of communications ; beyond that point
the force moved as a flying column.

　　In European campaigns the army which invades the
territories of its adversary can generally cover its communications ; it is indeed one of the main principles of strategy
in regular warfare that an army must do so if it is not to expose
itself to the gravest dangers. The fighting force protects its
communications itself by the direction of its march and as
a result of the extent covered by its frontage. But in small
wars this is impossible as a rule. What happens is that a body
of troops pushes far into a country the whole population of
which goes to form the enemy ; the fighting force at the front
deals with such opponents as it meets with or as strive to
prevent it reaching the point it aims at ; but behind the fighting
force the line of communications leading back to the base
requires a separate force, or several separate forces, as a guard.
When this line of communications is of great length, and when

the inhabitants of the theatre of war are ever on the alert to harass the regular troops, the detachments necessary to render the line secure accumulate until they become a most serious drain on the available resources in men.

In an earlier chapter it has been pointed out how **Examples.** the fear of exposing the communications of the expeditionary force to menacing tribes, the intervention of which in the struggle had not been foreseen, brought the troops to a standstill completely in the Ambela campaign. During the Spanish invasion of Morocco in 1859, their army advanced towards Tetuan from Ceuta, and the line of communications was only exposed to hostile enterprises on one side owing to its being contiguous with the shore ; nevertheless it was the case that the route was never secure and that only strong detachments could be sent along it with safety. In 1874 the enemy closed in upon the line of communications of the main British force advancing into Ashanti, and completely severed it at times. During the Boer war in 1881 the hostile demonstrations against the communications of Sir G. Colley's force at Mount Prospect led to his marching a part of the troops at his disposal back to clear the road ; the result of this move was the fight near the Ingogo, in which the column was brought to action by the Boers in a most unfavourable position. Unless, in fact, an adequate force is detailed to protect the line, or lines, of communications there is always great risk of their being cut temporarily or permanently.

It is surprising what forces this guarding of the com- **Large numbers of** munications absorbs. In the Afghan campaign the number **troops** of troops employed on the Khaibar line between Kabul **absorbed.** and Peshawur in March 1880, was more than 15,000 men ; at the same time the Kabul field force consisted of only about 12,000 men. General Skobelef made great efforts to get every available man up to the front for his operations against Denghil Tepe in 1880, the detachments on the communications being reduced to the lowest possible limits consistent with the safety of the various posts ; yet, while the army at the front mustered a bare 8,000 men, the troops on the communications mounted up to about 4,500, or to over one-third of the whole force. In desert campaigns, where the wells mark the only points suitable for posts on the routes leading back to the base, large forces are seldom required for the defence of the line of communications, because the number of posts to protect is of necessity small. But, considering small wars as a whole, this loss of fighting strength due to the drain caused by the obligation of guarding the communications is a distinctive and a very inconvenient feature.

Abandoning communications altogether. It is partly due to the difficulty of guarding a line of communications and to the drain which this creates on the strength of the army as a whole, that in operations of this sort cases so often occur of regular forces abandoning their communications altogether. But there are also other weighty arguments to influence the commander when it becomes a question whether such a procedure, a procedure seldom attempted in a great campaign, should or should not be adopted.

Liberty of action which the force gains thereby. An army cast loose from its communications enjoys great liberty of action. The very fact of its being so situated shows that it is independent as regards supplies. It can turn in any direction, and the enemy can only foil its plan of campaign by meeting it upon the battle-field. This is the reason why the system of flying column—self-contained bodies of troops roaming through the theatre of war—is so largely adopted in irregular warfare. Small flying columns form, as a matter of fact, a most effective protection for the line of communications of an army. They can move out and deal with any gathering of hostile warriors threatening the line in decisive fashion, and are in the meantime unhampered by solicitude as to their own communications inasmuch as they can always return intact to their starting point. By employing such columns freely, a chain of communications may be maintained, which in reality consists merely of detached links. To deal with a foe who resorts to guerilla warfare, flying columns must be largely employed in any case, as will be seen in the next chapter.

When the army itself abandons its communications and thus becomes a flying column, the fact of its being a self-contained force, advantageous as this is in certain respects, has also very serious drawbacks. For it follows as a matter of course that the troops are burdened with wounded and with great supply trains and columns carrying military stores—sufficient to make good whatever is expended during the whole time that the army is cut off from its base. This means a mass of transport, and all this transport has to be protected. The size of the train relatively to the strength of the force depends of course upon the length of time which it is to be adrift; but it is in all cases bound to form a troublesome charge, and it may become a veritable mill-stone round the neck of the commander if it swells to excessive dimensions.

It involves the army being accompanied by large convoys.

The conditions of one phase of the Tirah campaign of 1897 were no doubt exceptional, still they afford a most remarkable example of comparatively speaking large forces moving through a theatre of war as two flying columns. In this case the Anglo-Indian army burst into Tirah from the rear, striking the head of the valleys which form that remarkable tract of country. The object was to overrun this territory of the Afridis and Orukzais and, having entered it as it were by the back door, the obvious trend of the invading army was towards that part of the enemy's country which borders upon the Panjab. In moving in this direction the invaders were approaching their own country, and they could advance in full confidence of finding supplies and every requisite prepared for them. Communications were therefore abandoned and the army, split in two, descended the valleys of the two rivers which drain Tirah, each moving independently as a large flying column.

In the various campaigns which the British and Egyptian troops have carried out against the followers of the Mahdi, the principle of moving as a force independent of communications has often been well illustrated, and the difficulties caused by the great transport train necessary under the circumstances, has been made manifest. In the operations of the Desert column between Korti and Metemma, for instance, the force was practically a flying column, and it was greatly harassed by its convoy of supplies and stores. When the enemy was found in force near Abu Klea, a zeriba had to be formed for the convoy to remain in under protection of a part of the troops, while the rest went out to fight their way to the wells.

During the French advance from the Wémé river to Abomey in the Dahomey campaign, General Dodd's force was practically a flying column with a large convoy to protect; this convoy often proved a sore inconvenience during the numerous engagements which took place.

At Ahmed Khel, when Sir D. Stewart's force was marching from Kandahar to Kabul without maintaining its communications, the necessity of guarding the great trains upon which the army depended, prevented an effective pursuit of the Afghan tribesmen after they had been beaten off.

During the march of half Sir W. Lockhart's force down the Bara valley from upper Tirah, the transport columns were a constant source of anxiety, extending as they did over a great distance on the march and thereby greatly scattering the force in an extraordinary difficult country.

Question greatly affected by the length of time which the operation involves.

There is of course a great difference between an army merely casting itself loose from its communications for an operation which can be concluded in a few days, and the same army becoming a flying column for a considerable time and with a view of making some lengthy march—the supplies and stores required for some very short period seldom become a really serious burden to the force. The final advance to Kumasi from beyond Amoaful was made as a flying column, supplies for four days being carried; but the troops readily agreed to make their rations last six days, and in consequence there was practically no convoy at all. The conditions were altogether different in the case of Sir D. Stewart's march from Kandahar to Kabul, a distance of about 260 miles which took about six weeks to cover, and also in the case of General Duchesne's final advance to Antananarivo, abandoning communications a distance of 100 miles.

Partial abandonment of communications.

Often the abandonment of communications is not complete. Although Sir H. Stewart's force which crossed the Bayuda

Desert to Metemma was to all intents and purposes a flying column, it left in rear of it as it advanced a chain of defensive posts ; in virtue of their existence it was possible to send strongly guarded supply convoys backwards and forwards between the column and its base. This was the principle also in the later days of the South African war of 1899–1902 when the campaign had become one against nomad bands of guerillas. In warfare of this nature there is always risk of the communications being cut, and the situation in the theatre of war in fact is sometimes such that it is really very much a matter of opinion whether a line of communications can be properly said to exist or not.

But in the case of Sir D. Stewart's march quoted above and of Sir F. Roberts's march from Kabul to Kandahar a few months later, there was no doubt upon this point. The forces absolutely abandoned their lines of communications for the time. They were completely adrift. For a space they disappeared into the heart of the enemy's country, and to the outer world their position and their progress were quite unknown till they reappeared near the goal they were aiming at. Such incidents are of very rare occurrence in regular warfare—the solitary instance of such an operation upon a great scale of late years has been General Sherman's famous march through Georgia to the sea. But as long as an army is fully equipped, is prepared for the enterprise, and is capable of dealing effectively with any opposition it may meet with, the undertaking is not necessarily dangerous or even difficult. And when, in addition to this, the force is proceeding to some secure point where it can depend upon establishing its communications afresh, the operation may become quite a simple one. In this latter respect the march from Kabul for the relief of Kandahar differed widely from the march of the Ghazni Field Force, for Sir F. Roberts had a beleaguered force as his objective, not merely a junction with a friendly army.

Examples of armies casting loose from their communications for a considerable time.

The last Afghan war furnishes another and even more striking instance of abandonment of communications. This was when Sir F. Roberts first advanced from the Kurum valley to Kabul. Unable to spare the troops necessary to guard his communications, he organized his army as a flying column and advanced into the heart of a difficult country against a great oriental city, a city noted as a hot-bed of fanaticism, guarded by a considerable body of fairly armed troops, and surrounded by warlike tribes who could be depended upon keenly to resent the intrusion of an invader into their territories. In this case a telling blow speedily delivered was imperative, and it was essential to strike at once. The force was compelled by the circumstances to cast itself loose from its communications, and its capture of Kabul was a signal exploit—a memorable feat of arms. But the operation was somewhat hazardous, and it serves rather as an illustration of the startling results which can in warfare of this nature be obtained by boldness and resolution, than as an example readily to be followed in the future except when there is no help for it.

It must not be forgotten that an army without communications in a hostile country, which meets with a reverse, is in a very serious plight. Especially is this so if the population is—as is so often the case—merely waiting for an opportunity to rise *en masse* and tread the invader down. Hicks Pasha's force appears to have been destroyed actually on the battle-field of Shekan ; but, isolated as it was in the desert and with no line of retreat secure, it is most improbable that, even if the termination of the fight had been less disastrous, the hapless army could ever have got back to the Nile. Not the least important function of a line of communications is that of serving as a line of retreat in case of need, the posts along it, fortified as they usually are, afford refuges and pivots of defence to the army in its rearward march. A force which has no such line to follow, may have to fight its way through ever increasing hostile legions right back to where it started from. It has no temporary asylum near at hand, where it can gain a brief respite from hostile attacks and recover from defeat, and owing to its isolation it runs grave risk of being utterly destroyed. The disastrous retreat from Kabul in 1844 is a case in point.

Then there is another matter with regard to an army which has abandoned its communications which should be mentioned here. Co-operation between it and other forces in the theatre of war is rendered very difficult because its movements are unknown. Information as to the course of events and of changes in the military situation cannot be imparted to it. It is in the dark as to the progress of the operations as a whole. The broad strategical conditions of the campaign may be transformed without its commander being aware of it. He cannot communicate with other forces with which it is desirable that he should act in combination, in case he is obliged to vary his plan. The inconvenience which may arise from this is remarkably well illustrated by what occurred in the beginning of 1885 in the latter part of what may be called the fighting phase of the Nile campaign.

Inconvenience which may arise from the force being unable to communicate with bodies with which it may be co-operating.

The columns which advanced from Korti respectively to Metemma and towards Abu Hamed, were flying columns—communication between them and Korti took some days. When Khartum was discovered to have fallen the whole situation in the theatre of war completely changed, and the object which the expedition had in view, namely the relief of that fortress, ceased to exist. The British Government having resolved that the Mahdi must be crushed at Khartum, Lord Wolseley decided that an autumn campaign would be necessary.

He was not aware that Sir R. Buller's column had in the meantime been obliged to fall back with its transport crippled, and to abandon the steamers which had come from Khartum. Unacquainted with the actual condition of the force, he ordered it to move on Berber and to meet General Brackenbury's column there. Then, when he heard of its retrograde movement from Metemma to Gakdul, he determined, not knowing how completely its transport had broken down, that the Desert Column should return to near Korti and that it should then follow the River Column along the Nile, and he issued orders to that effect. It was not till a few days later that Lord Wolseley learnt that the Desert Column was quite incapable of undertaking any enterprise involving mobility. He was also unaware that the River Column had met with unexpected difficulties, and that in consequence it was doubtful if its supplies would hold out. It was only when this news arrived that it was decided to recall both forces to near Korti. Thus, detailed orders were twice over issued under a misapprehension of the existing conditions. This misapprehension arose from the fact that the two forces were flying columns and that they had no means of direct and immediate communication with the commander-in-chief.

Conclusions as to abandonment of communications.

It is clear, then, that many objections exist to an army abandoning its communications and advancing as a flying column. Under certain circumstances the course is perfectly justifiable, conditions will arise in small wars which may compel such procedure to be adopted, it saves the drain upon the available resources in men which a line of communications almost of necessity involves. But it is not a strategical manœuvre to be undertaken lightly, except as a temporary expedient or as a minor operation of war, and it is absolutely essential that a force which in this manner casts itself loose in the theatre of war, should have an organization calculated to meet the special requirements of the case and based on a full acquaintance with the conditions of the campaign.

CHAPTER XI.

GUERILLA WARFARE IN GENERAL.

IT has been pointed out in earlier chapters that guerilla Guerilla warfare in general.
warfare is a form of operations above all things to be avoided.
The whole spirit of the art of conducting small wars is to strive
for the attainment of decisive methods, the very essence of
partisan warfare from the point of the enemy being to avoid
definite engagements. The inconveniences and dangers to
regular troops when the adversary adopts this attitude, are
fully recognised by competent commanders. But no amount
of energy and strategic skill will at times draw the enemy
into risking engagements, or induce him to depart from the
form of warfare in which most irregular warriors excel and in
which regular troops are almost invariably seen at their worst.

It is only proposed in this chapter to treat of the strategical aspect of carrying on guerilla warfare—or rather of the
means by which adversaries depending on this system of
conducting hostilities can best be dealt with. In those which
discuss mountain and bush warfare, outposts, surprises,
ambushes and raids, the methods by which the hostile
procedure can be best met as a question of minor tactics,
are touched upon in more detail.

The aptitude which such opponents as regular armies
have so often in these campaigns to cope with, display in
harassing the troops who have penetrated into their fastnesses,
is known to all. They revel in stratagems and artifice. They
prowl about waiting for their opportunity to pounce down
upon small parties moving without due precaution. The
straggler and camp follower are their natural prey. They
hover on the flanks of the column, fearing to strike but ready

to cut off detachments which may go astray. It is not only, so to speak, the rank and file who are masters of this branch of the military art, leaders are produced who excel in controlling the scattered bodies engaged in it, and who give to it direction and vitality. A glance back over the small wars of an hundred years reveals few chiefs of imperishable renown in the ranks of the foes who have opposed the forces of civilization, few personalities figuring large in history. But a few great names are handed down to us, and these are not the names of men who led great hosts to battle, they are the names of commanders of guerillas and banditti. No one to-day remembers who led the Khalsa armies at Sobraon, or the Beluchis in Scinde, but Abd el Kader and the Circassian Schamyl figure among the great soldiers of the age. Charette and Andreas Hofer still live in history, not as patriots only but also as masters of one form of the art of war. Tantia Topi owes his reputation not to Kalpi and Cawnpore, but to the months when, with a dwindling following and bound to a declining cause, he kept the field while the British hunted him in vain. And De la Rey, De Wet and Botha never fully displayed their rare gifts of leadership till the Boer armies had been dissipated, and till the great struggle in South Africa had degenerated into a thoroughly irregular campaign.

Guerilla warfare is what the regular armies always have most to dread, and when this is directed by a leader with a genius for war, an effective campaign becomes well-nigh impossible. The guerilla has ever been a thorn in the side of the organized force. It was so in the Peninsular war, where the Spanish partisans proved a formidable foe to the French invaders. Fra Diavolo and his brigand bands were almost a match for the veterans of Massena in Calabria. The Cossacks, masters of this method of conducting operations, contributed almost more towards bringing about the terrible disasters which befel the Grand Army on its retreat from Moscow, than did the rigours of a Russian winter or the combinations of the able commanders of the pursuing armies. Before the last Russian intervention in the Balkans the Turks found the Montenegrins far more difficult to subdue than the organized Servian armies. It is because of this that the art of combating the guerilla method of conducting operations deserves especial attention when small wars are in question. Moreover, experience proves that even when there have been at the outset armies to beat in the field, the campaign will drift on in desultory fashion long after these have been overthrown, and that in small wars guerilla operations are almost invariably a feature of some phase of the struggle.

The terrain has much to say to effective conduct of partisan warfare on the part of the enemy. The Philippines and Brittany like Castille and Trans-Caucasia, present theatres of operations eminently suited to operations of this class. New Zealand, the kloofs and bushland of Kaffraria, Burma, and Achin, all fitted to a nicety the guerilla tactics of opponents designed by nature to pursue this form of war. Hilly and broken ground or districts clothed in jungle growth and thickets especially lend themselves to these very desultory operations. On the prairie, on the veld and on the steppes, on the contrary, guerilla methods can only be adopted by mounted men, whose mobility at least partially compensates for the lack of cover as they approach their foe. *Influence of terrain.*

Surprise is the essence of such operations—surprise, with retreat ere the opponent can recover, as a sequel, and in consequence the combinations of the enemy are of necessity framed on a small scale. Surprises with large forces are difficult to carry out. The Boers, it is true, managed some of their most effective strokes with comparatively speaking strong commandos, but the withdrawal of any large force when once committed to action is always most risky. Guerilla warfare, in fact, means almost of necessity petty annoyance rather than operations of a dramatic kind. Such capricious methods of conducting operations are best met by a resolute plan of *Promptitude and resolution essential to deal with guerillas.*

campaign and by an organization favouring rapid and energetic counter-strokes. Surprise can, to a certain extent, be
guarded against by measures taken for security. But the
escape of the enemy can only be frustrated by having troops
ready to follow up at once and to follow up effectively.

Abd el Kader.　　The French operations in Algeria during many years of
war will ever serve to illustrate what is the right way and
what is the wrong way of dealing with an antagonist who
adopts the guerilla mode of war. Abd el Kader was a partisan
leader of the foremost rank. He intuitively grasped
the conditions of the case. He recognized at once that
his followers could not hope to beat the trained soldiers
of France in open battle. His personal ascendancy over the
nomads of the south and over the wild Berber hill-men, enabled
him to play the strategist from wherever his wandering abode
might be, over a vast extent of country. For years his bold
and sudden strokes bewildered the French leaders. He had
full information of their slow, deliberate movements. He
knew when a garrison was drained of troops and he straight-
way fell upon it. He cut communications and he swept away
convoys. But by the time the French had assembled their
forces for a counter-stroke, and had dragged their guns and
impedimenta to the spot, the hostile body which had done
the mischief had vanished into the desert, or had flown to
some hill refuge whither the cumbrous column could not
follow it.

General
Bugeaud's
mode of
crushing him.　　But when the right leader came upon the scene from
France a great change came over the spirit of the struggle.
General Bugeaud added to great natural gifts a ripe experience. He had served an apprenticeship in guerilla warfare
years before in Spain. He knew the game, and his appearance on the scene as chief marked a transformation. " Vous
aurez beaucoup à oublier," he said to his assembled lieutenants,
and he altered the whole system of campaigning on the
spot. He perceived that he had to deal not with a hostile

army but with a hostile population, that this population consisted largely of clans and tribes of fixed abode, and that to bring them to reason he must reach them through their crops, their flocks, and their property. He established numbers of mobile detachments all over the country to watch centres of disturbance, and to strike at once on sign of trouble. These columns owed their strength to rapidity of movement rather than to numbers, they were kept equipped and supplied with a sufficiency of pack transport, artillery and baggage being reduced to a minimum. Their rôle was not merely to disperse the gatherings of the enemy, but also to chastise the rebels in their homes. The razzias or raids of the Arabs had been a terror to the French, but General Bugeaud instituted razzias by way of counter-stroke and turned Abd el Kader's own methods against the nomad leader. " Il se quand bat il veut, il cherche, il poursuit l'ennemi, l'inquiete, et se fait craindre," wrote Saint Arnaud. Abd el Kader had at last met his match, and the cause he had upheld so long with conspicuous ability and unfaltering courage, declined from the day his great opponent landed in Algiers, in 1841, invested with full powers.

In campaigns where the hostile tactics have been limited to surprises on a small scale and to ambuscades, and which have drifted on in desultory fashion for long periods, the want of prompt energetic action on the part of the regular troops has generally been mainly responsible for their failure to bring the war to a speedy conclusion. In the protracted Maori war the British operations were carried out with marked deliberation. It is true that at times, when the enemy stuck to his pahs and accepted battle, the operations were attended with great success, but the system of mobile columns ready to act at a moment's notice was not put in force, and therefore the Maoris played a game of hide and seek, and considering their inferiority to the regular troops they kept it up for a vexatiously long time. The

Campaigns when want of mobility and decision on the part of the regular troops against guerillas has had bad effect.

I

Russians during the long years of war in Trans-Caucasia against the fiery partisan leader Schamyl utterly lacked the system of decentralized vigour which Bugeaud employed so effectively under somewhat similar conditions in Algeria. The Kaffir war in 1851–52 was throughout of a guerilla character, the enemy not being formidable although greatly favoured by the topographical features of the country, but the British forces lacked mobility and the commissariat and transport services were not organized to meet the case. The slow progress made by the Germans in 1904–05 in suppressing the revolted tribes in South-West Africa appears to have been mainly due to the lethargic movements of forces constantly hampered by inadequate transport. The hill campaigns of India illustrate guerilla warfare excellently; the climate does not favour rapid energetic movements, the troops are always hampered by much baggage, and only certain of the native Indian troops are mountaineers and a match in activity for the hill-men; but the fact that the marauding hill tribes dwell in villages, the locality of which is often well known, compensates to a certain extent for all this because they can be punished by having their homes destroyed and their fields laid waste.

The broad principles of the strategy to be employed against guerillas.

Vigorous leadership and the rapid movement of columns from place to place will not, however, suffice by itself to subdue determined adversaries who have resorted to the methods of partisan warfare. An elaborate strategical organization is necessary as well. The principle of constantly harassing the enemy and of giving the hostile detachments no rest, can only be put in force if the theatre of war is carefully prepared for it beforehand. Experience shows that, if possible, the whole area of operations should be sub-divided into sections, each of which has its own military force or aggregate of military detachments told off to it. This was the system adopted by Hoche when operating against the Chouans in Brittany, it was the system introduced by Bugeaud to a certain extent when he took over the command in Algeria, it was the system under which the conquest of Upper Burmah was made good, and it was the system which, when developed to an extent hitherto unparalleled in war, eventually compelled the Boers to submit to the British forces under Lord Kitchener.

When the theatre of war has been sub-divided into sections, each section must have its defensive posts, its depôts of supply and its columns. There must be places whither raided flocks and herds can be brought. The sections must be further parcelled out into convenient and well-defined areas for the purpose of clearing the country of the supplies which may be useful to the enemy, to ensure that this process shall be carried out methodically and completely. How far such clearance is to be carried out depends of course on the circumstances of the case; but it is essential that it should be carried out systematically, whether it takes the form of devastating the country, or whether it be limited to the seizure of the supplies which may be necessary for the troops.

Before proceeding further and discussing details as regards the strength and composition of flying columns, it will not be out of place to refer to the case of a recent campaign which lasted for years, a campaign in which a huge army of regular soldiers strove vainly to suppress insurrection in a territory with a vast extent of coast line although the disciplined troops had sea power at their command, a campaign which was only terminated by the intervention of the military and naval forces of a great neighbouring state. As this was a case where the trained and disciplined soldiery signally failed to overcome the irregular warriors arrayed against them, it may be worth while to briefly examine the causes which led to this unusual result, and we cannot do better than to quote the opinion of Lieutenant Barnes, 4th Hussars, who was present for some time in the theatre of war while the struggle was at its height,

The war in Cuba.

and who thus had especial opportunities for making observations and for forming judgment.

"Although the Spanish Government for more than three years in Cuba maintained an army numerically far stronger than the insurgent forces, much better armed and organized, and superior in courage, they were utterly unable to subdue or even to check the revolt, which spread steadily westward until the whole island was disaffected. Some explanation of this remarkable fact may be found in the following considerations :—The Spanish troops were obstructed by the intense hostility of the inhabitants. They could get no good information of the rebel movements, while the rebels were never in doubt about theirs. An insurgent was distinguished from the peaceful cultivator only by his badge which could be speedily removed, and by his rifle which was easily hidden. Hence the Government forces, whether in garrison or operating in the country, were closely surrounded by an impalpable circle of fierce enemies who murdered stragglers, intercepted messages, burned stores, and maintained a continual observation.

" The country was densely wooded, and in the eastern districts mountainous. There were no good roads. This absence of good communications had a most paralyzing effect on the military movements ; the mobility of the intangible enemy was, however, unimpaired. Moving swiftly by the tracks in the forests, the rebels harassed all the Spanish columns and occasionally destroyed one. Finally, the climate was deadly. Small-pox, malaria, and yellow fever filled the hospitals and drained the fighting units.

"All these are obstacles to success rather than causes of failure—these latter must be looked for in the tactics and conduct of the Spanish forces. There was a complete absence of any general plan. Columns moved about haphazard in the woods, fighting the enemy where they found them and returning with their wounded to the towns when they were weary of wandering. Their method of warfare was essentially defensive. They held great numbers of towns and villages with strong garrisons. They defended or tried to defend, long lines of communications with a multitude of small blockhouses. They tried to treat the rebels as though they were merely agrarian rioters, and to subdue the revolt by quartering troops all over the country. The movement was on a scale far exceeding the scope of such remedies ; it was a war, and this the Spanish Government would never recognize. Over all the petty incidents of guerilla skirmishing, the frequent executions and the stern reprisals threw a darker shade.

" There appeared to be only one way of stamping out the revolt. It was a case for the subaltern with his half company operating independently and fighting the enemy wherever found, sometimes getting destroyed, but usually hurting much more than he was hurt. This might have been combined with a liberal use of mounted infantry or of cavalry acting as such, all working on some general system and operating in one district after another. It would then have become a very bloody and ferocious struggle, but the rebels having fewer men would probably have had enough of it first. But the Spanish troops are not adapted for this sort of disseminated work, most of the regimental officers having risen from the ranks and therefore lacking the self-reliance and initiative which are indispensable qualifications."

It must be remembered that the Cuban insurgents came of an intelligent race. They were well armed and most determined. To coerce such a people into submission is no easy task, as was found in 1901–02 in South Africa. But it is clear from the above account that the broad principles which must guide the conduct of regular forces engaged in operating against guerillas were not put in force. Mobile columns acting resolutely on the offensive were not employed. No attempt was made to parcel the revolted area out into districts and to stamp out rebellion in one district after another. The campaign against the Cuban rebels teaches us what to avoid rather than what to do.

The sub-division of the theatre of war into sections, each with its commander, its chains of posts, and its mobile columns may be said to be the first step towards dealing with guerilla warfare effectively. It must be remembered that operations of this class generally cover a wide area and that considerable doubt often exists as to the position of the enemy's centres of activity. Clearing the country of supplies and, in some cases, rendering it impossible for an enemy to exist in the country at all owing to no food or shelter being left, may become part of the programme. If this is to be done methodically it can be most effectually carried out by areas, each with its responsible commander. If one area is disposed of easily while another gives serious trouble, troops can if necessary be transferred from one to the other and a re-arrangement of boundaries may take place. It is the only plan by which a form of operations, which will always be harassing to regular troops and which may take an inordinate time to conclude unless method be brought into play, is likely to be carried out efficiently and economically. The

The sub-division of the theatre of war into sections.

failure to work on these lines has been commented upon above in the case of the Spanish efforts to subdue the Cubans. In Burma and during the later stages of the South African war of 1899–1902, this system formed the basis of the plan of campaign.

The extent of the various sections depends on the nature of the country, the amount of cultivation, the thickness of the population, the strength of the enemy, and so forth. No rule can possibly be laid down on such a subject. But in open territory like the veld, and when the enemy consists of mounted men, the areas will naturally be larger than in close intersected country such as hill and bush warfare takes place in. The area of the sections is, of course, also largely governed by the numbers of the troops available for their subjection.

Fortified posts and depôts.

Each section must have a certain number of posts told off to it. By dint of well constructed defence works, such posts can be rendered absolutely secure, without their proving a serious drain on the fighting force which may be available—the essence of operations against guerillas is to be found in utilising the troops available as far as possible for mobile columns, and that being so the garrisons of fortified posts should be reduced to a minimum consistent with safety. In these posts supplies are collected; and if there are many of them, columns and detachments can move in all directions with little transport, always sure of finding the food which they require to keep them in the field. These supply depôts are replenished from time to time by convoys; and, as these convoys, unless they are under strong escort, always offer the enemy opportunities of attack under comparatively speaking favourable circumstances, a multiplication of fortified posts where convoys can find shelter facilitates the replenishment of supplies and reduces the proportion of the troops required for convoy duty. In the South African war the difficulties of convoying supplies, added to the necessity of securing the railways, gave rise to those remarkable lines of blockhouses, which eventually served the purpose of ring defences enclosing many of the areas where Boer resistance was most strenuous and where Boer activity most marked. The larger fortified posts, where considerable stores of supplies are collected, serve as main bases for the flying columns, and at these not only food and forage, but also ammunition and equipment are often stored. It is to these larger posts that captured live stock is generally brought for safety.

The nature of the fortification varies according to the circumstances of the campaign. In the Kaffir war of 1851-52 large forts existed which were perfectly secure from the attacks of an enemy most disinclined to leave his kloofs and mountain fastnesses except for a raid ; Sir G. Cathcart indeed took considerable exception to the elaborate works constructed. On the other hand in Algeria, where a determined enemy was in the field who could at times come down upon a garrison in considerable force, large forts were necessary for security. In the operations in Rhodesia in 1896 the " base " of a column often consisted merely of some wagons in laager, with a few men and perhaps a Maxim acting as garrison. The character of the defences depends in fact on the nature of the theatre of war, or the extent to which the posts are isolated, and on the strength of hostile resistance.

As flying columns necessarily play so important a part in operations of this class, their strength and organization deserve special attention. The system which General Bugeaud introduced in Algeria was not new—General Hoche had worked on similar lines against the Chouans in Brittany with brilliant success. The principle of flying columns has since been used with much effect in the Western States against the Red Indians. It has also been put in force in Afghanistan, in Burma, in Rhodesia, and more recently in the prolonged struggle against the Boers.

Flying columns.

The troops forming such columns must be thoroughly
equipped for the tasks they have to perform, and they should
be able to travel light. Mobility is the first essential. The
guerilla trusts to sudden strokes, and it is of' the utmost
importance that the marauding party should not have time
to disperse and that it should be attacked before it can withdraw and dissolve. Hoche urged the leaders of mobile
columns to accustom their men to fatigue and hardships
and to keep them in condition. The detachments of United
States troops operating against the Red Indians depended for
success mainly on mobility, and in the later stages of the South
African war mobility was the main essential looked for in
columns.

The question of the strength to be given to columns depends upon the circumstances of the case. In Burma they
seldom numbered more than 300 men, with one or two guns.
In Algeria, where the enemy was brave, resolute, and capable
of suddenly gathering in formidable strength, small bodies
would have been unsuitable ; General Bugeaud recommended
three or four battalions with cavalry and two guns as a proper
strength. Practically, however, the columns should be as
small as possible consistent with safety. Their composition,
of course, depends upon the conditions of the campaign and
upon the terrain--on open ground a large part of the force
generally consists of mounted men, in thick bush infantry
alone can be used. In Abd el Kader's days portable artillery
scarcely existed, and it was wheeled guns to which General
Bugeaud so much objected. Guns on mules are by no means
out of place in a flying column of dismounted troops, and may
prove very useful; machine guns are generally very well adapted
for this sort of work. Where it is proposed to raid live stock,
some mounted troops are indispensable to bring the booty in.

Columns of
mounted
troops in
certain
theatres of
war. In the campaigns against the roving Indians on the prairies,
the United States leaders always depended largely upon
mounted troops ; great distances had to be covered and

the cavalry became highly efficient at this sort of work. Some of the marches were astonishing, and they often finished up with a skilfully executed surprise of the hostile marauders; infantry were sometimes carried in wagons, but the most brilliant exploits in these campaigns were carried out by mounted troops alone. In Kaffirland, and in South Africa generally, only mounted troops can hope to get on terms with the enemy if he does not mean fighting. Similarly on the steppes the mobile columns are formed of mounted Cossacks and irregulars. The Kirghiz freebooter Kutebar, in the days when Russia was preparing for the incorporation of Khokand, defied all efforts to effect his capture and his subjection for a decade; as long as he was at large his meteoric appearances and his impudent hardihood made him at once a peril to Russian progress and a scourge to the clans which had welcomed the arrival of the Cossack—only the most lightly equipped of mounted troops can hope to cope with such a foe. As observed above, mounted troops are essential to bring in captured cattle, and, when the enemy's livestock forms an objective, cavalry columns are the most effective means of sweeping the booty in from over a wide area. In the desultory warfare in Central Asia against the nomads, whose sole wealth consists in flocks and herds, the Russians employed raids of mounted men with conspicuous success. In the Kaffir campaign of 1877 small mobile columns of mounted police scoured the country raiding the cattle of the enemy, and they greatly assisted thereby in crushing the rebellion.

The suppression of the rebellion in Southern Rhodesia in 1896 affords an admirable illustration of the right method of dealing with guerilla warriors of a certain type. The Matabili, conquered and deprived of leadership and cohesion, were not in themselves a formidable fighting race, and they eschewed all fighting in the open except on one or two occasions during the prolonged operations. The Mashonas were still less warlike. But the territory affected was of vast extent, the

Suppression of the rebellion in Southern Rhodesia.

available British forces were small, and certain large tracts of country were singularly well adapted for the display of guerilla tactics by nimble savages such as the insurgents were. The troops employed to stamp out the revolt were for the most part mounted, but they were assisted by dismounted friendlies. They were broken up by General Carrington into mobile columns, varying in strength according to the task set before them, but often consisting of only a mere handful of men. Although the food supply of these in their rapid movements over great distances sometimes proved a difficulty, the fine climate and open air life rendered all ranks capable of enduring great fatigues and of covering an immense amount of ground within the 24 hours. Some portable guns and Maxims were available and accompanied the more important columns, rendering useful service.

The principle enforced, and rigidly carried out, was that each column had some definite task to perform, and must push through with it in spite of distance and of natural obstacles. The scattered impis of the Matabili were hunted down relentlessly and compelled to fight or to submit. On one or two occasions—as in the Matoppo Hills—the enemy gathered in considerable numbers, and, profiting by the nature of the terrain, accepted battle after a fashion. But such favourable opportunities for giving the rebels a lesson did not generally present themselves, and the campaign was essentially one of surprises and ambuscades on one side, and of vigour and determination on the other. In 1897, during the final operations against the Mashonas, it was found that the only way of compelling their submission was to hunt them into their cave strongholds, destroy their kraals, and finally capture them in their caves—a by no means easy task; the method adopted is given in some detail in Chapter XII. The operations were not of a dramatic kind, but they were singularly effective. It was the system of Bugeaud and of Hoche adapted to the special conditions of veld and koppie warfare, and the campaign serves as a model of what such campaign should be.

The evolution of the mobile columns which played such a paramount part in the later stages of the South African War, The columns in the South African War. throws a flood of light upon the subject of dealing with determined opponents fighting in guerilla fashion. In many respects the conditions of the struggle were extraordinarily favourable to the Boers for prosecuting partisan warfare, although they were not favourable in all respects. Their commandos enjoyed extraordinary mobility. The vast extent of the country created almost insuperable difficulties as regards supply for the British troops. The Boers fought with a grit and determination worthy of the highest admiration, and they were gifted with never-failing cunning and with rare foresight. But, on the other hand, the veld presents for the most part a singularly open country, and it is in broken and wooded territory that the guerilla enjoys the greatest liberty of action. The British moreover had an enormous preponderance of force, and their resources in all respects were practically unlimited.

When it became apparent that the collapse of the Boer armies, the capture of all the most important points in the Transvaal and Orange Free State, and the appropriation of the railway communications throughout the country, did not mean that the war was over, but that it was going to definitely assume a guerilla character, an elaborate system of flying columns was set on foot. But in the early days these columns were for the most part only flying columns in the sense that they were self-contained as regards supplies. They consisted largely of infantry. Their transport was made up of ponderous ox-wagons travelling slowly. No self-respecting column was without its heavy gun. Their movements were lethargic, their spheres of operations were cramped owing to the comparatively limited distances which they covered day by day, rarely did they inflict serious loss upon the enemy, and considering the mobility of the enemy it is not to be wondered at that the roll of prisoners taken by them was small. But in spite of this, these slow-moving columns did most excellent work. They cleared the country of livestock and of supplies with a thoroughness which the more mobile forces of a later date could not have attempted. The torpid columns of the early months of 1901 paved the way for those sudden strokes and rapid movements, which culminated in the drives of the last few months of the war.

Gradually it came to be recognised that to deal with the roving commandos effectively and to put an end to resistance, columns must attain a maximum of mobility. This could only be achieved by eliminating dismounted men and forming the columns practically entirely of mounted troops. But this imposed great difficulties owing to the bulk and weight of the forage which had to be carried. The number of supply depôts had to be increased, and, as these had to be scattered all over the theatre of war and their replenishment demanded expenditure of force, lines of blockhouses were instituted to facilitate the movements of convoys—lines of blockhouses which served a very useful purpose later on in the time of the drives. Thanks to this system the now genuinely mobile columns began to do brilliant work, to make important captures of prisoners, and to give a display of the art of war in dealing with a guerilla enemy operating in an extended theatre such as has not been seen before in any country. They covered great distances. They marched often at night. Their efforts were constantly directed towards surprising the scattered Boer detachments and giving them no rest. When by these means contact was gained with hostile commandos, they struck at once and struck hard. There was nothing new in the principle underlying their operations, the novelty lay only in the methods by which the principle was put in practice.

Danger of very small columns.

Although the columns organized to put down guerilla warfare should be as small as possible they must not be too small. If there be any fear of the enemy combining his forces to attack columns in detail, or of acting on interior lines as it is called, there must be troops enough to deal with whatever hostile forces can be assembled. In the early days of La Vendée, separation proved fatal to the Republican forces. The peasants gathered from time to time in great force and overwhelmed the detachments of regulars— the system of small columns introduced later by General Hoche was adapted to different conditions, to a more purely guerilla warfare than when the insurrection was at its height. In Mexico small columns of French and of Imperial troops suffered very severely when the troubles first broke out against Maximilian's rule, because the enemy was able to bring considerable forces against them. In Upper Burma, where very small columns were adopted during the prolonged period of pacification, no serious disaster occurred. Considering the great number of columns operating in a vast extent of almost unexplored country for many months, this is very noteworthy; but on one or two occasions it would have been advantageous had they been stronger. Sir F. Roberts's instructions were that "the troops should make their presence felt everywhere," and in view of the enormous area to be overrun, the columns had to be reduced to a minimum strength. During the operations against the Angoni Zulus in the Mpseni country in 1898, an insignificant force of 400 local troops with two guns, by dint of rapid marches and resolute initiative, completely broke up a numerous and warlike tribe, seizing their cattle when they fled, and attacking them whenever they made any attempt to stand. The smaller the column the more mobile it will generally be ; the more mobile it is the more suddenly it can deliver its strokes ; and the essence of combating guerilla warfare is to hit unexpectedly and hard. The enemy's game likewise is to hit unexpectedly, but generally not very hard.

Need for independence.

It is very important that flying columns should be made as independent as is possible within their own sphere of operations. Sir F. Roberts's instructions in the case of Upper Burma were that the " utmost latitude of movement " should be given to their commanders. This principle appears also in General Hoche's system, and to a less extent in that of General Bugeaud. In summing up the lessons of La Vendée General v. Boguslawski writes :—" The leaders of the columns must be officers who, in certain cases, understand how to depart from the plan of operations on their own responsibility, if the general situation appears to have altered." In the later stages of the South African war column commanders were always allowed great independence, except when some combined operation was being carried out by several columns.

Difficulty of controlling movements of separated columns.

In dealing with guerilla warfare like that in Rhodesia, one of the greatest difficulties to be contended with is that it is impracticable to issue definite orders to a force operating at a considerable distance from head-quarters. The inconvenience caused by this on the Nile early in 1885 was alluded to on p. 123, although there the operations were not directed against guerillas. During the campaign in Uganda in 1897–98, which covered an immense extent of country, messages had to be sent by native runners ; it sometimes took as much as six days to communicate with a subordinate, and twelve days to get a reply. The same difficulty occurred in Sierra Leone in 1898.

Under such circumstances a great deal of latitude must be left to subordinates, whose judgment should remain as far as possible unfettered. It is one of the awkward problems which an officer with the general control of operations over a large territory finds himself confronted with. On more than one occasion in Rhodesia contemplated junctions of separate columns did not come off, but their leaders knew that what they had to do was to strike at any hostile gatherings with which they obtained touch, and they constantly acted on

their own responsibility in consequence. In no class of warfare is the need of self-reliant subordinate officers so urgent
as in operations of this nature, and the lack of such may spoil
the best matured combinations of the chief. It has been seen
that the Spanish failure in dealing with the Cuban insurgents
has been attributed partially to the want of an abundant
supply of such leaders, a want which will generally make itself
felt in any army in which the bulk of commissions are gained
from the ranks.

The " drives " instituted in the closing days of the South
African war may be called the last word in strategy directed
against guerilla antagonists. In principle the drives combined
the system of sub-dividing the theatre of war into sections,
of utilizing highly mobile troops, of acting with the utmost
energy, and of getting the full benefit out of fortified posts.
The plan was practically perfect in theory, and the lines of
blockhouses were there ready to form the barrier against which
the commandos were to be forced. But its execution was
extremely difficult. There was always risk of a gap being left
somewhere, or of the enemy breaking through lines which
were necessarily stretched almost to the breaking point.
The " drives" achieved great results however, and they present
perhaps the most remarkable feature of that long drawn out
campaign against the Boer guerillas. The method is obviously
one which could only be used after prolonged operations
and after ample preparation, and it would rarely happen that
such heroic remedies would be necessary in operations against
the class of enemy ordinarily met with in small wars.

The South African "drives."

In no class of warfare is a well organized and well served
intelligence department more essential than in that against
guerillas. Hoche instituted an elaborate system of espionage
in Brittany, paying particular attention to this very important
subject. Guerillas trust to secret and to sudden strokes, and
if the secret is discovered their plan miscarries. On the
other hand, all movements intended against them must be

Need of a good intelligence department in guerilla warfare, and of secrecy.

concealed or they will be scared away. Guerilla warfare means that the regular troops are spread about a hostile country where all their movements can be watched by the enemy and where their camps are full of spies. Experience proves that partisan leaders can seldom be trusted, and that in all dealings with them great circumspection is essential. Hoche discouraged parleying with the rebels by subordinate officers, distrusting their chiefs. " Parle comme si tu avais confiance en tout le monde " was the motto of General Bugeaud " et agis comme si tu ne pouvais t'en rapporter a personne." Such conditions call for a very efficient and watchful secret service for a trustworthy corps of spies and for a wide awake police, with a capable intelligence department controlling the whole.

A well organized corps of scouts drawn from the more intelligent members of the community who may side with the regular forces, is an invaluable adjunct to the intelligence department. Dealing with the partisan operations of South African races or, in territories like Cuba and Mexico, of rebels, settlers in sympathy with the disciplined forces can generally be found, whose knowledge of the country and the people well qualify them for such work. Moving about secretly by night scouts of this class can detect and locate the hostile gatherings, can discover where the enemy has concealed his flocks, and can lead the columns to the spot where it is proposed to strike. In bush warfare, to be dealt with later on, scouts are generally natives who cannot be trusted far out of sight ; but Europeans who have long lived an open air life in a theatre of guerilla warfare, who are accustomed to track footprints and who are adepts at the hunter's craft, will move miles ahead of the fighting force and can sometimes fix the quarry at several marches distance.

Lack of an efficient intelligence service was one of the many causes of the Spanish failure in Cuba. In the Peninsula the French commanders never got over the difficulty of establishing some organized method of obtaining information as to the movements and intentions of the Spanish guerillas. Until Bugeaud came upon the scene the French in Algeria paid insufficient attention to this all-important matter, and the Russians operating against Schamyl and the tribesmen of the Trans-Caucasian hills were generally completely at fault as regards intelligence. In the later days of the South African war the paramount importance of a well equipped intelligence department was fully recognized, and its work exercised a great influence on the course of the operations. The Germans operating in South-West Africa have sorely felt the want of an adequate intelligence service—it is only in armies accustomed to the varying conditions of irregular warfare that the importance of this subject is fully appreciated.

The adoption of guerilla methods by the enemy almost Carrying off necessarily forces the regular troops to resort to punitive destroying measures directed against the possessions of their antagonists. property. It must be remembered that one way to get the enemy to fight is to make raids on his property—only the most cowardly of savages and irregulars will allow their cattle to be carried off or their homes to be destroyed without making some show of resistance. Antagonists who will not even under such circumstances strike a blow, can only be dealt with by depriving them of their belongings or burning their dwellings. When operations are being carried out against guerillas scattered over great tracts of country, it has generally been found very useful to send raiding parties consisting of mounted men great distances, to carry off the enemy's flocks and herds or to destroy encampments and villages. As already mentioned the Russians have put this method of warfare in force in Central Asia, and the French made large use of it in some of their Algerian campaigns. In Chapter XVI raids will be considered from the tactical point of view, here it is only necessary to draw attention to them as one means of bringing guerillas to book. The raiding plan is of course somewhat different from the methodical clearing of the whole country such as was carried out in South Africa in 1901–02.

The objection to raids pure and simple is really one of principle. To filch the property of irregulars when they are absent is not the true spirit of waging war against such opponents ; the proper way to deal with them is to kill them or to wound them, or at least to hunt them from their homes and then to destroy or carry off their belongings. But it must be remembered that the French in Algeria and the Russians on the steppes have had to deal with nomads who thought fit to adopt guerilla tactics, and who never fought if they could help it ; British troops have had practically no experience of such conditions.

Raids designed to destroy hostile depôts of food or ammunition of course stand on a different footing altogether, their value in any class of warfare can hardly be overrated ; but guerillas, savages, or semi-civilized adversaries rarely have such depôts, therefore the question of operations against them hardly arises in small wars. The system of raiding the enemy's cattle was employed to a certain extent by the British forces in Kaffirland in 1877, and in the suppression of the Rhodesian rebellion ; but it was not found that these enterprises had much effect upon the Mashonas in 1897, who held out till tackled in their caves. In those campaigns great difficulty was experienced in getting the enemy to fight, as the French found in Algeria and the Russians in some of their steppe campaigns, but the South African native races are not nomads, and it is always nomads who especially prize their flocks and herds. Of course if the force is actually short of food, raids may become absolutely necessary ; and should a body of troops for any reason have been compelled to adopt a defensive attitude for a time, a bold raid will tend to re-establish its prestige, and will encourage all ranks at a time when they may be depressed owing to their unsatisfactory position. But regular troops who can find no better means of stamping out the resistance of determined guerillas than by cattle lifting raids will probably take a long time to perform their task.

When the operations take the form of pacifying a dis- Pacification turbed district, as was the case in La Vendée and as is, indeed, of revolted districts. usual during at least some period of a guerilla war, much judgment is needed. The enemy must be chastised up to a certain point but should not be driven to desperation. General Hoche in La Hoche's system is thus described by Thiers. Vendée.

" Hoche devised an ingenious mode of reducing the country without laying it waste, by depriving it of its arms and taking part of its produce for the supply of the Republican army. In the first place he persisted in the establishment of entrenched camps * * * . He then formed a circular line which was supported by the Sèvres and Loire and tended to envelope progressively the whole country. This line was composed of very strong posts connected by patrols, so as to leave no free space by which an enemy who was at all numerous could pass. These posts were directed to occupy every hamlet and village and to disarm them. To accomplish this they were to seize the cattle which usually grazed together and the corn stowed away in the barns ; they were also to secure the principal inhabitants ; they were not to restore the cattle and the corn, nor to release the persons taken as hostages, till the peasants should have voluntarily delivered up their arms."

This was a case of restoring order in a great tract of civilized country where the insurrection was prompted largely by religious feeling. It was a case of civil war, and the brilliant French soldier-administrator substituted this system for the devastation which had been tried by his predecessors and which had failed.

Similarly in Burma great care was taken not to exasperate Upper the people of the newly acquired province, and to punish Burma. only the dacoits and marauders who invested the country and were reducing it to anarchy. The country was divided into groups of posts, each group having troops enough to garrison all the posts, while a flying column was always ready to take the field. The operations were especially directed against the dacoits, villages which harboured them were destroyed, cattle were carried off and crops impounded ;

but great care had to be exercised not to punish villages which were merely victims of dacoity. Fines were sometimes inflicted to make the villagers give up their arms if it was thought they were in league with the marauders. But in these operations the population was friendly to the regular troops and the operations were not directed against the people as a whole.

Severity sometimes necessary.   In the Indian Mutiny, a campaign for the suppression of a rebellion where the most drastic measures were justified by the events at its outset, guerilla warfare was not a feature, except in the Central Provinces and in some few localities after the rebel armies had been overthrown. The nature of the campaign was indeed such that the insurgents were so roughly handled in action that the country was practically pacified on the battle-field. But in South Africa in 1851-52, in 1877, and again in 1896, rigorous treatment was meted out to the enemy in crushing out disaffection, and with good results ; the Kaffir villages and Matabili kraals were burnt, their crops destroyed, their cattle carried off. The French in Algeria, regardless of the maxim, " Les représailles sont toujours inutiles," dealt very severely with the smouldering disaffection of the conquered territory for years after Abd el Kader's power was gone, and their procedure succeeded. Uncivilized races attribute leniency to timidity. A system adapted to La Vendée is out of place among fanatics and savages, who must be thoroughly brought to book and cowed or they will rise again.

Conclusion.   The subject of how best to deal with an enemy who deliberately adopts guerilla tactics, and who persists in resistance in spite of such damage as regular troops can inflict in destroying villages, carrying off live stock and trampling down crops and so on, presents a very awkward problem. Elusive guerilla bands are difficult to surprise and it is only by surprise that loss can, as a rule, be inflicted on them. Hill warfare and bush warfare, to be dealt with in later chapters, are essentially contests against guerillas operating in exceptionally awkward country who can always escape if they wish to. Wholesale destruction of the property of the enemy may sometimes do more harm than good, and it is, in any case, by no means easy to carry out. In the preceding paragraphs the subject has only been dealt with in very general terms as the conditions vary in different cases ; a plan which may be highly effective in the one may fail altogether in the other, but the principle of dividing up the theatre of war into sections, each treated to a certain extent by itself, will generally be found to be applicable, and a happy combination of mobile columns and of defensive posts in the various sections should then bring about success within a reasonable time.

CHAPTER XII.

TACTICS OF ATTACK.

Offensive tactics generally imperative.

IN the majority of small wars the regular troops generally have to adopt the offensive on the battle-field as a matter of course. The enemy declines to attack, trusting to advantages of position and to such cover as nature provides or as can be improvised. The Sikhs, the most formidable fighting race which the British Army has had to deal with in the east, adopted defensive tactics from choice, when engaged on what was essentially an offensive campaign. Brave and fanatical warriors who fight in masses and adopt shock tactics sometimes, it is true, compel the regular army to act on the defensive, to march and to fight in square and to forego the moral advantage of being the attacking side, but such conditions are the exception and not the rule.

The great importance of impressing the enemy with the feeling of inferiority, the advantage of a dominating attitude in the theatre of war, the value of moral effect, have been dealt with in earlier chapters. A daring and resolute plan of campaign affords the best guarantee of ultimate success, and the same great principle holds good on the battle-field, as the history of the small wars most unmistakably proves. When decisive victories have been won by insignificant bodies of regular troops over great masses of barbaric foemen as at Plassey, Isly and Meani, it has almost always been due to the assumption of a bold offensive, and this gives to the study of the tactics of attack against such antagonists, a special interest.

How theory of attack differs in small wars from regular warfare.

As a broad principle of the conduct of these campaigns, the importance of successes in action being decisive has been already pointed out. Since fights are difficult to bring about, and inasmuch as it is on the battle-field that the issue must be decided, it is obvious that when an action has been brought on, mere victory is not enough. The enemy must not only be beaten. He must be beaten thoroughly. Let there be no mistake about this—the theory of attack when regular troops are pitted against irregulars, differs fundamentally from the theory of attack designed to meet the case of great operations between armies of the first class.

On the European battle-field the end to be attained in attack is, in the ordinary course, to drive the enemy out of his position. The general, intent upon the progress of the action in his coign of vantage, his finger on the conflict's pulse, is no less rejoiced than is the panting soldier in the firing line, when the hostile musketry slackens and dies away—a sure sign that the defenders are going to quit their ground. " By all that is holy he is limbering up! Stole away! "—King-lake's immortal story of the hillside beyond the Alma exactly presents the spirit animating all ranks in an assault upon a disciplined army in position. Up to the last moment there is painful uncertainty whether the venture will succeed or not. To the columns sheltering in front of the Cemetery Hill at Gettysburg, or below the Grivitza position during the second attack on Plevna, the mere disappearance of the foe to their immediate front would have meant triumph of the most far-reaching kind.

But in combat with irregular warriors something more than this is wanted. The issue of the assault will seldom be in doubt, nor will it often entail losses of any military importance. The position which the foe has taken up rarely has any intrinsic importance of its own, and therefore its evacuation by the defenders will seldom appreciably benefit the troops beyond clearing the way for further advance. The mere expulsion of the opponent from ground where he has thought fit to accept battle is of small account; what is wanted is a big casualty list in the hostile ranks—they have been brought up to the scratch of accepting battle, they must feel what battle against a disciplined army means. It is this fact which justifies the plan of operating against the line of the enemy's retreat, and which often makes some form of enveloping attack advisable.

Artillery preparation. But before dealing with this very important subject of the direction which attacks should take, and detailing the reasons for adopting the various courses likely to suggest themselves, the question of artillery preparation, which plays so important a part in modern tactics, deserves attention. It is a question which affects the development of a fight, from whatever side the attack may be directed.

The experience of recent great campaigns proves that artillery preparation is generally of great value of attack in regular warfare. The first duty of the guns of the attack is to silence those of the enemy, the next is to overwhelm the defenders with their fire at the point or points selected for assault. In small wars, however, it is only the second phase of this artillery preparation which need generally be taken into consideration, because even if the enemy has guns he seldom can use them with effect. The main object of the artillery preparation in warfare of this nature is as a rule simply to make as it were a breach in the enemy's line of battle for the infantry to break in, and this is of course under certain conditions an almost indispensable prologue to the assault.

When and when not expedient. But this procedure is not always necessary and it often is not advisable to adopt it. Artillery admittedly exercises great moral effect in every kind of warfare, and this is especially the case when in conflict with uncivilized forces, owing to their tendency to exaggerate the potentialities of the arm. Asiatics have always set great store on the possession of guns. Irregular warriors who can put a few field pieces into their line of battle are apt to attach a most exaggerated importance to them—it is a characteristic of such opponents, and one which regular troops can at times turn to good account, as will be shown further on. When the antagonist happens to possess guns he particularly dreads artillery fire, and even if the enemy has no guns and does not know artillery, he is greatly terrified when the shells begin to seek him out. The consequence is that, in either case, a preliminary bombardment tends to drive the enemy out of his position and to scare him away before the attack develops, which is just the thing that is least wanted. The French attacks on Bacninh and Hung Hua in Tonkin in 1884 ended in the Chinese being driven out by artillery fire with very little loss, when it was most desirable to have inflicted a heavy defeat upon them. Similarly in Madagascar in 1896 the French found that the use of guns made it almost impossible to effectively cut the retreat of the Hovas, who generally fled immediately any shells burst near them. Sometimes in pursuance of some special object it may be expedient to drive the enemy off in this fashion—the tribesmen evacuated the formidable Sempagha position under the fire of artillery in the advance into Tirah. But as a general rule, certainly at the outset of a campaign, the withdrawal of irregular adversaries from a position where they have shown themselves prepared to accept battle, is a distinct misfortune, and on this account it is a mistake to be too free with shell fire in the early stages of a fight.

Moreover, artillery preparation sometimes shows the enemy what is to be the point of attack, which may be by no means desirable. It is of course incompatible with anything in the nature of a surprise. The sortie from Kandahar against the village of Deh Khoja in 1880, is an example of this ; a half hour's bombardment from the ramparts served to alarm the Afghans and to warn them of the project, so that they flocked to the point of danger from all sides. This objection to artillery preparation is, however, by no means so generally applicable as is the objection that premature gunnery tends to frighten the adversary away without a fight. " The effect of artillery," says Lord Wolseley, " is absurdly small upon an enemy who does not fight in large or even in formed bodies,"

Objections to it.

referring of course to actual not to moral effect. The chances
of dealing decisively with a timid opponent may be destroyed
by the discharge of a few introductory projectiles which inflict
little or no loss.

But it must not be supposed that artillery preparation may
not at times be most essential. If the enemy be strongly
posted and be resolved on offering a determined resistance, a
preliminary bombardment may be indispensable. A very
remarkable example of the value of an artillery bombardment
is afforded by what occurred at Omdurman, where the
fire of the gunboats and howitzer battery the day before
the decisive battle had the effect of driving the Khalifa's
army out of the town ; it seems in fact to have been largely
due to this bombardment that the enemy elected to fight in
the open with results so happy for the Anglo-Egyptian army.
In the Indian Mutiny the guns did splendid service in most
of the actions in paving the way for the infantry, a very
favourite manœuvre being to send out some artillery on both
flanks so as to enfilade the hostile position to a certain extent ;
but in that campaign the rebels were well armed and often
fought with desperation. The three minutes of concentrated
artillery fire previous to the successful assault on the bluff
at Dargai appears to have greatly assisted the infantry,
although from the nature of the ground it probably caused
little actual loss to the tribesmen. If the enemy be posted in a
defence work, a preliminary bombardment is most desirable
supposing that the resistance is likely to prove formidable—
Mahmud's zeriba on the Atbara is a case in point. Instances
might be multiplied to show the need of guns to prepare the
way for the infantry in such cases. The nature of the hostile
position, the fighting qualities of the adversaries, the question
whether the actual capture of the ground occupied by the
opposing force as affecting the situation at the moment is
of more importance than giving the enemy a lesson—these are
the points which must be taken into account when deciding

whether the guns are to be used freely from the outset or not.

When it happens to be a matter of urgency to achieve rapid success the use of artillery freely before the infantry can get to work may be most desirable, even if it has the effect of driving the enemy off without his suffering seriously. An example of such a case is furnished by the relief of Fort Gulistan on the Samana ridge in 1897 by General Yeatman-Biggs. The tribesmen had captured another post, that of Saragheri which lay between Fort Gulistan and the relieving army, and, as the force advanced, the hill of Saragheri was found to be covered with hostile crowds. Great anxiety existed with regard to the fate of Gulistan and the tribesmen were driven off by artillery fire. The infantry got no chance and the hostile losses were only slight, but the column was in consequence little delayed and it was soon afterwards seen that the imperilled garrison was still holding out.

It also sometimes saves time.

It is moreover necessary to point out that there have been cases where the failure to carry out a preliminary bombardment has led to most unfortunate results. The story of Chillianwalla is well known. At the battle of Wad Ras near Tetuan in 1859 the Spaniards attacked the village of Amsal without artillery preparation, and they were several times repulsed; they only carried it eventually after losing very heavily. Want of artillery preparation seems to have been a main reason for the very severe losses of the Dutch in their attacks on the Achinese stockades in 1873–74; that guns were very effective against these works is shown by the fact that the Kraton at Kota Raja, the main hostile stronghold, was evacuated under a concentrated bombardment. It stands to reason that it is far preferable to frighten an enemy out of his position by artillery fire alone, than to suffer a reverse owing to attacking without any preliminary bombardment by guns. Artillery preparation is essential at times; it is only when it is not essential that the question arises

Instances of want of artillery preparation.

whether the nature of the case renders it expedient or otherwise.

And while on the subject of artillery, an important principle of offensive tactics with reference to the enemy's guns may here be mentioned. This is that, when such opponents as the regular troops have to cope with in these wars bring guns into the field, it is most desirable to capture those guns. The great importance which irregular warriors attach to this arm has been referred to already. Asiatics are inclined to calculate the strength of an army by the number of its guns. It is true that the ordnance which such adversaries bring into the field is seldom formidable. The material is usually obsolete. The ammunition is ineffective. The fuzes are almost always useless. But it is not on account of the assistance which his artillery affords the enemy on the battle-field that it is a valuable prize to strive for. It is on account of the moral effect which the loss of the guns produces in the hostile ranks, that their capture offers so attractive an objective for the regular troops. Retreat can be explained away, and gaps in the ranks waved aside with a pious ejaculation. But the loss of guns is not so easily accounted for. A barbaric host which marches out to war with a great train of cannon—symbols of military power as they are held to be throughout the land—but which returns without them, brings back with it incontrovertible evidence of its own defeat. Artillery is a favourite plaything of the semi-civilized potentate, chieftains put their trust in it, the rank and file regard it as a mighty engine to destroy their foes, and so it comes about that when they see their guns are lost they think that their only hope of victory is gone, and a *sauve qui peut* is very likely to be the upshot.

Moreover, such artillery as these armies bring into the field is not difficult to capture. The battery seldom forms a mobile unit. The guns are dragged up into position somehow, but there is no means of carrying them off at a

moment's notice when the assailants press the attack home
to the spot where they have been placed.

In those actions of the last Afghan war in which the enemy had guns
and where the British proved successful—Charasia, the Peiwar Kotal and
Kandahar for instance—they were generally all or nearly all captured. In
the Indian Mutiny the rebel guns were generally well served and were
fought with great tenacity; but the enemy seldom succeeded in carrying
them off, and large numbers of them swelled the booty after the later British
successes in the f¹⁴d; in that campaign the hostile artillery was really
formidable at first, and the rebels with justice had confidence in it, some
of their field batteries moving in excellent style. The great losses in guns
which the mutineers sustained were no doubt partially due to the resolution
with which they were kept in action to the last, but the result of these
losses was that the enemy lost all confidence and in the end fought
with no hope of victory. During the China war of 1860 the large number
of guns captured by the allies at the two actions fought on the march from
Tientsin to Pekin—Shankiawan and Palikao—had a most depressing effect
upon the Chinese levies.

A good example of the moral effect of capture of artillery is afforded by
the following incident. In 1854 the Khokandians assembled in great force
before Fort Perovski, the Russian advanced post on the Sir Daria, and
practically blockaded it. The commandant resolved on a bold stroke. He
sent out such troops as he could spare to attack the enemy unexpectedly.
The small force, however, soon found itself in a critical situation, being
threatened from all sides; but in their endeavour to wipe the Russian
column out, the formidable hostile forces made the mistake of leaving their
artillery almost without protection of other troops. Perceiving this the
officer in command of the Russians delivered a vigorous attack upon the
guns, and captured them. The effect was immediate. The Khokandians
took fright, fled in wild disorder leaving many trophies in the hands
of the insignificant Russian force, and Fort Perovski saw no more of them
for a time.

The assailants should be prepared to turn captured guns
upon the enemy if possible ; in the French attack upon the
Hova position covering Antananarivo, their turning force
captured two guns on the extreme right of the defenders and
used them with good effect, the accompanying batteries
having been much delayed by the terrain.

It is indeed interesting to note that artillery is often not
only a source of embarrassment to irregular warriors but Trust of
irregular
warriors in
their guns.

becomes a real danger. Schamyl's cause declined when he increased the number of his guns; he would not abandon them when attacked in force, and was driven by their possession to abandon his guerilla tactics. In the instruction book of the Bokharan forces occurred the passage, "Special care must be taken of the guns, and it must be remembered that the strength of one gun is equal to that of 1,000 soldiers"; the Russians did not, however, find the Bokharan artillery to be very damaging. General Skobelef in his campaign against the Turkomans used to say, "If I had the right I would present the Tekkes with a few old guns." Still it would rarely be the case that an enemy should be deliberately permitted to carry off his artillery; for even when this compels him to adopt unsuitable tactics it is the result of an exaggerated belief in the virtue of the guns, and if the guns are captured the moral effect is proportionate.

Importance of capturing trophies.

Just as the enemy's artillery is always a most desirable objective on the battle-field in campaigns of this nature because of the prestige gained by taking it, so the capture of trophies should also constantly be kept in view. British troops no longer take their colours into action, although prizing them none the less on this account as emblems of regimental distinction; but Asiatics and irregular warriors in many other parts of the globe generally bring banners into the field. Fanatics prize their standards highly and look on them as sacred, their loss is regarded as a disaster and as prophetic of ultimate overthrow. There is of course no material benefit to be gained by capturing them, but the moral effect of securing them is great. As, in planning the campaign, the seizure of some ancient city or historic stronghold should be rated far above its military importance, so on the battle-field the wresting of trophies of this nature from the enemy is to be accounted as a very proper object to be attained. It must never be forgotten that in small wars moral effect ranks almost before material gain.

Desirable as it is to ensure that success in action shall Difficulty of
mean not merely the defeat of the hostile forces but their ensuring
destruction, the conditions of the case will often render such decisive
decisive results quite impossible. Rugged, rocky hillsides may
be the scene of struggle. The fight may take place in
thickets and in tangled jungle growth, where control of the
troops engaged is almost impossible. The terrain in
which a fight takes place indeed rarely lends itself to decisive
tactical combinations. But, quite apart from the topographical conditions which so often prevail in operations of this
class, there are two notable characteristics of irregular warriors
which tend to hinder the achievement of decisive victory.

In the first place such opponents are apt to lose heart Reasons for
prematurely at the spectacle of assaulting columns advancing this.
steadily upon them. The moral effect of deliberate attack
of this nature affects the nerves of the best of troops, to
irregular warriors it is appalling and uncanny—and they give
way before it.

In the second place, when such adversaries do give way,
they retreat with amazing rapidity. They evaporate and disappear. They disperse in all directions and conceal their arms,
and on this account effective pursuit becomes most difficult ;
cavalry alone can attempt it, and the ground is often unsuitable
for mounted men to traverse. The French in Tonkin seldom
got to close quarters with the Chinese, even when these had
carefully prepared their ground and when their attitude in the
preliminary stages of the fight appeared to foreshadow a
desperate resistance ; so precipitate was their retreat when
the assailants began to drive their attack home, that they got
away with little loss. Both at Charasia and Ahmed Khel
the Afghans fled so quickly from the field when the fate of the
day was decided against them, that from that moment
they suffered few casualties.

A very good example of the rapidity with which regular warriors effect
their escape is afforded by the very successful action at Landaki in 1897, by
which Sir B. Blood forced an entrance into Swat.

The tribesmen were defending the " Gate of Swat," a typical military defile, where a great rugged spur from the hills south of the valley of the Swat river stood out like a buttress, allowing only a narrow passage between its declivities and the river. The enemy fully expected that an attempt would be made to force the defile and had gathered in strength at that point, while sangars crowded with hill-men crowned the spur. Sir B. Blood determined to occupy the enemy with artillery fire and with part of his force, to hold the cavalry ready for a swoop through the defile, to send a strong force up the hills under General Meiklejohn to turn the hostile outer flank, and by cutting off the enemy's line of retreat into the hills, to hustle him over the spur down into the plain beyond, where the cavalry could finish off the job in style.

The troops under General Meiklejohn had proceeded a considerable distance up the hills, and were within effective musketry range of the crest of the spur before the enemy seemed quite to realize the nature of the movement. Then, however, the tribesmen broke and fled precipitately, and by the time the spur was captured they were already disappearing over the plain beyond making for the foot hills. The victory was singularly complete, some 200 of the enemy were killed, and an entrance into Swat was forced at a trifling sacrifice ; but thanks to their great fleetness of foot the hillmen managed to escape out of the trap which was being laid for them, without their suffering as heavily as had been hoped from the horsemen whom they with good reason greatly dreaded.

Objection to purely frontal attacks, advantage of flank attacks.

The fact is that purely frontal attacks are a mistake because, in the first place, the enemy gives way before them and because, in the second place, from their direction the hostile line of retreat is left unthreatened. Frontal attacks combined with flank attacks are infinitely preferable if circumstances permit of the manœuvre. Or the attack may be solely directed against the flank and even against the rear of the opponent. In regular warfare flank attacks are held to be expedient owing to the heavy loss sustained in frontal attacks when there are modern arms of precision in the defenders' hands ; but in small wars, although frontal attacks may sometimes be dangerous for the same reason, the great objection to them is that they do not ensure decisive victory. A case like Dargai is really exceptional, although it is at the same time most instructive. At Dargai the extraordinary strength of the enemy's position as against a frontal attack led, on the one hand, to very heavy loss in the assaulting columns and, on the other, to the tribesmen sticking to their ground far longer than they would have done had their flank been threatened ; it was the absence of any turning movement on the part of the regular troops which caused the victory to be so decisive, but at such a heavy sacrifice.

It is somewhat singular that, taking into account the tendency of irregular warriors to threaten the flanks and rear of the regular forces, such adversaries seldom seem to be prepared for attacks upon their own flank or rear. When they prepare their positions for defence they do not take the contingency into account. Of course it is not always so— the tribesmen had made especial arrangements for securing their flanks with sangars at the Sempagha Pass when Sir W. Lockhart attacked it in 1897. But an examination of the general course of actions in many campaigns in very different theatres of war and under most varying conditions, shows that it very frequently is the case. The oft-quoted Chinese complaint of the ignorance of the barbarians who did not know that guns could only shoot out of their muzzles and not backwards, and who in consequence attacked the Celestials, not in front as they expected but in rear, may have been mythical ; but it has a spice of truth in it. It does not seem to occur to irregular warriors that they may not necessarily be attacked at the point where they have made their most elaborate preparations. It is somewhat singular that it should be so, because such antagonists are always in great terror of having their retreat cut, and if they find the regular troops getting round their flanks they generally abandon their positions in hot haste ; still experience shows that it is the case. The following three examples illustrate the unpreparedness of the enemy for attacks in rear and flank; but many others might be quoted.

Enemy seldom prepared for flank attacks or attack in rear.

In 1853 a Russian force advancing into Daghestan found the Tavliens in force in a fortified position behind the River Metchik. The bulk of the troops were directed to assault the lines in front, but a part of the force

Examples.

was sent to make a detour through the forests and debouch in rear of the enemy. Schamyl's followers were preparing to offer a strenuous resistance to the attack which they saw the troops in front of them preparing, when suddenly they became aware of the movement against their rear. They were completely unprepared for this, although the nature of the country should have suggested its possibility. They incontinently fled, abandoning their works, while the column threatening their rear was still some distance off and before it had fired a shot.

The forcing of the Khan Band defile by General N. Chamberlain in 1857 also illustrates this. This was a narrow gorge south-west of Dera Ghazi Khan. It had been the scene of a combat in which the Sikhs some years before had suffered very severely at the hands of the Bozdar tribe. The route passed through this narrow gorge, the hills on the left being practically inaccessible while those to the right were difficult. Plan III. facing p. 166, shows the enemy's position and the line followed by the attack. The Bozdars had some sangars in the gorge itself, and others on the hills to the right so as to take in flank the troops as they forced the passage —these latter breastworks were close to the defile and formed the left of the enemy's position. General Chamberlain, quitting the trough of the valley with the bulk of his force some distance from where it narrowed into a gorge, advanced against the extreme left of the hostile line of defence by making a detour over the hills. The sangars on the flank were not arranged to meet such an attack, and were easily captured. The hill-men had in fact assumed as a matter of course that the troops would follow the valley and endeavour to force the defile itself, although it was obvious that there was really nothing whatever to hinder a turning movement such as General Chamberlain carried out with complete success.

The battle of Suruj Kund near Multan in 1847, also serves as a good example of this. The Sikhs having taken up a strong position and entrenched it, General Markham was sent with the British and Indian troops, to fall upon the left flank of the enemy, while some Sikh and other troops, auxiliaries to the British, remained in front and eventually assisted to complete the victory. " The battle of Suruj Kund," wrote Major Herbert Edwardes who was with the auxiliaries, " may be described as the most gentlemanly ever fought. A mere manœuvre of fine soldiership turned a large army out of a strong entrenchment, and routed them with the loss of five guns before they understood the attack. It was the triumph of discipline over an irregular army. A regular army in the same entrenchments would have changed its front, but the rebels not being attacked as they intended to be attacked were unable to fight at all. General Markham placed his force upon the hostile flank and simply rolled up the line. The hostile Sikhs could make nothing of it."

Flank attacks give better chance of a decisive victory.

As a consequence of the omission on the part of the enemy to protect his flanks, an attack on one, or even on both, of them can generally be carried out without meeting with

serious resistance. When such a direction is given to the
assailants, or to a portion of them, it is clear that its tendency is to bring the regular troops, or some of them, upon
the hostile line of retreat. The direction of the attack has in
fact the effect of compensating to a certain extent for that
precipitancy of retreat which irregular warriors, thanks to their
fleetness of foot, can indulge in, and which so greatly militates against a decisive success. The enemy cannot get
away so easily, and if the adversary has guns a flank attack
is far more likely to secure their capture than a frontal one.
In a word flank attacks tend to bring about decisive victories,
to ensure the very objects which in warfare of this nature
are the most difficult to obtain, and it stands to reason
that, the more the flank attack is directed against the rear of
the enemy, the worse is his chance of escape in most cases.
Of course peculiarities of terrain may modify this, but as a
general rule it will be so. It must however be borne in mind
that irregular warriors are always very nervous about their
line of retreat—as shown at Landaki, mentioned on p. 160 ;
they are very apt to beat so precipitate a retreat when they
feel their flanks threatened, that they get off in spite of the
best arrangements.

When the question arises of attacking a hostile position **Containing
force, in case**
in flank or rear, it is always a matter for consideration whether **of attacks on**
a containing force should be left in front, and whether this **the flank or
rear of the**
force should, if existing, join in the attack. If there is any **enemy.**
fear of the enemy abandoning his position before the flank
or rear attack develops, it is generally well to occupy him
in front. At Assaye Sir A. Wellesley brought the whole of
his small army upon the Mahratta flank. At Kandahar,
on the other hand, the enemy was to a certain extent contained by troops on his front and by artillery fire, although
the main attack fell on Ayoub Khan's right flank. At El Teb
the British square manœuvred so as to come upon the flank
of Osman Digna's entrenchments, no containing force remaining

in front. At Kirbekan, where the attack was directed against the enemy's rear, a very small containing force was left in front; the guns of this detachment took part in the action but the rest of it was not engaged.

Action of Kirbekan, a rear attack.

This battle of Kirbekan is so remarkable an example of an attack upon the rear of a strong position occupied by irregular warriors, that it deserves to be narrated in some little detail. The Mahdists held a position with their right flank resting on the Nile, which is shown in Plan IV, facing p. 166. Close to the Nile, and at right angles to it, was a chain of rocky knolls on which the enemy was posted, sheltered behind stone breastworks. About 600 yards off, in echelon to the left rear, was a remarkable ridge of trap rock with almost precipitous sides; this also extended on a line at right angles to the Nile, and it was occupied by the Arabs. In rear of the hostile position, at some little distance off, was the mouth of the rocky Shukuk defile; and it was most important to cut the enemy off from retreating into this. General Earle decided to march right round the enemy's left and to attack the hillocks in rear and the ridge at its right extremity. Two guns with an infantry escort were left in front of the hillocks to occupy the enemy, and the camel corps was deputed to demonstrate against the front of the ridge, while the rest of the force was detailed for the turning movement.

The operation was signally successful. The Dervishes grimly stuck to the position, although they must have seen the march of the column which was to attack them from the rear from the ridge. On reaching the right rear of the hostile position, the knolls and the ridge were attacked simultaneously. The Arabs stood their ground well and suffered heavily, although a proportion escaped before the attack commenced. But the victory was complete, and the hostile power in that part of the theatre of war was absolutely broken and destroyed in this one single action.

Co-operation of containing force.

In this fight the small force left in front of the hostile position was merely a containing force. It made no direct attack. As a rule, however, the force in front co-operates more directly in the combat in such operations, and the attack takes the form of a combined assault in front and in flank or else in rear. If it can be arranged that the frontal attack shall occupy the attention of the enemy and keep him on his ground, and that the flank attack shall develop just as the flight begins so that the fugitives can be shot down by the troops working on to their line of retreat, an ideal tactical situation has been created. The action at Ferkeh on the

Nile in 1896 is a case where the main attack was on the hostile front and where a smaller force appeared on the enemy's line of retreat at the psychological moment; the Dervish force on this occasion was little, if at all, superior in numbers to the regular troops, and it was practically destroyed. General Négrier's method of assaulting the Chinese works in Tonkin, which were generally isolated on hills and knolls, was most effective; while the bulk of the infantry, supported by artillery, moved direct against the objective, clouds of skirmishers pushed rapidly ahead, worked round the flanks and brought a cross fire to bear on the enemy in retreat; the Chinese seldom let the French get to close quarters and, but for this enveloping form given to the attacks, they invariably would have practically all escaped. In the desultory fighting in Burma, where the dacoits and other hostile bodies generally held villages or some form of stockade, the cavalry used to work round both flanks before the infantry attacked, so as to be ready to deal with the fugitives. These minor operations in Tonkin and Burma serve to illustrate the principle of combined front and flank attacks very well.

If the hostile position is very strong, and if a frontal attack is therefore likely to lead to hard fighting, the main assault is generally best made upon the flank; a minor direct attack upon the front will be very effective when the flank assault has begun to make itself felt. The conditions in this case, of course, differ entirely from those described above as prevailing in Tonkin and Burma, where the enemy was disinclined to offer a determined resistance. As an example of cases where, owing to the strength of the adversary's position, the main attack has been on the flank while the assault on the front has been only a subsidiary and secondary operation, may be cited the attack on the Peiwar Kotal.

Main attack on the flank.

The capture of the Peiwar Kotal by Sir F. Roberts, in 1878, is illustrated by Plan V, facing p. 166, which shows the general course of the action. The Afghans held the pass over a lofty ridge with difficult approaches.

Peiwar Kotal

A frontal attack upon their position would clearly have entailed severe losses, and so Sir F. Roberts determined to attack the enemy's left with the bulk of his force, the plan being a surprise after a night march. Part of his army was to attack from in front when the main movement against the hostile flank had succeeded. Reaching the extreme left of the Afghan defences at early dawn, the turning force was completely successful, rolling up the left wing of the enemy in great confusion towards the centre. It was however, found, that advance along the ridge became after a time almost impracticable, and a further turning movement was then undertaken, directed on to the line of retreat of the defenders. The enemy thereupon began to give way all along the line, and this enabled the frontal attack to be driven home. The victory was complete, the enemy's guns were all captured, and the Afghan troops fled in the utmost confusion having suffered considerable losses.

Enemy inclined to draw all his forces to meet the flank attack and so opens the way for a frontal attack. Antagonists of this character, if attacked in flank, are much inclined to draw all the forces over to that side to meet the onset, thus enabling a movement against their front to make great way. As actions in such warfare are seldom on a large scale this is generally quite feasible ; the distances are small and the massing of the bulk of the defending force on one side or the other can be rapidly effected. The consequence is that a frontal attack, after the hostile forces have been drawn off to strengthen the threatened flank, may succeed in gaining some great and even decisive advantage, even when made by a relatively small body of troops, if the troops are handled skilfully.

At Charasia, in 1879, the Afghans had taken up a strong position in the hill, on either side of a defile through which the road led to Kabul, and were especially in strength to the left of it. Sir F. Roberts disposed his forces for the attack so as to launch the greater part under General Baker against the Afghan right, while a small body under Major White was to occupy the enemy in front of the defile. Plan VI, opposite, shows the Afghan position. As General Baker fought his way forward, driving the Afghans off, numbers of the enemy hurried over from near the defile to reinforce their comrades on the threatened right. Major White, finding the enemy in front of him to be no longer very formidable, attacked with great vigour, and he was so successful with his small force that he completely overthrew the hostile left and secured the defile. Hereabouts was posted the enemy's artillery which was all captured by the small force, the rôle of which had in the first instance merely been to contain the enemy on that side.

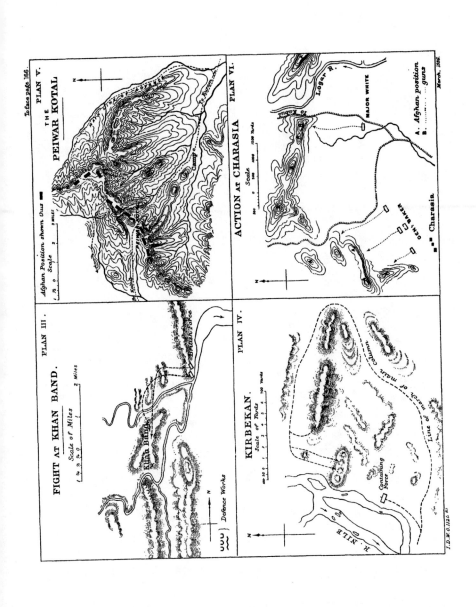

PLAN III.

FIGHT AT KHAN BAND.

Scale of Miles

⅛ ¼ ½ 0   2 Miles

N

UUU| Defence Works

British Force

Kula Bank

PLAN IV.

KIRBEKAN.

Scale of Yards

400 200 0   1   2   3   4   5   6   700 Yards

N

Line of march of main column.

Containing Force

R. NILE

PLAN V.

THE

PEIWAR KOTAL

Afghan Position shown thus ▬

Scale

½ ¼ 0   2   3 MILES

N

Kuram R.

PLAN VI.

ACTION AT CHARASIA

Scale

500 0   500   1000   1500 Yards

N

Logar R.

To Kabul

MAJOR WHITE

CAVALRY

A. Afghan position.
B. .... guns

▬▬ Charasia.

March, 1895.

I.D.W.O.1121.B.

For the execution of combined attacks of this kind careful calculation of time and a correct appreciation of the
general probabilities of the action about to take place, are
necessary. At Kirbekan, the hour at which the guns of the
containing force in front of the enemy's position were to
commence firing, was carefully laid down. If combination be
essential to success, it is imperative that the two detached
forces shall actually co-operate at the proper moment. It
may be impossible to communicate between them, and the
terrain may be such that neither force knows exactly what
the other is doing; at Charasia the two forces, although
some distance apart, could watch each other's movements to
a certain extent. As a rule it is best to allow the detached
commanders some latitude of action, because something unforeseen may at any moment arise; but if mutual co-operation
be the essence of the operation it is imperative that there be
a thorough understanding between the separate portions of
the force engaged. Further on, in discussing the general
question of divided forces co-operating to achieve some common object on the battle-field, some instances will be adduced
to show how difficult it often is for a commander to handle
detached bodies actually in action, and to illustrate the
strange mistakes which occur. Everything depends on both
the force which is in front, and that which is turning the flank
or which is manœuvring against the rear of the opposing
army, having been given a correct impulse to start with.

It has frequently occurred that one or the other has,
either owing to some misapprehension or else to unforeseen difficulties, entirely failed to perform its share of the
task. Thus General Duchesne during his final advance on
Antananarivo in 1895, finding the Hovas in a very strong
fortified position on the Amboluminas range, arranged to
attack them both in front and on their left rear; the column
destined to turn the flank marched off some time before daybreak, while the advance of the columns against the front was

made ostentatiously in the morning; but the enemy fled precipitately as soon as the frontal attack developed itself and before the turning force could join in; the advanced troops and cavalry of this latter managed, however, to cut in on the hostile line of retreat, and to do good execution.

Calculations as to the length of time which will be required for a force to march to a certain point over ground which is often not very well known, are apt to prove inaccurate even if some unexpected action on the part of the enemy has not upset them. Moreover any divided action of two distinct forces moving some distance apart, is always liable to miscarry owing to some misunderstanding. The attack on Ali Musjid in 1878, serves as a good example of a turning force failing to perform its share in an attack owing to its meeting with unexpected difficulties of terrain. The serious reverse suffered by the French at Bang Bo, in 1885, may be cited as an illustration of a mistake with regard to a turning force having a most unfortunate sequel.

Ali Musjid. (1) Ali Musjid in the Khaibar pass was a well placed and somewhat formidable fort, and the Afghans had made elaborate preparations to hold the position. The plan of operations was to send one force over the hill to the right of the pass, aiming at a point some distance in rear of the position so as to intercept the enemy's retreat: to send another force, moving on a line inside of the first, to assail the position in reverse and on its left flank, and to move the remainder of the troops up the pass and attack in front. The first force, under General Tytler, started at 6 P.M.; the second, under General Macpherson, at 2.30 A.M.; and the main body at 7 A.M., this last being under Sir S. Browne, who was in command of the whole. Sir S. Browne arrived before the position, bombarded it, and commenced his infantry attack in the afternoon. But it soon became apparent that the turning forces had not reached their destinations and that the project of striking simultaneously from two sides had failed, so the action was discontinued. General Macpherson's force had been delayed by the almost insuperable difficulties of the road, and was therefore unable to co-operate. General Tytler's force, however, succeeded in striking the defile higher up, and late in the afternoon it managed to cut off a considerable part of the hostile which was retiring. During the night the fort was evacuated, and it was occupied next morning without further fighting.

French disaster at Bang Bo. (2) Bang Bo lies a few miles within the Chinese frontier. General Négrier had pushed the Chinese before him and captured Langson, and had

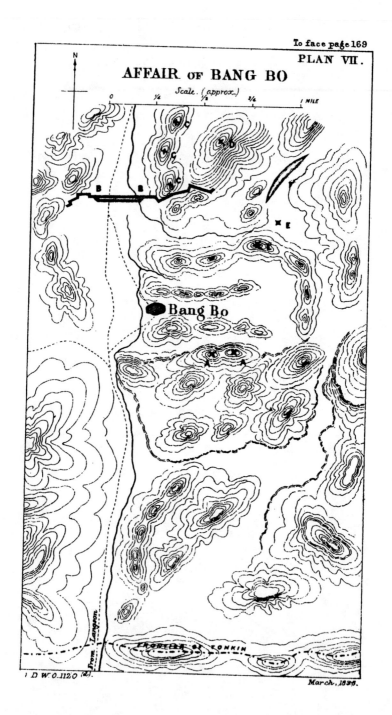

AFFAIR OF BANG BO

Scale. (approx.)

Bang Bo

followed them up into their own territory, driving them out of Tonkin by a series of brilliant tactical operations.

The route beyond followed the trough of a deep depression in the hills. A few miles beyond the frontier the French found the enemy in position on some heights (A in the sketch opposite), stretching across the valley and narrowing it into a gorge, and they carried these by a spirited attack in the afternoon. From the high ground another line of defences was observed about two miles ahead ; this consisted of a strong entrenchment (B) right across the sole of the valley, of some works on knolls (C, C), and of a small work on a commanding hill (D). The troops bivouacked for the night, part of the force having pushed on and occupied two abandoned works (E, E).

General Négrier determined on a combined turning movement and frontal attack next morning, and he directed his right wing to advance at an early hour and to capture the hill (D) from the right, thus taking in reverse the Chinese line of defence, which was evidently well prepared and strongly held. When this point had been captured the frontal attack was to be delivered.

The morning unfortunately broke with a thick fog. The right wing could only advance very slowly, feeling its way to the front for about three hours. Then the fog began to lift and the troops destined for the attack on the hill (D) pressed forward ; but they were suddenly brought to a standstill by the deep ravine (F), which it was found impossible to cross. The Chinese, perceiving the movement against their left, sent men to occupy the hill (D) which had not been held by them at all till then, and when the fog completely lifted General Négrier saw these men moving up the hill. Hearing no firing he assumed that the Chinese were not holding the eminence, and that the troops he saw were French who had crept close up unobserved in the mist. Under this false impression of the tactical situation at the moment, he at once launched the remainder of his force against the entrenchments in the valley. These proved to be most formidable, and the attack on them failed. The right wing endeavouring to attack the hostile position on its immediate left gained some ground, it is true, but it was compelled to retire before a vigorous counter-attack. The Chinese then advanced over their main entrenchment in pursuit of the troops who had been repulsed in the frontal attack, and the consequence was that the two divided French wings were only withdrawn out of action with such difficulty and after such determined fighting, that General [Négrier felt himself compelled to withdraw to Langson, having lost one-eighth of his force.

Advantageous, in fact, as are flank attacks combined with assaults on the front of the enemy's position, owing to their increasing the probability of gaining a decisive success, there is always a chance of the combination failing unless all goes right. If the ground be favourable for cavalry action, mounted

Cavalry in flank attacks.

troops are very valuable in flank attacks, thanks to the rapidity with which they can act against the enemy in retreat. The action of Badli ke Serai between the rebels and the force moving from Meerut to Delhi after the outbreak of the Mutiny, is an excellent example of such action by mounted troops ; the cavalry and horse artillery were sent to operate against the enemy's flank and rear while the infantry attacked in front, and the result was a completed rout of the mutineers. This war indeed furnishes numerous other instances of the same kind. At Kali Nuddi after the relief of Sir J. Outram, at Lucknow by Sir C. Campbell, the cavalry was similarly sent round by a concealed detour to fall upon the rebels in retreat; the enemy was driven from his position by the infantry, but was retiring in good order till the cavalry swooped down ; the effect of the troopers' onslaught was tremendous, the mutineers' force being utterly dispersed and suffering very heavy losses. In the Chitral Expedition of 1895, the cavalry sent round to operate against the flank of the tribesmen on the Swat river, who were occupied by the infantry in front, scattered the enemy like chaff by its sudden appearance, although the ground was by no means favourable for the action of mounted men. The fire of cavalry dismounted may be particularly effective on an enemy's flank.

Artillery in flank attacks.

The effect of artillery accompanying a flank attack is also very great. At the Peiwar Kotal the guns with the turning force did fine execution. A main object of such operations is to act against the enemy in retreat, and as such adversaries are very quick in withdrawing, guns are often the only means of inflicting loss when the hostile force gives way. In the Mutiny the horse artillery performed signal service in this manner, working with the cavalry. When guns get upon the flank of an enemy's position they can moreover often enfilade it with great effect.

Imperative necessity of following up a preliminary success.

In all attacks upon irregular warriors, or upon armies of inferior morale, it is not only essential to drive the assault home with vigour, but to follow up any success gained with the utmost energy and decision. The impression created amongst such opponents by even a trifling preliminary success is very great, and once they are got on the move they must be kept upon the move. This is a broad principle of offensive tactics, whether the assault be delivered in front, in flank, or as a combination of both directions of attack. It is at the root of the whole system of conducting operations in warfare of this nature, in which moral effects counts for so much. Of course when the opposing force occupies several distinct lines of defence—a system to which such adversaries, notably the Chinese, are much addicted—infantry may after capturing the first line be able to reach the second in time to come to close quarters with its defenders; but this seldom happens. Once the first line is forced, resistance as a rule collapses to an extent which can never be hoped for when fighting against regular troops. Dash is not only essential to start with, but advance must continue without a pause till the enemy has been driven from his last position. This was the system followed in the Indian Mutiny and by General Négrier in Tonkin. The adversary does not understand it, and becomes hopelessly demoralized.

In small wars the principle is so clearly established *Need of* that the enemy once on the move must be kept on *initiative on the part of* the move, that the responsibility assumed by the sub- *subordinates* ordinate commander who presses on, is not so great as in *in attack.* a struggle against regular troops. There is little risk of the enemy rallying. The more quickly and resolutely he is followed up the smaller does the chance become of his showing further fight. In hill and jungle warfare, to be dealt with especially further on, initiative is especially desirable on the part of junior officers. The following striking incident at the battle of Kandahar deserves mention, as it illustrates so well the importance of individual initiative in not allowing the enemy to recover from the effects of a first reverse.

The Afghans held the long ridge, shown in Plan VIII, facing p. 176, and the villages of Ghundigan and Ghundi to its right front. Sir F. Roberts' plan was to attack the right flank of the enemy, and the action commenced by two brigades advancing parallel to each other and capturing the two villages about simultaneously. The enemy retreated round the right of the ridge to the village of Pir Paimal and to the reverse slope of the ridge. As the two brigades advanced, sweeping round the ridge, that on the right struck the village of Pir Paimal and captured it; but then the advanced troops found themselves suddenly in face of nearly the whole Afghan army close to, and on the ridge above, the village.

Hostile reinforcements were hurrying up, and the enemy was bringing a heavy artillery fire to bear on the British troops sweeping round the end of the ridge. If the Afghans were to make a counter-attack on the advanced detachments, a serious check might befall the hitherto victorious troops. The situation was critical. The enemy was showing unexpected tenacity and was in strong force. There was no time to lose. Major White, whose regiment, the 92nd, was furthest to the front, at once formed it for a final attack. Charging the enemy he drove his men in like a wedge between the masses on the low ground and those on the ridge, and captured two guns. This sudden onslaught completely changed the aspect of affairs, the enemy broke and fled in all directions, and all further resistance practically ceased.

Cavalry to be at hand to complete victory. The value of cavalry in completing a victory if the ground be at all suitable, can scarcely be exaggerated. In the present day this arm of the service is, at least in regular warfare, accustomed to work in large independent bodies on the battle-field, and experience has shown that under normal conditions this arrangement is the best; the tendency of modern tactical organization is to reduce the amount of divisional cavalry to a relatively insignificant body. But in small wars some bodies of mounted men should generally be kept at various points ready to assist the infantry, in preference to the cavalry being all practically kept as one-force. This is of course speaking of cases where the armies in action are some thousands strong; with very small bodies of troops the cavalry is necessarily on the spot. The reason why this dispersion of the mounted troops is desirable is that there shall be mounted men ready at all points to follow up success at once; the enemy gets away so quickly that if the troopers are not on the spot they may be late.

When there is ground in rear of the hostile position where Other arms to play into the hands of the cavalry. cavalry will be able to work effectively, infantry and artillery should endeavour to drive the enemy in that direction so as to give the mounted troops a chance of inflicting heavy losses. It is often the case that a force of irregular warriors will be found occupying rugged hills, on the far side of which are stretches of level ground; the enemy will endeavour to avoid these stretches of level ground when driven from his position, but with good management the infantry and artillery may make retreat by any other line impossible. At Landaki mentioned on p. 160, the very rapid flight of the Swatis, and the delay which arose in getting the cavalry through the defile by the river owing to the road being broken, saved the tribesmen from the mounted troops, whose prowess they had learnt to dread; when Sir B. Blood had broken out of the Malakand position a few days before, the infantry had driven the tribesmen down on to a level valley, where the 11th Bengal Lancers and Guides cavalry had given them a lesson which will be remembered for years.

The great problem when attacking irregular warriors in position is not so much to decide how to capture that position, for the chances are that this will not prove very difficult, as to make certain that the victory shall be a real victory causing the enemy heavy loss. This end may be achieved in various ways under diverse sets of conditions. But, given the suitable situation, no more effectual way of achieving a decisive and lasting triumph can be found than to compel the broken straggling array, which has been driven from the ground whence it bid the troops defiance, to stream across a level tract of country, where the cavalry can deal a *coup de grâce.*

At the battle of Kandahar the plan was that the whole Importance of the cavalry acting at the right moment. of the cavalry was to make a wide turning movement outside the infantry, was to cross the Argandhab and was to fall upon the enemy in retreat, but owing to unforeseen circumstances it was greatly delayed and came up very late; a few squadrons following the infantry and ready to strike promptly, would have been of the utmost assistance after the last stand was made by the Afghans. In broken intersected country the charge of a small detachment of cavalry may be of great value as a minor episode of the conflict, and it is essential that the troopers should be at hand, to strike when an opportunity offers and thereby to complete what the infantry has begun. The cavalry operations against the hostile flanks and rear in the Mutiny and in the Egyptian campaign of 1882 were admirable, and were highly effective owing to the ground being generally favourable. Under these circumstances massing the cavalry seems to have been a good arrangement. But on battlefields less suited for the combined action of great bodies of horse, and in attacking an enemy who, once the infantry have come to close quarters retires at a rate completely outpacing the trained foot soldier, it is most expedient that the cavalry, or at least some of it, should be distributed so that some of it may be available to strike home then and there.

Artillery to be pushed up to the front to play on enemy when he gives way. And as with the cavalry so it is with the artillery. Irregular warriors can always escape from infantry, but they cannot so readily escape from the effects of artillery fire. On this account some of the guns ought to be pushed up to close quarters in good time, so as to be at hand when wanted. In a later chapter dealing with artillery the importance of forward tactics of this arm of service will be illustrated by examples. At the battle of Staweli, where the French decisively defeated the forces of the Dey of Algiers which had taken up a strong position to bar their advance on the capital, the artillery was pushed up right into the hostile position, and it completed the rout of the enemy by its fire at short range. In the Mutiny the guns were always handled with great boldness. In warfare against undisciplined opponents or against forces of inferior morale, the rôle of artillery is not so much to prepare the way for the infantry as to complete the work which the infantry have been unable to carry through to the end.

One point deserves to be specially noted. Many examples might be cited from campaigns of recent years to show that when dealing with irregular warriors it is often practicable for a commander of disciplined troops to completely impose upon the enemy as to the strength of the force, and to impress the foe with the idea that a far larger body of soldiers is at hand than is actually the case. It is especially in attack that the circumstances lend themselves to deceptions of this kind. Of course such ruses are not prohibited by a defensive attitude—Lieutenant Grant's action at Thobal already mentioned on p. 83, is a remarkable example of one ; but from the nature of the case it is when acting on the offensive that they are most likely to succeed.

Attack often offers opportunities for deceiving enemy as to available strength, and thus for gaining successes with insignificant forces.

(1) Towards evening on the second day of the final move of the 2nd division of the Tirah Field Force down the Bara valley, the tail of the rearguard under Major Downman was unable to get into camp before dark, and it found itself towards dusk in a position of considerable difficulty. It happened that a small party of the Gordon Highlanders was detached to one flank covering the rearguard's retirement, and this came suddenly under heavy fire from some houses. With four of his men Captain Uniacke made a rush for the nearest, shouting words of command and pretending that he had a large force at his back, captured it, and, as the Afridis bolted, he kept up the deception by shouting and using his whistle to attract the attention of the troops further in rear. Major Downman on arriving decided to collect his troops at the houses, and the rearguard eventually passed the night there, isolated but in safety.

(2) Lieut.-Colonel Baden-Powell's capture of Wedza's stronghold towards the close of the Rhodesian operations of 1896, is another excellent illustration. It would be hard to find a better example of bluffing the enemy in campaigns of this class. The stronghold consisted of several kraals perched almost on the crest of a mountain some three miles long, which was joined to a range by a neck. A sketch plan of the action faces the next page. While the defenders numbered several hundreds, the entire British force only amounted to 120—the original plan had been for another column to co-operate in the attack which was unable to do so. Colonel Baden-Powell commenced operations by sending 25 mounted men to the neck (A in sketch) with orders to act as though they were ten times as strong ; the guns were to bombard the crest, which the rest of the force, some hussars,

demonstrated against the outer end of the mountain and against the back of it. After some desultory skirmishing the mounted infantry pushed their way up to the point designated, leaving horses below with seven horse holders; but the enemy began to assemble in force and to seriously threaten the hill party.

Colonel Baden-Powell perceiving their somewhat critical position, sent to the guns and hussars to make a diversion. But these had been unexpectedly delayed on the road and were not yet at hand, so he took the seven horse holders and with them moved round to C in rear of the position; then, scattering the men, he ordered magazine fire, so as to give the idea that there was a considerable attacking force on this side. The ruse was completely successful. The rebels who had been pressing over towards the neck hastily spread themselves all over the mountain, and the arrival of the rest of the troops at this juncture completed the illusion, the guns coming into action at B. The hussars moved round the mountain, and were dispersed to a certain extent, so as to represent as strong a force as possible and to impress the enemy. It was decided that no assault should be delivered that day; but the deception practised by the assailants was carefully kept up during the night. Fires (shown D in the sketch) were lighted at intervals round great part of the mountain, which were fed by moving patrols, and the men forming these patrols had orders to discharge their rifles from time to time at different points. Everything was done to make Wedza and his followers believe that a whole army was arrayed against them. The next day the kraals were captured with ease, most of the enemy having slipped off in the darkness.

The separation of force on the battlefield. The question of combined front and flank attacks has been already dealt with; it necessarily involves separation of forces at least temporarily. When the enemy is holding a regular defensive position and accepts battle, the breaking up of the attacking force into distinct bodies working to a certain extent independently of each other will seldom go further than one portion attacking in front and another in flank. But cases sometimes arise when it is necessary, or when it seems desirable, to attack an enemy from several points, and this generally involves separation with its attendant advantages and disadvantages. It is especially on occasions when the enemy is in small force and not deliberately drawn up for battle that these conditions present themselves—they are constantly occurring in hill and jungle warfare or when the enemy adopts guerilla tactics.

BATTLE of KANDAHAR

Scale

Pir Paimal

Ghundigan

Ghundi

A.....Afghans

WEDZA'S STRONGHOLD

Open undulating plain

MOUNTAINS

Open plain

Routs followed by Hussars

Fortified Kraals.....

Scale (approx)

MILE I   3/4   1/2   1/4   0   I MILE

I.D W.O. 1120(e)

Jan.y, 1899.

The reasons for and against tactical separation are analogous in many respects to those already given in Chapter IX for and against strategical separation.

A main advantage is the moral effect which it exerts. *Advantages of this.* The enemy finds it very trying to be attacked simultaneously by different columns. Some must menace the line of retreat, and irregular warriors above all things fear a situation where their escape, should it become expedient to fly, is jeopardised. If it is intended to completely disperse a gathering of such opponents no better means can be adopted than to attack them from several points if it be practicable. In the attacks on the Waterkloof group of mountains in 1851–52, several columns were always formed to advance from different sides meeting on the top, and the Kaffirs were always totally dispersed with considerable loss of cattle, &c.; but the very difficult nature of the wooded ridges and ravines was such as to prohibit heavy loss being inflicted on the Kaffirs themselves. Another advantage of attacking from several sides—and it is a very important one when some village or stronghold, the exact nature of which is not known, is the objective—is that one or more columns may be unable to effect a lodgment, and that the operation may be successful in spite of this; there is always the chance that one of the detachments may force its way in. Many examples could be cited of successful attacks by several columns marching independently on localities, villages, stockades, &c., and attacking simultaneously, and of the operations proving entirely successful. Of these the following will suffice.

(1) For the capture of Nareh near Constantine in Algeria in 1849, *Examples.* Colonel Canrobert divided his force into three distinct columns. One starting at night some hours before the others, was to make a detour in the mountains, and was to occupy high ground on the far side above the collection of villages about to be attacked; it was then to wait till it saw the other two ready to attack. The other two, starting later, moved more directly on the objective, their orders being that they, with the column sent ahead, should fall on Nareh from three different sides soon after daybreak. The operation was completely successful, the timing of the

movements was most happy, and the *coup de main* had a great effect in the surrounding districts which were all in revolt against the French.

(2) The capture of Yangi Kala two miles south of Denghil Tepe by General Skobelef previous to the attack on that stronghold in 1880, is another good example of separation prior to an assault. The expeditionary force arrived and halted to the west of the fortified village, which was a straggling place with many enclosures and gardens and a few small mud forts of the usual oriental type. One column was sent round south of the place to attack it on its south-eastern and eastern sides, another was to assault the western side ; the cavalry pushed on on both sides so as to threaten the Tekkes' retreat northwards to Denghil Tepe. The operation proved completely successful, for the enemy soon became demoralized on finding the Russians advancing from different sides and on perceiving that there was a risk of being cut off from the fortress.

(3) Another good example is afforded by the capture of the strong stockade of Sittang, near Pegu, in 1825, during the first Burmese war. The stockade was on an eminence, protected on the left by a river and on the right and rear by dense jungle which made approach on those sides difficult. Three columns of attack were told off, the right and centre to assault and escalade the front face, the left to make a detour through the jungle and to assault the right face. This left column when it reached its destination gave the signal for attack to the others by bugle call. The dispositions proved completely successful, and all three columns practically escaladed the very strong defences simultaneously. The Burmese fired one or two most effective volleys, but they became terrified at the concentric attack and made for the exit at the rear, afraid of being cut off. One-fifth of the storming force was, however, placed *hors de combat* in the few moments that the defenders stood their ground, showing that had these not become panic-stricken the assault might have failed altogether, and that in any case it would certainly have cost the British heavy sacrifices had the enemy offered a really stout resistance.

Disadvantages. The dangers of tactical separation of this kind lie partly in the opportunity which it affords to the enemy to beat the different columns in detail, and partly in the risk of miscalculations as to time. Moreover, success may be imperilled by misunderstandings with regard to orders, or by confusion arising in the various fractions of the force in their endeavours to co-operate with each other. There is always the further danger that detached columns may fire into each other.

Enemy may beat fractions in detail. Uncivilized opponents and troops of inferior organization and morale seldom understand the principle of working on interior lines, or of reaping the advantages which arise when their antagonist divides his forces. But, actually on the battle-field, when the defenders are in a central position which the attackers are approaching from different sides, it is sometimes obvious even to leaders of no great capacity for war, that they may be able to fall upon the various fractions coming against them and crush to a certain extent in detail ; they can see what is going on, as sometimes also can their followers, and they are therefore more likely to seize their opportunity of acting on interior lines tactically, than where it is a question of strategical combination against detached forces approaching convergently from points in the theatre of war far apart from each other. Still in those cases where separation of force in carrying out an attack against enemies of this class has resulted in failure or disaster, this has usually been due not to the tactical skill of the adversary but to mistakes or mismanagement on the side of the assailants.

A very serious disaster befel a column of United States troops during the Red Indian wars on the Little Big Horn, which illustrates the danger of tactical separation. The column consisted of 12 troops of cavalry, with a train of pack animals. On getting touch with the Indians it was formed into four parties, one of five troops under Colonel Custer commanding the column, and two of three troops each, one of them under Major Reno ; the fourth of one troop formed the baggage guard. The force was moving down the valley of a stream. When it was reported that the enemy's settlement was only two miles off, Major Reno's party was sent to the front to move rapidly against the enemy, it being understood that Colonel Custer would support. The two other parties had got altogether separated from this main portion of the force. Major Reno found the Indians in great force and being unsupported he was, after a hot fight and heavy loss, compelled to take refuge on a bluff close by, which proved a satisfactory refuge. Fortunately he was joined here by the two parties which had gone astray, and with their assistance was enabled to hold his own against the determined attacks which the Indians kept up for many hours. Colonel Custer's force appears to have moved to the right of the valley—firing was heard on that side. Apparently it got back eventually to near the river some distance lower down than where Major Reno's force had taken up position—this at least was conjectured from the tracks. But what occurred exactly is not known, for the force was annihilated and nothing but the bodies of men and horses served to tell the tale of the disaster. It appears to have been the case that the five troops fell in with an overwhelming force of Indians, and that these afterwards came to attack Major Reno's party. Fortunately that officer secured a good position, and had partially entrenched his men while there was yet time.

Difficulty of manœuvring detached forces effectively.

When several detached columns are intended to co-operate in a combined attack, there is always the danger of an error with regard to time or distance marring the effect. This occurred as already described in the case of the flank attack on Ali Musjid, and also during the first advance on Wedza's stronghold as mentioned on p. 176, although in neither case did harm come of it. The manœuvring of such divided forces by the commander of the whole, is always difficult to carry out successfully once they are started upon the enterprise. The great object to keep in view is to assign to each a task within its powers, taking the nature of the terrain, the amount of opposition to be encountered and so forth into account. It is always better to err on the safe side— to allow too much time rather than too little. To each column a proper impulse should, if possible, be given at the outset, then the less interference there is with their independence the better. Of course unforseen circumstances may arise which render a change of plan at the last moment imperative ; but in the absence of such a contingency it must never be forgotten that the secret of success lies in trusting subordinates till they are found to be going wrong, that orders sent from a distance may be issued under a misapprehension of the exact circumstances at the moment, and that there is always great risk of their causing confusion.

The unfortunate sortie from Kandahar against the village of Deh Khoja during the blockade in 1880 illustrates this very well. The sortie took place after daybreak, preceded by a short bombardment from the guns on the walls (the plan opposite shows the position of the village relatively to the city). The cavalry moved out of the Idga gate and made a wide detour round to the east and south-east of Deh Khoja. The infantry under General Brooke were formed into three small columns and advanced out of the Kabul gate towards the south-west end of the village, which was held in some

PLAN X.

DEH KHOJA.

Scale.

0   ¼   ½   ¾   1 MILE

N

CAVALRY

Khairabad
(Village)

Deh Khoja

Idga
Gate

Kabul Gate   LEFT COLUMN

CENTRE COLUMN

RIGHT COLUMN

KANDAHAR

Garden

I.D.W.O. 1120 (P)

March, 1896.

strength by the Afghans and was prepared for defence. Large hostile bodies were seen hurrying up to reinforce it during the preliminary operations.

The centre column, which was accompanied by General Brooke, with part of the right column, forced their way into the village at its southern end. The rest of the right column occupied the garden close by, and with the cavalry kept the enemy's reinforcements in check, while the left column lined some walls to the south and west, and acted in reserve ; one and a half columns, in fact, penetrated into the place, while the remainder halted outside. By dint of hard fighting General Brooke and the troops with him forced their way along the streets. They had just reached the north end of the village when an order came from Kandahar to retire. General Brooke thereupon gave the necessary directions to those with him, and the dangerous operation of withdrawing from a particularly awkward position in face of a fanatical enemy was at once begun.

The troops in the garden, the cavalry, and also the left column, all retired on the Kabul gate under orders from Kandahar. Those in the village were, however, attacked with great determination by the enemy who speedily perceived the retrograde movement, and they only extricated themselves with the utmost difficulty. Some escaped by the north end and some by the south, but very serious losses were suffered in the streets and in retiring back to Kandahar. Half the force in fact was left in the lurch in the village, while the other half, which had been far less heavily engaged, retired practically without fighting. General Brooke himself was killed and the sortie ended in a distinct reverse.

This affair at Deh Khoja shows how difficult it is to control detached bodies in action. But there is another danger in such a case, and this is that the troops may shoot into each other by accident, or that one column may mistake another for a hostile body. This actually occurred at the action of Suruj Kund, already mentioned in this chapter ; while General Markham's force attacked the Sikh left and rolled up their line, an auxiliary contingent attacked the right front of the hostile position ; the contingent was mistaken for the enemy and fired into. The same thing occurred at the first attack on Kimmendine, near Rangoon, in 1824, where the artillery of the flank column fired into the centre one in the jungle from a distance, causing some loss. This sort of misunderstanding frequently occurred on a small scale in the later days of the South African war ; little damage was generally done and the mistake was as a rule detected very

Detached bodies may fire into each other.

quickly, but an unrehearsed scuffle of this kind is very apt to give the show away when anything in the shape of a surprise on the enemy is in contemplation.

The following examples are of interest as showing how misunderstandings may arise in operations of this character under varying circumstances and for different reasons. They serve to show that, when separate forces are endeavouring to act in combination in terrain where the view is restricted, there is great risk of some misapprehension either of orders or of the conditions existing at some particular time.

(1) In the Maori war in 1863, Colonel Warre operating in the Taranaki obtained information of a hostile pah, and he determined to surprise it. A party was sent round to arrive in rear of the position at a fixed time. Colonel Warre was to make a demonstration in front to draw the enemy into their rifle pits out of the pah. When that had effected its purpose the detached force was to occupy the pah. Both forces arrived at the right time. That detached to the rear, however, became impressed with the idea that it had been discovered and it did not attack in consequence. The result was that the demonstration drew the enemy out of the pah as had been anticipated, that there were no troops to seize the opportunity and to force their way into it when it was practically deserted, and that in consequence the well concocted plan came to nothing.

(2) A very singular instance of a misunderstanding of this kind leading to a serious disaster, is afforded by the Achin war of 1874. A plan of the ground faces page 184. During the operations after the capture of Kota Raja an attack upon a fortified village named Longbatta was arranged for, which was to be carried out by a combined movement of two separate columns ; one was to move against the front and the other to make a detour and attack the right. The plan shows roughly where clearings existed : elsewhere the jungle was dense, the thick undergrowth making all movements of troops most difficult.

The column destined for the frontal attack never reached the place at all. It was delayed by the obstacles in the way, it kept too much to the right, and eventually after some hours, got to the Panjaret village much exhausted. The left column after a most trying march reached Longbatta, and captured it after some fighting. It then received an order from Kota Raja to take another village close by ; but the order was misunderstood, and the column moved against Lung, a place considerably further on across more open ground. The Achinese at once endeavoured to re-occupy Longbatta, so part of the column had to go back and hold it, while the rest pushed on and succeeded in capturing Lung. Here, however, they were promptly attacked by very superior numbers of the enemy. The officer in command ordered a flourish on the trumpets to be sounded to apprise the rest of the force that he was in difficulties, but this signal was unfortunately misunderstood. The right column had heard the firing and was marching as best it could through the jungle towards the sound of the cannon ; but the trumpet call was taken by it to mean a pæan of victory, so it marched straight back to Kota Raja.

The part of the left column which had moved on to Lung had therefore to fight its way back unsupported to Longbatta, and it suffered very heavily in its retreat. The co-operation between the two columns had failed completely in the first instance. Then the mistake about the village, and the subsequent misunderstanding with the trumpets, caused half of one of the two columns to be left isolated and to be almost annihilated.

(3) The combat of the Zlobani mountain in Zululand took place under totally different conditions from those obtaining amid the swampy flats near Kota Raja with their dense tropical vegetation. The Zlobani mountain was one of the singular, flat topped hills with almost precipitous sides which are a feature of the topography of south-eastern Africa. It was, as appears from the sketch facing next page, oval in plan, the longer axis three British miles long running east and west. It lay some miles east of the camp at Kambula.

The object of the attack on it was to raid the cattle which it had been ascertained the Zulus were concealing there. Colonel Wood decided to send a mounted force under Colonel Buller along the south to make an assault on the east or further end, as the main attack. Colonel Russell with another mounted force was to create a diversion at the west end and was to act in support. Colonel Buller's force surprised the enemy at dawn, scrambled up with some loss, dispersed the Zulus on the top, and secured the cattle ; it was then decided to retire by the western end. Colonel Russell meanwhile had occupied a lower plateau at the western end and had ascertained the success of the main attack. All was going well when a large Zulu army suddenly came in sight, approaching from the south-east and marching towards Kambula past the south of the mountain.

Colonel Wood had followed Colonel Buller, and, on ascertaining that all was right, had re-descended and moved along the south of the mountain. Here he became aware of the Zulu army's approach, and he at once sent orders to Colonel Russell to move his force back to the Zinguin Neck west of the mountain, where it would cover Colonel Buller's retreat. Owing to some misunderstanding as to the locality intended, however, Colonel Russell moved off to a point some six miles to his west.

Not only the British on the summit, but also the Zulus who were hiding among the rocks and kloofs of the hillside, had seen the impis on their march, and they promptly began harassing Colonel Buller's force. Having no support to fall back upon, and the descent of the western end of the mountain being barely practicable, this suffered very severely. Owing to the great hostile army to the south, which, however, fortunately did not come into action, the situation appeared to be even worse than it was. It was only by a supreme effort that panic was allayed and that the force succeeded in reaching the bottom without a very serious disaster. The troops felt themselves to be in the utmost peril. Colonel Russell's force, had it taken up the position intended, would have been a moral support of the utmost value to the hard pressed troopers as they scrambled down the steep declivity with the Zulus gathering all round them, even if it had been unable to actually intervene in the fight. Once at the bottom, Colonel Buller's force, consisting as it did of mounted troops, was able to retire without much molestation.

Note on the battle of Adowa. It may be mentioned here that the unfortunate battle of Adowa furnishes a most striking example of the risks of separation in the field. This combat does not, it is true, illustrate tactics of attack, nor indeed does it illustrate tactics of defence ; it was a haphazard affair, the Italians not having intended an assault on the Abyssinians and the opposing armies having come into contact unexpectedly. Still in a work of this kind it would be an omission not to draw attention to what was the most prominent feature of this battle, a battle which ended in the most serious disaster which regular troops have encountered in any modern small war. The fact that the Italian brigades were so scattered when the Abyssinians came out against them arose to a certain extent from a misunderstanding, as has been already mentioned on p. 46. But the upshot was that they were beaten in detail and that an army of 15,000 men, consisting for the most part of European troops, was utterly routed by a host of irregular warriors.

Risk of counter-attack. As will be seen in Chapter XXI dealing with infantry tactics, less depth and fewer reserves are generally necessary in infantry attacks upon irregular enemies than is the case in regular warfare. The same holds good as a broad principle of attack tactics in small wars as a whole. The losses are less severe and the risk of counter-attack is smaller than in attacks delivered against disciplined troops. But although counter-attack has less to be feared, and although the relative strength of reserves as compared to that of troops in front line need not be so great, reserves can never be dispensed

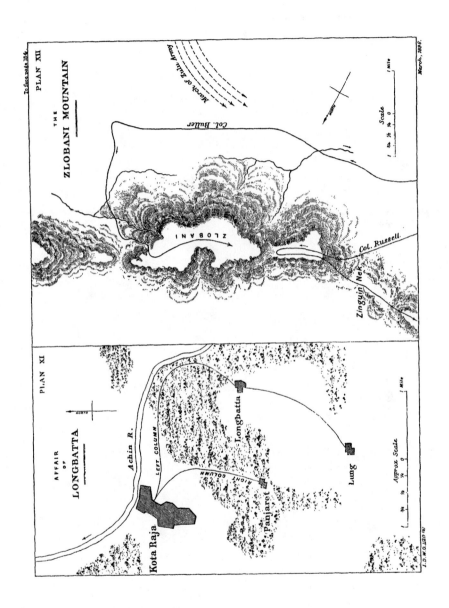

PLAN XII

THE
ZLOBANI MOUNTAIN

March, 1896.

PLAN XI

AFFAIR
OF
LONGBATTA

with altogether. Reserves are especially needed in fighting against fanatics who may make a sudden rush by way of counter-attack. In the main this is a branch of infantry tactics to be dealt with under that head in a later chapter, but the question of absence of reserves when there is risk of counter-attack, to a certain extent involves the other arms also.

(1) At Denghil Tepe in 1879, General Lomakin was obliged, owing to the smallness of his force, to deliver the assault with practically no reserves. When the stormers found it impossible to penetrate into the defences and fell away under the heavy fire poured into them by the Tekkes, there were no reserves to lean upon. Fortunately the guns afforded a refuge to the Russian infantry as this was swept back by the defenders, who charged out over their battlements in great force and with much determination. The retreating infantry masked the artillery for a while but cleared the front in time to allow the guns to deliver some rounds of case into the Turkoman swarms. These sufficed to drive the Tekkes back into their stronghold in confusion.

(2) At the battle of Tetuan in 1859, where the Spanish army made a direct attack upon the Moors entrenched in a strong position, the enemy unexpectedly charged out over their defences on one flank just as the assault was about to be delivered. This sudden counter-attack, however, in reality favoured the assailants, because it enabled them to fight their way into the position with the flying Moors, who had no chance against the Spanish muskets in the open. But the incident illustrates the possibility of such foes delivering unexpected counter-strokes of a character which may call for a solid front on the part of the regular troops.

(3) The charge of the ghazis at the battle of Bareilly in 1858, is another good example of a hostile counter-attack. An attack on the rebels was being prepared and the artillery on the British left, which was to take the enemy in flank, had been in action for some time. Suddenly a crowd of fanatic swordsmen charged down upon the extreme right of the British. Fortunately, the infantry, although taken somewhat aback, had time to close their ranks, and they effectually dealt with the ghazis. Scarcely were the ghazis disposed of than a large force of the rebel cavalry swept round the right flank and caused considerable confusion in rear.

(4) As instances on a small scale may be cited a sudden charge of spearmen from the hills on the right of Mahdist position at Kirbekan down upon the infantry just preparing to storm them, and a fanatical rush at the action of Kotkai in the Black Mountains Expedition of 1888. The enemy in this latter case was giving way and the attacking troops were pressing forward with all speed to complete the victory, when suddenly, out of a masked nullah running diagonally across the battle-field, a body of swordsmen made

Margin note: Examples of hostile counter-attack.

a desperate attempt to break the line ; all of them were killed, but they inflicted some loss and might have caused very serious confusion but for the steadiness of the troops.

Need of co-operation between infantry and artillery to meet counter-attacks.

The examples cited above serve to show that there is often a chance of a very sudden counter-attack being delivered by a fraction of the hostile force, even if, speaking generally, irregulars are not very prone to attempt such offensive returns. To meet counter-strokes guns are very useful. The case of Denghil Tepe, although rather in the nature of a counter-attack after an assault has failed, illustrates the value of artillery in support ; it provides a further argument for the forward action of this arm, the need of which has been already pointed out if a decisive victory is to be gained without a turning movement. Good troops have little to fear from a sudden rush of bodies of fanatics if the ground be open ; but in a broken intersected terrain where there is no field of fire, such antagonists may create serious disorder, if they come on with resolution and unexpectedly, and may even break through the line if reserves are not at hand. General Skobelef in his instructions to the troops in the Turkoman campaign of 1880, laid the utmost stress on the artillery being up to support the infantry in attack, and upon the infantry being kept well in hand. " The main principle of Asiatic tactics is to preserve close formations." " The artillery must devote itself to closely supporting its comrades without the slightest regard for itself." Such were his maxims, and although such tactics are inapplicable under many of the conditions which small wars present, the rules laid down for guidance by so illustrious a leader command consideration.

Tendency of enemy to threaten flanks and rear of attacking force.

When the question comes to be considered how a regular force about to attack the enemy should be drawn up in operations of this class, there is a point which at once attracts attention ; the fact that irregular warriors are very prone to shirk meeting a direct attack tends to drive them into harassing operations directed against the flanks and rear of the regular troops. Their instinctive appreciation, moreover, that the flanks and rear of the troops advancing against them are the most promising points for counter-attack, often causes them to give a great deal of annoyance. In bush fighting, when the enemy does not act purely on the defensive, and when the adversary depends upon stockades and similar defences concealed in the jungle, the flanks and rear of the regular troops are constantly threatened. As will be seen in Chapter XX the French operating against opponents of these proclivities in Dahomey made considerable use of the square formation while acting on the offensive. At Amoaful and Ordahsu in Ashanti the same kind of tactics on the part of the enemy were experienced, as also in Achin, and in both these campaigns especial arrangements had to be made to guard the flanks and rear of troops advancing to the attack. This enveloping system of undisciplined adversaries is not peculiar to the bush however, the same thing is experienced in the hills on the Indian borders, by the French in Algeria and the Russians in Central Asia, and recently the Somalis have been found to adopt the enveloping method when prepared to accept battle. The Moors employed it in 1859, and in consequence of their tactics Marshal McDonald at the battle of Tetuan advanced in a formation like a wedge, his flanks being thrown back—an order of battle not altogether unlike Marshal Bugeaud's at Isly.

This battle of Isly is of especial interest as it is probably the most decisive victory gained over irregular forces by any troops other than British since the battle of the Pyramids. Marshal Bugeaud drew up his army in the form of, as he himself described it, " the muzzle of a boar "—a triangle in fact with blunted apex ; and in this wedge-like order of battle he went straight at an immensely superior force of Moors. The formation was arrived at by echelon of battalion columns— battalion columns being the normal infantry order of attack— and the artillery and non-combatants were within the triangle.

The battle of Isly.

The marshal had given directions that the battalions were to form battalion square if the Moorish horse charged home. The enemy does not appear to have penetrated through the gaps at any time ; the hostile onslaughts were not indeed very formidable, in spite of the enormous numerical superiority of the Moors. And although a formation with great gaps in it will seldom recommend itself as an arrangement for meeting charges of hostile cavalry, especially when there is a great deal with the force which needs protection, it served its purpose extremely well in this case at Isly, the French gaining a brilliant victory at a trifling sacrifice.

An illustration of an échelon formation.

Marshal Bugeaud's battalions having been drawn up in heavy columns, as was the system in those days in all regular armies except the British, robs this battle of much of its interest at the present time. But it is a remarkable fact that what was one of the most decisive battles in any small war of the last century, was won by one of the greatest of masters of irregular warfare with a force drawn up in échelon formation which advanced right into the heart of a huge hostile army and compelled this to attack. When the Moors rushed down upon the French, these of course stood to receive the attack ; but their deliberate advance, which moreover was only checked at the moment of impact, created them in reality the assailants and makes the battle of Isly an example of offensive tactics.

Remarks on the échelon formation.

This method of drawing the troops up in échelon has the advantage of assuring a good development of fire, and it protects the flanks. When General Egerton advanced to the attack at Jidballi he formed the infantry in double échelon from the centre, with the mounted troops on the flanks ; the échelon however formed square when close to the enemy. An échelon formation does not meet the difficulty of an enveloping attack made in great force and with reckless determination. The very rapid advance of fanatics such as are met with in the Sudan and sometimes in Algeria enables these to make sudden onslaughts upon the regular forces from any side, and mere facing about does not satisfactorily meet a hostile counter-attack in great strength upon the rear of a body of troops advancing in échelon formation. Moreover if the enemy succeeds in getting through the intervals there is great risk of the troops firing into each other. On open ground there is little danger of the enemy, however fierce his attack may be, getting to such close quarters ; but experience has shown that among thickets and in broken terrain such foemen manage sometimes to reach the muzzles of the rifles. In view of the success which has generally attended the employment of the square formation under these conditions, it seems doubtful whether the échelon order of battle makes an efficient substitute ; but in attacking adversaries less prone to rely on shock tactics it would no doubt at times prove very satisfactory even in bush country.

A special chapter is devoted later on to the square formation. Marshal Bugeaud's order of battle was not of course a square ; but his idea while advancing to attack the Moorish camp was to be prepared for the onslaught of the hostile cavalry from most sides, and the object of the square is the same—to be ready to meet assailants trusting to shock tactics from whatever direction they come. The échelon formation or the square formation—defensive formations in reality—are employed on the offensive where the enemy is in great strength and is inclined to deliver strokes against the flanks and rear. Under such circumstances the regular force must advance in an order of battle which can show front at a moment's notice in any direction, covering its impedimenta. Here, however, we are rather concerned with threats against the flanks and rear of a body of troops acting on the offensive, than with regular attacks upon them.

Where the flanks and rear of the attacking troops are merely threatened, the sound principle to act on seems to be not to take these threats too seriously. The French when

Importance of pressing and not paying too

attacking very superior forces in Tonkin usually adopted an échelon formation, to counteract the overlapping tactics of the enemy and prevent them from becoming a serious danger ; but except for taking this precaution they pushed ahead disregarding the threats against their rear. It will almost always be found that if the advance be resolute and the assault pushed home, the clouds of foemen hovering on the flanks melt away and cease to be a danger. The case of Ordahsu in the Ashanti war illustrates this ; the British troops pushed boldly on, disregarding the tendency of the enemy to harass the flanks and rear, and no evil came of it. This method of combat on the part of the enemy has, it must be remembered, very little in common with the enveloping system of attack which the Zulus employed with such success at Isandlwhana, and with such manœuvring power at Ginghilovo and Ulundi—in Zululand the regular troops acted on the defensive on the battle-field and in square or laager, the enemy being the assailant. The very fact of disregarding feeble tentative hostile operations against the flanks and rear, shows the enemy that the regular army holds him lightly, and, as has been so often insisted upon, moral effect is all powerful in these campaigns.

General Romanovski's decisive victory over the Uzbeg army at Yedshar is worthy of mention in this connection. The Emir of Bokhara had about 40,000 men, the Russian force consisted of only 3,000 ; but in spite of disparity of numbers General Romanovski attacked without hesitation. The enemy enveloped the Russian force and made desperate attacks upon the baggage which was guarded by only a few companies, and these were at times in great peril. But the Russians pressed resolutely on, the baggage escort meanwhile repulsing the hostile onslaughts as best it could and pushing on whenever it had a moment's respite. The enemy could not stand against the determined advance of General Romanovski and the fire of his guns, and at last became panic-stricken and fled.

At the battle of Wad Ras, in 1859, the Moors seriously threatened the Spanish flanks while the attack was being developed. But although it was found necessary to detach some troops to make head against them, the main position of the attacking army pressed on, unhindered by the manœuvres of the enemy. When the village of Amsal in the centre of the hostile position was captured the Moors disappeared in all directions. The Sultan's army being numerically far superior to the Spanish force, was able to overlap the assailants, while at the same time offering resistance to the main attack.

In Chapter XI a passing reference was made to the successful operations in 1897 against the Mashonas in their caves. Inasmuch as it is a not uncommon trick on the part of the natives in that part of the world to take refuge in caves, and as their doing so has baffled troops at times, a short description of the method adopted with such happy results by Captain Hon. F. de Moleyns, who conducted the campaign, may be useful.

Attacks on caves in South Africa.

A rebel gathering having been located in some kraal, the first step towards dealing with it was to get within striking distance of it unobserved. To achieve this end Captain de Moleyns used to make a night march to the close vicinity of the point to be attacked, choosing moonlight nights when possible, because moonlight would be desirable on subsequent nights while experience showed that the enemy kept no look out except close in to the kraal.

The kraals were situated near the caves, and were generally prepared for defence. If the surprise was complete—as was generally the case—the troops when they advanced to attack at dawn found the Mashonas in the kraals, and the first step was to drive them out. It was always found that after some resistance the defenders fled to their caves, a movement which was not interfered with, it being in fact exactly what the assailants hoped for. As soon as the kraals were cleared, picquets were placed all round the caves and an impromptu siege began. Under a heavy fire directed into the mouths of the caves—these could be gradually located by watching the puffs from the hostile muskets and rifles—the picquets slowly closed in till they had formed as restricted a ring as the amount of available cover admitted of, and then a rigid investment was instituted.

The close investment having been completed, the next operation was to blow in the mouths of the caves. Explosives were prepared in heavy and light charges. These were brought up near the cave to be dealt with, care having been taken that its fire was completely silenced. A small charge with a short fuze was then hurriedly placed at the mouth of the cave; on this exploding the heavier charges were deposited before the natives could recover from the shock of the first, and the explosion of these had invariably the effect of bringing out some women and children. These were encouraged to bring out more, and in the end nearly the whole community would gradually be captured, although some used to manage to slip through the ring of picquets at night in spite of all precautions. Of course the

Mashonas sometimes managed to pull out the fuzes of the charges, and the operation did not necessarily proceed quite so smoothly ; but the result was always arrived at by patience and perseverance in from three to five days.

After three strongholds had been captured by this method the rebellion was practically crushed. The remaining rebels, finding that their cave fortresses were a source of weakness rather than of strength, gave up their arms and surrendered, and the campaign came to an end.

In these operations the broad principles which should guide the conduct of campaigns against irregular warriors were fully observed. The enemy having chosen the guerilla form of warfare was followed up in detail, and the blow against each fraction was driven right home. The point kept specially in view tactically, was to make certain that the foe did not escape when once brought to battle.

Hour for attack.

One more point with regard to the tactics of attack deserves attention, and this is the question of the hour at which attacks should be delivered. Night attacks are discussed in a later chapter together with other nocturnal operations, and the objections to them are there set out ; they are seldom

Attacks at dawn.

advisable, but experience has shown how very effective attacks at dawn of day are if practicable. It is a very general custom in undisciplined and irregular armies to withdraw a large part of the force by night and to send it back in the morning. The French army advancing on Algiers in 1830 took full advantage of this at Sidi Khalif, where the Dey's forces were finally overthrown ; it had been ascertained that the enemy used to. entirely withdraw at night out of the position which had been carefully prepared, so General Bourmont attacked in the early morning and captured it with little difficulty. The same thing was observed at Deh Khoja, already referred to in this chapter ; had there been no preliminary bombardment from Kandahar this village would probably have been captured without serious resistance.

It is somewhat singular that in view of the inclination which such enemies display for attacking at early dawn themselves, they rarely seem to anticipate danger at this hour.

The fact, however, remains, that if a body of troops can manage by a night march to arrive before the position of an irregular force, or even of an army modelled to a certain extent on the European system but not ranking as a regular force, it can generally deliver a most effective attack. Owing to the insufficiency of the outposts on the side of the enemy, or of their total absence, the approach of the assailants is seldom discovered if conducted with skill and regularity. The difficulty lies in the night march; if that difficulty is got over successfully there is generally good prospect of a surprise and a victory. It should be noted that one great advantage of attacking at daybreak is that the enemy finds it very difficult to ascertain at once what especial point the assailants are aiming at. The movement of columns round a hostile flank with the intention of falling upon the foe at dawn from all sides are difficult to execute by night, but a sudden concentric attack in the grey of the morning often has achieved a great success—the guerilla phases of the South African war of 1899-1902 provided many examples.

A good instance of such an attack at break of day occurred in Algeria in 1845. Abd el Kader had, with the suddenness characteristic of his methods of making war, unexpectedly appeared in the Metija near Algiers, where the whole district had broken out in revolt. News reached the capital that he was at a place called Cherck el Tobul in the hills. General Gentil commanding in Algiers thereupon made a night march to the enemy's camp. The movement was kept secret, the march was swift and sudden, and the force reached the camp before dawn and surprised it at daybreak. The rebels were wholly unprepared and were completely routed, tho Emir himself only just managing to escape.

Ludlow Castle, outside Delhi, was captured during the siege in 1857 by an attack delivered about dawn; the troops got up unobserved to close distance under cover of the darkness.

The attack on the Afghan flank at the Peiwar Kotal already described on p. 166, was delivered at dawn, and Sir H. Kitchener's force arrived before the Atbara zeriba soon after daybreak.

The well known case of Tel-el-Kebir is a very remarkable example of such an attack. The movement of a large force in battle formation by night right up to within striking distance of a formidable line of entrenchments held by a large army, was a signal achievement of war. Its arrival before the works was admirably timed and the result was a complete victory. The Egyptians were practically surprised, their outpost service had been neglected, and the outposts, such as they were, were too close in to give any adequate warning of a contemplated assault.

Attacks early in the day expedient, to allow of effective pursuit.

In fact attacks at daybreak, if they can be managed, afford considerable chance of very decisive success, so this seems to be perhaps the most favourable time for delivering an assault on a strong position.

It may be added that, when fighting certain enemies, the only chance of getting at them at all may be by attacking at daybreak after a night march. It was found in the suppression of the Matabili rebellion that approach under cover of darkness was absolutely necessary, otherwise the rebels slipped off and got their cattle and belongings off as well. One of the most successful actions of the campaign was brought about by assaulting the koppies among which a hostile impi was posted at dawn, after a march of 20 miles which lasted nearly the whole night.

In any case it is always expedient to attack early in the day if possible, so as to allow time not only for driving the enemy out of his position but also for carrying out an effective pursuit —this is a principle, however, which applies also in regular warfare. It must never be forgotten that in small wars decisive success, not perhaps as a tactical operation but as an effective operation of war, depends not only upon beating the enemy but also upon following up the success forthwith. The hostile forces must not be permitted to slip away and dissolve when only half beaten if it can possibly be avoided. A decisive tactical victory, won in the afternoon, may have a less lasting effect than a less pronounced triumph on the actual battle-field, achieved early in the day, provided that the success in action has been merely the prelude to an obstinate pursuit and general advance of the victorious troops.

CHAPTER XIII.

TACTICS OF DEFENCE.

THE subject of the defensive in small wars affords little scope for exhaustive discussion. A defensive attitude is almost always to be deprecated, and only under certain special circumstances is it to be recommended. The operations of regular troops in such warfare must never be allowed to stagnate ; the troops must be up and doing, striking their adversaries when these attempt resistance, hunting them down when they shun combat. An army acting on the defensive tacitly admits a certain superiority on the part of the enemy, and the very essence of the proper conduct of campaigns against irregular and undisciplined foes is bluff.

Defensive attitude unusual, but sometimes unavoidable.

Still, defensive tactics are sometimes forced upon the regular troops. In the chapters on squares, hill warfare, &c., some cases which impose upon them a defensive attitude will be referred to. If the enemy attacks in great force and with reckless daring it is usually best to receive the onslaught and not to press forward to meet it. The tactics adopted by the Zulus and Mahdists when flushed with confidence were best met at a halt in close formation, even on ground where arms of precision could tell with full effect. In the jungles of Dahomey the sudden hostile attacks on flanks and rear could be confronted most satisfactorily by the troops on the spot acting on the defensive till the edge was taken off the hostile appetite for combat. In every campaign detachments of regular troops will sometimes have to accept the position of letting the enemy attack them.

Where a small force of regular troops is opposed to great hostile masses, no matter how ill-armed or how deficient in

(10830)   N 2 morale those masses may be, circumstances render it almost imperative to act on the defensive. Many examples might be cited of small detachments being hemmed in and besieged in these campaigns—it may not be possible for them to fall boldly upon the enemy and fight their way through, there may be women and children to guard, valuable stores to protect too bulky to be moved, some post to be held which can not be abandoned. In such a situation, although the regular troops may spasmodically act on the defensive and teach the enemy to respect them, they must upon the whole maintain a defensive attitude in spite of the drawbacks attendant on that attitude—an attitude which naturally gives encouragement to the opposing warriors, who are as easily roused to warlike enthusiasm by a show of weakness on the part of their adversaries, as they are prone to discouragement and despondency when these show a bold and resolute front.

Small bodies of regular troops hemmed in.

It is hardly necessary to point out that, when a small force of regular troops is cooped up in some post by masses of savages or semi-civilized antagonists, its position is one of great anxiety, because the circumstances of the case are such as to give the enemy a great moral advantage. Under such circumstances the hostile gatherings swell apace and gain in courage from hour to hour. If the body of regular troops be very small the situation becomes especially full of peril from the very fact that, owing to its inability to depart appreciably from an attitude of passive defence, the enemy increases in assurance till he plucks up courage to risk an assault in full strength, when numbers may tell decisively.

Even then defensive must not be purely passive.

In such cases it is of supreme importance to maintain as active a defence as possible, to worry the enemy incessantly, to compel him to believe that the garrison is full of fight and that it has not lost heart under untoward circumstances. Even if counter-attack in the shape of sorties makes no material gain, it means a moral gain. The opposing force can probably spare those placed *hors de combat* in the fight far better than the regular troops can—every man counts in a hard pressed garrison. But the flash of enterprise will not have been without its effect if the sortie has been planned with skill and has been executed with vigour and determination. A purely passive defence is improper in warfare of any kind, but in a small war it is absolutely fatal. The enemy must be taught that the apparently insignificant force of regulars has not lost heart and that it represents an active power to be reckoned with. Fortunately this is a principle which officers commanding small detachments isolated in a hostile land and surrounded by swarms of enemies, seldom forget, as experience shows.

During the siege of Potchefstrom in the Transvaal, which was one of the chief incidents of the Boer war of 1881, a sudden sortie by a small party against the hostile trenches which were slowly nearing the little fort, had a most excellent effect. It greatly alarmed the Boers, in addition to achieving its immediate purpose of destroying some of their advanced works.

During the remarkable defence of Tuyen Kwang in Tonkin in 1885 by the French, which lasted nearly three months, two or three effective sorties by very small parties proved most valuable. Without perhaps achieving any success of importance, these plucky enterprises kept up the spirits of the garrison and prevented the Chinese from growing too confident.

A sally by a small detachment under Lieutenant Harley during the siege of Chitral in 1895, was not only brilliantly successful in destroying the hostile approaches, but exercised a great moral effect upon the enemy.

Similarly during the siege of Fort Gulistan by the Orukzais in 1897, a gallant sortie under a native officer of the Sikhs had an excellent effect; three hostile standards were captured, and it is said that the three sections of the tribesmen represented by these went off to their homes. The enemy had got up to within 20 yards of the walls.

Examples of minor counter-attacks under such circum-stances.

None of these episodes were in themselves great operations of war, but they contributed towards preventing the hostile swarms which were hemming in the small hard pressed garrisons from thinking that they were completely in the ascendant. These bold feats of arms, moreover, served greatly to encourage the troops. They converted the defence for the time being into an active defence. Such counter-strokes must be sudden and they must be pushed home with decision. There is no need for a large party, the smaller the detachment told off for the enterprise, the better may be the chance of achieving a successful surprise and the better can the detachment be kept in hand at the critical moment. And even if the sally fails in its object, if the enemy's trenches are not cleared, if his approaches cannot be blown up, if the little force is obliged to regain the defences with nothing to show for the effort it has made, no great harm will probably come of it. " If we fail in only one-third of our enterprises," said the Duke of Wellington, " we should not complain, but make up our minds to this as a general rule." A show of activity raises the spirits of troops driven to adopt a defensive attitude. A counter-attack of this kind shows the enemy that the defenders have not lost heart.

A counter-
attack on a
large scale
must not
miscarry
where the
army is in
difficulties. On the other hand, if any considerable portion of the defending force assumes the offensive for a special purpose, it is very unfortunate if the undertaking miscarries. A failure under such circumstances means that an important fraction of the force has suffered a check, and the moral effect upon the troops, who from the facts of the case are working under depressing influences, may seriously affect their fighting efficiency in the future. When a counter-attack on an important scale is contemplated, it is imperative that the whole scheme shall have been considered in all its aspects and that its details have been worked out thoroughly. The sortie to Deh Khoja from Kandahar is an example of such an enterprise undertaken on an important scale, failing ; it amounted to a disastrous reverse to a force condemned practically to a passive defence, a part of which force had already met with serious mishap at Maiwand. What occurred at Kabul in 1841 is an even more striking illustration of the danger of an ill-considered and badly-executed counter-attack.

The British army was beginning to find itself in critical circumstances, in consequence very largely of a want of enterprise at the time when the great hostile movement, which ended by accomplishing the annihilation of the force in the defiles of Jagdalak and Gandamak, had not yet come to a head. This being so, the ill-judged and ill-planned attacks upon the Bemaru heights had most calamitous results.

On the first occasion the main object was to capture and carry off two guns which the enemy had planted on the heights ; but the enterprise was only undertaken late in the day, and its execution was hurried and ineffective. One of the guns sent out in support stuck in a ditch, and the other was not given time to make any preparation. The first attack of the infantry on the heights failed, and they were thereupon charged and swept back by masses of Afghan horse. Then the British artillery opened an effective fire, and after a time a second attack partially succeeded and the enemy abandoned the two guns. But it was by this time getting dark and the upshot was that only one of the Afghan pieces was brought in and the affair was really a failure.

On the second occasion the attack was made before dawn. The Bemaru village was not captured by surprise simultaneously with the heights, as it should have been, and only one gun was taken out. An attack, later on, upon the village failed. This gave time for the enemy to swarm out of Kabul to attack the partially successful British troops in great force, and to drive them off the heights with heavy loss after a keen struggle. The army was demoralised by previous failure, and by the manifest mismanagement of the affair, and the net result of the two attempted counter-strokes against the ever growing Afghan forces was to still further depress the already shaken troops.

With anything approaching an equality of force to that of the enemy, a passive defence is, of course, wholly inadmissible. It may no doubt occasionally be resorted to for a time—sometimes with great advantage when it is intended to draw the hostile forces on to attack ; but it must only be adopted provisionally and as a temporary measure. Passive defence may be adopted as a ruse to tempt the enemy into some rash action even when the regular army is as strong as the enemy. It may sometimes be justifiable so as to afford troops a rest, or to enable supplies to be brought up in anticipation of an active campaign, or to cover the arrival of reinforcements sufficient to act with decisive effect. Otherwise, except under the circumstances dealt with in earlier paragraphs where the regular force only represents an insignificant total in face of a formidable gathering of irregular warriors, passive

Evils of passive defence if not imperative.

defence is out of place. The history of British small wars of the present generation, however, unfortunately provides three deplorable examples of serious defeats which can be directly attributable to an attitude of passive defence. In none of these cases did the circumstances restrict the troops to this attitude. There is every reason to believe that in each case active defence, if not actual attack, would have completely changed the complexion of affairs.

Examples.　　　After the failure of the attack on Laing's Neck in the Boer war of 1881, the enemy began to cut the communications of the British force facing the hostile position, and to raid long distances into Natal. It was decided to march a part of the force back to Newcastle to reopen communications. No sooner had this detachment left camp than the Boers, mounting their ponies, moved round over the hills to intercept it ; and in this they succeeded. The British force was compelled to take up a position near the Ingogo river, which proved to be particularly bad—a low undulation was occupied, an undulation fringed below with rocks which gave perfect cover to the enemy while the troops were exposed on the sky line. The Boers, approaching in small parties and making skilful use of the folds of ground to hide their movements, formed a ring round the position and fired on the guns and infantry from behind the rocks, while the British force remained a passive target for the hostile bullets till darkness closed in and put an end to the fight. The losses were very heavy, and the troops only succeeded in withdrawing to where they had come from during the night, by extraordinary good fortune. The Boers were in no overwhelming force, they were scattered while the British were concentrated, and the distance to be traversed in a rush was small, so that everything pointed to the certainty that a vigorous charge with the bayonet would have great effect. The Boers at the point selected for the effort would have rushed to their mounts, for they had no weapons with which to meet shock tactics, and they would thus have given the rifles of the infantry and the guns a chance which they never got throughout the disastrous engagement.

The circumstances at Majuba hill were somewhat similar a few days later. The British force had during the night gained the summit of this flat topped hill with its steep and broken sides, a hill commanding the Boer position at Laing's Neck, but not within rifle range. After a momentary and not unjustifiable panic on discovering the British at daybreak on the hill above them, the Boers boldly prepared to attack it. Its sides afforded excellent cover, inasmuch as terraces gave rise to considerable areas of dead ground. The troops for the most part were drawn up on the summit away from the edges, only a few men being told off to fire down the slopes. The Boers succeeded in creeping up unobserved to immediately below a small detached koppie, held by a party who flanked the face up which the main attempt was being made. A sudden and most effective volley practically cleared this koppie, and following close on the heels of the survivors, the Boers reached the crest. If ever there was an opportunity for a bayonet charge it was this ; but in place of a counter-attack the enemy was met by a mere desultory fusillade, the troops were unaware that their assailants were not numerically a formidable body, uncertainty and the fatal feeling of inferiority which mere passive defence engenders led to panic, and the men broke and fled. It is not a pleasant story, but it is a most instructive one. At the Ingogo river there was the excuse for not delivering a counter attack that, in crossing the 200 or 300 yards from the British position to where the Boers were crouching behind their rocks, serious loss must have occurred. On Majuba hill it was a mere matter of a rush of a few yards, and of keeping up the confidence of the troops by making them feel that if they were caught in a trap there was a way out of it.

The other instance referred to is Maiwand. Here it was not a case of confronting Europeans armed with rifles in the use of which they were trained from childhood, but of fighting Asiatics—Asiatics in considerable force it is true and well supplied with guns, but none the less Asiatics. The British force, quitting ground where a purely defensive action might have been fought with some hopes of success, moved out to meet the Afghan army and formed up on a stony plain for battle. Ayoub Khan's force was allowed to slowly deploy from column of route, and to form a line of battle to a certain extent enveloping the troops. The hostile guns were enabled to bring a concentric fire to bear on the British position, which lasted for some hours and demoralised the native troops, infantry and cavalry. When after a period of purely passive defence under trying circumstances, a great ghazi rush supervened, the native troops gave way and the line was completely broken. It is said that Ayoub Khan's Herati regiments suffered so severely from the British shells that they retired twice, and that they would have fled at the first attack. Whether or not this be the case, there is no doubt that a passive defensive under such circumstances was inexcusable. The British Empire in India would have a very different history if a passive defensive attitude had been adopted at Plassey and at Meani, where the hostile superiority of force was far more marked than it was at Maiwand at the outset, and where, when the armies came in contact, the enemy was drawn up for battle instead of being in motion and in column of route.

It is a relief to turn from the consideration of passive defence, totally opposed as it generally is to the fundamental principles upon which small wars should be conducted, to that of active defence. It is not always practicable to attack, and it is not always desirable to do so. At times regular troops will find themselves acting on the defensive in small wars, even

Active defence.

when the disparity between the forces is not so marked as to render this necessary. When this is the case a great chance often presents itself of seizing upon the moment when the enemy is disordered by advance, to deliver a crushing counter-attack. It is almost impossible to exaggerate the value of cavalry at such a moment. When irregular warriors get into disorder, or when their heart fails them just when they are about to drive their attack home, the bravest of them are easily thrown into panic, and once a panic sets in they dissolve into a helpless mob. Cavalry then gets its chance ; but even if there be no cavalry a rapid and resolute advance of foot soldiers may achieve much, and all preparations for such an advance should have been made in anticipation of the event. In such cases as Ahmed Khel in Afghanistan, as Ulundi and Ginghilovo in Zululand, and as Abu Klea, where the enemy approaches suddenly in great force and with much ferocity, the force of the attack breaks itself in the assault, and the survivors disperse after their onslaught has failed— they do not give the regular troops time or opportunity to deliver a counter-attack, unless a force of cavalry be at hand and the terrain permit of the action of this arm. As a general rule, however, the hostile attack is not pushed home with such vigour and suddenness, and in consequence there are more opportunities for a telling counter-stroke.

Remarks on defensive order of battle. On the defensive a great development of fire is essential, and unless there is risk of a fanatical rush strong reserves are not required. In view of the tendency of irregular opponents to circle round the flanks these should if possible rest on ground very favourable for defence, or else they should be well protected by cavalry or guns ; at Maiwand the flanks were quite *en l'air,* although the cavalry succeeded in keeping the enemy at a respectful distance from the one most exposed. It will sometimes be expedient to keep special reserves intended to deliver the counter-attack, concealed in rear of the fighting line. No definite rule on this head can be laid down,

To face page 203

PLAN XIII.
ACTION
OF
KAILUA
Scale
0
1/4
1/2
3/4
1 MILE
From Bang Bo
REDOUBTS
Kailua
ENTRENCHED
CAMP
COUNTER ATTACK
LANGSON
N
French
Chinese

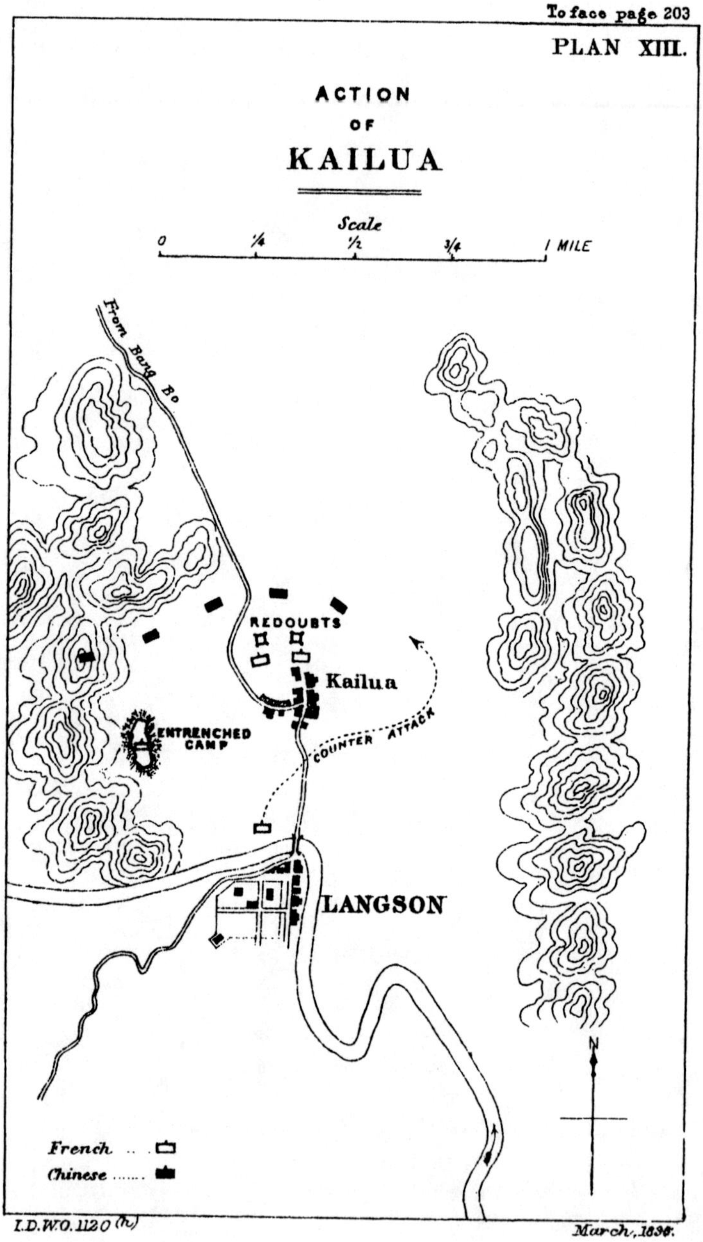

I.D.W.O. 1120 (h)

March, 1886.

it is seldom possible to decide in advance exactly how and where a counter-attack will be delivered ; but the force should be so disposed as to ensure that, whenever in the course of the action it is proposed to change from the defensive to the offensive, there may be troops on the spot to make the counter-stroke with power and effect.

The combat at Kailua in front of Langson where General Négrier de-feated the Chinese after the reverse suffered at Bang Bo described on p. 169 is an excellent example of a skilfully planned active defensive. The French position is shown on the rough sketch opposite, the reserve being in rear of Kailua on the right. The small entrenched camp on the left, the two re-doubts and the village of Kailua, all formed valuable defensive pivots, so that the position, although commanded, was a formidable one. *The engage-ment at Kailua as example of active defence.*

The Chinese were drawn on by the outposts as these retired into the plain, General Négrier having given orders to reserve fire so as to attract them to close quarters. They developed their principal attacks against the left where, encouraged by the cessation of fire on the part of the French, they pressed up close to the line. Fire being then suddenly opened they lost heavily and fell back some distance. They, however, came on again coura-geously on this side in spite of heavy losses, the French always reserving their fire till it should be thoroughly effective. Then General Négrier ordered part of the reserve to move out round the right of Kailua and to fall upon the enemy in flank from the rear. This decided the day. The Chinese left was rolled up, the reverse on this side immediately caused panic, and the whole force fell back completely defeated. Unfortunately just as the day was won General Négrier was severely wounded, and the victory was not followed up as it should have been.

The advantages of the square formation for meeting enveloping hostile attacks, and for ensuring that a firm front shall be offered to an enemy, the direction of whose sudden onslaughts can never be foreseen with certainty, will be pointed out and dealt with fully in Chapter XVII. But when the direction which the hostile assault will take can be foreseen approximately, and when the ground is fairly open so that the opposing force cannot creep round the flanks and make a sudden rush upon the rear, the need for square for-mation is not so very apparent even when fighting against savages who charge up recklessly to close quarters. An order of battle in irregular line with flanks thrown back, with the *Advantages of a line formation over square, even when the enemy is addicted to shock tactics.*

cavalry ready to act on the flanks and with the guns distributed so as to ensure shell fire being brought to bear on any point from which the enemy is delivering a determined attack, is excellent. If there is a fairly good field of fire there should be no fear whatever of the line being broken as long as good fire discipline is maintained, and in such a formation more rifles can be brought into play and a more extended position can be occupied than if square be adhered to. Strong reserves, which seriously reduce the number of rifles in the front line, are always out of place ; but small local reserves are desirable, especially towards the flanks.

Examples.

At Ahmed Khel the enemy was found in strong force on high ground to the left, and across the front, of the route which was being followed by Sir D. Stewart's force marching on Ghazni. All the troops available were formed for attack and the guns opened fire. Then a swarm of ghazis suddenly charged down towards the troops, and a mass of hostile cavalry which had been seen on the right of the Afghan position attacked the British left. The consequence of this was that the British force was at the moment of the hostile onslaught drawn up in a long line with intervals, the guns being on the right. While the Afghan cavalry fell upon the left of the line, the fanatic swordsmen attacked the front and centre. The infantry held their ground. On the right the guns kept the enemy off, although it was found necessary to withdraw them somewhat and to throw back this flank so as to form a front against the hostile onslaught on this side ; some squadrons were also sent to prolong the line here. The attack of horsemen on the left, in the meantime, had caused considerable confusion, the native cavalry being caught at such a disadvantage that the Afghan horsemen were eventually only checked by the infantry in rallying squares. Finally with the great development of fire which the long line was able to bring to bear, the enemy was repulsed with overwhelming slaughter.

Matters had been critical for a few moments because of the tremendously sudden nature of the hostile attack, for which on so large a scale previous operations in Afghanistan had afforded no precedent. But a defensive line of battle, taken up more or less at haphazard, proved excellently adapted to the circumstances. And the reason of this was that it admitted of a great development of fire.

At the fight of Tokar in 1891, the Egyptian troops were suddenly attacked by the Mahdists in great force, but managed at the last moment to occupy a semi-circular position supported by the ruined buildings of the old village. Formed up roughly in line, they beat off the enemy. The Arabs worked round the flanks, however, and caused some havoc among the baggage in rear.

Colonel Macdonald's brigade beat off formidable enveloping attacks at Khartum by dint of changes of front in line. The combat is described on pp. 387, 388.

The flanks are in fact the great difficulty. The enemy instinctively shirks the frontal fire of the line, and in consequence the attack of irregular warriors is almost always enveloping. Zulus, Sudanese, and Moors are all equally addicted to sweeping round the flanks of their opponents, and at Adowa the Abyssinian attacks were so delivered as to envelope the separate brigades of the Italians. Guns on the flanks are excellent, as shown at Ahmed Khel; but if so placed their fire may be lost to a great extent at the start. Artillery pushed out well to the front of either flank at the outset and withdrawn later to cover the flanks, is an excellent arrangement; the objection to it is that, with troops which cannot thoroughly be depended upon—native auxiliaries for instance—the sight of the guns retiring may have a bad effect, and withdrawing the artillery even a small distance certainly gives the enemy encouragement. At Maiwand the withdrawal of the smooth bore guns from want of ammunition appears to have had a very unfortunate result.

Difficulty as to flanks.

In discussing defensive tactics in small wars, theory must to a large extent take the place of teachings from actual campaigns. The spirit of attack animates the regular troops and their leaders in this warfare, and defensive actions are therefore the exception and not the rule. History cannot in fact be drawn upon to the same extent as in dealing with offensive tactics.

Occupying a position and awaiting attack in it, leaves to the enemy the choice of fighting or not fighting. Some opponents when in fighting mood may be trusted to attack, but they can never be depended upon to do so with absolute certainty, and if the enemy declines action there is some risk of no fighting coming off, which is of course in most cases a most undesirable consummation. Therefore when a

The enemy may decline to attack.

position is held in these campaigns in the hope that it will be attacked, arrangements should generally have been made to quit it and to assume the offensive in case the opponents shirk the engagement. The Mahdists seldom showed disinclination for battle at the outset of a campaign, but the action at Agordat in 1893 shows that even these reckless fanatics could not always be tempted into assaulting a position which had been prepared to meet their attack.

In preparation for the advance of a large force of the enemy, the Italian troops had occupied and prepared a position for defence. The Mahdist army approached, but passed by on the other side. The Italian general determined to force a fight, so he moved out of his position towards the hostile army. Under the altered circumstances the Dervishes at once accepted battle. The enemy attacked with great spirit, compelling the Italians to fall back a little with the loss of their guns by the suddenness of the onset. Then, however, the effect of arms of precision speedily began to tell, the troops advanced again, recovering the guns, and in the end completely dispersed the enemy.

Conclusion.
It sometimes comes about that a body of regular troops falling back before irregular warriors, can turn the tide by occupying a strong position. As, however, some special points with regard to retreats deserve notice and can best be dealt with in a separate chapter, defensive tactics under such special conditions will be most advantageously treated under that heading. The whole question of the defensive in small wars is wrapped up very much with that of squares and of defence works. A brave and enterprising enemy acting in masses brings about the system of laagers, zeribas, and squares. But as a rule the antagonists with whom regular troops have to cope in small wars, do not fight in this fashion and they should be attacked without hesitation unless very strong grounds exist for not doing so. Resolute initiative is the secret of success. A defensive attitude is generally unsound in principle, and it is not assumed in practice without good reason by a leader who understands how to deal with irregular warriors.

CHAPTER XIV.

PURSUITS AND RETREATS.

THE question of pursuits and retreats is in small wars to no <small>Enemy not</small> small degree influenced by a peculiarity of irregular warriors, <small>prepared for a vigorous</small> so marked in most cases as to be a distinctive characteristic. <small>pursuit if beaten, or for</small> This is that after the first excitement they are slow at following <small>following up</small> up a victory and that on the other hand they are not prepared <small>their victory with energy</small> for being vigorously pursued if beaten. "Nothing," says <small>if triumphant.</small> Lord Wolseley, "will demoralize the undisciplined enemy more than rapidity of movement and an unhesitating display of energy and a constantly renewed and prolonged effort on your part. If he on his part obtains a victory, its very success seems to exhaust him and render his subsequent movements slow. He halts to plunder or to rejoice over his victory, and is correspondingly dazed and panic-stricken if, when you obtain a success, it operates upon you in different fashion and quickens your movements and gives increased energy to the blows you follow it up with."

Irregular warriors once defeated are so apt to become panic- <small>Their mobility</small> stricken, that regular troops following in pursuit can generally <small>makes them</small> act with great boldness ; this applies not only to savages and <small>difficult to pursue.</small> semi-civilised races, but also to guerillas of a higher type. But, on the other hand, the rapidity with which such opponents naturally make off renders effective pursuit very difficult. Irregular warriors when beaten on the battle-field withdraw at first with the utmost celerity and vanish from the scene of conflict with quite dramatic suddenness ; but after having gone some miles they do not anticipate being followed up and they are greatly dismayed if they do not then find them-selves safe. This being so, it is obvious that a force of cavalry

at hand on the battle-field, ready to be launched against the
enemy when he gives way, is most essential; otherwise the
extreme mobility of the fugitives enables them to evade
their pursuers. "To have a few parties of horsemen ready to
follow up is a most important point if a decisive tactical
triumph is contemplated—more so than is the case in regular
warfare. Undisciplined forces when beaten become a mere
flying rabble at the mercy of the troopers, and travel too fast
for infantry to get on terms with them. In small wars the lack
of mounted troops for this purpose has often been greatly felt.
In the early days of the Indian Mutiny, during General Havelock's advance from Allahabad to Cawnpore, and afterwards
from Cawnpore to Lucknow, want of cavalry prevented the
full fruits of the brilliant successes gained over the rebels in
successive fights from being reaped. After the fight at
Kwintana in Kaffir-land in 1877, again mentioned on p. 232,
the small force of mounted men was insufficient to carry
out an effective pursuit. Hicks Pasha had no cavalry at
Marabia when his square so signally defeated the Mahdists;
once these were out of range of guns and rifles they were
safe.

Infantry in
pursuit.

But it must not be supposed that because, to start with,
infantry finds itself quite unable to catch irregular warriors
who have been vanquished in combat, it should necessarily
on this account despair of coming up with them again. If
there be no cavalry available to keep the enemy on the move
there is always considerable probability of hostile bodies
never dreaming that the victors will have the energy and
resolution to push on again immediately after their triumph,
collecting again after having fled panic-stricken for some miles.
When undisciplined forces, who have been driven pell-mell
from their ground, and who have reassembled some distance
from the battle-field thinking that their rapid flight has
secured them from further attack for a time, suddenly see
the troops pressing on them, they realise that they are dealing

with a foe who means business. A strenuous pursuit, even if
it be slow, always has a great effect.

It is impossible to insist too strongly on the importance Need for great
of determined and vigorous pursuit. The remarkable achieve- vigour.
ments of small British forces in the Indian Mutiny were largely
the result of the extraordinary efforts of all ranks to make
every successive victory as complete as possible by following
up the defeated mutineers relentlessly. Great liberties can be
taken by mere handfuls of men in these cases, owing to the
inevitable demoralization of irregular warriors after they have
been beaten. Still, opposed to wily antagonists it is well to
make sure that they really are beaten and are not playing some
trick ; it is advisable to keep a careful look out for ambushes
even when the foe appears to be in full flight.

A good instance of this energetic following up of the enemy is supplied
by the sequel to Sir C. Campbell's victory at Cawnpore. The cavalry and
horse artillery had, before the action, been sent to make a long detour
so as to be ready to fall upon the hostile line of retreat; but owing to
mistaking the route they were not at hand when the mutineers broke. The
infantry could do nothing, so Sir C. Campbell took a field battery and with
his own staff and escort dashed after the enemy. Several guns were
captured and fortunately, just when the swarms of fugitives were becoming
too thick for this singular pursuing force to continue its intrepid career, the
missing mounted troops turned up and completed what had been so well
begun.

Owing to the rapid flight of irregular warriors after a Detached
reverse, it is often expedient before commencing the action force to strike
to have a detached force thrown well round the hostile flank retreat.
ready to pounce down upon the enemy when he retreats.
This is an extension of the principle, already enunciated in
the chapter on Tactics of Attack, of flank attacks which will
bring part of the force within striking distance of the opponent's rear. There is, of course, the risk which attends all
detached movements, that the force designed to strike in on
the hostile line of retreat may not for some reason reach its
place in time—the cases of Cawnpore above mentioned, and
of Ali Musjid referred to on p. 168, might be cited as

examples. But a manœuvre of this class if brought off successfully can hardly fail to add greatly to the completeness of the victory, and it may prove to be the only means of striking at the enemy when in retreat. When such an arrangement forms part of the scheme of operations, it is of course advisable that the detached troops should keep their presence concealed to the last possible moment owing to the terror which undisciplined forces always display if their rear is threatened ; a premature appearance may upset the whole plan of action.

Tendency of the enemy to disperse in all directions.

It has already been remarked that in this class of warfare effective pursuit is rendered especially difficult by the tendency of the enemy to disperse in all directions when defeated. The fact that some of the adversaries met with in these campaigns evince extraordinary courage does not much affect this. Fanatics who attack with the most reckless daring are in this respect little better than the most cowardly among the lower races, once they see that victory is hopeless and the battle over, it becomes with them a genuine *sauve qui peut*. It is an inconvenient habit of irregular warriors that if they get a moment's respite after defeat they conceal their arms and pose as harmless people of the country, in which rôle they cannot well be molested by the troops—this frequently occurred in the Indian Mutiny, and it happened also after the battle of Kandahar. The tendency of the enemy to dissolve completely, makes pursuit in certain respects especially difficult ; but it must not be forgotten that it benefits the regular troops in that very small parties can venture great distances afield when following up a beaten foe. In any case it imposes upon the commander, and upon subordinates who may see an opportunity of acting decisively, the duty of following up a success instantly so as if possible to come up with the fugitives before they have time to scatter and elude their pursuers.

The terrain is of course frequently such as to render effective pursuit virtually impossible. Cavalry can very rarely act in the Indian hills, and infantry is soon out-distanced by the agile tribesmen. In the bush it is simply impossible to keep up with the enemy in flight. In such theatres of war as Daghestan and Trans-caucasia, as New Zealand and Achin, as Dahomey and Ashanti, victories have rarely been completed by a successful pursuit. In hill warfare and in bush warfare this difficulty as to following up successes is in fact one of the chief obstacles in the way of a decisive campaign.

If by any chance the enemy retreats in some semblance of order, guns and cavalry have a great chance just as is the case in regular warfare. Such conditions are somewhat unusual. When they occur the pursuit must be executed with no less vigour than when the enemy has dispersed ; care must however be taken that the troops following up the fugitives do not become too much broken up ; the operation must in fact be kept thoroughly under control. The object of pursuit is to convert the retreat into a rout and to give a *coup de grace* to the formation and the cohesion of the beaten force, already seriously shaken by what has gone before. For Use of cavalry such work horse artillery in association with cavalry is of and horse course invaluable if the ground be suitable ; in the Indian pursuit. Mutiny this combination on more than one occasion achieved most striking results in pursuit.

The affair at Jaora-Alipore after the defeat of Tantia Topi at Gwalior by Sir H. Rose is a remarkable example. 600 sabres and a horse artillery battery under Colonel Napier were, after some delay, sent in pursuit of the rebels. The enemy was found 4,000 strong, with 25 guns posted in a favourable position. But the stand was of short duration, the rebels being routed with the loss of all their guns and baggage.

The conduct of a retreat is justly held to be the most Retreats. trying of all operations of war. It is always easier to play a winning than a losing game, no matter who may be the opponent. But in face of irregular warriors retrograde move-ments present certain features of special difficulty.

(10830)   o 2

　　　Retreat after a reverse at the hands of such antagonists is
generally rendered particularly awkward by the necessity of
carrying off the wounded. This is of course always indispensable when fighting against uncivilized foes. It constitutes
one of the greatest difficulties which regular troops have to
contend with in hill warfare. It is also a serious impediment
to their operations in bush warfare, and even in open country
the presence of a convoy of wounded with an army retreating
in face of adversaries who massacre all who fall into their
hands, greatly aggravates the anxieties of a situation which
is, at the best, an unfavourable one. It is always desirable,
when it can be done with safety, to send off the sick and
those who have been placed *hors de combat* in action well in
advance before the retirement commences. But if the
enemy be in a position to envelope the flanks or to strike in
on the line of retreat, or if—as was the case at Maiwand and
Adowa—the people of the country through which the withdrawal takes place offer hostility, it is obviously unsafe to
detach the helpless from the immediate protection of the
army. It may even be necessary to adopt the awkward
square formation in such a case, and the retirement of the
whole force is sure to be retarded very seriously.

Retreat draws
down upon
the troops the
waverers in
the hostile
ranks.
　　　One of the most unfortunate results of the retreat of a
force of regulars engaged with uncivilized antagonists is that
it tends to convert the waverers in the hostile ranks into active
participants in the fighting. It is very generally the case in this
class of warfare that when a fight is imminent, crowds of the
people of the country assemble at a safe distance to watch its
course, ready to join in the fray if their compatriots should gain
the upper hand. If the disciplined army achieves a victory
they quietly disperse, but if it is defeated they are the first to
rush down upon it and to inflict all the injury they can. Many
examples of this might be given—the case of the attempted
relief of Kahan mentioned on p. 61 is a typical one. At
Charasia the hills all round the scene of conflict were crowned

with tribesmen who would have at once thrown themselves into the mêlée had Sir F. Roberts' slender force failed to drive the Afghan troops from their formidable position. In the combat at Tokar in 1891 only part of the Dervish assemblage actually attacked the Egyptian troops, the remainder held off aloof waiting for the result of the sudden rush which Osman Digna had arranged. The commander of a body of disciplined troops who finds himself obliged to retreat from a battle-field is very likely to find the forces which have already successfully opposed him doubled, and even trebled, just when that most difficult of all operations of war, a retreat, has to be commenced.

Numbers of instances might be cited to prove the eagerness of irregular warriors to take immediate advantage of their adversaries' retreat. Their efforts may soon relax in pursuit, but at the outset this is full of energy and confidence. If the regular troops recoil before them they swoop down exultingly upon the foes whom they think they have overthrown. In the excitement of supposed victory their leaders lose what little control over them they had. The change is instantaneous. One moment, as they feel the pressure of discipline and superior armament weighing heavily upon them, they are dejected, demoralized, bent chiefly on escape. The next, when they see their dreaded adversaries halt and turn, they become stirred with the wildest enthusiasm and rush out recklessly giving their pent-up ferocity full vent. *Enemy's eagerness at first to follow up a retiring force.*

At Denghil Tepe in 1875, the Turkomans, who had been utterly disheartened by the Russian bombardment, and who had only manned the ramparts of their fortress in despair when they found themselves hemmed in, no sooner saw the assaulting columns falling back in confusion, than they charged out furiously after the Russian troops. Their counter-attack was delivered with tremendous force, and had it not been for the guns, Lomakin's little army might have been not only defeated but destroyed. Yet up to this moment the Turkomans had shown little inclination to meet their antagonists in battle. *Examples.*

The final advance of the Afghans at Maiwand, after they had for some hours hesitated to deliver an attack, seems to have been to a certain extent brought about by the retirement of some smooth bore guns ; these ran short of ammunition and were therefore ordered out of action.

At the remarkable action of Bang Bo, near Langson in Tonkin in 1885 referred to in Chapter XII, a French attack upon some Chinese entrenchments failed, almost for the first time during the campaign. The Chinese were much disheartened by successive defeats at this time. No sooner, however, did they see the hostile assaulting columns in retreat, than they came out after them and followed them up eagerly—so much so that the French were not only repulsed but nearly suffered a very serious disaster.

In 1852, a large gathering of the Mohmund tribe collected in the hills north of Shabkhadar, a fort near Peshawur where Sir C. Campbell was in command of the troops. One afternoon a large number of the enemy threatened a raid down from the hills into the plains and they actually advanced some distance on to the level. Sir C. Campbell issued from the fort with a small force of cavalry and two horse artillery guns, and, attacking the tribesmen in flank on fairly open ground, drove them into the hills with considerable loss. But as the evening began to close in, Sir Colin was obliged to fall back. The Mohmunds no sooner observed this than they turned back and followed up the little British force with great spirit, so much so that the guns were obliged several times to unlimber and fire grape shot. The force, however, regained the fort without serious loss.

Although irregular warriors at first keen in pursuit their ardour soon cools.

But if irregulars are keen in pursuit at the start their ardour soon cools and their energy is short lived. In the first enthusiasm of victory they are wildly excited and enthusiastic in pursuit, at the first symptoms of wavering in the ranks of the troops even those in the hostile ranks who have been hanging back irresolute and afraid, pluck up courage and are ready to dash to the front with the bravest. But, on the other hand, after the first flush of victory their enthusiasm rapidly dies away, the tension slackens and the temptation to stop and plunder becomes too great to resist. Such enemies do not grasp the importance of making their triumph complete and enduring ; if the leaders realise it they fail to keep their followers up to the mark. Once the battle is won undisciplined warriors think their task is over, most of them thirst for loot and those who do pursue do so in leisurely fashion, allowing the vanquished army to elude their clutches. It is not only savages and Asiatics who display this peculiarity, guerillas and insurgents have often shown the same tendency. Many examples might be quoted, but the following will serve.

After the very disastrous reverse suffered in the second attack on the Bemaru hills near Kabul by the British in 1841, the troops, although completely demoralized, were not followed up by the Afghans right back to the cantonments as they should have been. Had the enemy acted with vigour the whole army might have been destroyed.

Early in the Mutiny, after the outbreak of Dinapore, when the mutineers had gone off to Arrah and were besieging the little handful of Europeans at that place, a party was despatched from the cantonment to attempt the relief of the garrison by a night march. The force after marching unopposed in the dark to near Arrah, fell into an ambush, was surprised and was routed. But, nevertheless, the remnants of the detachment succeeded in getting back to their boats many miles off on the Ganges, and they escaped to Dinapore. Had the rebels pursued with determination the whole party, already exhausted by a trying night march, must have been annihilated.

The Afghan pursuit after Maiwand was feeble to a degree. For a mile or two the enemy followed up with the utmost determination and the 66th regiment, in endeavouring to stem the hostile advance by retiring fighting and with deliberation, suffered overwhelming losses; but as soon as that portion of the infantry which maintained a bold front was disposed of and the Afghan tactical triumph was complete, their pursuit slackened. A good deal of loss was suffered by the defeated troops on the way back to Kandahar from villagers, but little from Ayoub Khan's army.

After the French reverse at Bang Bo near the Tonkin frontier in 1885, the Chinese had a great opportunity of irreparably injuring the beaten force by a vigorous pursuit. But they followed up slowly and hesitated to press their antagonists close. This gave General Négrier's troops time to recover from defeat, and to meet the victors on level terms at Kailua a few days later, where an ample revenge was taken for the misfortune of Bang Bo.

After the battle of Adowa the Abyssinians made no attempt at an organized pursuit, although in their ranks were included formidable bodies of horse. The Italian troops happily ceased to be molested within a very few miles of the scene of disaster, except by the inhabitants of the district they were traversing, who turned out to harass the fugitives and to cut up stragglers although they gave formed bodies of soldiers a wide berth.

In the later stages of the South African war it happened on numerous occasions that detached British forces or independent columns were obliged to retire before Boer commandos or gatherings, often after having suffered to a certain extent a reverse. The Boers were, when they chose, very unpleasant as pursuers; they moved with great rapidity and dash, and as the British side was always hampered with a certain amount of transport, its extrication was often a source of great difficulty. But they seldom stuck to their work for long, and would sometimes abandon pursuit just when matters were beginning to look very ugly for the retreating force.

Annihilation of regular forces due generally to their being completely isolated or to special causes.

Where regular forces have been completely annihilated in these campaigns, as occurred to Hicks Pasha's army in the Sudan, the circumstances have generally been such that the beaten army was so placed that retreat was impossible. In the steppes Russian forces have similarly disappeared, victims of the enormous distances which in such a territory must be traversed to achieve a military object. The retreat from Kabul in 1841–42 was through difficult mountain defiles and gorges infested with foes ; the gradual extinction of the doomed army was far more due to the tribesmen between the Afghan capital and Gandamak than to the forces of Akbar Khan which followed at its heels. It must be remembered that the retreats which so often take place in hill warfare and which are frequently attended by serious loss are mere local movements as a rule ; they exemplify eagerness on the part of the enemy at the commencement of the retirement rather than obstinacy in a prolonged pursuit.

Beginning of retreat the critical period.

The critical time is, therefore, as a rule the commencement of the retrograde movement, especially in hill warfare, as pointed out further on, on p. 328. It is then that the enemy is eager and determined and that the foemen, coming on in great force, their fleetness of foot brings them easily to close quarters. It is generally essential to conduct the retreat as a whole with deliberation, and to offer as bold a front to the enemy as possible, because any precipitation will only tend to draw down greater hostile bodies upon the troops. At the initial stage the movement cannot be too deliberate, except when it is a case of slipping off unexpectedly ; the slightest haste or flurry may prove fatal. At this period the presence of a few guns is simply invaluable to a regular army ; they can keep the enemy at bay and can then retire very rapidly to a fresh position and come into action again. In the later stages of the South African war the chief rôle of the guns, which

generally formed part of each column, was to keep the enemy
at a distance in case of a retirement. Cavalry and mounted
infantry can act with great effect as long as the enemy does
not consist of mounted men, owing to the fact that they can
maintain their ground longer than foot soldiers without risking
being permanently separated from the main body, and can on
this account guarantee to the rest of the force a good start
when the retrograde movement is initiated.

When an army retires thus in face of opposition a rearguard General
is always formed to keep the enemy at bay ; the need for this organization
is the same in small wars as in campaigns between disciplined of a retreat.
armies. But before referring to the special duties of the rear
guard and to the great importance of the main body keeping
touch with it, it will not be out of place to quote the instructions of a French commander who a few years ago achieved a
notable success in irregular warfare, as to the general conduct
of retreats in such operations. General Duchesne's memoran- General
dum to his officers at the commencement of his campaign in orders.
Madagascar contains recommendations which very happily
sum up the principles on which such a movement should be
conducted.

" *Retreat.*—In principle, retirement is always a mistake. Against an
enemy such as this expeditionary force is going to encounter, real danger
only commences with retreat. A force which can advance no further
should halt on commanding ground as near as possible to the enemy,
should entrench itself, and should await reinforcements.

" If, in altogether exceptional circumstances, retreat cannot be avoided,
three or four positions in échelon should be occupied by small parties (a
section at the most), covering all paths which are practicable, and capable
of being evacuated without one party masking another. At the given signal
the line falls back unmasking the most advanced of these positions, the
troops in which will thereupon fire volleys ; under this protection the line
will retire slowly, reforming at the same time. When out of range of fire
it will resume the order of march. The parties left in position will retire
one after the other, covered by the fire of those most in rear.

" It is a good thing in such a case to place a section of artillery in a position
from which it can retire under cover, with some rounds ready to delay
the enemy by rapid fire."

This conveys the idea of how a retreat would commence when a disciplined force falls back in presence of irregulars. The covering troops must be posted beforehand in well chosen positions, so arranged that the bulk of the army retires through the intervals. The movement must be conducted slowly and deliberately, and great care must be taken not to mask the fire of the detachments left to hold their ground facing the enemy. These have a very difficult task to perform, and the period during which the main body is withdrawing from contact with the hostile forces is a most critical one, any error perhaps leading to a deplorable disaster. The covering troops must be disposed so as to shield the flanks if there is any probability of the enemy working round with the idea of throwing hostile bodies athwart the line of retreat. It must be remembered that when the necessity for retirement has been foreseen betimes, these covering troops can often be posted on very favourable ground and should be in a position to act with coolness and determination. They become the rear guard of the retreating army, and their responsibility is only beginning when the main body passes through them.

Note as to retreat in face of very determined adversaries who rely on shock tactics.
It must be understood that the system laid down by General Duchesne, and which is generally applicable to retreats in small wars, does not meet the case of withdrawals in face of an enemy like the Zulus or the ghazi. Such warriors, trusting as they do to shock tactics, would make short work of isolated detachments in echelon or any other formation. Retiring before antagonists of this class some form of square formation for the whole force is almost indispensable. The entire force must move in the compactest formation possible, and it should be understood that the remarks contained in the following paragraphs dealing with rear guards are not generally applicable to the conditions which combat with antagonists of the "fuzzy wuzzy" type or with swarms of irregular horse, necessarily involve.

No matter what class of adversary be pursuing, the duty of a rear guard to a retreating army is a most trying one. In regular warfare it must at times even sacrifice itself to save the main body ; in small wars, on the other hand, it would very seldom be called upon to do this. The fate of a force which sacrifices itself in regular warfare is military destruction—overwhelming loss in the first place, then surrender at discretion. But in conflict with savages and semi-civilized opponents, and even in many cases with guerillas in a civilized country, there is no such thing as surrender. The fate of the force which sacrifices itself in a small war is in most cases actual destruction, and it is only in very exceptional cases that any body of troops can be expected to undergo this. Moreover, owing to the tendency of the enemy to work round the flanks, and owing to the fact that retreat in one of these campaigns implies almost necessarily a march through districts infested with guerillas and where the whole population is up in arms and stirred to action by the exhilarating spectacle of the invaders retiring, it follows that, if a rear guard allows itself to get separated far from the main body, it will almost inevitably be cut off. This being the case, it is, under ordinary circumstances, the duty of the main body to keep touch with the rear guard, the relations between them differing in small wars from what is generally accepted as correct in operations more *en régle*. It is not in accordance with the theory of rear guard action in this class of warfare that it should halt and force the enemy to deploy—the enemy generally pursues as a great irregular swarm without military formation. The object is to keep the foe at bay, and to do so more or less on the move.

In small wars, contrary to what is generally accepted as correct in regular warfare, a rear guard is in fact almost always entitled to count on support from the main body. Their duties in regard to each other, therefore, differ very materially from what is ordinarily laid down in books on modern tactics. In

regular warfare the great object being for the bulk of the army
to be relieved from pressure of pursuit, this presses on at its
best pace ; in the meantime the rear guard conforms to its
movements as far as practicable, halting when necessary and
thereby compelling the enemy to change from column of route
to order of battle—a process which means delay. But retreating in face of irregular warriors, the rear guard cannot be
left in the lurch ; it must keep on the move and the main
body has to conform its pace to that of the troops left behind
to hold the enemy in check. This is a very important point,
and one which is sometimes overlooked. Indeed it is perhaps
even more important in retreat than it is when advancing, to
keep the whole force compact and well in hand. If the enemy
means mischief—that such opponents are not always keen in
pursuit has been pointed out in an earlier paragraph—he will
work round the flanks. The adversary far exceeds the regular
troops in mobility so that these cannot evade him if he does
not wish them to. Therefore if gaps occur between main
body and rear guard the enemy will almost inevitably break in,
separating the two, and as this exposes the tail of the main
body there will be trouble. Occasions will of course occur
when a small rear guard may be left to hold some particular
point for some special reason. But under ordinary circumstances
the main body must keep touch with it, and this must be
very careful not to let the enemy work round the flanks and
cut off connection with the troops especially detailed to guard
its own rear. In hill warfare, where rear guard duties are
especially trying, the importance of keeping touch cannot
be overrated ; but this point will be again dealt with in
Chapter XIX.

Withdrawal
of rear guards.   The principle on which rear guards should retire is different
in the case of small wars from the principle on which this
difficult manœuvre should be carried out when both sides
consist of regular troops. In modern tactics the accepted
method is for the rear guard to deploy from time to time,

to compel the pursuers to do likewise, and then to rapidly fall back by march route to another position. The rear guard operates as it were spasmodically, alternating between a bold stationary attitude and a hasty withdrawal more or less intact. But retiring before irregular warriors a rear guard must generally be handled on quite different lines.

In small wars the principle is that the rear guard is constantly on the move, one fraction of it always covering the withdrawal of the remainder. The idea is always to present a bold front to the enemy with a portion of the rear guard. The whole of it must never be on the move at once. Some detachments must be drawn up in position and standing still while the remainder pass them, ready in turn to halt so as to protect the withdrawal of those left behind. The exact method of course depends upon all manner of conditions— nature of terrain, composition of rear guard, activity of enemy, and so on—but the underlying principle of mutual co-operation between the troops on the move and those at the halt remains the same. Sometimes guns can be sent off first to take up a position further back and to cover the infantry which holds its ground while the artillery is on the move. At other times the enemy may be checked momentarily by the threat or actual attack of cavalry while the other arms take up a new position. Or again it may simply be a case of infantry detachments passing through each other's intervals. But in any case a considerable portion of the rear guard will always be on the march, and there will be a constant retrograde movement in progress.

It has been laid down in an earlier paragraph that a retreat must be carried out deliberately, because any precipitation will tend to encourage the enemy and to render the pursuit more deadly. This same principle holds good as regards the rate of progress of the rear guard as a whole, but not necessarily with regard to the actual pace of its component parts. The detachments in immediate contact with the hostile warriors must generally, when the time comes for them to fall back, make the best speed they can, trusting to the fire of the covering troops. As a matter of fact the spectacle of troops hurrying off is very likely to draw the enemy on, and to cause the more intrepid spirits among the pursuers to expose themselves.

Field guns and cavalry can of course get away easily enough if the flanks are safe, but infantry do not find this so easy. Still there is not merely the feeling of support, there is a very genuine support to the fugitives in the existence of covering detachments standing firm and possibly able to bring an effective cross fire to bear on the ground being evacuated. But that does not alter the fact that these fugitives, if they be infantry, must as a general rule move at a double, and they may be obliged to run as fast as ever they can. The enemy is generally very fleet of foot, and the men left behind at the extreme tail of the retreating army cannot use their arms when they are in the act of falling back ; they may, moreover, mask the fire of the units supporting them. It is especially in hill and bush warfare that this system has to be adopted, for in such operations the detachments left behind to the last generally consist of mere handfuls of men. Its value was fully established in the hill fighting on the Indian frontier in 1897. The instructions in " Combined Training " only touch very briefly on the subject of rear guards in savage warfare ; its general instructions as to rearguards hardly meet the case of irregular operations and do not take into account the very rapid movements of savages. The question will be again referred to in Chapters XIX and XX dealing with hill and jungle fighting.

On the veld in 1901–02 it often happened that rear guards consisting mainly if not entirely of mounted troops, had to keep pursuing Boers in check. The principles as to withdrawal laid down above were then adapted to the special peculiarities of the case. Some detachments held the foe at a

distance while others hurried on to take up new positions.
If the rear guard resisted too long it was outflanked, if it did
not resist long enough the enemy got close to the baggage or
whatever was being herded home. Its manœuvres as a whole
consisted of part of it being constantly on the move and of
none of it halting for long. The forces generally being small
practically the whole of the combatants often formed the
rear guard, while the carts, wagons and impedimenta retired
at their best speed out of danger.

If the worst comes to the worst and the rear guard finds Counter-
itself cut off and severely pressed, a bold counter-attack will attack
often retrieve the situation. If this counter-attack can be the wisest
combined with the seizure of some valuable tactical pivot rear guard is
offering advantages for defence, it will sometimes bring the in serious
pursuers completely to a standstill. It must, however, be difficulty.
remembered that when the rear guard, or part of it, thus
transforms its attitude from one of steady retrograde movement into one of temporary advance or of standing fast,
the rearmost troops of the retiring main body, and also the
connecting links between this and the rear guard, run great
risk of being assailed in great force, because the enemy is sure
to be working round the flanks of the rear guard. Moreover
there is a probability that the main body will move on some
distance before it realizes that the rear guard is no longer
following it, and that the rear guard will in consequence be
left isolated and without support. All these points must be
carefully weighed when the decision is being taken. The
maintenance of touch between all parts of the force and skilful
arrangements on the part of those in command may obviate
these inconveniences and dangers ; but they are very likely
to occur and to create an awkward situation, especially so in
hill warfare.

The question of retirements in hill warfare will be again
dealt with in Chapter XIX, and will be illustrated by recent
examples. But the value of a sudden assumption of the

offensive when a rear guard is in serious danger will often be so great, and it is so desirable to emphasize its importance, that the following episode from the Tirah campaign may well be related here. It was a very remarkable feat of arms ; moreover a minor disaster which attended the operation serves to show the awkward position in which detachments between a rear guard and its main body may be placed owing to touch having been lost.

Lieut.-Col. Haughton at the retreat from the Tseri Kandao Pass.

A brigade had been sent on detached duty into the Waran valley, and after completing its work there was rejoining the rest of the army in Maidan. In doing so the brigade had to cross the Tseri Kandao Pass over the hills which separate the two valleys.

As the force quitted its bivouacs the Gurkhas were left as rear guard, while the 15th Sikhs were told off to hold the kotal which was about half way. The main body and baggage moved off early, and the latter reached Maidan almost unmolested. The Gurkhas, however, were pressed from the commencement of the retirement right up to the top of the kotal ; then they marched on leaving the 15th Sikhs to cover the retirement. As the Sikhs began to draw in their picquets from the heights above the pass the Afridis, as was their wont, grew bolder and bolder, and, taking advantage of the cover of a wood hard by, they crept down close to the rear guard. One company as it withdrew was suddenly charged by a crowd of swordsmen—almost the only occasion during the campaign on which the Afridis attempted a mode of fighting for which Pathans were formerly noted. But those who participated in this rush paid dearly for their temerity, the Sikh company meeting them with steady musketry and being most opportunely reinforced by another company. The carrying off of the wounded was, however, becoming a matter of serious difficulty ; so reinforcements were asked for. These arrived in the shape of two companies of Dorsets and of several companies of the 36th Sikhs under Lieut.-Colonel Haughton, who assumed command and who withdrew his force down the hill without much loss.

It was now getting dusk. The pursuit had been checked effectually. All the wounded had been sent on well in advance, and Colonel Haughton was debating how best to get through the awkward ground which lay at the foot of the hills, when suddenly the rear guard found itself fired into from all sides. The Afridis had learnt the danger of attacking the Sikhs in the open from their experience near the kotal, and had seen no chance of employing their tactics effectually in view of the skilful dispositions adopted as the rear-guard descended the slopes, but they had evidently been creeping round the flanks and now hoped to reap the benefit. There were still some miles of awkward ground to traverse. Night was closing in. The terrain hard by was intersected and broken. The situation was perilous and the outlook none too promising, but the resolute and skilful leadership of the commander averted the danger that was threatening.

Colonel Haughton perceived that the moment had come for a bold stroke. A heavy fire was being poured in from some houses 300 yards off to the flank. He fixed bayonets, and took his men against them with a rush. The Dorsets and Sikhs were upon the tribesmen almost before these realised what was impending. Some of the buildings were captured without very serious loss. Then, making the best of such defensive capabilities as the dwellings offered, the rear guard passed the night where it was, hemmed in to a certain extent and under fire, but nevertheless in comparative safety. At daylight it withdrew without much molestation and met the relieving force which had been sent out to its assistance.

But although the rear guard had by its well-timed counter-stroke saved itself from a situation full of peril, one most unfortunate episode had occurred which could not have been foreseen. When reinforcements were pushed up to help the 15th Sikhs, a half company of Dorsets had been left to hold a well-placed house near the road, so as to act as a *point d'appui* for the rear guard to retire on. The point where Colonel Haughton delivered his counter-attack and where he passed the night was some little distance short of the post which the half company had occupied ; but this party, hearing movements along the road below it, mistook the passers by for the rear guard, and, retiring from its house under this false impression, it suffered very severely in making its way to camp in the dark

Retreat is always a difficult operation, but regular troops Conclusion. obliged to fall back are in an especially awkward position in small wars. In warfare on the Continent between civilized armies, pursued and pursuers move at approximately the same pace, and if the retreating infantry keeps an unshaken front it has not very much to fear even from the pursuing cavalry. But this is not the case in small wars, where the enemy can always easily outpace the infantry. Therefore battalions, companies, or sections left to form front against the foes hanging on the rear of the retreating army, while the remainder move off, find it most difficult to extricate themselves when once embroiled. It is a most trying operation for the best troops ; but it is a point in their favour that, if they come through the ordeal of the first hour or two with success, they can generally hope to escape serious molestation afterwards. The tribesmen of the Indian hills have, it must be admitted, sometimes conducted pursuits with remarkable obstinacy, but this is not usual with irregular warriors. Even if their leaders recognize the necessity of following up success with vigour, the rank and file will not second their efforts. In regular warfare beaten troops are, from the tactical point of view, in reality in greater peril because the enemy's pursuit does not then cease on the confines of the battle-field —the victors come trampling on, resolved to leave no stone unturned to make their triumph assured. The difference is very marked, and the point is deserving of attention inasmuch as it involves an important principle of war.

CHAPTER XV.

The employment of feints to tempt the enemy into action, and to conceal designs upon the battle-field.

It is strange that the commanders of regular forces should Drawing the enemy on. so often succeed in small wars in drawing the enemy into action by subterfuge and stratagem. Irregular warriors individually possess the cunning which their mode of life engenders. Their chieftains are subtle and astute. All orientals have an inborn love of trickery and deception, the Red Indians have won an evil notoriety by their duplicity and craftiness, and even mere savages like the Maoris and the Kaffirs are constantly imposing upon regular troops by many forms of tactical artifice. But in spite of this, history affords numerous examples of such antagonists being lured out of strong positions or enticed into unfavourable situations, by bodies of trained soldiers handled skilfully—so much is this indeed the case that the subject merits a special chapter, the more so because the system can be turned to account both in attack and in defence.

That adversaries so strongly addicted to the employment Reasons why this can so often be carried out. of ruses and feints should often be so easily deceived themselves is, no doubt, in no small degree due to their contempt for the stolid methods of regular warfare. They see how cramped the movements are of the troops who have come to fight them. Lying in ambush to cut off stragglers, lurking by night around outposts, watching the camp routine of the regular army, they perceive that it is by the system of partizan warfare that they can best offer it resistance. Experience shows them that at this sort of work they often prove

more than a match for the trained soldier, and so they come
to underrate the capacity of their antagonists for turning the
tables upon them and for employing stratagem and artifice
upon their side.

The great importance of moral effect in these wars has
been already dealt with in earlier chapters, and the impressionable nature of the opponents whom the regular troops have
to combat in such operations, becomes a potent factor when
this question of feints comes up for consideration; it exposes
them to be enticed into premature attacks, or to be drawn
out of positions which they may have taken up deliberately
and with a sound appreciation of the military conditions
obtaining. If they are readily cowed by the steady advance
and resolute bearing of the regular army on the march and
in attack, they are also singularly quick at discerning signs
of wavering or of retrogression on its part, and this a
resourceful commander when he has such foes to deal with will
from time to time be able to turn to account.

How enemy's
eagerness to
follow up a
retiring force
can be turned
to account.

Examples illustrating the promptitude with which the
enemy turns upon the regular troops if these fall back, and of
the spasmodic intrepidity with which they throw themselves
into a pursuit in the first flush of triumph, might be multiplied—this characteristic has already been dealt with in
considering retreats. It is a feature of their mode of war
and one always to be reckoned with. Following an enemy up
persistently may not be understood by irregular warriors; but
they start a pursuit full of vigour and eagerness for the fray.
Now a wary commander who has his forces well in hand can
sometimes reap distinct benefit from this peculiarity of savage
and semi-civilized foemen. By simulating a retreat, or by a
well-timed show of hesitation, he can induce the hostile forces
to place themselves in a position of tactical disadvantage.
With some adversaries it is only by some such plan as this
that they can be got to put up a fight at all. Hill-men and
savages of parts of Africa dwelling in the bush are very difficult

to meet in open ground, they stick to their cover obstinately and never give the troops a chance unless, in hope of loot or excited to it by seeing the troops fall back, they rush out, carried away by an uncontrollable impulse.

Even when the adversaries are well disciplined and thoroughly under the control of their leaders, the excitement of seeing the regular troops wavering or in retreat snaps the ties which place them in subordination. In the enthusiasm of supposed victory they get out of hand. It is indeed noteworthy that this loosening of the bonds of discipline in a moment of success is not confined alone to the side opposing the regular forces. Most European nations employ native soldiers and local levies to a certain extent in the small wars which they become involved in. Experience has proved that the Sudanese troops of the Egyptian army, splendid fighting material as they are, can scarcely be controlled when they see the enemy on the run. In Tonkin the Turco officers used in the heat of action to make their men lie down and cease firing to make them tractable. The leaders may suspect a trap, but they cannot always check the rush to the front of men not thoroughly trained as soldiers, who see a prize almost within their grasp and fear to lose it. This being so, it is little wonder that bands of fanatics, of cut-throat mountaineers or African savages, cannot be kept in hand under such circumstances by their chieftains. *Hostile leaders cannot control their followers.*

A typical example of a successful feint is afforded by the battle of Kambula. The incident about to be related is an excellent illustration of the manner in which a commander of trusty troops may draw an enemy into premature attack, and by doing so may render a signal service to the entire force of which his detachment forms a part. It must be borne in mind that the Zulus, ill-armed and poorly organized as they were, were comparatively speaking highly disciplined and that they ordinarily obeyed implicitly those set in authority over them. *The Zulus drawn into premature attack at Kambula.*

The Zulu army marching to attack Kambula divided into three columns as it drew near the camp. One circled round the position to the right, another took a direction to the left, the centre moved straight on it. The right column reached its position first and halted out of range of the guns, whereupon Colonel Wood sent out the mounted men under Lieutenant-Colonels Russell and Buller to engage this right column. They rode up close to it, dismounted, and opened fire. Zulu discipline could not restrain the mass from springing up and bearing down upon the party of horsemen; these promptly remounted, and keeping up a running fight with the impi drew it on till it was close to the laager. There the Zulus came under heavy fire from the infantry on very open ground, and they lost so severely that they were compelled to fall back under the cover of some rocks and took no more part in the action. A third of the hostile army was, in fact, disastrously defeated before the regular attack upon the British position began.

Other examples.

This drawing the enemy on by pretended retirement or by sending out a small force to entice the hostile forces into premature action, as at Kambula, has been frequently practised with great success in this sort of warfare. At Sikak, the only regular battle which Abd el Kader attempted with the French troops, the fact that General Bugeaud was compelled to shirk engagement for a time on account of the need of getting his convoy into a place of security, really drew the Emir's forces on and committed them to a definite trial of strength so that the general was able to fight them on ground favourable to himself. The manœuvre is a time-honoured one and was often practised in the days when armies fought in compact masses under the absolute control of their chief. The Normans employed it with conspicuous success at Hastings. Regulars have generally used it with best results against less organized bodies. In 1521 Barbarossa lured the Arabs, Berbers, and Kabyles out of their entrenched camps at Millel by this ruse, and then inflicted a crushing defeat upon them. Jomini relates how in 1799 the French attacking Naples, which was being defended by the populace, pretended to retreat after they had gained a footing in the city, drawing the lazzaroni after them; having got the rabble clear of the streets the troops turned upon the defenders, beat them in the open, and forced their way through the streets at their heels.

Modern small wars afford some excellent examples of feints of this kind. They have often been practised in hill warfare and jungle operations, which will be dealt with in later chapters. They have been found practicable even in engagements on an important scale, and of this the following incident in the Mutiny may be quoted as an instance :—

Sir H. Havelock on his first advance from Cawnpore for the relief of the residency at Lucknow, found the rebels holding the village of Onao and drove them out of it. The space was somewhat restricted by swamps on either side of the high road by which he was advancing. Perceiving strong hostile reinforcements pressing up, he withdrew some way from the village to a favourable position where his troops were partially concealed. The enemy, encouraged by his retreat, came on to attack him, and so fell into the trap. The British suddenly opened fire, detachments wading through the swamps demonstrated against the hostile flanks, and the rebels fled, abandoning 15 guns.

In suppressing insurrections regular troops may be able to use this stratagem with good effect even when their opponents are intelligent and well armed ; those in revolt have not the cohesion or the trust in their leaders requisite to enable these to hold them back. A remarkable example of this occurred in 1821 during the Wallachian insurrection against Ottoman rule. *Value of the stratagem of pretended retreat in insurrectionary wars.*

The commander of a Turkish force, learning that a rebel battalion, specially noted as the holy battalion, was in the vicinity, sent some dismounted troopers to seek it out. The party of horsemen on coming up with the enemy left their horses under cover and advanced on foot. The battalion, taking the troopers for infantry, charged them at once and pursued them back to the village where their horses were. The Turks then mounted and suddenly fell upon the rebels, scattered as they were, and with their muskets unloaded. Being almost defenceless the Wallachians were nearly all cut down.

In this case it is seen how well adapted cavalry is for this sort of work. At the action of Futtehabad near Jellalabad in 1879 the cavalry and horse artillery were very successful in drawing a formidable body of Shinwarris out of a strong position while the infantry were coming up. The case of *Cavalry especially well adapted for this sort of work.*

Kambula already mentioned shows how effectively mounted infantry assumes the rôle of decoy, for in most cases the cavalry must act dismounted to produce a good result. Cavalry is, however, almost always preferable, because if the horses can be kept concealed there is not only a good chance of drawing on the enemy but opportunity may also offer of delivering very effective charges upon the adversaries when these are advancing in disorder. The following two examples may be given in support of that from the Wallachian war of independence, which has been quoted above :—

In 1860, a large body of Waziris without provocation made a raid from their hills into the plain near Tank, with the intention of sacking that town. Ressaldar Saadat Khan commanding the troop of cavalry at Tank collected some other mounted levies and advanced to meet the Waziris. He found them in awkward ground near the hills, but by retiring he gradually lured them right out into open country. Then suddenly he turned, first cut them off from the hills and then with his 200 sabres charged them. The enemy numbering 3,000 was thrown into complete confusion. The whole mass fled precipitately. 300 were killed, and many were wounded including the head man of the tribe. The cavalry in this brilliant exploit only lost one man killed, and a few wounded.

At the end of the Kaffir war in 1878, a mixed British and Colonial force was in position at a place called Kwintana. It was threatened by both the Galekas and the Gaikas, of which the latter (it afterwards transpired) were being held back by their chief Sandilli who did not think an attack opportune. To bring on a fight the mounted troopers were sent out with orders to advance and to then retire in haste before the enemy. The stratagem proved perfectly successful. The Galekas eagerly followed up the mounted troops as they fell back, and the Gaikas could no longer be restrained and joined them. The infantry was kept concealed in trenches till the Kaffirs were within easy range, then a few volleys sufficed to utterly defeat them.

Enticing the enemy into an ambuscade.

In this latter case the enemy was really drawn into a skilfully planned ambush. The French in Algeria managed on several occasions to profit by similar artifices, their commanders whose names grew famous in the years of warfare which followed on the capture of Algiers—Lamoricière Changarnier, Saint Arnaud, &c.—acquiring great skill in operations of this class. "War," says an Arab proverb, "is stratagem applied by force." Abd el Kader and his satellites were past masters in the art of carrying out surprises and planning ambuscades, and the French learnt this method of conducting war from those who they had come to conquer. One illustration from these operations will suffice.

Four battalions were marching over the pass of Muzaia in 1840, when they learnt that the Arabs were at hand in force. The baggage under one battalion was quickly sent off, two battalions were hidden in a fold of the ground close to the route, the fourth battalion, by getting touch with the enemy and then retreating rapidly, drew the hostile forces after them into the ambuscade which had been prepared. The two battalions which had been concealed suddenly charged out with the bayonet upon the Arabs, and threw them into complete confusion.

By a show of weakness, accidental or intended, irregular forces are often completely misled. That the enemy may sometimes be drawn on to a certain extent unintentionally was well shown at the action of Arogee in Abyssinia in 1868. In this engagement the Abyssinians were enticed out of a formidable position by a disposition of the regular forces which had not been ordained with the idea of drawing the enemy into the open. *Enemy sometimes drawn on unintentionally.*

Examples of Arogee and Nis Gol.

King Theodore's forces occupied some heights very difficult of access, covering the approaches to Magdala and overlooking a plateau upon which the British force necessarily debouched as it advanced upon the Abyssinian stronghold. The baggage of the leading brigade, moving by a different route to the bulk of the brigade, approached this plateau practically abreast of the rest of the troops. King Theodore, observing that the train of mules was apparently unprotected, ordered his soldiery to rush down and seize the booty. The British troops were hurried across to confront the enemy and to protect the baggage, and they moved so rapidly that they met the hostile swarms on the plateau where there was no advantage of position favouring the Abyssinians. The result was a decisive victory with trifling loss, which completely demoralized the King's forces and which paved the way for the capture of the mountain fortress a few days later without encountering serious opposition.

The march of Colonel Kelly's force to relieve Chitral in 1895 affords an interesting illustration of an unintentional feint on a small scale.

The enemy was holding some groups of sangars on the far side of the Nis Gol ravine near Mastuj barring the road to Chitral. The fire of the troops was beginning to have its effect, and when it was perceived that the Chitralis were preparing to evacuate their defences arrangements were made to cross the ravine, which was a very awkward precipitous sided nullah. The sappers and one company began scrambling down at one point with the assistance of ropes and ladders, but, after a few of the party had descended it so happened that a bullet struck some gun-cotton on the top and ignited it; the remainder of the men were thereupon ordered to retire a short way for fear of an explosion. Seeing this the enemy at once advanced defiantly out of their sangars on the other side. On quitting their cover the tribesmen came under so heavy a fire from companies preparing to descend by the road, that they fled right across the open, and numbers of them were shot down.

Drawing the enemy on by exposing baggage, etc.   The case of Arogee shows how the enemy will sometimes be drawn into attack by the hope of booty. The baggage column appeared to offer a tempting prey to the Abyssinians, although its march was not designed by the British commander with the idea of drawing them down from their formidable position. What occurred on that occasion shows that such opponents can sometimes be lured into action by exposing baggage, transport, cattle and so forth, apparently inviting capture. The undisciplined fighting man revels in pillage, and is difficult to restrain in any case if he sees booty apparently at his mercy; in rebellions the enemy may be moved by patriotism or may be stirred to action by some supposed wrong, but in most small wars the forces which the regular troops meet on the battle-field are really fighting mainly from the love of loot. Plunder is their motive in keeping the field, they fight for fighting's sake because a victory means spoil, and such adversaries can be trapped readily if the bait be tempting enough and if the escort be kept out of sight.

Drawing enemy on by artillery fire.   Although not exactly a feint Colonel Macdonald's use of the guns with his brigade at Khartum for drawing the enemy on deserves mention here.

The problem was to induce a mass of Dervishes who were preparing to attack from the west to deliver their onslaught before another mass to the north, also preparing to attack, delivered theirs. Colonel Macdonald ordered his batteries to open fire on the western force, and the effect was instantaneous. The Dervishes swarmed down from that side and the artillery and infantry fire just succeeded in breaking the force of the attack in time for part of the brigade to be formed up facing the southern mass when this advanced. As described further on, on page 387, the western attack was finally disposed of and the whole brigade formed up on a new front by the time the southern attack fully developed.

But there is another form of feint which is often as useful in warfare of this class as the feint designed to get the enemy to come out into the open. A show of indecision or a temporary retirement will sometimes induce opponents who are not very skilful in appreciating a military situation, to hold their ground when there is danger of their withdrawing and escaping an engagement. A great display of force may, as pointed out in an earlier chapter, have the effect of frightening the enemy away; conversely, concealment of strength tends to encourage the foe to risk an action. The results of the reconnaissance in force which was carried out by a part of Sir F. Roberts's force the day before the battle of Kandahar illustrates this very well; when the reconnaissance had achieved its purpose and the troops fell back, the Afghans followed them up some distance under the impression that the demonstration meant a real attack upon their position, and they were much encouraged and elated at their supposed victory; Ayoub Khan appears to have been largely influenced by the events of the day in his resolve to hold his ground. Thus the reconnaissance not only gained much valuable information for the battle of the morrow, but it had the further effect of assisting to keep the Afghan army in the position which it had taken up, and it thereby ensured a decisive engagement. The reconnaissance in force previous to the battle of the Atbara drew strong detachments of the enemy out of their zeriba; it probably served to greatly encourage the Khalifa's forces to stand their ground and to give the Anglo-Egyptian army a chance of utterly defeating them.

Just as such adversaries can, in spite of the wariness and cunning characteristic of races not wholly civilized, often be tempted into premature action, or can be enticed out of

[marginal note:] Inducing the enemy to hold his ground when inclined to retire.

[marginal note:] Feints as to intended point of attack.

ground favourable to their method of war, they can also be misled by feints and stratagems designed to give them a false impression of the point selected for attack by the commander of the regular forces. Guerillas often resort to such ruses, and they frequently succeed by these means in deceiving practised officers. Still they can at times be repaid in their own coin. In the fighting after the capture of Nilt Fort in the Hunza-Nagar country the frequent attempts upon the centre of the hostile position had drawn the attention of the enemy mainly upon that point; when, by a daring scramble up the precipitous hills, a party of the troops reached the extreme left of the tribesmen's position these were taken completely aback. On the afternoon before the attack on the Peiwar Kotal a great parade was made of throwing up batteries in front of the Afghan position to induce the enemy to expect a frontal attack. An interesting example of a successful feint of this kind is afforded by the fighting at Batoche in 1885, where the rebels collected by Riel were finally dispersed.

General Middleton found the half-breeds holding a long line of rifle pits stretching across the land enclosed by a wide salient angle formed by the Saskatchewan. The Government forces encamped opposite one end of this line of defence, formed a zeriba and remained facing the enemy four days engaged in skirmishes. On the third day the mounted troops made a demonstration against the hostile centre, and it was observed that a part of Riel's followers were withdrawn from that end of the line which was opposite the zeriba, to strengthen the threatened point. On the following day this demonstration was repeated by the mounted men, assisted by two guns, and these then returned quietly to camp. In the afternoon the whole Government force attacked the end of the rebel line in front of the zeriba. It had been greatly weakened there, and the troops had little difficulty in breaking through and in reaching Batoche. The undulating nature of the ground and the patches of woods and copses enabled the feint to be carried out in very effective fashion.

In some cases the enemy cannot be drawn into action.

Instances might be multiplied to show how valuable artifices of this nature may prove upon the battle-field in these wars, how the enemy can be induced by skilful manœuvring to forego the advantages he may enjoy as regards position, how he may be led to precipitate his attacks, and how he may be bluffed into withdrawing his forces from the decisive point. But before concluding the chapter it may be mentioned that episodes have occurred proving that irregular warriors cannot always be deceived or lured on in this fashion. The British frontier campaigns in India show that it is generally quite impossible to attract hill-men down to fight on the plains. All attempts to draw the Matabili out of the bush failed, and they showed clearly that they would choose their own time for attacking the colonial force. The remarkable action at Toski in 1899 is worth quoting as an example of a force which consisted largely of Moslem fanatics —warriors especially prone to allow themselves to be carried away in pursuit of a retreating foe—declining battle even after a portion of it had actually been tempted into action, simply as a consequence of the whole being dominated by a resolute will.

The action of Toski as an illustration of this.

Wad en Nejumi's singular march northwards past Wadi Halfa has been already referred to on p. 87. His goal was Egypt. Regardless of his threatened line of retreat and of the sufferings of his force from want of food and water, shutting his eyes to the hopelessness of the enterprise upon which he had embarked, unterrified by the imposing concentration of troops which he must have known were assembling to give him battle, he doggedly pressed on to near Toski. A little further on were some low rugged rocky hills where he would be in a position to offer effective resistance to the Egyptian forces. General Grenfell determined to prevent his reaching these, and as the event proved, the Dervish chieftain was equally resolved to gain their shelter.

Moving out from Toski to reconnoitre the Dervish position in the desert, General Grenfell found that the ground which the enemy must cross on his next advance was very open and favourable for an action. As all the troops which were mustering for the fight had not yet reached Toski, a reconnaissance of the mounted troops was determined on for the following day. The troops were ordered to show as broad a front as possible so as, if possible, to induce the Dervish leader to delay his advance.

When this reconnaissance got touch of the hostile forces next day, these were found to be just preparing to march. On sighting the Egyptian troops the enemy at once moved out against them, and the troops were compelled to retire gradually, drawing the fighting men of the Dervish army after them. General Grenfell thereupon sent for the infantry which had been held in readiness in camp; but before the infantry arrived Nejumi had evidently determined to avoid a battle and to make for the broken ground. The mounted troops were therefore sent to bar his way by making a long détour whioh brought them athwart the hostile line of march, and the infantry were hurried up with all speed. In the end the enemy was forced to fight and was, after a severe struggle, completely routed.

To start with, in fact, the Dervish force was tempted into a partial engagement. But Nejumi was so determined to effect his purpose of marching on, that he actually began a flank march past the mounted troops, covering his exposed flank by clouds of skirmishers. By his handling of his forces he showed himself a singularly resolute and capable leader, and, but for General Grenfell's promptitude in bringing the infantry up, and for his rapidly taking decision to force a general engagement, the strangely constituted Dervish army would have passed Toski, would have reached the broken ground further on, and might have given much trouble there.

Conclusion.

This question of feints and stratagems meant to goad the enemy into action has been dealt with at some length because, as it is notorious that the adversaries with whom regular troops have to cope in irregular operations are much addicted to ruses and deception, it might be supposed that they would naturally be difficult to impose upon. But the numerous instances quoted serve to show that this is not really the case.

It must be confessed that in the late South African war neither Boers nor rebels were easily deceived. As the campaign wore on and the cunning alike of commandants and individuals was shown in the hundreds of skirmishes which were taking place, it became more and more common to try feints and ruses so as to get the wary enemy at a disadvantage. But the stratagems seldom succeeded. The adversary was too wide awake. It is one of the many respects in which the contest for supremacy south of the Zambesi stands apart. In conflicts with a lower type of antagonist it is different. In spite of his native cunning the savage can be over-reached, the crafty hill-man can be deceived, and it is due to no fortuitous circumstance that occasions so frequently occur where irregular adversaries are brought to confusion by a trick. The discipline and cohesion of trained soldiers enables a skilful general to handle his force in such a manner as, without risk, to induce in the opposing forces the belief that they can cast prudence aside and can engage themselves on ground where the tactical superiority of the regular army has full scope. It is an important point to bear in mind in combats against irregular warriors, for to decisively beat such opponents it is almost always necessary to catch them in the open.

CHAPTER XVI.

SURPRISES, RAIDS, AND AMBUSCADES.

Surprise a favourite weapon of the enemy, but one which can also be used against him. "To conquer," wrote General Skobelef, when preparing for his campaign against the Turkomans, "you must know how to surprise." Although in small wars the enemy is generally well fitted by nature and temperament for devising ambuscades and carrying out surprises, it is by no means so difficult to put this method of warfare in force against him as might be supposed.

Best time of day for surprises. It has already been pointed out in Chapter XII that the forces which the regular troops are called upon to fight in these campaigns seldom protect themselves with outposts at night, and that on that account early morning attacks on them frequently meet with brilliant success. A night march followed by an assault upon the hostile position at dawn is perhaps the most effectual means of carrying out a surprise. The history of irregular warfare supplies abundant evidence of the fine opportunities which surprises at break of day afford a commander of regular troops. The capture of Kassala by the Italian troops in 1893 is an excellent example of this, and the affair of Cherek el Tobul and the capture of Ludlow Castle, both quoted on p. 193, are also notable examples of the same thing. The virtual annihilation of the Mahdist force at Ferkeh in 1896 was the result of the night march of two separate columns which at daybreak caught the unsuspecting enemy in a trap. In the latter part of the South African war the most remarkable successes gained by the British forces over the nomad commandos were gained by attacks at dawn after long night marches.

The question of carrying out surprise attacks at night can best be treated generally under the head of night attacks, dealt with in Chapter XXVII. But it may be pointed out here that while these are generally most objectionable in small wars if they are made on a large scale, it may often be expedient to annoy the enemy by small parties in the dark carrying out surprises of a harassing kind.

Irregular warriors seldom keep a good look out by night, but on the other hand they are generally thoroughly on the alert by day if they imagine the regular troops to be in their proximity. Therefore, if a surprise by day is contemplated it is almost always essential to lead up to it by a rapid march from a distance. Special troops must in fact as a rule be employed, and the enterprise must be conducted with dash and boldness. The Duc D'Aumale's surprise of Abd el Kader's smala described on p. 82 is a fine illustration of this class of operation ; the Arabs had no idea that a French force was anywhere near them ; the duke had made a forced march with his troopers, and the blow was as heavy as it was unexpected. For carrying out such enterprises a good knowledge of the theatre of war, careful preparation and bold execution are essential. In the campaigns against the Red Indians the United States troops succeeded on more than one occasion in surprising the wary enemy by making forced marches. But in the guerilla days of the late South African war it was found that something more than forced marches by day was necessary if the enemy was to be caught unawares ; it was only by forced marches by night and attack in the early morning that a surprise could be effected.

Cavalry, mounted infantry and camel corps are well suited for a surprise by day owing to mobility being so essential for such work. Remarkable results have moreover on occasion been achieved by cavalry carrying infantry on their horses. The Turkomans adopted this method in their sudden attack on the Russians in the Khiva campaign ; Abd el Kader on

By day a rapid march from a distance is generally necessary.

Mobility essential in troops employed.

(10830)   Q

the day after his defeat of the French at Macta in 1835, mounted 1,500 foot soldiers behind horsemen so as to fall upon the beaten troops at a favourable place ; Dost Mahomed in Afghanistan in 1841 made use of this same device. The plan has seldom been adopted by a regular army in irregular warfare, although the military history of Europe supplies many remarkable examples of such procedure in regular campaigns. It is true that on one occasion, in 1871, an attempt was made by the French to surprise some Arab insurgents by mounting infantry on mules by pairs, but the men were so exhausted when they reached the goal that they could do little fighting.

Another very effectual method of rapidly moving a force so as to effect a surprise is to put the men into carts ; but this can of course only be done in certain theatres of war. Colonel Skobelef moved two infantry companies in this manner in 1875 across Khokand. In the Mexican campaign in 1865 a small French force was conveyed 60 miles in 24 hours to relieve Monterey when threatened by the insurgents. The United States infantry have made forced marches to surprise the Red Indians by using carts. The Indian " ekka," familiar to all who have soldiered in the east, is a ready means of rapidly transporting troops.

Importance of keeping the project secret.

But to carry out a surprise in warfare of this nature, whether by day or by night, whether it be merely some minor episode or whether it takes this form of a momentous operation affecting the whole campaign, the most important point of all is to keep the plan secret. Officers who took part in the mobile operations on the veld which gradually wore down the Boer resistance, will realise the truth of this. " Aucun préparatif, aucun ordre ne fera soupçonner l'expédition. Les troupes seront spontanément assemblées a l'heure convenable. Des ordres écrits a l'avance et des instructions verbales seront alors donnés aux commandants des détachments "—so ran Marshal Bugeaud's instructions. There is always an element

of uncertainty in undertakings of this kind, and it is essential
that steps should be taken to prevent the secret from leaking
out.   Napoleon went so far as to ascribe success in such
operations entirely to luck.   "La réussite d'un coup de main
depend absolument du bonheur, d'un chien ou d'une oie,"
he wrote in his *Commentaires* ; but this applies rather to night
attacks than to surprises by day.   These latter depend especially upon their being unforeseen by the enemy, upon his
being unaware that any movement is contemplated and
his being ignorant that a force of regular troops is near him.

In Chapter V the difficulty of hiding movements and intentions from the enemy in small wars was commented upon.
The mysterious manner in which secrets leak out in such
warfare render it of the utmost importance to conceal to the
last any scheme which may be on foot to surprise the foe.
" Faire sentir la foudre avant qu'il ait vu l'éclair," was Monte-
cuculli's maxim.   The first condition requisite to score a
success is that the plan shall remain undivulged as long as
possible—it is to a rigid adherence to the policy of secrecy
that the remarkable sequence of successes by which the Sudan
was recovered may largely be attributed.   It is astonishing
how quickly the rumour spreads abroad, if the slightest
inkling is given to the force at large that it is to undertake some
operation of a special character.   Silence in such cases is golden
indeed, and this applies alike if the surprise takes the form of
an important operation of war like the transfer of the British
force from Alexandria to the Suez Canal, or if it be merely some
petty affair of intercepting an insignificant hostile detachment or seizing some paltry stronghold.

In 1891 a small Italian force was told off to surprise and capture a
troublesome chieftain named Debeb on the borders of Eritrea.   The secret
of what was intended was not kept, the whole party were apprised of what
was afoot, and a trifling unnecessary delay also occurred.   The consequence
was that Debeb and his following were found quite prepared for all eventualities, and that the small force sent to effect his capture was beaten off.

Great care must be taken that the enemy does not learn

what is impending by premature discharge of firearms. Rifles should not as a rule be loaded till the last moment, as a careless soldier may upset the most skilfully devised surprise by inadvertently firing off his weapon. During Sir F. Roberts's night march to surprise the Afghan flank on the Peiwar Kotal two native soldiers treacherously discharged their rifles in the hope of warning the enemy of the intended attack. A horse given to neighing when momentarily deprived of companionship is a serious danger. Close attention to details on the part of commander and officers, and a realization by the troops of the nature of the game they are playing, are essential if the *coup* is to succeed.

Enemy to be put on a false scent if possible. It is indeed always desirable to put the enemy on a false scent by every possible means when a surprise is contemplated. This can be done by various means. At night leaving the fires burning in the camp of a force which is to carry out some enterprise, will often lull the enemy into false security. The troops intended for the task may actually march in a false direction to start with—a good capture was made at Roos Senekal in the Transvaal by a column which quitted the place one day and which doubled back on its tracks that night. No undertaking offers greater opportunity for the employment of stratagem and artifice than a surprise. Guerillas such as regular troops meet with in campaigns like those of La Vendée, in the Peninsula, in Poland, and in 1901-02 in South Africa, are fully alive to this. In Algeria, the Caucasus, New Zealand, Somaliland, and other theatres of desultory war, the alertness and cunning of the enemy has been constantly demonstrated. A leaf might well be taken out of the book of some of the partisan leaders whose surprises and ambuscades have so often in small wars wrought confusion among bodies of trained troops.

General Philebert on one occasion in 1881, when operating against insurgents in Algeria, intended to surprise a place to the north of his camp ; in furtherance of this object he deliberately marched at night southwards, sounding his bugles, whereupon lights on the hills showed that the enemy was on the watch ; then General Philebert ordered complete silence and turned his column northwards again. Another time when on the march to surprise some villages, he found that his advance was observed, so he halted, encamped, and made a show of stopping where he was ; then, as soon as he was sure that the Arabs were no longer on the look out, he sent off a light column which was completely successful in its raid. Sir R. Buller in 1885 withdrew his force by night from Abu Klea, where it was blockaded by a large force of Mahdists, without molestation ; he left his camp fires burning and sounded the usual bugles so as to deceive the enemy.

The value of raids has been pointed out in the chapter on guerilla warfare ; they are often the only means of punishing the enemy and of bringing hostilities to a conclusion, and some point bearing upon these operations deserve a passing mention. Raids are a form of surprise. The idea of a raid is to affect captures or to do damage to the enemy's property by the action of a small force boldly handled and capable of covering a considerable distance in a short space of time. British troops have rarely attempted enterprises of this nature on a large scale and therefore the subject is to us an interesting one. *Raids a form of surprise.*

About raids undertaken to burn the villages or destroy the crops of recalcitrants there is not much to be said, to carry out such work it may indeed not be necessary to surprise the enemy. But when the object of the raid is to carry off live stock, secrecy and suddenness of execution are essential, otherwise the enemy will have driven off his flocks and herds and nothing will be found worth capturing. Experience has shown in South Africa that a native tribe about to commence hostilities will always send as much of its grain as possible, and the whole of its cattle, to some place of security beforehand ; the great object therefore is to ascertain where the tribal possessions have been concealed and to pounce down on them by a rapid well executed movement. The Arabs of Algeria, the Kirghiz and Turkomans of the steppes, and the Red Indians—all warriors enjoying in virtue of their horses or camels great mobility—have always displayed remarkable prowess in their forays. These wild uncivilized races may *Raids on the live stock of the enemy.*

indeed be said to have taught the regular troops opposed to them how such operations are best conducted.

The French proved apt pupils in Algeria. Adopting the Arabic name of razzia for their enterprises, they showed the enemy that this was a game both sides could play at. The capture of Abd el Kader's smala mentioned on former pages amounted to considerably more than a mere raid, it involved the overthrow of a considerable fighting force. It was the most remarkable example of an operation of this kind which occurred during the many years of desultory warfare which were needed to pacify the great African province, and the course of action which in that remarkable episode of war proved so signally successful—a forced march followed by intrepid attack when the enemy turned out to be present in force—may be taken as typical of the system of punitive raids which the French made their own. The idea of a raid is however rather to effect captures of hostile property than to fight, and the strength of the force detailed for the enterprise is not generally calculated with the idea of its giving battle to strong hostile forces.

For a razzia the force was in most cases composed mainly of cavalry, but a nucleus of infantry was generally found desirable. The general idea of an undertaking of this class is that the cavalry is detailed to surround the encampment or locality against which the enterprise is directed, the infantry then rushes in, cuts down all who resist, carries off women, children, flocks, and herds, and seizes any other booty which can be removed, burning the remainder. There is of course always considerable risk of a raid finding itself confronted by very superior numbers, by hostile forces so formidable that the plan of making a daring assault adopted by the Duc d'Aumale may be out of the question. The only thing for the raiders to do then is to retire as rapidly as they came. For success it is absolutely necessary that the foray should be a complete surprise. General Yusuf used to make a parade of marching

in the opposite direction by day and would then march back by
night and fall on the Arab encampment when this was
totally unprepared. Great care must be taken not to let the
men get out of hand, for fear that the enemy should receive
reinforcements and fall upon the raiders when scattered and
unprepared. Soldiers detailed for pillage are very liable to
become somewhat unmanageable, and, from the purely military
point of view, this is one of the strongest objections to raids.
A disciplined detachment which from any cause degenerates,
even if it be only for the moment, into a gang of marauders
is exposed to all manner of dangers, and finds itself in a
sorry plight if the enemy suddenly turns upon it. A bold
initiative is, however, the surest road to success in all such
operations, and is the best means of hindering the enemy
from gathering for a counterstroke.

In 1842 a column under General Changarnier in Algeria came upon a
mass of Arab nomads, horsemen, camels, women, children, flocks and herds,
all streaming along, protected by 1,500 horsemen. The General despatched
220 sabres supported by infantry to fall upon the Arabs. The odds against
the regulars were enormous ; but the French onslaught was so sudden and
was delivered with such dash that they succeeded in capturing 2,000 camels,
80,000 cattle, many prisoners and a huge booty, and bringing them into camp.

Bringing in the captured animals is one of the great Difficulty of
difficulties which follow upon a successful raid. This has often captured
been found to be the case by the Russians in Central Asia, cattle, etc.
by the United States cavalry in their raids upon the Red
Indians and by British troops in South Africa, as well as by
the French in Algeria and Tunis. The force told off for a
raid is almost necessarily small and it succeeds in the venture by the suddenness of its attack ; but when the prize is
secured the troops detailed for the undertaking become converted into an escort for the captured live stock. Even if
the enemy makes no attempt to recover his property, driving
great herds of camels or cattle or vast flocks of sheep to
some place of safety is by no means an easy task—sheep
move so slowly that they are especially troublesome. The

booty seems to melt away unaccountably. After some of their raids on the Turkomans and Kirghiz ending in the capture of quantities of live stock, the Russians were often within the space of a few days short of meat rations for the troops. The camels, cattle, sheep, or whatever the spoil may consist of, stray away at night even if the enemy makes no attempt to recover them.

If the enemy assemble in force while the booty is being brought back to camp, and if there be any risk of having to abandon it, the best plan will often be to kill the animals which have been captured if there is time to do it. Two very successful raids were effected by the punitive expedition against the Ogaden Somalis in 1898 ; the first time over 500 head of cattle were carried off ; but the second time, owing to the approach of night and the pursuit of the enemy, it was found necessary to kill all that had been taken. Slaughtering great herds of cattle or flocks of sheep is however a troublesome undertaking when a raiding force is being hustled. It must always be remembered that a raid may have been in the first place successful and that the party detailed for the purpose may be conveying its prize back to camp in triumph, but that if the enemy then assembles, attacks the convoy and defeats the troops hampered as they are, the operation as a whole will have been disastrous. The recovery of even a fraction of the booty will be interpreted by the enemy as a victory. The enemy will have had the last word, and may at the close have had the best of the exchange.

The raid upon the Zulu cattle on the top of the Zlobani Mountain already referred to on p. 183, was successful in the first instance. 2,000 head of cattle were captured and driven to the end of the mountain at which the descent was to be made. But the whole of the capture had to be abandoned when affairs took an unfavourable turn.

Ambuscades. The question of forming ambuscades in small wars is one which has hardly received the attention which it deserves.

Stratagems of this kind have hardly been so often attempted by regular troops in operations of this class as they might have been, considering that the terrain and conditions are often favourable to their successful execution. In the chapters on hill and jungle warfare it will be seen that in such theatres of war the enemy is constantly forming ambushes, and that being prepared for them is a matter of the first importance ; and it will also be shown that it is not impossible for the regular troops to lay traps of the same kind. But it is only on outpost service that the devising of ambuscades has up to the present been taken very seriously in campaigns against irregular forces.

The question of ambuscades is in reality nearly related to that of feints, already discussed in Chapter XV. Some of the cases quoted on pp. 230 to 233 are illustrations of this combination of ambuscades with feints, and show that it is often practicable to draw undisciplined opponents into a snare. It must be admitted that in campaigns against irregular warriors the regular troops fall into ambuscades more often than their adversaries do ; still many interesting cases have occurred when the enemy has been enticed into a trap and discomfited. The characteristics of a tumultuary assemblage of fighting men rather expose them to getting into pitfalls if they are cunningly devised. The eagerness with which such opponents at first follow up any success they may have gained has been noticed in earlier chapters, and the good results which may be obtained from tempting the adversary on by pretended retreat have been touched upon. Savages and semi-civilized races, fond as they are of stratagems, are not nearly so difficult to deceive as might be imagined. Opportunities often present themselves for preparing ambuscades for such foes, and when these have been skilfully planned remarkable results have sometimes been achieved. A good example of such action is afforded by an incident during General Sale's retreat from Gandamak to Jellalabad, which is thus graphically described by Kaye.

Ease with which the enemy can sometimes be drawn into them.

" Clever were the manœuvres by which on that day Dennie drew the enemy into his toils and heavy the retribution which descended upon them. Placing his cavalry in ambush he brought up his infantry, ordered them to advance firing and then wheeled them about as if in panic flight. The stratagem succeeded to admiration. The enemy, after a brief pause of wonderment, believed they had accomplished a great victory, sent up a wild shout and then rushed in pursuit of the flying Feringhees. They were soon on the clear open space to which Dennie had designed to lure them. The cavalry whom they had laughed at on the hills, able now to operate freely, dashed at them with sudden fury. The slaughter was tremendous the rout was complete."

But if savages and semi-civilized races are prone to be drawn into ambushes if judiciously arranged, it must be admitted that the insurgent in a civilized country, and the higher type of guerilla, are uncommonly wary birds. It did not prove particularly easy to catch the Boers napping, they seemed to have a miraculous instinct for scenting out an ambuscade. The Cubans seldom fell into a trap, and the veteran soldiers of France set their snares in vain for the Spanish guerillas during the Peninsular war, and for Fra Diavolo's banditti in Calabria. The operations of partisan warfare tend to stimulate the cunning and resource of the guerilla, and to place him on an altogether higher plane than the savage or the normal irregular when it comes to setting and to avoiding traps.

Remarks on the arrangement of ambuscades.

When cavalry and infantry are combined in an operation of this nature, it is usually the mobile cavalry which draws the enemy on, while the more easily concealed infantry falls upon the hostile detachments at the right moment. The Cossacks, when they were purely irregulars in the Russian service, were wonderfully skilled in the art of luring on an enemy, and they practised these manœuvres with equal success upon the splendid cavalry of Napoleon and upon the Tartar horsemen of the steppes. Parties of them used to spread out over a wide area, would worry the enemy into following them up by their fire from horseback, and would draw them on with marvellous patience to the point where, concealed in some hollow or behind some wood, a mass of these intrepid lancers was hidden, ready to dash out. Sometimes the Cossacks played into the hands of Russian infantry, but they seem to have preferred playing the game by themselves in their own way. The Boers were also very successful in using mounted men in this way; it was always dangerous to indulge in a vigorous pursuit of their detachments, except on a very broad front overlapping any ambush which might be intended; their skill in concealing their mounts was remarkable. To achieve success in any operation of this kind it is essential that the troops in ambush shall be thoroughly in hand and that there be no excitement. As in the case of effecting a night surprise, precautions must be taken against the premature discharge of fire-arms, and the enemy should be allowed to come close up before any attack is made on him. If the bayonet can be brought into play so much the better.

General Bugeaud arranged a very successful ambuscade at Takdempt in Algeria in 1841. He was withdrawing his forces from the place after destroying the works, but he left some troops concealed. As soon as they saw the French evacuating the town the Arabs entered it at the other side. They were quite unprepared to find troops hidden, and they suffered heavily when these attacked them.

General Prim after his victory over the Moors at Castellijos in 1859, drove the enemy some distance into the hills, but was then obliged to fall back as the evening was closing in. In doing so he posted two strong bodies of infantry among rocks on either side of the route which he foresaw the enemy would take in following him up. The Moors fell into the trap and suffered severely from the unexpected Spanish fire.

Drawing the enemy on is not of course a necessary part of arranging an ambuscade, although it tends to make irregular warriors throw off their caution and suspicions. Without some sort of feint to induce the enemy to press forward more or less recklessly the chances of bringing off a successful ambuscade are not bright. There is no more effective kind of ambush than one on the flank of a route which antagonists are about to follow; but undisciplined forces on the march are very much on the alert if they have any idea that regulars are in the neighbourhood, and there is scarcely an instance to be found in military records of a body of trained soldiers ambuscading the enemy under these conditions.

The forming of an ambuscade requires skill and eye for country. The great object to bear in mind of course is that the enemy shall not become aware of its presence till the concealed party is actually in a position to strike. In operations in the bush and jungle or on very broken ground this is not difficult to accomplish, especially if the hostile body can only move by one route ; but when the terrain is more open and the enemy moves on a wide front, great skill is required. If it be intended to act against a column on the march it will often be advisable not to deliver the blow till this has partially crossed the front, so as to cut it in half. Sometimes it may be expedient to delay attack till this can be delivered against the rear. When the moment for action arrives the concealed troops must be handled with the utmost boldness and dash, and it is essential that arrangements shall have been made beforehand for signalling when the time has come for the blow to fall. Several ambuscades some distance apart can at times be employed with great effect, although this arrangement has of course the disadvantage of involving a separation of force with its attendant risks. When several ambuscades have thus been formed, it is imperative that all the details shall have been carefully worked out and that the commander of each party shall know exactly what to do in any circumstances that may arise.

In 1813 a band of Prussian guerillas watching for a French convoy near Zwickau was disposed in two separate ambuscades. The parties were half a mile apart in two distinct woods, and it was calculated that when one attacked the advance guard, the other would find the rear guard about opposite to it. The arrangement was completely successful and practically the whole convoy was captured, rear and front being attacked and rolled up simultaneously.

Before concluding this chapter on surprises and ambuscades a few examples of successful ambuscades on the part of the enemy in small wars may be given. Very numerous

instances could be adduced, for in wars of this class the
enemies against whom the regular troops are operating excel
in such tactics. Some remarkable cases have of late years
occurred in West Africa in the case of minor naval boat
expeditions against petty potentates, and in the expedition
against the Yonnis near Sierra Leone in 1891, the enemy
showed much skill in devising ambushed stockades, and in
making use of obstacles so as to bring the troops to a standstill under their fire.

The following are interesting illustrations of the cunning
with which irregular warriors will at times entice troops into
a trap even in comparatively speaking open country.

In the early days of the French occupation of Algeria a squadron one day
engaged on reconnoitring duty perceived a number of Arabs on a wide plain
driving herds in front of them. The cavalry, thinking they had an easy
prize in their hands, charged down upon the enemy, but fell into a carefully
prepared ambush. They were received with a very heavy fire from a swarm
of Bedouins concealed among some scrub, and the troopers would have come
to utter grief but for the opportune arrival of another squadron which
managed to extricate them.

A somewhat similar incident occurred in the campaign in Tunis in 1885.
A reconnaissance party of French cavalry came upon a number of camels
guarded by a few Arabs, who at once mounted and drove off the camels into
a sort of defile. The troopers followed them up and fell into an ambuscade
which cost them dearly.

Some very successful ambuscades were devised by the
Anti-Republicans of La Vendée and by the Spanish guerillas
in the Peninsular war. In small wars of more modern date,
the Moors, Khivans, and others have displayed great dexterity in this kind of warfare, even when the terrain has not
especially lent itself to such operations. Irregular warriors
with their natural aptitude for creeping about and their
instinctive capacity for stalking unsuspecting adversaries,
are really formidable in this branch of the art of war ; military
records prove that even when, as in Burma and Rhodesia,
they have no intention of committing themselves to a stand-up

fight, they will manage by their stratagems to inflict loss and to create confusion.

The ambuscade at Shekan.

The most striking example of an ambuscade of recent years is supplied by the disastrous engagement at Shekan, in which a whole army was involved and was wiped out.

Complete and authentic details of the destruction of Hicks Pasha's army will probably never come to hand ; but from various sources it has been found possible to obtain a general idea of what occurred. Learning from spies the direction that the Egyptian force was about to take, the Mahdi moved the bulk of his followers to a valley through which it must pass, when he concealed them in the woods on either side of the route and in a wooded depression crossing the line of advance. Other contingents were told off to attack in rear.

All remained quiet till Hicks Pasha's squares reached the wooded depression. Then the fanatical Arabs sprang up and swarmed down from all sides. The troops, already somewhat demoralised, became panic-stricken at this terrifying onslaught and in a few minutes all was over. The most striking feature of the action was indeed the manner in which a great gathering of undisciplined warriors was bestowed and was kept silent and concealed till the moment of action arrived.

Other examples.

The following examples of ambuscades occurring under very various circumstances and in totally distinct theatres of war may be cited in conclusion.

In 1840 the Russian General Golosojef, advancing with a force of about 5,500 men against the guerillas of the Chechnaya, fell into a cleverly prepared trap and suffered heavy losses, although ultimately successful. The enemy had arranged a most skilful ambush along the banks of the little river Valerik and in the neighbouring thickets. The Russian troops were on the march suspecting no evil and without elaborate precautions. Suddenly a heavy fire was opened upon them when they were quite unprepared, and by its unexpectedness nearly caused a panic. In the end after a severe hand to hand encounter the regular troops proved victorious, but not before they had lost large numbers of killed and wounded at the hands of a numerically insignificant adversary.

In 1883 the French were practically blockaded in Hanoi, their settlement in Tonkin. It was determined to make a reconnaissance, and a force of 400 men with three guns marched out for the purpose. Some distance out, the road crossed a stream by a bridge and beyond this were some villages and enclosures. The advanced guard had crossed the bridge and the guns were actually on it, when fire was suddenly opened from all sides beyond the stream. The surprise was complete. The advanced guard retreated in disorder. The guns could not be turned where they were and they had to advance over the bridge and turn on the far side ; one stuck in the mud, and in the gallant and successful effort to save it Captain Rivière, the French Governor, and many others were killed. This disaster heralded the Tonkin war of 1884–85.

In the affair at Fish Creek during the suppression of Riel's rebellion in 1885 the half breeds had taken skilful advantage of ravines and opened a heavy fire unexpectedly on the advanced guard of the Canadian troops. The ambuscade was not successful; the ground had, however, been judiciously chosen, and had the rebel fire been better directed at first the advanced troops might have suffered considerably.

The disaster which befel Major Glasenapp's detachment early in 1904 at Owikokero in German South-West Africa is a remarkable example of an ambuscade.

The force consisted of 11 officers and 35 mounted men with a machine gun. It was on the march following up the Herreros through bush grown country when it came upon a herd of cattle which was promptly captured, those of the enemy with it who did not take flight being shot. Some men were left with the cattle and the force advanced, capturing two more herds ; to take charge of these some more men had to be left behind. Then the detachment, now reduced to 11 officers and 25 troopers with the machine gun, pressed on, hoping to come up with the fugitives and believing them to be merely a small rear guard.

The bush got thicker and thicker. On reaching a more open place the detachment was, however, suddenly fired on. An attempt to outflank the enemy disclosed the fact that the Herreros were in greatly superior numbers, and were endeavouring to surround the force. Retreat became absolutely unavoidable, and in this the little body of German troops lost very heavily. The machine gun had to be abandoned, many horses were shot ; the total casualties amounted to 10 officers and 22 troopers, and the enemy recovered their cattle.

The Herreros in fact appear to have drawn the detachment cleverly into an ambuscade. The detachment had been in pursuit of them for some days and officers and men were naturally eager to have a brush with the enemy who seemed always to be running away. The place selected for the ambuscade was admirably chosen, and it is possible that the herds of cattle were left to a certain extent as a bait—their capture certainly appreciably reduced the number of men in the German firing line. That the little band was not annihilated was due to the fine behaviour of officers and men under untoward circumstances.

CHAPTER XVII.

Squares in action, on the march, and in bivouac.

Square forma-
tion cannot be
satisfactorily
treated under
the head
either of
attack or
defence.

There are certain questions of tactics in small wars, apart from retreats and pursuits, or feints and surprises, which cannot be satisfactorily treated under the head either of attack or defence and which do not especially affect any one of the three arms. These can best be dealt with by themselves in special chapters, and under this heading come squares.

The square is adopted by regular troops in small wars as a battle formation to meet special situations, and it can be used both offensively and defensively. The formation is also often employed upon the march under certain circumstances. Recourse is had to it under many differing conditions, both as regards the terrain in which the operations are taking place and as regards the method of fighting of the enemy. Although common enough in the old days in what was then regular warfare, it now-a-days is a formation peculiar to small wars. It has been employed so largely in irregular warfare in modern times, the conditions which have brought it into favour vary so greatly in different cases, the experiences gained in actual practice where it has played a part have sometimes been so inconclusive, that the subject is really a very large one and deserving of careful study.

Object of
square
formation.

The *raison d'être* of the square, whether it be used as an order of march, as an arrangement for bivouac, or as a formation for battle, is to be found in the necessity which may be at times imposed upon a body of regular troops of being able to show a fighting front in any direction, and in the obligation which it incurs of protecting its supplies and wounded. In its military sense the term does not necessarily mean a rectangle

of four equal sides. It simply means a formation showing
front to flanks and rear as well as to the proper front. Such
squares have sometimes only three sides, the rear face being
left entirely or practically open—it all depends on circumstances. It is worth noting that a French square at Shott Tigri
in 1882 was arranged with its rear face formed of camels, but
that the Bedouins succeeded in carrying these off and up-
setting the whole arrangement.

The reason why a formation which offers a fighting front in
all directions may have to be adopted, is that in these campaigns
attack or counter-attack has from various causes often to
be expected from any point. Sometimes this is due to the fact
that, owing to superior numbers, the enemy can surround the
regular troops. It may result from the position of the enemy
not being known and from the conditions not admitting of
its being ascertained. It may arise from the great mobility
which irregular warriors enjoy upon the battle-field. The
cause may be found in the necessity of protecting supplies,
or stores, or wounded against marauding parties. But some
sort of square formation is constantly being imposed upon
the regular troops in these wars, because the nature of the
case demands an order of battle calculated to offer an all
round defence.

Irregular forces are fond of threatening the rear of regular
troops, partly because they anticipate that they will be
offered less resistance there, and partly because they hope
to loot the supplies and stores which they know will be following the army. At Ordahsu the enemy had made a clearing in
the bush, on purpose to attack the troops in rear after they had
passed the clearing, and they closed in as the column fought
its way forward. At Wad Ras, the final engagement of the
Spanish army in the war against the Moors in 1859, the Moors
pressed in on the rear of the invaders although these were
at the very time driving the bulk of the Sultan's army from
its position. The Zulus always endeavoured to envelope the

Enemy's tendency to operate against the flanks and rear of regular troops.

British forces—at Isandlwhana they captured the camp in
rear of the troops who were only formed up with the idea of
meeting a frontal and flank attack. In Algeria, Tunis, and
Tartary it has been the practice from time immemorial for
masses of horse to charge down from all sides. It is these
enveloping attacks and these hostile demonstrations against
the flanks and rear, which oblige the commander of the regular
troops to draw them up in square formation in spite of its
manifold drawbacks. The formation is adopted on the march,
at the halt when resting or when bivouacking for the night,
and as an order of battle, and because, even when the troops
are not actually in action it is always employed with the idea
in view that an engagement may occur at any moment,
it will perhaps be best to consider it first as a battle
formation.

Two forms of
square, the
rigid and the
elastic. The
rigid form
here dealt
with.

Before proceeding further it must be pointed out here that
there are in reality two kinds of square formation—the
rigid form and the elastic form, and that it is the first with
which we are here concerned. The elastic form of square is
employed in bush and jungle warfare, its essence consists in
the army moving or being drawn up in groups or detachments
more or less all round the convoy, the guns, the wounded, or
whatever impedimenta may be accompanying it, and this
kind of formation can best be dealt with in the chapter on bush
and jungle warfare. Indeed, a form of elastic square is often
employed on the march in hill warfare, when the heights are
crowned and the force as a whole consists of an advanced
guard of these flanking detachment and of a rear guard;
the idea then is the same—security against attack from any
point. In the present chapter it is the rigid square, designed
to meet the charge of horse or the fanatical rush of footmen
which has to be considered, a defensive order of battle forced
upon regular troops by irregular warriors who adopt shock
tactics and who enjoy superiority as regards numbers.

In the rigid square formation the combatant troops Usual formation. forming the square are drawn up practically shoulder to shoulder, as is laid down in principle in "Infantry Training." It is designed to meet the onslaught of adversaries who trust rather to spears and knives than to firearms.   In Zululand and the Sudan the brave warriors with whom the British and Egyptian troops had to deal, came on impetuously in vast numbers and with great rapidity and suddenness.   The French adopted the formation in Egypt and in Algeria to beat off the onslaughts of great masses of horse.   The square is in fact. employed under somewhat the same circumstances as battalion squares were formerly used in regular warfare, but with the great difference that when it is employed in small wars non-combatant services, wounded, and all that is not self-protecting with the force are collected inside the square.   Even the cavalry is sometimes inside the square.

In actual battle the square, as a rule, acts mainly on the Squares in action. defensive till the enemy is beaten.   Still it often happens A formation at once offensive and defensive. that the action of the regular troops takes in part the form of an attack.   This principle is well illustrated by the case already quoted of Isly where the French, in a formation on the principle of the square, moved straight towards the centre of the Moorish position and compelled the hostile forces, consisting largely of mounted men, to charge.   At Abu Klea the British square moved close past the position which the Mahdists had taken up in a dry river bed, and induced them by so doing to attack.   Sometimes, but more rarely, the square is actually used in attack, as at El Teb where the Mahdist entrenchment was turned and then attacked in this inconvenient formation.   But in the main the square is an order of battle which is employed when acting on the defensive.

An excellent example of the use of a square as a forma- Example of Achupa in Dahomey. tion enabling a small force to compel the enemy to attack it without great risk, and bringing about thereby an action in a position favourable to the regular troops, is afforded by the affair of Achupa in 1891 in the early days of hostilities between France and Dahomey.

The French only held a few points on the coast at this time, of which Porto Novo was the most important. The Dahomeyans were known to be advancing in force against this town. It was a straggling place with only one fort to defend it, and its garrison of 400 men was, owing to its extent, quite insufficient to hold it against a determined attack. Colonel Terrillon who was in command determined to march out and fight the enemy a few miles off. When the forces came in contact the French formed a square. In this order of battle they beat off the attacks of the Dahomeyans numbering several thousands, and they inflicted such severe losses upon their savage opponents that these retreated and that Porto Novo was relieved from all fear of attack. It is interesting to note that in this fight the native troops forming one side of the square, got out of hand in the excitement of victory and charged, leaving that side completely open for a short time.

Organization of squares in action.

The difficulties which arise in the manœuvring and the organization of the square are obvious. A shoulder to shoulder formation can be maintained easily enough upon the drill ground ; but when the terrain is uneven or intersected the force is very apt to get into confusion. The most careful supervision will not prevent gaps from occurring, the pace of the artillery and of the machine guns is not as a rule the same as that of foot soldiers, in the interior of the square are the non-combatant services impeding the view of the commander, and, the larger the square is, the more difficult is it to keep it intact. The great point to keep in mind seems to be to check the pace of the front face constantly so as to make sure that the sides are kept closed up and that the rear face is in its place. Frequent halts are desirable and the transport inside the square must be very carefully supervised. If the enemy threatens, the square should halt at once, the sides facing outwards and the rear face turning about. How hard it is to manœuvre one of these rigid squares and to keep the ranks closed up so as to leave no weak point for the enemy to profit by, is well shown by what occurred at Abu Klea.

The force forming the square consisted of 1,200 men, with three guns Abu Klea. dragged by hand. Inside the square were the camels for carrying the guns, and others for water, ammunition, and wounded. Its advance was covered by skirmishers. The ground was open but undulating. The hostile position in the dry river bed already mentioned was well marked by banners. It so happened, however, that when about 500 yards from the flags, the rear face became bulged out by the camels, and that at this moment the enemy, to the number of about 5,000, suddenly sprang up from the khor where they were concealed to the left front, and charged the square on its left side.

The skirmishers ran for the square and by so doing masked its fire at first. The guns were hurried out on the threatened side. The fire of the front and left faces and of the guns was so severe, that the enemy swerved to the right and brought the whole weight of their charge to bear on the left rear corner of the square where—partly due to the bulging out caused by the camels—there was a gap, and where the fire was in consequence not so effective as on the flank. The confusion at this point appears to have been increased by the tendency of the camel corps to push forward and meet the enemy. The result was that the fanatical spearmen broke into the square and that a desperate melée ensued, in which the British force lost heavily and which only ended when all the Arabs in the square had been killed in a hand-to-hand fight.

The first point which suggests itself when considering Question of skirmishers. this remarkable conflict of Abu Klea is the question of the skirmishers. Now it is obvious that a rigid square of this kind covering a very narrow front has no means within itself in at all broken ground of discovering if foemen are lurking near its path. Moreover, the best way of replying to casual hostile fire directed at such a square is by independent fire of skirmishers, because great delay must ensue if the troops forming the square reply to it—this was indeed at Abu Klea the main reason for the skirmishers being sent out. But if the enemy delivers a sudden attack they are terribly in the way, and so much is this the case that upon the whole it seems far better to dispense with them. When, two days after the action of Abu Klea, the square made its final advance from the zeriba which had been formed three miles from the Nile to reach that river, there were no skirmishers out. At Ulundi there were no skirmishers in front of the square although the mounted troops acted to a certain extent in this capacity. It was the same at El Teb, and when the square formation was employed near Suakin skirmishers were generally dispensed with.

How to deal with gaps. How to prevent gaps from occurring in a square is a question which is easily answered in theory. It is simply a matter of careful supervision and of constantly halting the front face to enable the sides and rear to close up. But in practice these intervals occur in spite of the most strenuous exertions. There is always the risk of the rear face being bulged out by the non-combatants as occurred at Abu Klea. In the disaster which occurred to Baker Pasha's Egyptian force near Trinkitat in 1884, the rear face of the square was in a state of chaos when the Arabs made their onslaught. That it is a matter of supreme importance to prevent the square from being broken stands to reason. Once the enemy penetrates it, it becomes a thoroughly bad formation. If the faces which remain intact turn round and fire on the intruders, they are liable to shoot into each other. It is, however, interesting to note in this connection that, the day before the disastrous fight as Shekan in 1883 in which the force was annihilated, the rear face of Hicks Pasha's square was broken by an Arab charge, but the enemy was driven out by the front face wheeling round. A square penetrated by an active and determined enemy is liable to be thrown into complete confusion and the whole aim and object of the formation is defeated when it is broken through. Gaps are so dangerous and so difficult to obviate altogether that it seems advisable to provide especially for the case of their occurring.

Suggestion as to reserves in squares. The best way of providing against gaps which may occur at a critical moment affording the enemy a passage into the square, would seem to be by detailing a reserve, or several reserves, within the square. The reserves should be distributed so as to ensure that they can at a moment's notice be pushed into an interval if one occurs at a critical juncture. After the experience of Abu Klea this system was adopted by Sir C.

Wilson, when commanding the final advance of the desert column from that place to the Nile near Metemma. Probably the best arrangement is a small reserve at each corner, for experience shows that a rush of fanatics or savages is generally directed at a corner—such warriors recognise instinctively that this is a weak point both because less fire can be developed and because there is most likelihood of confusion here. Of course there is a very serious objection to reserves, in that they withdraw men out of the firing line in a formation which at the best only admits of a limited development of fire except when the enemy attacks from all sides simultaneously. No instances appear to have occurred of recent years of a square being saved from being broken into by the action of a reserve ; but on the other hand when squares have been broken there never seems to have been a reserve at hand to thrust into the gap.

At Abu Klea the gap occurred at a corner. Corners are The corners. obviously a weak point because there is a loss of fire even if the square remains intact, and because the tendency in the sides of a square is for the men to feel inwards. " Infantry Training " lays down that the flanks of a battalion should not meet at an angle, with the especial idea of providing against this. As observed above, it is a good plan to place reserves at the corners, and it might be desirable to detail a senior officer to have a special control over each of the four angles of the square.

As regards the position of artillery or machine guns in a Position of square it used to be thought advisable to place them at the artillery. corners, partly because the corners are weak points and partly because the plan admits of fire all round except one quarter of a circle ; but it is very doubtful if this is necessarily the best arrangement. As already mentioned they were run out to the side attacked at Abu Klea. At El Teb the guns were kept in battery and run out when required. At Tamai the machine guns were in front of the square which was broken, and they fell for a time into the hands of the enemy. At Ulundi, on the other hand, the guns were for the most part at the corners. Of course when the enemy is not close at hand the guns can be run out to any side where their fire may happen to be desirable. But when the enemy actually charges, there is something to be said for their being at the corners, as long as they are in pairs ; a single gun may somehow be put out of action just at the critical moment, and machine guns are always somewhat precarious weapons to depend on in a rush. It never seems desirable therefore to place a single gun or machine gun at a corner ; if they are to be worked singly they are best in the centre of the sides.

When it is possible to place the guns at some distance from the square they may give the square great assistance should it be assailed. Their fire necessarily takes the assailant in flank. But this arrangement of course exposes the guns themselves to be rushed unless they are under special protection of other troops.

When the final advance to the Nile was made by the desert column from the zeriba which had been formed at the Abu Klea wells after the fight, it was decided to have the guns behind. They proved of great service to the force as it moved on towards the Nile by their effective fire on masses of the enemy who were preparing to charge it. Although firing at longer range than they would have been if with the square, they probably had far greater effect than had they been with it.

Position of Cavalry. Cavalry are generally best outside the square, this arm is of course for the time being merely an encumbrance when actually inside the square ; it would indeed often happen that there was no room for cavalry inside. At Ulundi the cavalry after reconnoitring to the front and obtaining touch of the enemy retired inside of the square ; but the Zulu system of attack was always enveloping, and had the mounted troops remained outside when the action developed they would have inevitably masked the fire of the square. At the fight on the Chengo river in 1897 between the Portuguese troops and the Gaza rebels, the small party of cavalry was kept inside the square ; the enemy came up near the square on all sides, but the cavalry suddenly issued from it, and, charging home, scattered the enemy in all directions. In the Sudan the cavalry has almost invariably been kept outside and quite independent of the square ; so placed, they can reconnoitre effectively, and mounted troops who can gallop away clear in case of emergency seem to be better adapted for acting as a screen under the circumstances, than infantry skirmishers who have to get back into the square if the enemy closes. The Russians when employing this formation in Central Asia have generally kept their mounted men outside the square. After one of the two squares was broken at Tamai the dismounted fire of the cavalry operating some way off, was of great assistance, taking the enemy in flank from a position of practical security. The distance which the cavalry should be from the square depends of course upon circumstances ; it should not be too far off to render prompt assistance, but it should not, on the other hand, be so near as to run the risk of masking effective fire from the square.

The question whether a single square is preferable to two or more squares is a difficult one to decide. When the noncombatant services to be protected are proportionately large, a single square is preferable because the actual available space in the interior of a single square is larger than that in two squares formed of the same number of men. Moreover, a single square will generally, but not under all circumstances, afford a greater volume of fire, inasmuch as the enemy will seldom attack more than one square at the same time. Question of forming two or more squares.

But on the other hand two or more squares mutually flank each other. If one square should be broken the others can afford it considerable support by their fire, and if it is thrown into complete confusion the disaster, however serious, does not involve the destruction of the whole force. Thus at Tamai, where the British force was formed into two squares, one of them, broken and thrown into disorder, was obliged to fall back some distance; the other then became of the greatest assistance in retrieving the fortunes of the fight, not only by its fire but by its moral support. Moreover, two or more squares are much more easily manœuvred than a single square formed of the same number of men. There is, however, always the risk of squares firing into each other if the enemy penetrates between them; some slight inconvenience was caused by this at Tamai. At Shekan the army was formed up in three squares, and it appears that these fired into each other in the confusion which occurred when the Mahdists made their sudden onslaught and thereby greatly added to the terrors of the moment.

When the enemy attacks in great force and envelops the regular army as in Zululand, a single square is clearly preferable; for if there are two or more squares the fire of certain of their faces must be lost to a great extent. But upon the whole, especially in close country when the hostile tactics take the form of sudden rushes, there is much to be said for having more than one square, if it be only on the principle of not putting all the eggs in one basket.

Square affords a target for the enemy.

The great objections to the square formation are the limited development of fire it admits of—this has been already touched upon—and the fact that it offers a particularly good target for the hostile fire. Even bad marksmen armed with indifferent, antiquated weapons can do damage when they have a square to aim at. Experience in Central Asia, in Zululand and in the Sudan shows that this is so. But, after all, the losses incurred from the enemy's small arms are seldom very appreciable even at comparatively speaking short range, and when the hostile tactics are such as to call for the adoption of a square formation, the enemy rarely is supplied with guns. It may, of course, happen that the opponents of the regular forces have guns and know how to use them; in that case a rigid square formation certainly affords them an excellent mark. Thus at El Teb the Mahdists had some guns, and until these were silenced they caused loss in the British square as it advanced. In Dahomey some inconvenience was caused to the French squares by the enemy's guns, which made good practice and which might have caused serious havoc had the shells burst. Still upon the whole this objection to the square, that it offers a target to the enemy, does not prove a very serious drawback to a formation which has been proved by experience so very efficacious in certain circumstances.

The limited development of fire which this order of battle admits of is a more serious matter than the target which it presents to the enemy, and there seems to be no safe plan of increasing this at a critical moment. Wheeling forward the sides in the direction where the enemy may be, cannot be attempted at close quarters in face of active warriors, who would be round the flanks in a moment—as appears indeed actually to have happened at Abu Klea. The restriction which it puts on the fire of the men, is in reality the greatest objection to the square formation, and there seems to be no remedy for this. *Limited development of fire from a square.*

The square has occasionally been used in actual attack as at El Teb already referred to, although the formation certainly does not readily lend itself to such action. A charge in square is obviously difficult to carry out, there is always a risk of confusion and of the ranks becoming broken, and the chance that the enemy may profit thereby to break into the interior. The square is essentially a defensive and not an offensive arrangement for combat; still the case of El Teb shows that it is not impracticable to assault a position with troops drawn up in this formation. The battle of Tamai on the other hand affords a striking illustration of the dangers which may arise out of the assumption of the offensive in square. *Square in attack.*

The story of this fight is briefly as follows :—A large gathering of Mahdists was concealed in a ravine. The two squares advanced in échelon about *Tamai.*

1,000 yards apart, that formed by the 2nd Brigade leading. As this drew near the ravine, groups of the enemy rushed out from its shelter to attack, but were mowed down by the fire of the square. Then a charge was ordered, and the front face of the square sprang forward to a point close to the edge of the declivity, halted, and began an irregular fire against the enemy on the opposite slopes of the ravine. The machine guns were run out to the right front corner of the square. There may have been some gaps due to the right side of the square not having moved so fast as the front face, or to the troops being unsteadied by their rapid advance. Whatever was the cause, it came about that when a mass of hostile spearmen suddenly rushed up out of the ravine against the right front corner, the fire of the square at that point was unable to check their onslaught. They captured the machine guns and rolled up the front and right faces. The rear face promptly closed up ; but it was unable to stem the torrent of Arabs, and the square formation was completely lost in the melée which ensued.

The square was in fact disordered by its own charge and, getting too close to the ravine, its fire proved ineffective at a critical moment. The Arabs, who were concealed in great force in the ravine, took advantage of these circumstances to deliver a determined counter-attack which threw the square into complete confusion.

It is of course essential that gaps and intervals should not occur, and in the rapid movements which always take place in delivering an assault, it is practically impossible to prevent their occurrence. If feasible, there should be a pause to induce the enemy to charge home—a feigned retreat might bring this about at such a moment. If marked disinclination to attack be shown by the adversary, and if the hostile position be so strong that it is dangerous to take risks, a move of the square towards a flank may bring about the desired forward movement on the part of the enemy. Even supposing that the enemy declines to be " drawn," a move like this towards the flank will probably cause the position to be evacuated ; then, while the opponents are in retreat, the square may be broken up, the troops may advance in line or *echelon* formation, and it may be possible to bring artillery fire and musketry effectively into play against the fugitives.

Capture of Bida.

The square formation does not in fact readily lend itself to offensive action beyond what is involved in advancing upon the enemy and leading him on to charge. This employment of the square is well illustrated by the tactical conduct of the operations which resulted in the capture of Bida by Major Arnold early in 1897—an operation which admirably shows the advantage of the square when regular troops are acting against masses of foemen whose musketry fire is not very alarming.

Major Arnold's force consisted of under 600 constabulary, with seven guns and six maxims, the guns being dragged by hand at great labour. The attack on Bida was carried out as follows:—The infantry advanced in square with the guns in the centre, the movement necessarily being very slow owing to the delays caused by hauling these latter along. A halt was made on commanding ground near the town and the guns were brought into action upon masses of the enemy thronging its outskirts. Thereupon the square was surrounded by hostile swarms who hurried up from all sides, but the steady musketry and maxim fire kept the Fulahs at a distance, and their fire was of the wildest description. Then after a time the square advanced afresh, took up a good position within 600 yards of the town, and a bombardment of this by the artillery was begun which lasted some hours. The enemy could not stand this, the hostile parties gradually broke up and lost heavily from the long range fire of a 12-pr. which was with the force as they took to flight. The battle of Bida was one of the most signal successes ever won by British arms in Africa.

Before considering squares on the march it will not be out of place to point out that in spite of its obvious inconveniences, this order of battle has proved admirably suited to the conditions on many occasions. In the form in which it has on occasions been employed in Algeria, which was adopted at Ulundi, and which has played so great a part on the battle fields of the Sudan, it has undoubtedly been a success. When good troops drawn up in this formation have got into difficulties, as at Tamai and Abu Klea, it has generally been attributable to difficulties of ground, or else to the square not being properly formed at some critical juncture. On open ground even indifferent troops have with comparative ease beaten off formidable attacks—at Marabia, south-east of Khartum, Hicks Pasha, in 1883, completely defeated a most determined Mahdist attack with untried Egyptian troops formed in square, and he moreover inflicted tremendous loss

Square formation has frequently proved most effective.

upon the enemy. When troops even of poor quality are drawn up in this compact formation, a thorough fire discipline can generally be maintained as long as the terrain is fairly open and as long as the hostile onslaught has none of the features of a surprise. The consequence is that arms of precision are made the most of, and that the fanatics or savages as they make their daring charges are mowed down by scores. If there is a fairly clear field of fire, the enemy as a rule indeed never reaches the square. The masses of infuriated assailants melt away under the rain of bullets. The leaders are shot down, and the onslaught of the intrepid warriors is brought to a standstill before they can get close enough for the hand-to-hand struggle which they are striving for.

Even in the scrub and bush around Suakin, where the field of fire was most limited and where the maintenance of the rigid square formation was most difficult, it invariably proved triumphant in 1885. In those operations the hostile rushes used to be very sudden, and the rifles of the troops had not full scope ; but even so the square was found an order of battle which commanded success. However unsound and ill adapted to the circumstances the formation may have seemed in theory, it met the case on every occasion in that campaign in spite of the scrub and bush. Theory cannot be accepted as conclusive when practice points the other way; the objections of the square are manifest, but it has scores of times fulfilled its purpose.

Square formation as an order of march. Forming square on the move.
Having dealt with the square as an order of battle or in actual presence of the enemy, it now becomes necessary to regard it as an order of march. The formation is obviously inconvenient for any prolonged movement. On this account commanders will generally, when it can be considered safe, arrange their order of march not actually in square but rather in some formation which will allow the troops to rapidly assume square if the enemy be met with in force. As long as the

transport and non-combatants are kept well closed up, and
provided that there is a strong compact rear guard to form a
rear face, the flanks can easily be drawn in to form the sides,
and the square is then complete. But if there be the slightest
risk of a sudden fanatical onslaught, if the country be overgrown, or if nullahs abound where the enemy can muster unobserved, an arrangement of this kind is not very safe. A
hostile charge may be delivered while the force is in the act of
changing from the marching formation into square, and
pressed home at such a moment may throw everything into
confusion.

In this connection it is interesting to note that the disaster which oc·
curred to Baker Pasha's force near Trinkitat in 1884 seems partially to have
been due to the fact that his troops had not time to complete the square
when they were attacked by the Mahdists. His men were, however, so
untrustworthy and so insufficiently trained, that there is not much to be
learnt from that disastrous fight. The force would probably have been
rolled up no matter what formation it was in.

When there has been a probability of very sudden hostile
attack, the square formation has frequently been adopted as
an order of march as the only means of safe-guarding the
convoys which accompany the regular force, and the troops
have marched great distances so drawn up. Even when
a force is going deliberately into action, there are always non-
combatant services to be protected in these wars—the safe-
guarding of these is one main cause of the adoption of the square
as an order of battle. But a moment's consideration will
show that when a force is on the march the numerical strength
of the non-combatant services, and the area of ground which
they occupy whether in movement or at the halt, must be far
greater than when the force has cast off all possible impediment preparatory to engaging deliberately in a fight. Supplies
for days and even for weeks involving a, relatively to the size
of the army, gigantic transport column, may be accompanying
the force on the march. The convoy will sometimes be so
great that the number of combatants are quite insufficient to

form a square round it possessing any semblance of cohesion. On the march the square formation is in fact most cumbersome and is most difficult to maintain.

In spite of its drawbacks, however, the French have made considerable use of this order of march in their small wars. In Egypt when operating against the Mamelukes, in Algeria and in Tunis, the liability to very sudden attack of formidable bodies of horse often left them no choice except to march in square. General Logerot in Tunis always marched in square with an advanced guard in front. The Russians have sometimes adopted it as an order of march in Central Asia, notably during the suppression of the Turkomans in the khanate of Khiva after the occupation of the oasis in 1874. In the Sudan, and especially around Suakin, the British and Egyptian troops have often been compelled to carry out marches in square under most unfavourable circumstances.

Difficulties of marching in square.

It is, of course, highly inconvenient when regulars have to march in square with a mass of non-combatants and transport inside. Progress must inevitably be slow. The baggage animals, crowded together as they are, get into disorder. From the very fact of their being in a restricted space their supervision is most difficult. The pace of the whole force is reduced to that of the slowest animal. But in spite of its manifold disadvantages, marching in square is often the only plan by which a movement can safely be carried out, and the inconveniences inseparable from the arrangement have to be accepted. The advance to the Abu Klea wells is an example of such a march, although in that case the bulk of the transport had been left behind in a zeriba there nevertheless was a mass of camels inside the square.

Hicks Pasha's three squares at Shekan had inside of them the enormous mass of transport which the carriage of 50 days' supplies of food and a few days' store of water for his force necessarily involved. This huge train of animals must have been a terrible incumbrance in that last desperate fight with the Dervish hordes, and it probably contributed towards bringing about the fatal results of the hostile attack. Such a case would no doubt seldom arise in war—it is obviously an extreme case for an army to abandon its communications and to launch out many days' march into a theatre of operations, destitute of supplies and even of water and held by an enemy so formidable as to compel the adoption of square formation. Under ordinary circumstances the method which would be employed in such conditions is that of forming a zeriba or fortified bivouac in which the convoy is left under protection of a fraction of the force, while the rest of it goes out as a fighting square to give battle to the enemy, as was done at Abu Klea.

The history of small wars of recent times probably affords Suakin, 1885. no example of the employment of square formation upon the march, under conditions so unfavourable as was the case in 1885 at Suakin. The sudden rushes of fanatical spearmen in this bush-overgrown theatre of operations made it obligatory that the square should be of the rigid form with ranks closed up. The convoys to be guarded consisted of camels—a most inconvenient form of transport when the animals are crowded together. Water, a most difficult thing to carry, was a main item of supply to be conveyed by the camels. The mimosa scrub greatly hampered movement and tended to break up the ranks. The heat and dust were most trying to the troops. Everything seemed to conspire against success. But the square formation was found to work, and resolute onslaughts by masses of fanatical Hadendowas were beaten off with comparative ease, although progress was very slow. One reason for this was that from the nature of the operations the size of the convoys could be satisfactorily apportioned to the numerical strength of the forces guarding them.

At Suakin the method adopted was to form depôts a few miles apart along the line of operations which it was proposed to follow. Convoys were sent out guarded by troops told off for the purpose, who formed square round the transport. On reaching the depôt the supplies and stores were deposited and the convoy returned. By working on these lines the strength of the convoy could be kept within limits which did not exceed what the troops could safeguard in this formation, and the system was strictly in accordance with the principle, already referred to in Chapter V, of holding back the troops and of pushing supplies ahead of them. But when a force is moving as a flying column for some considerable distance in an unproductive theatre of war, its transport for supplies soon grows into an unwieldy mass, which occupies more space than the troops can possibly surround in shoulder-to-shoulder square formation. When Sir H. Stewart's force advanced from the Jakdul Wells on Abu Klea, it had with it nearly 3,000 camels ; the number of combatants in the force was, including officers, only about 1,500 men—a number quite insufficient to have formed a square round such a mass of transport on the move without leaving numerous gaps.

Artillery and cavalry with reference to squares on the march. Artillery in motion is defenceless. When therefore the square is adopted as an order of march to meet the case of very sudden hostile onslaughts, it is obvious that the guns should be inside ; outside they run the risk of being rushed before they can get into action. Whatever position the guns are to take up when they come into action, whether at the angles or in the faces, this should be fixed in advance ; on the move they should march inside the square close to the positions they are to take up, so as to be ready to get to work at once if the enemy makes a rush. They should be kept well clear of the transport, and when hostile attack seems imminent it has been found best to drag portable guns along by hand. Machine guns would be treated in a similar manner.

Cavalry on the other hand will of necessity always be outside the square on the march. Mounted troops are invaluable for reconnoitring purposes and can be of great assistance in this manner to the square. Their retirement inside the square in case of attack will seldom be advisable unless, as at Ulundi, the enemy is in great strength and surrounds the force, or unless there is plenty of time for the retirement to be effected deliberately and in good order without masking the fire of the square. Under ordinary circumstances, in fact, the cavalry keeps quite independent of the square. During the advance to the Abu Klea wells, and also at Suakin in 1885, the cavalry moved at some distance from the squares. Hicks Pasha seems to have adopted the same arrangement. Should the square be attacked, the cavalry, if remaining outside, must be guided by circumstances; it is in a position to act very effectively against the enemy when beaten off, as was well illustrated at El Teb. It can threaten the flanks and rear of the enemy while actually attacking the square. When cavalry vedettes are scouting in front of a square on the march, they should be instructed to retire to a flank in the event of coming upon a formidable hostile gathering, so as to unmask the fire of the infantry and artillery. In Dahomey, where the nature of the terrain and the weakness of the cavalry detachment militated against the effective action of this arm, the mounted troops were generally on the flank on the march; when the enemy showed in force the troopers sometimes retired behind the column and formed the rear face of the fighting square; but in that campaign the square was rather of the elastic order suitable to bush warfare, than the rigid square designed to meet shock tactics.

In a case where the square formation has been adopted on the march as security against the risk of attack by strong bodies of fanatical horse, the position of the cavalry must be something of a puzzle. Presumably the force of cavalry will be small. It may be obliged to scout ahead of the square. If it bolts for the square to escape a hostile onslaught it gets in the way. If it gallops away the enemy will pursue and perhaps disperse it. Under such conditions the cavalry will necessarily have an anxious time and the proper course for it to pursue is not easy to determine.

Bivouac in square.

As regards forming bivouac in square there is not very much to be said. When this is found to be necessary it is almost invariably also desirable to convert the bivouac into a temporarily fortified post or zeriba, or, in case the force is accompanied by wagons, into a laager. The French in Egypt generally bivouacked in square. Sir J. Outram's force bivouaced in square on the night before the fight of Khushab in Persia, after it had been attacked unexpectedly by the enemy. It is a very good arrangement if no means exist of making a zeriba, or if the circumstances are such as to necessitate provision against very sudden and dangerous rushes from all sides. As a rule however, owing to the very cramped space left inside, it is very inconvenient to bivouac in rigid square formation, *i.e.*, the men simply lying down where otherwise they would be standing. Still it might under certain circumstances become necessary to so pass the night, as, for instance, in a case where the force has been overtaken by darkness before it can form any defences.

Conclusion.

Square formation has been treated of at considerable length, more with a view of illustrating under what varying conditions it has been employed in irregular warfare, than of laying down rules for guidance as to when it should be adopted and how it can best be organized. It is not popular in certain quarters. In theory there is indeed much to be said against it. But as long as regular troops burdened with the impedimenta with which they cannot dispense, are pitted against warriors who, whether as a consequence of their great numerical superiority, or of their rapid movements, or of the nature of the theatre of operations, can attack them at close quarters from any side at will, it will not be easy to substitute for it a better formation.

CHAPTER XVIII.

PRINCIPLES OF LAAGER AND ZERIBA WARFARE.

CONDUCTING operations under shelter of laagers and zeribas is peculiar to small wars. Even in irregular warfare it is a method of carrying on a campaign which is only practised under certain special conditions—it is indeed only applicable to some cases. But in many of these campaigns improvised defences have been constantly constructed whenever a force halts, the principle of employing laagers and zeribas on all occasions has been a distinctive feature, and their constant utilization has occasionally indeed governed the whole course of hostilities to a very remarkable extent.

General principles of laager and zeriba warfare.

The principle is an excellent illustration of defensive tactics superimposed upon offensive strategy. The regular troops invade hostile territory, or territory in temporary occupation of the enemy, and in doing so they maintain strategically the initiative. But, no sooner do they find themselves in presence of the irregular forces prepared for battle than they form the laager or zeriba as the case may be, and either await attack or else leave their impedimenta in it and go out to fight without encumbrances. In any case they have a secure bivouac and adequate protection during the hours of darkness.

Laagers and zeribas are really an extension of the principle of the square. They afford lines of fire in all directions, and they offer resistance to attack from any side. They provide security for the baggage, for the transport, for the food, and for the non-combatant services. Under favourable circumstances they can be formed so quickly that they may be said to represent a defensive battle formation assumed actually in the presence of the enemy. The arrangement of bivouac in square so largely adopted in Algeria, Tunis, and Central Asia, was generally accompanied, when it was possible, by the construction of some defences approximating to what is understood by a zeriba.

Tactically a defensive system.

Laagers and zeribas possess from the tactical point of view all the attributes of fortifications, their employment means a defensive attitude—an attitude tending indeed towards passive defence. Where shelter is improvised merely to ensure the safety of the non-combatant portion of the force while the remainder gives battle in the open, this is not objectionable. It is when the fighting force surrounds itself with abattis or with rings of vehicles on every possible occasion, that what is here called laager and zeriba warfare has such drawbacks, because such a method of conducting operations is in the main an adoption of the defensive when in action. And even when the troops are not actually in action, the formation of laagers and zeribas has the same effect upon them as acting on the defensive has—it heightens the respect which they entertain for the antagonists whom they are going to fight.

Objections to this.

It is perhaps to some extent a matter of opinion whether this system of constantly shutting up the force within a kind of fort, which has been so largely adopted in many campaigns, has an injurious moral effect upon good troops. But the natural inference which all ranks are inclined to draw therefrom is that the army cannot in the open cope on level terms with the foe, and many experienced leaders hold that this must have a depressing influence upon their men. Sir C. Napier, after his brilliant success at Meani in Scinde, felt himself compelled to form an entrenched camp, because formidable bodies of Beluchis were still in the field ; but he camped his force outside fearing lest the troops, flushed though they were with victory, might infer from their occupation of the lines that their cause was a failing one. Trusting to fortifications during the day time—at night it is different—undoubtedly argues inferiority to the adversary. Laagers and zeribas do not breathe the spirit of attack. The soldier who daily fences himself round with abattis and obstacles to keep the enemy off, may come to think that deprived of this shelter he is no match for the savage whom he has come to beat. Putting the moral factor on one side, this method of making war has in many cases much to recommend it; but in war the moral factor can rarely be ignored with safety.

On the other hand, when the regular army is hampered by the responsibility of safeguarding a great column of transport, when in fact it is merely an escort for its own supplies, laagers or zeribas are almost compulsory, supposing the adversary to be strong and enterprising. In the jungle and the bush where the hostile forces may creep up unseen and pounce down suddenly, some form of defence work round the camp, or even during a midday halt, may be indispensable. To stem the rush of swarms of fanatics, or to check the onslaughts of savages who swoop upon the regular troops regardless of losses caused by modern arms of precision, obstacles are invaluable. In theatres of war where sudden attacks of masses of irregular horse are to be expected, the constant formation of laagers or zeribas may be obligatory. But even then it is to a certain extent a contravention of a broad principle governing the whole art of war—the principle that success should be sought for in attack, in preserving the initiative in tactics as in strategy, and in reaping to the full the benefit of moral effect by assuming and maintaining a dominant bearing. *Situations where laagers and zeribas are very necessary.*

It was laid down in Chapter XI that the right method of dealing with antagonists who adhere to the guerilla system of warfare, is the organization of mobile columns capable of going considerable distances and designed to follow up the hostile parties and give them no rest. The temporary bases *Their value in dealing with guerillas.*

of these columns generally require defensive arrangements of some kind, and therefore in operations of this class laagers or zeribas will generally be made considerable use of. Moreover, mobile columns are almost necessarily small and they must be to a certain extent hampered by transport. By making use of laagers or zeribas this transport can often be left behind while some especial dash is being made. During the suppression of the rebellion in Rhodesia, columns were often separated from their wagons for two or three days at a time, these were formed into laagers and a small guard rendered them practically secure ; maxim guns in them were found very useful, adding greatly to their defensive strength. It is, of course a most important point in these cases to reduce the numbers left behind in charge of the impedimenta of the column to a minimum, so as to have as many rifles as possible for the active operations which are being undertaken; and with this in view, some form of defensive post for the temporary depôt is, as a rule desirable.

Conditions
necessary
for their
construction.

The formation of zeribas and laagers demand the existence of certain conditions. Zeribas, in the ordinary acceptance of the term, are enclosures fenced in by abattis and thorn bushes, and to construct them there must be jungle, bush, or scrub on the spot. Laagers, on the other hand, are formed of wagons, and it is only in certain small wars that wheeled vehicles accompany the troops. These temporary defensive enclosures are sometimes supplemented by breastworks of pack saddles and stores, by shelter trenches, and so forth. But the idea of this class of rapidly improvised fortification is (to use the phraseology of the engineer) not so much to provide cover for the defence as to oppose obstacles to the attack. It is designed to secure the regular troops against the shock action of their antagonists, rather than against their fire.

Campaigns
in which
zeribas and

Zeribas assumed great prominence in the campaigns in the Sudan. Here the hostile tactics consisted chiefly in sudden rushes of reckless fanatical spearmen.   As a rule mimosa laagers have
been largely
used. bushes and scrub were available on the spot.   Around Suakin the thick jungle growth favoured the unseen approach of large bodies of the enemy, but, thanks to it, the construction of brushwood fences offered was simple and they provided the best method of meeting the tactics of the Mahdists.   Hastily improvised defensive enclosures of this kind can, of course, be supplemented by trenches and parapets, and they may eventually be converted into fortified posts which can be held by a small number of men.   In Dahomey the French, bivouacking in square, protected themselves with shelter trenches and abattis having the character to a certain extent of zeribas ; these defensive enclosures were, however, formed chiefly as a protection for the night.   Zeribas were made free use of during the Somaliland campaign of 1903–04.

Laagers have always been a special feature of warfare in South Africa and North America.   On the veld and prairie the pioneers of civilization moved in small bodies, with their families and property borne in great wagons adapted to these roadless rolling downs, and often found their vehicles a sure bulwark when attacked.   Sheltered behind the bulwark which the wagons formed, their firearms had full play and the hostile charges were stemmed and broken.   It became the regular programme after a move to draw up the wagons in the form of a square or oblong enclosure, the cattle, horses, &c., being picketed or fastened up in the interior, and saddles and other gear being used to form a breastwork between the wheels.   Regular troops campaigning in these countries have adopted the same method and have found it to answer.   The United States troops when operating against Red Indians were constantly forming laagers, or corrals as they were called. During the suppression of Riel's rebellion in 1885, laagers were generally established by the Government troops when they got into camp after a march.   In the Zulu and Matabili wars laagers were always constructed when at the halt, if wagons were available, as long as there was any possibility of attack.

Their special advantages. Economy of outposts.

One great advantage of forming laager or zeriba is that it economises outposts. The troops bivouac along the faces, and can man them at a moment's notice. The line to be defended is clearly defined. Each unit has its place. The line of defence is practically identical with the line of outposts, and a mere fraction of the force serves to secure it against surprises—a point which is of great advantage both by day and night.

Security at night.

At night the fact of being within a defensive enclosure gives security to the troops, and gives, what is of almost equal importance, a distinct sense of security. In a later chapter it will be seen that although night attacks by the enemy are somewhat unusual, irregular warriors are given to harassing their opponents under cover of darkness and that marauding is always to be expected. The wagons, abattis, &c., serve to check this, and to avert what is a great annoyance even if it is not a serious danger.

They generally, but not necessarily, enable the regular troops to select their ground and time for fighting.

Another great advantage of forming laagers and zeribas is that they generally enable the commander of the regular forces to select his own ground, and to a certain extent his own time for fighting. This may not of course necessarily be the case, but it usually is so. Sir H. Stewart's force marching from Abu Klea for the Nile, was practically compelled by the enemy to form a zeriba on unfavourable ground; but, under the shelter of this zeriba, the column was able to transform itself into a purely fighting force and was enabled to march out to fight, selecting its own time. The result of this was that the column brought off its fight on favourable ground, and that it was effectively supported by the guns in the zeriba without being hampered by their presence when in movement. The following example from the Red Indian campaigns may also be quoted; in this case a laager, which had to be formed under sudden pressure of the enemy in an unsuitable position for defence, saved the troops from destruction when in a most critical situation

A small cavalry force with a convoy of wagons was marching in 1879 to the White River Agency, in Colorado. The cavalry moving in front of the wagons came suddenly upon the enemy in strong force near the Milk River, and the mounted troops were speedily obliged to fall back. Thereupon the vehicles were hastily formed into a laager close to the river, and to complete the ring, for which there were not wagons enough, wounded horses were shot and the carcases were used to form a sort of breastwork on one side. The position was most unfavourable for defence, but, thanks to the wagons, the troops held out for a week till they were finally relieved, having been reinforced in the meantime. The losses in men and horses were very heavy in the interval, but the force was saved.

Sir H. Stewart's force and the United States troops in these cases had to form a defensive host as best they could in a hurry on unfavourable ground. There is always the chance that small bodies moving about a theatre of irregular warfare may be suddenly attacked by superior forces, and may be obliged to construct a zeriba or some kind of laager on the spot. But the most remarkable examples of attacks on laagers and zeribas of late years have been where these have been deliberately established, and where in consequence the commander of the regular troops has chosen his own battle-field. At Ginghilovo in the Zulu war, and at Imbembesi and Shangani in the Matabili war, the position of the laagers had been deliberately selected. At Tofrek near Suakin in 1885, the site of the zeriba had been carefully chosen. By having a temporary fortress of this kind the commander of the force may elect to fight inside of it, most favourably placed if the enemy can be induced to attack, or he may prefer merely to use the laager or zeriba to shelter the non-combatants while the fighting portions sally forth and give battle in the open. This latter plan was the one adopted at Ulundi, at Tamai, and at Abu Klea. The French in Dahomey frequently left their stores and transport under improvised cover of this nature, issuing out of their zeribas to fight in their own time and on ground practically selected by themselves. When this arrangement is adopted the laager or zeriba relieves the force of the encumbrances which hamper it at other times, and it serves, moreover, as a refuge, should the fates prove unpropitious on the battlefield.

They afford the troops repose during prolonged operations.

An army penetrating far into the territories of a brave and warlike race must occasionally have some rest and security from alarms. For rest it must come to a halt ; but the very fact of its coming to a standstill is in a manner a confession of weakness and the enemy, taking it to mean a want of confidence, gathers courage. For this reason the regular troops are especially exposed, during a halt of any duration, to onslaughts of their adversaries who will have been emboldened by the temporary inaction. But within laagers and zeribas the troops rarely have much to fear, and if the enemy is tempted to attack them he is generally beaten off with comparative ease. In fact, when the soldiery really need repose the assumption of an attitude of defence, and even of passive defence, may not be unjustifiable ; it may indeed at times be almost imperative.

Zeribas may become defence posts upon the line of communications, or may serve as supply depôts in advance of an army.

When, as is so often the case, the broad plan of campaign at the outset is to push supplies into the heart of an enemy's country under limited escort, with the idea of forming great depôts for the army which is eventually to crush the resistance of the enemy, some plan of constantly forming laagers or zeribas and fighting on the defensive is imperative. With time, zeribas—not laagers if these are taken to mean enclosures formed of wagons, camels, and so forth—develop into defensive posts. As the force advances they remain behind it—links upon the chain of communications. Sometimes, as observed above, zeribas afford a means of pushing the supplies ahead of an advancing army, a system the necessity of adopting which at times was dealt with fully in Chapter V. Thus, in 1885, when it was decided to advance south-westwards from Suakin, a convoy strongly guarded was sent out with orders for the troops to construct a zeriba in which to leave the loads under the protection of a portion of the force, the troops were then to return with the transport to the base. The zeriba was formed, in spite of a desperate attack upon it when half constructed, and then relays of convoys were sent out to it daily till sufficient supplies had been collected for the force to advance beyond it. In this case the zeriba acted at first as a secure supply depôt thrust out in advance of the army; then, when the army passed it, it served as a fortified post on the line of communications. This well illustrates one phase of what may be called laager and zeriba warfare.

The truth is that adequate reasons exist in certain theatres General of war, and under certain conditions, for adopting this method conclusions. of making war temporarily, and sometimes for adhering to it throughout the campaign. In many struggles of recent years the practice has invariably been to form laager and zeriba whenever the troops were halted by day, or halted for the night or longer. In Dahcmey, in Zululand and among the Matabilis, in the campaign against Riel, and in Central Asia in many cases, the regular army has adopted the system and has adapted it to varying circumstances with great success. Some think it to be derogatory, some fear its evil moral effect upon the troops. But if kept within limits, if employed only when clear necessity arises, if not permitted to cramp their energies or to check judiciously applied offensive action on the part of the troops, there is much to be said for a military system which safeguards the supplies of an army and which grants it temporary repose.

CHAPTER XIX.

HILL WARFARE.

Explanation of term " hill warfare." HILL warfare may fairly be said to constitute a special branch of the military art—typical hill warfare, that is to say, such as Anglo-Indian troops have been fitfully employèd upon for two generations beyond the Indus, culminating in the memorable Tirah campaign. It is not proposed in this chapter to deal with general engagements in mountainous country, like the storming of the Malakand Pass under Sir R. Low or the attack upon the Peiwar Kotal; nor is it intended to deal with the case of operations against irregular forces, which may be occupying or may have taken refuge in patches of hilly country, as the Matabili rebels did in the Matoppos in 1896. It is the campaigns of regular troops against hill-men fighting in guerilla fashion in their own native mountains and in defence of their own homes, campaigns almost the most trying which disciplined soldiers can be called upon to undertake, which create the conditions of genuine hill warfare and which deserve to be considered as a subject quite apart.

Its difficulties in all parts of the world. The memorable operations of 1897-98 on the Panjab frontier attracted general attention to the importance of training our troops with a view to meeting the exigencies of this hill warfare, in consequence of the exceptional difficulties which beset the regular forces and of the heavy losses which were incurred before operations were brought to a conclusion. But it is no new thing for disciplined soldiers to find the coercion of mountaineers an arduous and a perilous task. Strong bodies of French and of Bavarian troops under experienced leaders suffered catastrophe after catastrophe at the hands of the Tyrolese peasants in 1809. Anglo-Indian battalions accustomed to triumph on the plains of Hindustan against tremendous odds, found in Nepaul that the disciplined army did not necessarily emerge victorious from combat with the hill-men of that rugged region. The military might of the Ottoman Empire, when still near the zenith of its greatness, failed for years to subdue the highlanders of Greece. Hill warfare presents, in fact, features of peculiar difficulty to regular armies, and its successful prosecution demands exceptional methods and exceptional leadership.

It will not be out of place before entering on a closer consideration of the subject, to examine for a moment what are these special difficulties involved in hill warfare. Some of them are obvious enough. It hardly needs demonstration that a rugged mountainous country destitute of roads, renders the movement of organized bodies of fighting men slow and laborious, quite apart from what the enemy may do. Any intersected terrain favours the people of the country who are acquainted with its intricacies, at the expense of invaders to whom it is unknown. Wheeled transport cannot be employed in such theatres of war, and vast trains of pack animals which stretch out a portentous length when on the march have to take its place. Supplies are rarely abundant in the mountains. All these are points that strike one at once; but there are others which are not quite so self-evident.

In the first place there is the wear and tear caused by isolated marksmen perched on the hill tops, who fire down upon the troops in camp and on the march, whose desultory enterprises render outpost duties very onerous, who inflict appreciable losses among officers and men, and who thin the columns of transport with their bullets—this is more prejudicial to the efficiency of the army than is generally supposed. "Sniping."

Then again there is the unfortunate fact that, from their very nature, these operations are constantly imposing upon the regular troops the undesirable rôle of acting as a force Retirements unavoidable at times.

retiring before irregular warriors. Columns have to visit outlying valleys for punitive purposes and must then rejoin the main body ; and even when penetrating into the heart of a hostile mountain district the rear of the army, as it passes successively the homes of different tribes and clans, draws these down upon it, and, as a result of the general direction of its march retires before them. Furthermore, it is the one great fundamental rule in war against undisciplined opponents, against Asiatics and savages and guerillas, always to seize and to keep the upper hand, to advance constantly and to harry them till they beg for peace ; but in struggles against mountaineers occasional local retreats on the part of the regular troops cannot be avoided however resolute and vigorous may be the general plan of campaign. It is not only the tactical difficulty which attends these minor withdrawals, but also the elation in the hostile ranks at the spectacle of columns falling back, which has to be reckoned with and which gives to hill warfare a character of its own.

Care of the wounded.

It has already been pointed out how greatly the responsibility for saving the wounded from falling into the enemy's hands affects the tactics of regular troops in small wars. In no form of operations is this fact so strongly brought home to a disciplined army as in hill warfare against savage, bloodthirsty clansmen. The removal of wounded men is especially difficult owing to the nature of the ground. Every wounded man creates a little knot of men which offers the sniper a favourable target, one injured man thus begets others, and the progress of that part of the force in close contact with the enemy, becomes seriously—sometimes fatally—delayed.

Special risk to officers in Indian frontier fighting.

Another point must not be overlooked in Indian frontier fighting where the hostile gatherings often number many who have served their time in native regiments. This is that officers are very likely to be singled out by marksmen, who can readily recognize them by their clothes and appearance. This is

especially the case with British officers in native regiments,
who can be detected at a considerable distance, and the value
of whose lives the Pathan is perfectly well aware of. This is
a very serious matter, and one for which unfortunately there
seems to be no remedy in campaigns on the Panjab border.

Then there is the naturally warlike character of the
average hill-man to be taken into account. He is a fighter
all the world over, and always has been. The history of
Europe proves it. Russian experiences in the Caucasus
prove it. Anglo-Indian conflicts with the Bunerwals and
Mohmunds and Afridis and Miranzais prove it. It is true
no doubt, that even the most truculent of Pathan clans, even
Zakka Khels and Mamunds, do not display the reckless
bravery which the Zulus did in the days of Ulundi, and
which has so often won admiration for the forces of the
Mahdi and of the Khalifa. They do not give themselves away,
but for all that they are warriors to the core. The guerilla of the
hills plays the game in his own way. Amongst their boulders
and gorges the tribesmen of the Indian frontier are most
formidable foemen; they are active, cunning, determined,
and often take a long time before they acknowledge
themselves vanquished, although once beaten, they take it
like good sportsmen, hoping for better luck next time. Of
late years, moreover, a new feature has been introduced into
warfare in their territory. They have acquired a stock
of modern rifles, which have made their tactics far more
difficult to cope with than when they trusted to antiquated
matchlocks having neither range nor accuracy. It was the
martial instinct of the Afridis and their excellent arms which,
brought into play in a theatre of war presenting unprecedented
difficulties to a disciplined army, made the Tirah campaign
one of the most dangerous and arduous struggles which
British troops have been engaged in since the Indian mutiny.

Moreover in hill warfare regular armies have to contend
not only with hostile bullets and charges of swordsmen, but

Enemy generally warlike and nowadays well armed.

Stones and trees can be thrown down on the troops.

also with the missiles which nature provides for the defenders of a mountainous country. The enemy rolls down rocks and stones, often with murderous precision. A large proportion of the defenders of the Malakand Pass in 1896, trusted entirely to the effect produced by dislodging boulders. The disaster which befel a party of soldiers in the Koragh defile near Chitral at the outbreak of those disturbances which led to Sir R. Low's advance, was also mainly caused by crowds of Chitralis who hurled down stones from coigns of vantage. It is interesting to note that instances have occurred where mountaineers have rolled down trees upon the troops.

One of the most serious disasters which the French forces met with at the hand of the Tyrolese in 1809, befel a column of all arms advancing from the south, not far from the Brenner Pass. The guerillas had cut down numbers of trees high up on the mountain side above the road, and these were suddenly precipitated from various points upon the soldiery. Whole companies were swept down over the precipices into the torrent below. The confusion caused was indescribable, the losses overwhelming. A formidable body of highly disciplined troops was rolled back in confusion, routed by a mere mob of ill-armed peasantry.

Having drawn attention to some of the peculiar difficulties which beset regular forces engaged in hill warfare, the special methods which it imposes on them can be now dealt with in detail.

Size of columns.

Hill warfare almost necessarily obliges the regular troops to employ pack transport. The inconvenience of this form of transport has been already pointed out in Chapter V, and the enormous length of columns which it gives rise to, has been commented on. If the roads are very difficult—and there are certain to be some short lengths of narrow defile on most marches—the transport has to move in single file, and then it must be assumed that each animal will take 3 to 4 yards of road. If there are 5,000 mules to a column, and if that column makes a march of 10 miles along a narrow mountain track, the rearmost mules will still be in the old camp waiting to move off, when the head of the column has already reached the new camp. The result of this is that in genuine hill warfare columns must be small. It is found that four or five battalions, a battery and a field company of engineers, with their baggage and supplies for four or five days, make as large a force as can conveniently be included in a single column. A very practical argument in favour of small columns is that, if the amount of transport is small there is a reasonable prospect of its being of good quality, which is essential if the force is to possess mobility.

If operations are to cover an area of any extent, it is generally best to employ several small columns. It is the only way by which reasonable mobility can be secured. But it does not follow on this account that the force, as a whole, is to advance by several lines of operations. It may sometimes be best, bearing in mind the broad principle of holding back troops and pushing supplies ahead of them into the heart of the theatre of war, to advance by only one line in the first instance, not necessarily in strong force, with the idea of massing food in some central position well within the enemy's territory. But then, when the supply magazines have been established and the whole force moves up, its further operations will be carried out in small columns working independently in different directions. *Several columns usual.*

In warfare of this character the enemy is apt to retire into mountain fastnesses with his women and children and belongings, and these must be visited and, if necessary, cleared. Very determined hill-men may decline to come to terms till every little valley and gorge has been harried. All this takes time and to get the work done numerous small columns must be employed, even if the transport question did not dictate a dissemination of the force when it is on the move.

Marches must generally be very short, so as to ensure that the rearguard gets in before dark. When there is any likelihood of opposition, and if the size of the columns and the amount of supplies it is taking with it oblige it to include *Length of marches.*

some thousands of pack animals, a march of 5 miles is about as much as can safely be attempted. A very small column with only a few hundred animals could, however, cover a considerably longer distance than this between dawn and the closing in of the evening. It is really a matter of calculation, as long as there is no opposition. But if the head of the column has to fight its way forward and is delayed by deploying in difficult ground, the time which will be taken cannot be accurately calculated and even a 5 miles' march may prove inconveniently long. The importance of getting into camp before dark will be shown in later paragraphs.

The troops generally on the lower ground, the enemy on the heights.

Inasmuch as in hilly country the routes naturally follow the course of valleys, and as habitations, cultivation, and level patches suitable for camps are generally found in depressions, regular troops engaged in operations in such theatres of war are, when not in immediate combat with the foe, practically compelled to remain on the lower ground. This is so whether they are on the move or at rest. The consequence is that the enemy occupies the crests of the hills which the army passes on the march, or which surrounds its bivouac when it comes to a halt. Hill-men moreover always retire to the high ground when the troops advance against villages or show dispositions for a fight. As a result, what is

"Crowning the heights."

technically known as "crowning the heights," is at almost all times an essential part of any operation in hill warfare, and it can rarely be altogether dispensed with even when the troops are at rest. But although this principle is fully recognized nowadays, and although the precaution of occupying commanding ground whence hostile parties could inflict loss on the army below seems an obvious one to take, it is nevertheless a fact that the system has only of late years come to be adopted as a matter of course—as the following examples show.

Examples of neglect of this.

In the Nepaul war the lack of flankers on the heights was the paramount cause of failure on the part of several of the columns.

In 1823 a Turkish commander, well aware that all Hellas was up in arms and full of fight, advanced through the historic pass of Thermopylæ without previously occupying any points on the steep declivities which abut on the land side of the defile. The Greeks suddenly appeared on the hill sides, and swooped down upon the Sultan's troops as they wound along below in column of route. The column was cleft at many points and was crumpled up. The slaughter was appalling, guns and transport were abandoned, and the Ottoman troops, paralysed by the sudden onslaught when they might have defended themselves, and panic-stricken when they found that their belated efforts to show a bold front were unavailing, fled in wild disorder towards Thessaly.

During the retirement of the avenging army from Afghanistan in 1841 through the Khaibar Pass, the advanced brigade under General Pollock got through unmolested, the heights having been crowned. But this precaution was neglected in the case of the rear brigades. These suffered appreciable loss at the hands of the Afridi tribesmen, whose demand for money in payment of safe conduct had been peremptorily rejected.

In connection with this question of crowning the heights, it is desirable here early in the chapter to point out a very notable characteristic among hill-men. This is their antipathy to attacking up-hill, and their almost unreasoning dread of having opponents above them. They are ready enough to pick off antagonists who show up on the skyline from their hiding place below, but they will not advance from them even when their numbers are insignificant. It is not very easy to account for this, unless it is simply the result of the moral advantage which those perched on an eminence appear to enjoy over those at its foot. An assault down hill, of course, gets over the ground more quickly than when it is delivered up an ascent, but on the other hand it is easier to creep up hill unseen than down hill. However, there can be no doubt—whatever the reason may be—that mountaineers are very nervous about having opponents above them, and that in hill warfare this is an important point for the regular troops to bear in mind, because it influences the whole question of tactics to a considerable extent. It enables picquets to hold knolls far out of reach of any support. It offers a means of obliging the enemy to evacuate strong positions, if higher ground be near. It

Enemy's dislike of attacking up-hill and of being commanded.

may afford security to hard pressed troops who find an eminence at hand, offering them a temporary refuge, which they can occupy and hold.

Seizing the high ground in attacking a defile.

The principle of crowning the heights generally comes into play in the case of forcing the passage through a gorge or ravine. Hill-men are very much inclined to mainly depend upon breastworks within the ravine itself when making their arrangements to defend such a place. In any case seizing the high ground on either side of the defile will generally be the best method of forcing it when the enemy is prepared to offer a resistance. The capture of the heights of course turns any defence works down below, often taking these in reverse; and, once they have been secured, fire from them may cause considerable loss to the enemy retreating along the ravine—as occurred in the case of General Pollock's attack on the entrance to the Khaibar which is quoted in General Clery's "Minor Tactics." But it is not general actions of this kind which claim special attention in hill warfare; these have been already dealt with in Chapter XII.

Occupying the heights in moving along a valley or defile.

Before going into the operation of how to crown the heights in some detail, it will not be out of place to point out how well this obligation illustrates the inconvenience of conflicts with guerillas as the adversary. As will be explained below, this crowning the heights is a most troublesome and difficult operation, fatiguing to the troops, breaking them up into small parties which may easily meet with some mishap, and tending to delay the column. But in spite of its inconveniences and drawbacks and of the wear and tear on officers and men, it may have to be undertaken day after day for weeks upon weeks even when the enemy seems to be quiescent, because it is never known when these hill-men may collect and where, and because in guerilla warfare it is never safe to assume that there is no enemy because there is no enemy to be seen.

Moving flanking parties and

Many valleys exist where flanking detachments would almost move as rapidly along the hill tops as the column with its impedimenta would make its way below. Where there are no subsidiary valleys, and no ravines and gorges jutting out from the main valley into the mountains on either hand, moving along the heights in parties is not necessarily a very tedious task; but such topographical conditions are in all parts of the world the exception rather than the rule, and this is certainly the case on the high lands of the Indian frontier. Many of the valley systems beyond the Indus may almost be likened to the backbone of a fish, so many are the nullahs and clefts on either side of the main depression, and it is obvious that the movement of flankers parallel to a column traversing this main depression will in such a case be a slow and most exhausting process. Therefore it has come to be very generally recognized as the best arrangement in very difficult country of this nature for the flanking parties to be stationary instead of moving.

The plan adopted may be roughly described as follows :— The advanced guard starts as a strong force, relatively to the column as a whole, and moves off some time before the main body. As it advances, it detaches parties on either hand to seize convenient hill tops commanding the line of route, and to hold them while the column passes. As the rear guard comes level with the different parties these withdraw from their posts and join it—the rear guard sweeps them up, as it were, on its march; and this has one great advantage, namely, that the rear guard, which as a rule gets most of the fighting, gets stronger and stronger automatically as it approaches its goal. Of course this method is not without its obvious inconveniences. Units are broken up, and at the end of a rough day's work the rear guard becomes rather a heterogeneous body. Moreover the troops which start first are apt to be the last, or among the last, to get in. Still, where the operation involves traversing a network of ravines and the flanking parties have to be stationary, an arrangement on this principle seems to answer better than any other. It should be noted that the flanking picquets on descending from their posts are often sent on at once to camp, if the rearguard be not pressed, in recognition of the hard work they have gone through. It is hardly necessary to point out that a stationary picquet, which can, if necessary, strengthen its position with sangars and which soons learns the surroundings and the defensive capabilities of its post, affords a more effective guard over a given stretch of ground thán does a party of the same strength which has been clambering up and down for miles on end, meeting at every step new under-features and new obstacles during the time that it traverses that same stretch of ground.

During the memorable march of Sir W. Lockhart's 2nd Division down the Bara valley in 1897, the leading brigade did not at first find flanking picquets for the rear brigade; but it was found by experience that it was better for it to do so. And it is interesting to note that, when on the evening of the last day but one of the march the Afridis boldly attacked General Westmacott's rear guard which had taken up a position on a ridge for the night, he had under his command, besides detachments of his own five regiments, a whole wing of the 2nd Gurkhas belonging to the other brigade, which had been on picquet duty.

Some difference of opinion exists whether it is best for one battalion to undertake flanking duties on both sides of the valley, or whether the picquets should be found by separate battalions for the two flanks. The former plan has the advantage that the entire control along a certain stretch is under one commanding officer. On the other hand, inasmuch as, when one battalion has been expended another has to be told off, it tends to mix up different units more than if whole battalions are told off to one side. Should the enemy be in force on one side and require to be driven off before the column can advance, this task can probably better be entrusted to a single battalion which would then picquet the heights on that flank.

Remarks on flanking picquets. It is of course impossible to lay down any rule as to what the strength of flanking picquets should be. They must

be strong enough to hold the post they are detailed for, and
to safeguard the stretch told off to them. But experience
proves that the guerilla hill-men are not fond of attacking
well posted parties, and that very small detachments can
remain isolated in safety if their position has been carefully
selected. " It is a common error," says Lieut.-Colonel Martin
in his pamphlet, " Mountain and Savage Warfare," " to have
far too many men on these flank picquets, which, if well
supported by one another and their supports, are far safer if
they consist of a few men properly posted ; and a few men
are, as a rule, sufficient for their requirements, whereas a
large number are not only a waste of power but may give
the enemy a better target to fire at and are more difficult to
withdraw." Still, this presupposes that the ground admits
of the picquets effectively supporting each other, and of their
having supports to lean upon, which in very broken ground
may be impracticable. But on this point the experience of
the Tirah campaign is all in favour of very small parties ;
for throughout those long and trying operations, where isolated
detachments were constantly posted at different points along
the lines of route and round the camps and bivouacs, not one
single one was overwhelmed by day or by night.

Of course it sometimes occurs that particular knolls and
spurs may be held by the enemy and that the capture of
these entails a force of some strength being told off for attack.
But when such a point has once been secured a small picquet
will generally suffice to hold it.

As regards the positions to be taken up by flanking
picquets, the considerations governing this question have
been greatly modified of recent years by the improved armament of the tribesmen. Formerly, when the enemy's fire
was innocuous at ranges over 500 yards, the picquets had
not to push out far afield into the hills. But with antagonists whose musketry is accurate at ranges up to a mile,
it is necessary that flanking detachments should occupy

the knolls and crests situated at distances of 1,500 yards, and sometimes more, from the point to be protected. When troops or baggage are moving along in column of route offering a favourable target for the enemy's marksmanship, it is almost indispensable that the picquets should be so placed as to keep the tribesmen out of range of the column. In any case the picquets must make it absolutely certain that small hostile parties do not creep down clefts and gorges, and get close to the route with a view to sudden attack upon baggage or followers. As a rule a picquet would climb up to the knoll which it is to occupy with bayonets fixed, and in scattered formation so as not to present a target, and it should avoid showing up the sky-line towards the enemy, or indeed getting on the sky-line with regard to any point where foemen may possibly be lurking. It is very important that the commander of a picquet should know when he is to quit his post, because as a general rule its withdrawal is the most difficult part of its task ; but as retreats and retirements will be dealt with later on, this point will be referred to then.

In the case of convoys passing along a valley, the system of stationary picquets is almost invariably adopted. On a line of communications through mountainous country the picquets would usually be sent out from the post at either end of the march which the convoy is to undertake, meeting half way. In this case the country is generally well known and it may be assumed that the enemy's enterprises will not be of a very determined character.

Remarks on moving flanking parties.

When in place of stationary picquets the flanking parties follow the heights and march parallel to the force moving along the valley, it will generally be advisable for the leading party and the rear party to consist of relatively strong bodies, especially the latter which is particularly likely to be molested. Great care must be taken to keep touch between the parties, and to ensure that they keep approximately abreast of their proper points in the column. It cannot well be absolutely

laid down that either the column or the flanking parties are
to set the pace. Practically, the column will move as fast as it
can ; the advanced flanking parties keep abreast of the head,
and the rear flanking parties of the tail ; but it may turn out
that, owing to ravines or rocks or to opposition on the part
of the enemy, the flankers cannot go fast enough, and then
the column must be checked. Of course if the rate of movement of the flanking parties is faster than that of the columns,
they must relax their pace.

Before closing this question of crowning the heights in hill
warfare—the occupation of the commanding ground round
camps and bivouacs is treated under the head of outposts in
Chapter XXVI—it is worth while pointing out that the
system is really very analogous to the square formation, which
is adopted in very different terrain as a safeguard against the
operations of a very different kind of enemy. In both we see
the idea of all round defence, the need for which so seldom
arises in the open field in regular warfare. In the one case
resistance has to be offered to the enterprises of gangs of
cut-throats against extended columns, in the other the sudden
onslaught of hosts of reckless foemen has to be prepared for
against a column which can be kept compact. The fighting
formation in the one case is almost the antithesis of that in
the other, and yet both may be said to originate from the same
cause and both are peculiar to small wars.

Comparison of system of crowning heights to square formation.

It has already been pointed out one of the chief difficulties
which the conditions of hill warfare create, is that the regular
troops are so often obliged to undertake retrograde movements.
The inconveniences which arise from this have been briefly
referred to in an earlier paragraph, and the history of the Indian
border wars proves how very serious they are. These retirements are often a disagreeable necessity. On the other hand
it is to a certain extent within the power of the authorities
controlling the conduct of operations in the hills, to reduce the
number of occasions when withdrawals are imposed upon the

Retirement a necessity at times, but general conduct of operations should be such as to render them as infrequent as possible.

troops, and it is clearly most desirable to keep down this number to a minimum.

Reconnais-
sances, in
reference to
this.
It is often the case in hill warfare—almost constantly on the Indian frontier—that the regular troops are called upon to advance into mountainous districts of which very little is known. An army of trained soldiers encumbered with all the transport and paraphernalia which it necessarily involves, cannot be launched into such terrain without its having been previously examined to a certain extent. It thus comes about that a reconnaissance is often the first step before any operation is undertaken. Under cover of detachments, their strength varying according to circumstances, staff officers push ahead to see what there is to be seen and to report to their chief; when, however, they have found out what they want, the force forming the reconnaissance has to return to the point whence it started—from the enemy's point of view it retreats. Now as these reconnaissances cannot sometimes be dispensed with, and as the retirement which they involve is apt to be misconstrued by the hill-men, it seems very desirable that such operations should as far as possible take the form of a surprise, that the information should be obtained after a rapid, sudden march, and that the troops should be back again in camp before the enemy has had time to collect. If the reconnaissance can be carried out on these lines, the retirement may be unmolested and will not consequently appear to have the character of retreat in face of the foe. In view of the extraordinarily speedy movements of mountaineers, of their system of beacons on the hill tops, and of their other modes of rapid communication, it is by no means easy to make a reconnaissance far into their territory and to get back before they can assemble. Still, if it can be so arranged, it will probably save loss in men, and it will certainly save some momentary loss in prestige.

Forces de-
tached for
particular
Then there is the question of detachments sent off on punitive expeditions against particular villages or clans.

When these have performed their task they must generally objects, in rejoin the main body, and this involves a local retirement. reference to it. That the force detailed for such a purpose must withdraw eventually is of course unavoidable ; but it would seem to be a sound principle in these cases not to hurry over the operation, but to make the time spent on the operation as far as possible dependent upon the attitude of the people of the locality. To march into a valley early in the morning, overcome resistance, destroy dwellings, burn fodder and blow up towers, and then to retire in the afternoon hotly pursued by an infuriated community, does not intimidate truculent highlanders ; on the contrary they think that they have got the best of the transaction. On the other hand questions of supply, and the exigencies of the general plan of campaign, may not admit of the troops which constitute a minor expedition remaining detached for several days in some particular valley, merely for the purpose of proving to a petty clan that the regulars are in a dominant position. There are so many considerations to be taken into account that the only general rule on the subject that can be laid down is, that the operation should be concluded as deliberately as circumstances admit of, and that if practicable the force should not withdraw as long as the enemy shows any inclination to follow it up.

The operations against the Mamund clan in 1897 are a case in point. The intervention of these Mamunds in the Mohmund campaign was as unexpected as it was inconvenient. Occupying a side valley on Sir B. Blood's line of communications from the borders of the Mohmund country back towards Malakand, their sudden hostility was necessarily a source of some anxiety, and it was not known that, owing to their numbers and to their very warlike nature, these tribesmen were foes who required to be taken very seriously.

A single brigade attempted to crush the clan in a single day. The operation involved a march of some miles, the destruction of several villages, and then a return march to camp. The task proved to be altogether beyond the capabilities of the force within the time, and the troops suffered heavy losses. But by deliberate methodical operations extending over several days the same force not very strongly reinforced, later on crushed all the fight out of the Mamunds, finishing its little campaign in triumph in spite of the fact that the enemy was continually getting assistance from beyond the frontier, which coincided with the head of the valley.

Holding cap-
tured heights,
in reference
to it.

Another phase of hill warfare which brings up this question of retirements is the case of hill crests or kotals which may have been captured from the enemy, but which cannot easily be held owing to the exposure which the troops would suffer, or to want of food, or for some similar reason. The only thing that can be said on this point is that a victorious army should if possible pass the night upon the battle-field (unless, of course, it can advance beyond it), and that if practicable arrangements should be made beforehand with this in view. But events cannot always be foreseen, and it must be remembered that heights are constantly cleared of the enemy when the conditions of the case render their subsequent abandonment advisable, without the enemy necessarily re-occupying them. One hears a great deal from time to time about " positions " in hill warfare. But the fact is that almost every mountain crest becomes a position when the enemy occupies it, and that the crest is captured and cleared, not because it is a point of strategical or tactical importance, but because the enemy is there. Still when high ground has been wrested from gatherings of hill-men it should not be abandoned at once, if it can be avoided ; even if it can be held for a few hours the withdrawal from it will not appear to the enemy so much in the light of a retreat.

The case of
Dargai.

In this connection the two actions of Dargai in 1897, which attracted such attention at the time, may be instanced. The first movement against the heights above Chagru Kotal from Shinawarri camp had been a reconnaissance in force to view the country, the main column approaching the Dargai position from its right rear (south-west) after a most difficult march over unknown country, while a smaller force actually captured the heights by a frontal attack from the east before the main column came in sight. Strong reinforcements kept joining the defeated tribesmen from the Khanki valley to the north, and, had it been decided to hold the heights, a whole brigade would probably have been required to occupy a very isolated position, and one for the occupation of which no preparations had been made.

The intended line of march of the field force was northwards over the Chagru Kotal, east of the Dargai heights, down into the Khanki valley. Sir W. Lockhart, well acquainted with Pathan methods of warfare, foresaw that the tribesmen who had come from the Khanki valley would withdraw as soon as they found the troops passing their front and threatening their line of retreat. But the troops on reaching the Chagru Kotal on the second day were launched direct against the heights, and although this operation resulted in a very gallant feat of arms which excited general admiration, it was not in accordance with the design of the general in chief.

Had it been foreseen that the enemy would gather in such force on the Dargai heights after they had been abandoned, it would have been a matter of consideration whether all the risks and inconveniences attending their retention by an isolated body of troops ought or ought not to be incurred. Had the sequel been foreseen—a direct attack upon an extraordinarily strong position which two days before had only been captured by a brilliant assault, when held in far less strength by an enemy threatened in rear—the position would no doubt have been held at all costs. But these subsequent events could not have been foreseen. The original operation was a reconnaissance. Reconnaissances are an unfortunate necessity, a preliminary to the advance of an army into little known districts which cannot safely be dispensed with. As has been pointed out in an earlier paragraph, reconnaissances in hill warfare very often involve the disagreeable consequence of the enemy closing in on the rear of the troops when these withdraw on the completion of their task. If heights captured from the enemy were always to be held as a matter of course for fear that they might be reoccupied by the hill-men, the whole army would soon be frittered away in isolated detachments posted on ground most inconvenient from the point of view of supply and water.

There is one very important point in manœuvring in the hills which should not be lost sight of when the tribesmen are well armed, as is now so often the case. Troops should never—except when about to charge, at which time the

Troops not to get into clusters under enemy's fire.

enemy's marksmanship is certain to be erratic—collect into clusters and groups affording a favourable target for the hostile rifles. Whether advancing or retiring within range of the enemy's musketry, formations should be loose and dispersed. When casualties occur some men may, of course, have to get together to carry off the injured ; but under no other circumstances should compact bodies of men, however small, come under steady fire of these hill-men who often make very good shooting as long as they are not flurried. This is in the main a question of infantry formations which will be dealt with later on in Chapter XXI, but it is well to emphasize the point here before dealing with various details of combat in hill warfare.

Remarks on attack in hill warfare.

Attack has been already dealt with in Chapter XII, and a few observations upon infantry formations in hilly country will be included in Chapter XXI. But some general matters in connecton with assaults on hill tribesmen may conveniently be touched upon here.

Experience shows that in hill warfare the broad principle that the making of a good bag should be a principal aim in offensive tactics, when dealing with guerillas, is especially applicable. They are not easily caught, these mountaineers. Expert cragsmen, as nimble as goats among their declivities and boulders, knowing every cleft and every nullah, it is wonderful what mobility they possess. If their flanks or rear are threatened they disappear as if by magic. Unless detachments manage to get where they can pick off the fugitives as they bolt, the assailants find after their weary scramble up the hill sides that the bird has flown untouched, and they have to satisfy themselves with the empty honour of gaining possession of a knoll or crest which is of no use to them. If possible, therefore, the flanks of hostile gatherings should be turned by unseen parties of active men and picked shots. The elements of concealment are indispensable, and it must be remembered that above all things the

detachments making the detour do not too soon show up above
the tribesmen nor in rear of them, otherwise the enemy will be
off. For the same reason the frontal assault must not be premature or the enemy will get away undamaged. This seems
to be the theory of attack in such operations, but quick eye
for country, agility, and experience are required to put the
theory effectively in practice.

It would be difficult to find a better example of the art
of handling men on a small scale in attack against guerilla
mountaineers, than the scuffle which took place between the
Gurkha "scouts" under Lieutenant Lucas and the Chamkanis
on some heights above Thati in 1897.

The Gurkha
scouts attack-
ing above
Thati.

> There were 80 of these scouts engaged. On this particular occasion they
> were moving rather ahead of one flank of the column operating against Thati.
> When the enemy was observed in some force on high ground, they first had to
> scramble up some precipitous slopes. Then on approaching the crest they
> found in front of them three successive spurs, each one sangared and held
> by large bodies of tribesmen. Lieutenant Lucas waited until he saw
> the leading company of the 5th Gurkhas coming up in support; then,
> telling off one half of his command on one flank to sweep the first lot of
> sangars with independent fire, he himself led the other half from the other
> flank to charge this nearest position. To the wild delight of the Gurkhas.
> the Chamkanis, on seeing the little party rushing forward, stood up, fired a
> desultory volley and got their knives out. It looked as if there was to be
> a scrimmage such as the scouts had been thirsting for. But the enemy
> could not stand the combination of approaching bayonets and of a withering
> fire, which the happy dispositions adopted for attack brought about.
> They wavered a moment and then fled, leaving behind them several
> dead to the credit of the firing half of the scout company. The two other
> spurs were cleared in the same way, and finally, when the hill-men streamed
> away over the crest and across terraced fields below, the Gurkhas shot them
> down from above with deadly effect. Twenty or thirty of the enemy were
> killed and not a single scout was even wounded, for these Pathans are poor
> marksmen at a moving target, and their shooting goes to nothing when they
> feel that they are being got at.

In this capital little bit of work the right principle of
carrying out an attack on hill-men is very well illustrated.
It was not merely a case of advancing with a rush and driving
the enemy out helter-skelter by a resolute offensive, but

(1083)   U

care was also taken to have detachments, halted and well
posted, ready to bring a damaging musketry fire to bear on
the fugitives. The sangars were not merely cleared of their
defenders ; the defenders were treated to a torrent of bullets
as well just when they had to quit their cover. There were
no turning movements, no attempts to manœuvre the hill-
men out of their positions, they were tackled and in a military
sense wiped out.

Turning movements not to be undertaken too readily.   Writers on tactics are always harping upon turning movements, and in some valuable papers which have appeared
in India on hill warfare, there has been perhaps rather too
much tendency to dwell upon their value. Quite unintentionally the idea has been conveyed to a certain extent, that
when troops find tribesmen holding some spur or crest they
are at once to begin working round the hostile flanks. This
system should by no means be adopted as a matter of course—
on the contrary, it is wholly out of place except under given
circumstances. If hostile parties are strongly posted and
well covered, and if a direct attack on them will involve serious
loss, then by all means should troops be sent to operate against
their flanks and rear so as to turn them out. The detailing
of small bodies to work unseen round the hostile flanks so as
to reach points whence an effective musketry can be brought
to bear on the enemy when driven out by direct attack, will
always be a sound and wise arrangement. If a picquet has to
occupy some knoll it must turn the enemy off the place by
whatever means seem most certain to achieve the object. But
under other circumstances turning movements do not pay in
the long run. If it is merely intended to clear spurs and crests
of tribal gatherings, artillery fire will often do the trick and
save the infantry a climb ; but war carried on on these lines
has few terrors for the guerilla mountaineer. The young
men who do most of the fighting and who are generally the
last to consent to negotiations being opened, do not worry
over crumbling watch towers and burning byres, nor do the

sufferings of women and children greatly appeal to them; but they do not like being killed and wounded any better than other people. The moral is obvious.

Mountain guns can travel over very awkward country, and in the disposition of mixed forces for attacks upon hill-men this fact is not perhaps always quite sufficiently kept in view. The killing effect of artillery firing up at sangars from much lower ground is insignificant, although it may clear the enemy out of his defences. If the guns are told off to remain down in the valley or on the lower spurs and to stick to theoretically good " artillery positions," their real value is ofter entirely thrown away. They should, if possible, get on to high ground so as to be able to play on the retreating enemy —of their mobility their own officers are the best judges; and as long as the force is advancing their escort need rarely give grounds for any anxiety. In Chapter XXIV, which deals especially with artillery, the desirability of very forward tactics on the part of this arm in small wars is insisted upon; this principle is of paramount importance in hill warfare, because portable guns cannot move rapidly like horse or field artillery, to make up for having been originally left too far back in the line of battle.

Cavalry can of course do nothing on hill sides or in narrow valleys; but the terror which horsemen inspire among mountaineers renders this arm particularly valuable whenever there is fairly level country within the area of a day's operations. If the other arms can drive the hill-men on to ground where cavalry can work, troopers may be enabled to perform splendid service, and their presence in wide open valleys such as are so often found jutting up into the mountains, will often afford most useful support to the flanks of troops moving along the slopes. The services of the sowars during the operations in the Mamund country in 1897 were extraordinarily effective, owing to the almost exaggerated idea which the clan entertained of their capabilities. On the occasion when the village

Mountain guns and cavalry in attack in hill warfare.

of Zagai was destroyed the enemy was, to start with, taken somewhat by surprise, but as soon as the designs of the force were detected the tribesmen hurried from adjoining valleys to participate in the fray; those coming from the left had to cross an open space held by some] lancers, but they would not face the music, and after a considerable delay they started to reach the vicinity of the village by a long circuit round the hills, only arriving when the fight was over. Given practicable terrain, cavalry can be of immense service as an auxiliary to infantry and artillery even in hill warfare. The difficulty about cavalry is that its forage demands much transport, and that the resulting increase of the baggage train may not be justified by the few rare occasions on which the arm is likely to come into play.

Remarks on the destruction of villages. The destruction of villages is a task which is so often imposed upon regular troops in hill warfare that a few points with reference to this particular class of work may be included here. Although the habitations of the enemy are sometimes perched on crags and pinnacles, and are occasionally found clinging to steep declivities, they are as a rule constructed either on terraces or else down in the valleys, and owing to the topographical features of the country they will therefore generally be commanded by adjacent heights and spurs. If a strong force is available to deal with the village, it should have no difficulty in occupying the high ground and in keeping the enemy off. But if only a small body of troops be detailed for the enterprise, the occupation of surrounding spurs may be impracticable, and in that case the work of demolition will probably be carried out under considerable difficulties.

The work must be carried out deliberately. Mountain guns do not have much effect upon Pathan villages without a heavy expenditure of ammunition. If the houses are of wood they have earth piled on the roofs as a rule, and they will not burn unless holes are made in these. The demolition of towers, although an easy engineering operation in itself, takes some little time. It is often very difficult to find the stores of grain, &c., if the enemy has been expecting the visitation, and unless these stores be dealt with the job is incomplete. The destruction of a village in fact cannot be effected in a moment, and to ensure that the work shall be carried out thoroughly the parties charged with doing the damage require to undertake the task methodically and with deliberation; many of the dwellings of the Zakka Khels in the Waran Valley, which had been dealt with in November, 1897, were three weeks later found almost reconstructed.

The first step towards ensuring that destruction may be effectual is to arrange that it shall if possible be carried out by the sappers and their assistants unmolested. Under a hot fire, and with the enemy perhaps inclined to threaten the line of retreat, working parties will almost inevitably fail to make a lasting impression upon the dwellings given over to them. Therefore unless the whole operation is to be carried out in strong force capable of brushing away resistance, it will be judicious to give to it the character of a surprise. When the principle of " military execution " was applied in deliberate fashion to the valley of the Mamunds, General Jeffreys, having only a small force at his disposal, always concealed his intentions; the troops would march up the valley and would then suddenly turn off towards the locality selected for the visit, the consequence being that the place was in flames and its defences in ruins before the tribesmen could gather in any force to interfere.

Assuming that the village about to be dealt with lies in a re-entrant in the hills, as is so generally the case, and that it is held by the enemy, the best procedure will generally be to push forward troops on either flank to capture the spurs between which it nestles. This is a case when guns can be used early in the fight, because it is desirable to make sure of the spurs, even at the cost of simply driving off the tribesmen (who will inevitably collect on the heights above the

Principle of attacking a village.

habitations) instead of trying to tackle them. Once these spurs are occupied, the enemy will almost for certain evacuate the village, and come under cross fire from the troops who have gained the high ground ; it will, moreover, be easy to keep hostile parties at a distance who might otherwise try to annoy the detachments engaged in destroying the place. The object being to destroy the village, other circumstances are made subservient to this object, and the guns can be used freely against the guerillas on the heights. Supposing the destruction of the buildings to be only an item in a programme of general attack, a different procedure would of course be followed, inasmuch as the plan suggested here is not calculated to cause much damage among the opposing personnel except those actually holding the village.

Presence of women and children in villages. In the Pathan country the presence of women and children in a village may be taken as a sure sign that the men belonging to it do not mean to fight. This fact need not of course influence the decision to destroy it. But, from the tactical point of view, it is useful to know hostile intentions, because there may be more than one place to be dealt with, and the enemy may mean fighting at one and not at another.

Stone throwers. It is well to remember that those hill-men who are detailed to hurl down rocks and stones upon the troops, are as a general rule unarmed, or that at least they have no weapons of a formidable kind. To deal with them it is of course necessary to get level with, or above, them ; but it will generally be found that very small parties can do all that is required. Foemen assembled at the head of a stone shoot are practically defenceless as long as the troops do not attempt to approach them from below.

The difficulty of communicating orders during action in hill warfare. On level open ground the communication of orders rarely presents much difficulty ; they can be rapidly conveyed by mounted men, and on such terrain moreover, a force is generally in fairly compact formation. But in action against guerilla mountaineers in their own country, mounted orderlies cannot be used. In addition to this the regular troops are apt to be scattered in relatively speaking small parties over an extensive battle-field, the terrain being so broken that messengers on foot cannot traverse it at a very rapid pace. A hilly country favours signalling of course, and this is always made free use of in operations in such terrain; but when the army engaged becomes broken up into very small units as is so often the case, this means of communication cannot be entirely relied upon, and its effective employment depends on conditions of weather and light, which may fail.

Mistakes as regards orders have frequently caused difficulty and loss in hill warfare, owing to isolated parties misunderstanding the intentions of the commander and marring his plans. And before suggesting how best to avoid such *contretemps* two examples from the campaigns of 1897 on the Indian frontier may be given, showing what unfortunate results may attend the non-receipt or misconception of an order.

Practically the last serious combat of the Tirah campaign ended in a disaster owing to this. A column had crossed the Shin Kamar kotal, and some of the troops had advanced a little way down the valley on the far or northern side. The route on either side of the kotal was overshadowed by hills on the flanks, the whole depression running north and south. The enemy showed in considerable strength on the hill tops ; but there is every reason to believe that the return journey would have been attended by no very serious fighting, had not a company, owing to some mistake which has never been quite explained, withdrawn from a knoll situated immediately west of the kotal and dominating it. This knoll was promptly seized by the enemy, and the retirement of the troops beyond was so seriously jeopardized by its loss that it became necessary to recapture it at all costs from strong hostile bodies elated by an apparent success. The knoll was stormed ; but there were many casualties, and the troops forming the rear guard thus found themselves encumbered with numbers of wounded. In the final withdrawal from the knoll, the troops, hampered as they were by the wounded, suffered further serious losses, and the rear guard was in the end only extricated with the utmost difficulty from its awkward situation. In this unfortunate affair five officers and 22 men were killed and many were wounded, among the officers killed being Lieutenant Colonel Haughton, whose leadership in the Tseri Kandao retreat, mentioned on p. 224, and on other occasions during the campaign, had been the admiration of all.

The first attempt to cow the Mamunds has been referred to in an earlier paragraph. The day's fighting is remarkable for the number of lessons in the art of mountain warfare which it teaches, and one of its most memorable incidents was the unfortunate result which attended the non-delivery of an order to a certain company at the proper time. After having been heavily engaged for some hours the brigade retired, keeping the enemy at a respectful distance at most points. But a Sikh company on the extreme right had pushed high up into the hills, and before the order to withdraw eventually reached it, it had become completely isolated and was being hard pressed by very superior numbers. To extricate it the Guides had to turn back, and it only reached the foot of the hills towards dusk with both officers wounded and short of ammunition, having had a desperate scuffle. It was largely due to this *contretemps* that the whole brigade was benighted, and that, while most of it regained camp in detachments, some troops were cut off and remained in a situation of much danger till past midnight.

Precautions to be observed.

It is obviously important to devise, if possible, some method of avoiding such unfortunate occurrences; but this is not easy. The ordinary precautions tending to ensure the correct transmission of messages should of course be observed—messages should be written down, should if practicable be sent twice by distinct orderlies, should be clear and concise; if the receiver of a message is in any doubt as to its meaning he should if possible refer back to the sender, and so on. But all these precautions may fail under the difficult conditions which are likely to arise in a tussle with hill-men on awkward ground, and therefore it seems most desirable that the officers should be informed of the intentions of their chief at the outset, and that before executing any change of plan, sufficient time should be allowed to elapse to ensure that outlying detachments shall have learnt what is going to be done. Especially is it important that the whole force should be aware of the alteration in the direction which the operations are to take, when a retirement is to commence; orders to distant parties must be despatched in ample time to reach them before the withdrawal begins, otherwise small bodies of troops in close contact with the enemy

may be left in the lurch just at the most critical moment.
Signalling is of course invaluable in these circumstances, and
signallers should, if practicable, accompany every detachment
sent off independently for any purpose.

In the above-mentioned affair with the Mamunds a great Importance
deal of loss was caused by the force being benighted. This being
brings us to a matter of great importance in hill warfare. benighted.
It may be laid down as a fundamental rule of conduct that the
day's operations, whether they take the form of an attack
or of a march, should be so devised as to ensure that the troops
shall if possible reach their bivouac by sundown. This
cannot, of course, always be arranged. It is often a matter
of mere conjecture how long a march will take, although
it has been laid down in an earlier paragraph that marches
should be very short. On the occasion of the first visit to
Dwatoi from Maidan in the Tirah campaign, although the
distance was only seven miles, the rear guard did not reach
its destination till evening on the day after the march commenced, and it was out all night in the defile. The opposition
met on the road may be very determined, and may cause
unexpected delay to the whole force. Circumstances may
render it compulsory to move a certain distance before
halting, whether this entails being out after dark or not. On
several occasions in the frontier campaigns of 1897, when
troops and transports failed to reach their destination before
nightfall, being overtaken by darkness while still on the
march, their being thus benighted was unavoidable.
But it was not always unavoidable, and no lesson is more
clearly taught by the experiences of those operations than
that such belated movements of troops or transport are
fraught with the gravest dangers.

In the darkness the enemy is enabled by superior knowledge of the country to work round the flanks and to get to
close quarters. The column becomes split into fragments.
Detachments lose their way. Transport drivers become terror-

stricken and can no longer be controlled. The difficulties of
the route increase a hundredfold, and it is impossible to send
orders or to maintain a tactical control. Such being the
consequences when troops are benighted while on the move
in hill warfare, it is obvious that when practicable the day's
work should be calculated on the basis that it shall be completed within the hours of daylight, whatever the operation
may be.

The withdrawal over the Tseri Kandao Pass, already
referred to on p. 224 and elsewhere, was one of those cases
where the movement could not have been concluded before
dark under any circumstances if the enemy gave trouble,
the distance being about eight miles. On that occasion the
goal was the great encampment of three of the four brigades
forming the field force, and it was desirable, if possible, to
reach this haven of refuge and to complete the transfer from
the Waran valley to Maidan in a single day. But the result
proved that it would have been better to take two days.
When a route is fairly well known and the rate of march can be
calculated with approximate accuracy, there seems to be little
excuse for sending off transport in such quantities or at such
an hour as to risk its being benighted, either wholly or in part.

When the Tirah field force crossed the Arhanga Pass
from the Mastura into the Bara valley, nearly the whole of
the baggage had to be left behind temporarily. The route
was difficult, and the subsequent movement of the great mass
of transport in single file was necessarily a slow and laborious
operation. On two successive nights transport was still on
the road after dark and 11,000 rounds and over 500 kits were
in consequence lost. The tribesmen had not recovered from
the effects of the Sempagha fight and did not seriously molest
the transport in the darkness ; but it is clear that at that early
period of the campaign the importance of avoiding these night
movements was not fully realised, and that, what is now considered one of the fundamental principles of conducting these
kind of operations, was not appreciated.

Still, in spite of the best laid plans, it must sometimes Course to be occur that the whole of a force, or its transport, or its rear pursued if troops are guard, may fail to reach its destination before nightfall, and benighted. the question arises how, under such circumstances, it should act. The answer to this seems to be plain, and is, indeed, written down with unmistakable directness in the records of the frontier campaigns of 1897. Troops about to be benighted must make up their minds to stop out till morning breaks, and they should prepare for this before darkness actually sets in. While it is still light some position should be selected where the force can be concentrated on ground favourable for defence, where the transport, if there be any, can be parked under proper protection, and where the best can be made of what cannot fail to be an awkward situation. The decision must be come to in good time, so that dispositions may be completed before the darkness closes in ; the cold and exposure of a night in the open without great coats, &c., must be faced, in preference to the perils of continuing the movement after sundown. Of course this rule only holds good in presence of an active enemy and in a country where the troops are liable to be scattered and taken at a disadvantage. A compact column on favourable ground has not much to fear from ordinary hill-men at night or at any other time, and at night the enemy's sniping from a distance is not very damaging.

It happened on more than one occasion in Tirah that a An early rear guard was left to its own devices at nightfall ; the main decision to be arrived at as body of the force moved on and reached camp practically to intended course of unmolested, while the troops who had borne the burden and action when heat of the day had to choose between remaining out till night approaches. morning or straggling on as best they could. Further on, in dealing with retirements and rear guards, the importance of the main body making its pace conform to that of the rear guard will be pointed out, as it has already been pointed out in Chapter XIV. But, although this principle need not perhaps be carried so far as to make it an axiom that because the rear guard is benighted the main body must stop out all night also, it should be carried so far as to ensure that towards evening the whole force should know what is going to happen, and that the commander of the rear guard and his subordinates shall learn in good time what is to be the further programme. When heavy losses occurred at night in the Indian hill warfare of 1897, it almost always arose owing to misunderstandings, or owing to the fact that the approach of darkness was not taken into account at an early enough hour to allow of special arrangements being made.

Guns to be sent on.

Officers of mountain artillery have, with good reason, a strong objection to being caught by the darkness while on the move, or to spending the night in any position where the enemy can creep up close under cover. The mules get shot, and in any case the guns are of very little use in such circumstances. Guns must therefore, if possible, be sent on in sufficient time to reach the destination, provided of course that they will find supporting troops when they get there.

McCaskill's brigade marching down the Khaibar in 1841, when Afghanistan was being evacuated, was belated in the defile. The Afridis fired into the long column from the heights, and rushing down at one point captured two guns, after causing heavy loss to the detachments when taken at a disadvantage. The guns were afterwards recovered, as the enemy made no attempt to drag them off.

The first day's bout with the Mamunds, in 1897, marked as it was throughout by dramatic incidents, supplies no more remarkable picture than that of the four guns of No. 8 Bengal Mountain Battery, which passed the night at the village of Bilot. With a half regiment of Sikhs and 30 sappers they were making their way back to camp, when an order came for them to halt and to cover the retirement of the Guides, who, after rescuing the isolated Sikh company as narrated on p. 312, could be heard fighting their way steadily back to camp on one flank. At this juncture a sudden tropical storm stopped the fighting and threw everything into confusion. Only the artillery and sappers received the order with reference to the Guides ; this little party got to Bilot, where after the weather cleared firing was resumed and matters assumed a most critical aspect. Most fortunately a dozen of the Buffs turned up by accident, and their magazine rifles probably saved the guns. For these before long were firing case shot at 20 yards range. Both officers were wounded, the other having been killed in the afternoon.

Many of the detachment and of the mules were hit, and the position of the whole party was such as to cause the gravest anxiety, when, after several hours and in the nick of time, two Sikh companies arrived. As a consequence of this nocturnal combat two of the guns were practically put out of action till the casualties could be replaced.

Before making a few observations on the conduct of movements by night in presence of an aggressive enemy, when for some reason or other the troops have not been able to halt in good time and to take up a good position, some examples of halting, and of not halting, will be of interest. All are taken from the Tirah campaign.

Examples of troops being benighted.

When Lieut.-Colonel Haughton, who was commanding the rear guard on the first move to Dwatoi mentioned on p. 313, perceived that owing to the extraordinary difficulties of the road he could not get through before dark, he halted the baggage, parked it on suitable ground, picqueted the hills all round, and passed the night on the road in security.

All the way down the Bara valley the Afridis continually pressed on the rear guard. On the last day but one of the march to Barkai, General Westmacott's brigade was heavily engaged all day covering the baggage and transport; this was in great confusion, the drivers being demoralized with terror and cold, and the valley presenting extraordinary difficulties to movement of any kind. The enemy was roughly handled several times during the day, but, coming on with a boldness not shown before, was evidently inspired with the dread that the loot might after all escape. Towards dusk there were still two miles to be traversed, and General Westmacott then took up position on a ridge for the night. The tribesmen committed themselves to an attack, which was pushed home with desperate bravery, but they were repulsed at all points with heavy loss. Not a mule or a follower was cut off, and what may be looked upon as the last serious fight in Tirah proper, ended in a notable triumph for the regular forces.

Two days earlier, when the other brigade had brought up the rear, it had also been found impossible for the rear guard to get in before dark—the affair has already been mentioned on p. 175. Towards evening it was gradually outflanked; but the enemy was not in strong force, and the guns proved of great assistance till they were obliged to push on to camp two miles distant for fear of being benighted. Between the tail of the rear guard and the camp the river ran in an awkward ravine, and the route passed through what was a typical military defile. Through a misunderstanding between the brigades the flanks had not been picqueted. The consequence was that desperate efforts had to be made to induce the followers, who were benumbed with cold, were utterly exhausted and were terrified out of their wits to push on to camp. In the meantime the enemy got in between the tail of the rear guard, now consisting of several companies, and the camp. The transport and drivers suffered appreciable losses, which, however, turned out afterwards to have been less serious than was at first supposed.

But while this was going on Major Downman with the rearmost troops had occupied the buildings where he passed the night in complete security, practically unmolested and within sight of the camp. The difficulty had occurred quite close to the picquets around the bivouac of the division. It is absolutely impossible to keep transport in such a situation from straggling and from becoming more or less unmanageable when the darkness closes in, and considering that the heights had not been crowned, it seems fortunate that the losses in the followers and animals were not much heavier than they actually were.

Before quitting Maidan Tirah, Sir W. Lockhart visited the Chamkani and Massuzai country to the west of Tirah, and General Gaselee's brigade was sent out in advance to open the road. Although opposition was not very determined the country proved exceedingly difficult, and it was foreseen early that the whole brigade could not get over the pass which had to be crossed, before dark. General Gaselee therefore sent part of his brigade on, kept part of it in the pass itself, and left the baggage well protected at the foot of the pass. He thus spent the night with his force in three distinct detachments, each detachment, however, being able to take care of itself. An attack was made on the baggage during the night, which was repulsed with loss.

These incidents seem to point out clearly the course which should generally be pursued. When a force is on the move an understanding should be arrived at as to the intended procedure before dusk actually descends. This affects not merely that part of the force which is about to be benighted, but it also affects other parts which have reached, or which are close to, their destination. If the rearmost detachments of the force are in difficulties in the late afternoon and cannot get in before night, they should be reinforced betimes and should be halted on favourable ground. It is far better for the force to be broken up into detachments which, even if isolated, are well posted, than for part of it to be drifting along in the darkness, encumbered with an ever-growing crowd of helpless wounded officers and men who cannot be abandoned, and at the mercy of savage cut-throats who can attack it from all sides.

Troops on the move at night.   Assuming, however, a body of troops to be benighted on the road and to be unable, owing to care of transport or some such reason, to halt in any defensive position where it can keep the enemy at bay, the great point seems to be to keep the troops in compact bodies prepared to assume the offensive when an opportunity offers. When it is dark the enemy cannot see to aim except at very close ranges, and if the troops are of good cheer and make occasional rushes with the bayonet, the wary foe will keep at a respectful distance. Nullahs should if possible be avoided, they are very dangerous if the heights on either side are not picqueted. But, above all things, there must be no straggling on the part of the men, or they will almost inevitably be cut up. The disaster to part of the Northamptonshire Regiment in retiring after the first reconnaissance to Saran Sar in Tirah, an account of which is given at the end of the chapter, occurred, as will be seen, while they were retiring through a shallow steep-sided nullah in the dusk while the rearmost companies were hampered by many wounded. The party of the Dorsets which came to grief during the Tseri Kandao retirement, mentioned on p. 225, seems to have moved in two separate bodies, one of which was brought in almost intact, while the other got into a nullah where the men appear to have become separated and to have been cut up singly or in small groups. To show the importance of the light question, it may be mentioned that the rear guard in this remarkable Tseri Kandao affair spent the night in two separate parties in buildings some little distance apart, but that Lieut.-Colonel Haughton was careful to take his party over to join the other one before it was light enough for the enemy to fire accurately. The advantage of keeping in groups during a night march is well shown by the following incident, which occurred during the night move of baggage over the Arhanga Pass, referred to on p. 314.

Some Afridis had concealed themselves on roofs of houses close to the road, and suddenly jumped off them as the convoy passed and got among the mule drivers. Lance-corporal Simpson of the Queen's had collected 13 men, and was moving with these in a compact party with bayonets fixed.

Some of the enemy tried to rush this little body, but they were bayoneted or shot. The N.C.O. then took his men a little way up the hill side and fired volleys into the raiders; these tried to get above him, but he again moved a little way up the slope and fired steady volleys. The moral effect of the cool, intrepid conduct of this little party under its young leader was invaluable to the rest of the escort, for it is not the Pathan's game to run unnecessary risks on a night foray. To find a party with fixed bayonets when he expects solitary individuals is an unpleasant surprise, but to be greeted with steady volleys at such short range that even in the dark they may prove deadly, quenches his thirst for plunder effectually.

Sir W. Lockhart's maxims.

Inasmuch as the dangers of straggling and of small parties getting into nullahs and ravines and falling into ambushes, are appreciable by day as well as by night, and inasmuch as some of the points drawn attention to above in reference to night work are really applicable to all hours of the day, it will not be out of place before proceeding further to quote some remarks made by Sir W. Lockhart to the Northamptons and Dorsets, in Tirah, in commending them for their conduct under most untoward circumstances. " We must remember," he said, " that we are opposed to perhaps the best skirmishers and the best natural shots in the world, and that the country they inhabit is the most difficult on the face of the globe. The enemy's strength lies in his thorough knowledge of the ground, which enables him to watch all our movements unperceived and to take advantage of every height and every ravine. Our strength, on the other hand, lies in our discipline, controlled fire, and mutual support; our weakness is our ignorance of the country and the consequent tendency of small bodies to straggle and to get detached. The moral of all this is that careful touch must be maintained, and that if by mischance small parties do find themselves alone they should, as much as possible, stick to the open and shun ravines and broken ground, where they must fight at a disadvantage and run every risk of being ambuscaded."

Advantages which experienced troops

The regiments which are ever looking towards the border highlands from the Panjab plains, know all this by experience and by tradition. The youngster who marches for the first *enjoy in this class of warfare.* time into the mountains has often heard it from the men decked out with many medals in his company; the subaltern has been told it by his seniors. The Sikhs, the Gurkhas, the Dogras and the Panjabis know full well that what is practised in camps of exercise in the North West Provinces or the Deccan, is designed to meet conditions totally different from warfare in the hills. On the threshold of the border highlands they shed their text-book tactics as it were a garment. Filing among the ravines and gorges, and scrambling over the crags and mountain crests, they adapt themselves at once to the conditions of the conflict, and the stealthiest Zakka Kehl or Orukzai knows that these native regiments of the Sirkar are not to be trifled with. But with British troops it is different. Battalions find themselves suddenly engaged on operations of a new and uncanny kind, the like of which often not one single individual in the corps has before experienced. So it comes about that when in a tight place neither officers nor men know instinctively what to do, they break up into groups, some group goes astray, loses its way, gets into a *cul de sac*, and, endeavouring to save its dead and wounded, is wiped out coolly and methodically by a not very superior body of the enemy not nearly so well armed or so brave as are the victims. Happily, the peculiar tactics which hill warfare demands, and with which native regiments, seasoned by many a border scuffle are well acquainted, are now being practised when opportunity offers in time of peace, and the petty disasters which so greatly swelled the lists of casualties in Tirah and which cloud the records of that great campaign, ought not to recur in the future.

The principle inculcated by Sir W. Lockhart that small *Danger of even small ravines unless the heights are held.* parties should keep clear of ravines and broken ground when possible, does not apply only to detachments. It holds good equally in the case of large bodies of men, unless the crests and knolls dominating the ravines and depressions in the broken ground have been picqueted. The plan of crowning the heights is just as applicable to a shallow nullah as to a great depression in the mountains. The topographical under-features of any valley in the hills presents alternating spurs and ravines more or less accentuated. At first sight it might appear that the ravine would present a safer line of movement than the spur, because the former offers better cover; and it is no doubt generally the case in advancing to the attack that the ravine would be the preferable route. But when in difficulties, or when the object is to get from point to point with as little loss as possible, the spur will almost always be the line to take, and troops experienced in hill warfare are well aware of this. The case of Saran Sar quoted further on illustrates this principle well, and it will be found in studying the movements of regiments which have seen much service in the hills, that they are always on the spurs when they are retiring or otherwise in an awkward situation.

It is interesting to call to mind that the closing scene of the disastrous retreat from Kabul in 1840 gave evidence that the survivors, a mere handful of officers and of men of the horse artillery and the 44th Regiment, in their last hour recognized instinctively that the ravine was no place for them. They were in a depression parleying with the emissaries of Akbar Khan, the tribesmen gathering in threatening array on the heights around them, when somehow fire opened. They made a rush for it, cleft a path for themselves up a hill side through their astonished foemen, and seized a knoll where they fought it out to the bitter end with stones and steel.

Value of counter-attack when troops get into difficulties. This final effort of a doomed remnant showed not only that the gallant party realized the value of ground, but that the terrible experiences of the march through the Afghan defiles with the crests on either hand swarming with Ghilzai tribesmen, had not stamped out the spirit of attack which is the fundamental principle of conducting warfare against irregulars. In operations against guerilla hill-men this great principle must never be forgotten. When the worst comes to the worst, a bold onslaught may save the situation. A single straggler lost in the darkness may save himself if he rushes in with his bayonet. A small party with a charge and a shout may hunt away the hostile swarm which has hemmed it in. And this is one reason why a nullah is so dangerous, because the sides may be so steep that it is impossible to assume the offensive, and because in any case the slopes will break the force of a rush.

Still, it would be a mistake to suppose that it is only the regular troops who get caught in such places. Gurkhas and other soldiers versed in the art of hill warfare manage occasionally to trap the wariest of mountaineers. At setting snares, devising ambuscades and work of that kind, some of the native corps on the Panjab frontier are quite a match for the guerillas whom they have to deal with; and there is no reason why British soldiers, supplied as they always are with a goodly proportion of officers who are keen and practical sportsmen, should not acquit themselves satisfactorily as guerillas if they only got the practice. The following two incidents which occurred in Tirah, are worth quoting in this connection :—

Examples of catching the enemy in ravines.

When the first column sent down the defile from Maidan to Dwatoi was returning, the rear guard consisting of 36th Sikhs was somewhat pressed and several casualties occurred. Some ponies were sent back to help the wounded along; but, at a narrow place in the ravine, a number of Afridis scrambled down the rocky sides hoping to capture these, being apparently unaware that the rear guard was close by, coming up the gorge. A party of Sikhs managed by a skilful movement to get round above the enemy, and down into the ravine beyond. The looters were fairly trapped. Precipitous walls of rock shut them in on two sides, egress up or down the gorge was barred by the 36th, and the Sikhs dealt with them with the bayonet.

On another occasion some Zakka Khels made a bold attempt to cut off the tail of a convoy proceeding back from Maidan towards the Arhanga Pass. A company of Madras sappers working not far from the spot, hurried to extricate the convoy, and in doing so drove the enemy up the valley towards the pass where some companies of the Gordons happened to be. One company of the highlanders hastened down each of the two spurs flanking the ravine. The Afridis were almost surrounded, and lost about 40 men, having only accounted for one soldier and for four followers of the convoy.

It will be observed that on both these occasions the

tribesmen came to grief in an attempt to loot; and it should always be remembered in dealing with such antagonists, that cunning as they are, nimble, resourceful, and acute, they have human weaknesses. They are thieves by nature, and are by profession accustomed to harry villages, to rob and murder travellers, and to cut off traders. They have a passion for plunder, and sometimes forget their caution in efforts to acquire it. Just as the Abyssinians rushed down from the heights at Arogee in hope of loot, and suffered for it as narrated on p. 233, so the wily mountaineers will sometimes make a blunder and pay the penalty of greed. It is a point worth noting, in view of luring such opponents into ambuscades and of catching them at a disadvantage among the baggage animals when they rush out from their hiding places to effect a capture.

General question of rear guards and retirements.

Early in this chapter it has been pointed out how one of the greatest difficulties under which the regular forces labour in typical hill warfare, is that owing to unavoidable circumstances portions of the force employed are so often obliged to retire, for various causes. As already demonstrated these retirements are often misconstrued by the enemy into confessions of defeat. It is not the unfortunate moral effect of these withdrawals alone, however, that makes them so objectionable, but also the fact that they at times place regular troops in positions of great perplexity and peril, and that they involve perhaps the most difficult operations which trained soldiers are ever called upon to undertake in conflict with irregular forces.

In Chapter XIV the question of retreats has been already dealt with, and most of the points laid stress on therein apply to the conditions of guerilla hill warfare. It is necessary to draw attention, however, to the fact that rearguards have a very important and often most difficult part to play in the hills whichever way the army is going, whether it be advancing or retiring; because mountaineers are generally fully alive to the fact that detachments with-drawing before them, as a rear-guard must, are tactically in a disadvantageous situation. In discussing withdrawals and retirements and rear-guards it must be understood that these are not necessarily the movements of the tail of a retreating army. At the same time it stands to reason that troops covering the actual retreat of a column, are more likely to get into difficulties than are troops who are merely protecting the rear of an advancing army, because in the one case the enemy has the moral advantage and not in the other.

The broad principle enunciated in Chapter XIV that retirements should be conducted deliberately and that rear-guards as a whole must withdraw slowly maintaining a bold front, holds good in hill warfare. In operations of this par-ticular nature, the enemy is to the full as eager and zealous in pursuit as is found to be the case in campaigns against irregular warriors of other kinds; hill-men are indeed especially noted for their energy and skill when following up retiring troops. The importance of keeping touch in a retiring column, and of the main body as a general rule adapting its pace to that of the rear-guard in conducting a withdrawal in face of guerilla highlanders—points already emphasized in Chapter XIV—can scarcely be overrated. That a bold counter-attack will often prove the best way out of a difficulty has been proved over and over again in hill warfare. But there are certain other respects in which rear guard operations in mountainous country present abnormal features.

In the first place, experience proves that hill-men are Persistency of exceptionally persistent in pursuit. As a rule an uncivilized hill-men in pursuit. foe is desperately in earnest when the regular troops first begin to fall back, and this first phase of a retirement is, therefore, its most critical time; but the history of small wars shows, on the other hand, that an army once fairly launched in retreat is not ordinarily followed up with much obstinacy by savage warriors. This, however, is not the case when the trained soldiers are opposed to mountaineers fight-ing in defence of their hearths and homes. We have only to look back to the melancholy story of the retreat from Kabul to find an example of a formidable body of troops of all arms being harassed and dogged during its retirement for many days by ever growing swarms of hill-men, whom even the love of loot and the attractions of a rich harvest of plunder in the wake of the withdrawing army, failed to draw off from the trail. Moreover it is very generally the case that in mountain warfare the retirements and rear-guard affairs are limited to a single march and to a single day's work, so that the enemy hardly has time to weary of the game of hovering around the hindmost detachments until these reach a place of safety.

The fact that the retirement is generally down hill tells against the regulars.

Early in this chapter, the disinclination of hill-men to attack up hill was referred to, they like having their oppo-nents below them, and their whole attitude is governed by this question of relative levels. A moment's consideration shows that when troops have to retire in hill warfare, they will generally be retiring down hill with the enemy above them or easily able to get above them. Mountaineers stick to the crests and spurs while they can. The regular army marches and encamps on the low ground. Thus while the troops generally attack ascending, they also generally retire descending. Even if a force be retiring up a valley, the picquets on the flanks will be moving down hill to join the column, and the enemy pursuing these will have the command.

This is one reason why the tribesmen of the Indian frontier are so formidable in pursuit. They are enjoying not only the moral advantage derived from the regulars retreating before them, but also the, in their opinion, very great material advantage of being above their opponents and of being able to charge down on these when they fall back. Before breech-loading rifles penetrated into the border valleys, rushes down hill sword in hand were a very favourite manœuvre on the part of most Pathan clans. These onslaughts have rarely been attempted of late years upon regular troops who are advancing, but this national mode of fighting is not forgotten when the soldiers turn their backs.

In Chapter XIV it was laid down that retirements should as a whole be conducted slowly and deliberately. But this does not always altogether hold good in hill warfare, at least at the commencement of a withdrawal. Indeed it is often expedient to withdraw in the first instance very rapidly, because by doing so a good deal of ground may be covered before the enemy perceives what is going on. The nature of the country is of assistance to the regular troops in this. On open ground a withdrawal is perceived at once, the enemy follows up without delay, and any precipitate movement of the retiring force encourages him to desperate effort which detachments in motion may not be able effectually to cope with. In broken intersected country, on the other hand, even the very watchful tribesmen may lose touch of what is going on, and a smart retreat of the troops nearest them may come upon them as a complete surprise. But even in hill warfare quick withdrawals of this kind are only admissible just at the start with the idea of giving opponents the slip for a moment. Later on the withdrawal must, as a whole, be conducted as deliberately as in the case of retreat in open country.

Advisability of a sudden start and rapid movement at first when retiring

Retreats and rear-guard operations in mountainous country when the hostile forces consist of guerilla warriors who know the country, who can easily outpace the troops, and who possess the warlike instincts rarely wanting in the hillman, involve so much difficulty and danger, that the broad rule which really governs the whole conduct of small wars and which may be summed up in " fight the enemy wherever you get the chance " hardly applies to them. On the contrary, the rear guard should sneak off unmolested if it can. When a force is retiring through mountain defiles the most able leadership, and the most admirable conduct of the rank and file, will hardly prevent the enemy from having the best of it if there be a close pursuit. The retiring force suffers in prestige in any case, and in spite of superior armament, of cohesion, and of courage, the balance of probability is in favour of its having more casualties in its ranks than occur amongst its antagonists. Therefore the intention to fall back should be concealed to the last moment—unless of course it is hoped to lure the enemy into some rash action.

Changing a movement of advance into one of retirement. Should the army have been advancing, and should it become necessary during the day's operations to withdraw again, it is very important, supposing the enemy to be in force and inclined for fight, that the troops shall achieve some distinct success before turning to go back. To approach a hostile position and to then retire without attacking it, is sure to bring down the enemy in force with the possible sequel of a harassing and dangerous pursuit. If it can safely be attempted and if there be sufficient time, the enemy should be beaten first, and then the troops may be able to withdraw without very serious molestation ; at any rate the enemy will, after having been roughly handled, give them a wide berth for an hour or two, and will probably only follow them up at a respectful distance. Lieut.-Colonel Pollock in his " Notes on Hill Warfare," quotes the action of Shah Alam Kaghza, in the Waziristan operations of 1881, in proof of this, and his account of what occurred may be given here.

" The 1st Sikhs advanced up a spur covered with oak jungle, so thick that it was difficult to see more than ten yards off. About half way up they halted and the two half companies were ordered to lie down, fix bayonets and load. Suddenly a charge was made on them, the enemy appearing about ten yards off The fire they received sent them back, but the officer instead of allowing his men to get out of hand, pursued them steadily up hill, halting to re-form every now and then. This was a wise precaution as if the men had got out of hand and rushed up the hill, a rush of Waziris might have swept through them. As it was, at each hill the Waziris tried to rush the companies, but did not succeed. . . . After the charge we heard the general's bugle sounding our regimental call and the retire.

Colonel Price, who was a very able officer and quite understood the situation, refused to obey the order, as he was aware that if we retired through the thick scrub before the Waziris were beaten, the result would have been a heavy loss in men, so, instead, he drove them over the range and we halted for some time, and then retired without a shot being fired at us."

In a case like this there must be always some difficulty in changing from movement forwards into movement backwards, and it will generally be best to halt some time and to make sure that all out-lying detachments know exactly what they are to do. The intention of retiring should be concealed to the last moment, and it will perhaps be possible to get a good start of the enemy before he realizes that the troops are turning back. Sounding the " retire " on the bugle will rarely be a wise procedure, especially on the Indian frontier where the bugle calls are known to the tribesmen. Nothing should be left undone in the way of deceiving the enemy by actual manœuvre and by spreading false reports.

When General Westmacott's force which had moved down from Bagh to Dwatoi in Tirah to reconnoitre the route, turned back after a day's stay at Dwatoi, it got a clear start of the Afridis. The enemy had not expected that this withdrawal would take place. From the nature of the ground round Dwatoi, the drawing in of the picquets and moving off of the baggage could hardly have been effected without loss, had the tribesmen been on the alert and had they known the direction of the intended march.

When the details of conducting a retirement in the hills Details of come to be considered it becomes manifest how extremely diffi- retirement operations. cult such an operation may prove to be. Except when it is a case of withdrawal from a captured position, or of the marching out of a portion of a force from an encampment which remains in occupation of other troops, the conditions will generally be that the column has detachments out on knolls and spurs in the direction where the enemy is, and that, as it moves off, these detachments have gradually to be withdrawn to other positions. These retirements of picquets cannot always be effected without casualties.

The retreat of a picquet in face of active determined Withdrawal tribesmen who are on the watch to catch it at a disadvantage of picquets. when it quits its position, is a delicate operation requiring nerve and judgment. It may be assumed that its commander has noted his surroundings and decided on his course of action in good time in view of the contingency of recall, and it is most important that he shall have selected a good route and shall have informed his subordinates beforehand of the point where the next halt is to be. When the moment comes to retire, the bulk of the picquet should if possible slip off unobserved by the enemy, while a few especially active men remain behind to keep the opponents occupied and, should these perceive what is going forward, to hold them in check. The withdrawal should be in driblets, care being taken not to stand up before starting lest it attract attention, and in the meantime the files left behind should extend quietly so as to lead the enemy to think that the full muster is still in position. As soon as the main body of the picquet has taken up its new position the men left behind hurry off to join this, covered by its fire and taking care not to mask this fire ; practically the little party has to run for all it is worth, but it does not in reality incur so much danger as might be supposed, because irregular warriors are bad shots at a moving target, especially when they are excited and are rushing forward themselves. The re-united picquet should fire a few steady volleys and it should if possible make a pause before retiring again on the same principle. The men must avoid getting into clusters while on the move, otherwise they may give their antagonists a good target to fire at.

Picquets covering each other's retirements. Sometimes one picquet will cover the retirement of another, and if the ground be favourable and if all concerned are experienced in such operations, the system of one line of picquets retiring through another will work to perfection. Considerable losses may moreover be inflicted on the enemy by cross fire if he presses forward too eagerly to occupy abandoned positions. The great principle to be observed of course is that parties actually hurrying off shall have their retreat covered by the fire of other parties which are halted in favourable positions, and which can therefore aim steadily. If by mischance a man is wounded and has to be carried off by his comrades, the situation becomes very nasty, because it involves a little cluster of men for the enemy to aim at ; the steady fire of a few files from some secure position however has a wonderful effect in keeping back guerilla antagonists, for these, however bloodthirsty they may be, generally have a rooted aversion to exposing themselves to really dangerous fire. It is when isolated detachments retire with no support to cover the movement, that the regular troops get into difficulties and that ever-increasing swarms of clansmen get in among them and commit havoc. If it can be arranged for picquets to retire down parallel spurs, they will be able to afford each other very effective support ; the enemy will take good care not to attempt a move down the ravine between them and thus each picquet will have one of its flanks secured.

If a picquet be overlooked from higher ground and if in consequence it be impossible for part of it to slip away unnoticed by the enemy, the best plan may be for the whole of it to retire simultaneously and to make a rush for the next position decided upon. Such a movement, if there be no covering picquet to maintain fire upon the enemy, is undoubtedly dangerous. But if tribesmen perceive that a detachment is withdrawing in driblets, they will make great efforts to outflank its position and to make the retreat of the few men left to the last a most perilous undertaking ; then, if some of this rearmost party get hit, the whole of it may be sacrificed. In the event of casualties occurring, the best plan will often be to deliver a counter-attack or to make a show of delivering a counter-attack, and the wounded should if possible be carried back along a line well commanded by the fire of the covering detachments. It is a great point to keep the enemy from getting so close to the wounded as to be allowed an easy shot into the little groups which collect, and a heavy independent fire should be maintained by the covering detachments upon points where the enemy may be gathering, so as to disconcert the hostile aim.

Above all things is it necessary that, once the retreat is in full swing, successive withdrawals in face of an active pursuit should be carried out with deliberation as a whole, and that picquets, or portions of picquets, acting as covering detachments to parties falling back, should fire steadily and accurately. The enemy soon takes note of it should the fire be at all wild and acts accordingly, he becomes more and more venturesome and may finally try a rush. As long as these guerilla warriors can be induced to stick to their skulking tactics and to shun the open, they cannot get to close quarters with the rearmost parties while these are actually on the move, and that in itself is a great point gained.

Importance of parties nearest the enemy getting timely notice of intended retirement.

Obviously it is most important that commanders of picquets and of detachments in contact with the enemy should get timely notice of an intended retirement, otherwise they may lose touch with their supports, or they may be compelled to conduct their own retreat with a rapidity not in consonance with the requirements of the case. Owing to the difficulties apt to arise in transmission of messages, much judgment is required on the part of the commander of the retiring force, and of the commanders of isolated detachments. There is greater danger of some party or parties getting into difficulties when an action is abruptly broken off and an immediate withdrawal ordered, than when the force is retiring after a halt where there has been plenty of time for communication and where the troops nearest to the enemy have had opportunity for noting their surroundings. Detachments in close proximity to the foe cannot simply turn round and move off, arrangements must have been made in advance, while on the move they must be covered by other detachments or they are sure to come to grief.

Direction to be followed by retiring picquets.

In retiring, picquets and detached parties should follow the lines of the spurs as far as possible, they should avoid ravines unless these are swept by the fire of other detachments, and it is of course essential that they should take a line in general conformity with the direction followed by the force. The disastrous consequences of disregarding these rules are exemplified by the following unfortunate incident which occurred during the Tirah campaign.

A reconnaissance was being made by the Kurrum movable column up the long Karmana defile into the Chamkani country. No opposition was encountered in advance ; but when the retirement commenced, the tribesmen collected in some force and adopted their usual harassing tactics ; they were however kept in check without great difficulty. A picquet of the Kapurthala infantry which had been detached to hold a flanking spur, however, met with disaster. It was ordered to withdraw at the proper time and it received the message, but instead of descending obliquely rearward into the valley and joining the rear guard, the commander and most of the men made an attempt to strike the valley higher up with the idea of participating in the skirmish which was going on. The party got into difficult ground and came in contact with the enemy higher up than where the rear guard was—they in fact missed connection with it and thus became isolated. They found themselves, moreover, in an awkward side ravine and the tribesmen quickly closed the ends of this. The upshot was that they were eventually shot down to a man.

Experience shows that if the pursuers are roughly handled at any point, the fate of those slain by the troops rarely fails to exercise a most wholesome restraining influence on the remainder, at least for a time. It is most important to bear this in mind because a sudden counter-attack when there happens to be a chance of inflicting loss on the enemy, or a happily conceived ambuscade, or a feint by which the wary hill-men are induced to expose themselves, may stave off pursuit for the nonce and may even stop it altogether.

Pursuit often checked completely if enemy is roughly handled at the start.

The slaughter caused by the fire of the 15th Sikhs upon the Zakka Khels when these charged out on them on the Tseri Kandao kotal, as narrated on p. 224, was so great that, after it, the rear guard was able to withdraw to the foot of the hills unmolested. The rear guard, indeed, would probably have reached camp without further loss, but for night closing in and giving the foe fresh heart.

On the occasion of the second reconnaissance to Saran Sar, in Tirah, the scouts of the 3rd Gurkhas covered the retirement, while the regiment itself took up a position some way lower down and to a flank. The scouts, by prearrangement, suddenly fled down the hill. They were promptly followed by the enemy, who thus came under cross fire from the regiment. As a result of the ruse the tribesmen suffered so severely that they kept at a safe distance for the rest of the day. The fate of the little party of Afridis, which was trapped during the retirement from Dwatoi to Bagh, as mentioned on p. 323, had the effect of taking all the sting out of the pursuit.

Value of counter-attacks when in retreat. The check may often be merely temporary. It is never safe to assume that, because by some deft stroke the hill-men have been caught at a disadvantage, have been punished and have apparently drawn off, that they have really abandoned the idea of harassing the retirement altogether. The effect will frequently be—as happened at Tseri Kandao—to induce the enemy to creep round the flanks taking care to give the troops a wide berth, and to attempt an ambuscade or to devote attention to stragglers. Still, when in a difficulty, it may greatly relieve the troops to choke off the pursuers even for a few minutes, and no opportunity should be lost of doing so. It is extraordinary how swarms of hill-men gathering round a detachment of troops which is retreating and is apparently in peril of annihilation, will give way if this suddenly assumes the offensive. While some of the party advance boldly with bayonets fixed, the remainder may be able to remove the wounded a considerable distance and to take up a good position for covering the retirement of those who have turned on the enemy.

The value of a counter-attack is demonstrated by the following incident, as related by Lieutenant Winston Churchill, his graphic account of the earlier part of the withdrawal of these two companies of the 35th Sikhs being unfortunately too long to reproduce.

" The retirement continued. Five or six times the two companies, now concentrated, endeavoured to stand. Each time the tribesmen pressed round both flanks. They had the whole advantage of ground, and commanded as well as outflanked the Sikhs. At length the bottom of the spur was reached, and the remainder of the two companies turned to bay in the nullah with fixed bayonets. The tribesmen came on impetuously, but stopped 30 yards away, howling, firing and waving their swords.

" No troops were in sight except our cavalry, who could be seen retiring in loose squadron column. . . . . The Sikhs, who numbered perhaps 60, were hard pressed and fired without effect. Then some one—who it was is uncertain—ordered the bugle to sound the ' charge.' The shrill notes rang out not once, but a dozen times. Everyone began to shout. The officers waved their swords frantically. Then the Sikhs commenced to move slowly forward towards the enemy, cheering. It was a supreme moment. The tribesmen turned and began to retreat. Instantly the soldiers opened a steady fire, shooting down their late persecutors with savage energy."

It is hardly necessary to say that nullahs should be avoided during a retirement, unless commanding points on either side have been picqueted. No straggling should be allowed, and constant watch must be kept on the flanks, especially if the rear guard be covering the withdrawal of a baggage column. In following the line of a valley, as is so often the case when a force withdraws, the dangerous points for the baggage are where minor ravines and gorges debouch into the main one. Even if the heights are effectively crowned, parties of marauders can often get down these subsidiary defiles unseen, and can rush out to cut up followers, to throw animals into confusion, and even to overwhelm small groups of soldiers. These junctions should be held till the rear guard comes up, or at least till it is close at hand ; the troops for the purpose drop off from the main body as it marches along. It is especially important to take this precaution in case the heights have not been picqueted, as may sometimes be the case owing to their inaccessibility or to there not being sufficient men for the purpose. When it is a case of protecting a baggage column, the parties to hold the junctions should take up position before the transport reaches the place, *i.e.*, they should be detached from troops in advance of the baggage column.

Ravines to be avoided, and junctions of these with the valley to be specially guarded.

When retiring over unknown ground in the hills it is very important to send on trustworthy men to reconnoitre the ground, and to prevent any possibility of the force getting into a *cul de sac* or being brought up short by a precipice. Lieutenant-Colonel Pollock, in " Notes on Hill Warfare," mentions the following occurrence : " Some years ago, in

Men to be sent on ahead to find the route in unknown country.

retiring from the crest of the Kohat Pass, a body of men, not knowing the way, moved straight down the hill. The Afridis saw their mistake at once and pressed them back on to the precipice below them, and I think about forty men were shot or fell over it." Had the picquet of the Kapurthala Sikhs, referred to on p. 333, observed this precaution of sending men ahead, they would probably not have got into the defile where they eventually perished.

Pace of column to be regulated by that of rear guard.

Finally, in withdrawals and retreats in hill warfare, it is impossible to insist too strongly upon the necessity of touch being kept between the front and rear, and upon the recognition by all concerned that it is the duty of the leading troops to support the rear guard, just as it is the duty of the main body of the rear guard to support the picquets and detachments which are in immediate contact with the enemy. On no account must the units at the head of the column press on, leaving those in rear to look after themselves as best they can. The following paragraph of a memorandum issued by Sir W. Lockhart, while stationed at Maidan in Tirah, may be quoted on this subject : " Under no circumstances whatever should any of the troops return to camp without direct orders from the officer commanding the force engaged until the successful withdrawal of the whole force is assured, for if the troops in the front or in advanced positions have reason to think that they are not supported in rear, and will not be backed up till they have passed through the lines covering their withdrawal, they naturally are apt to lose heart and heavy loss or disaster may result."

The theory of rear-guard duties in hill warfare.

The theory of a rear-guard's duty in European warfare is that it must protect the rest of the army from attack, that it must keep the enemy at bay at all hazards so as to give the force the retreat of which it is covering plenty of time to get away, and that, if it achieves this object the fact of its being as a fighting body wiped out of existence is quite in accordance with the fitness of things, however regrettable it may be. That these conditions do not apply to small wars in general has already been pointed out in Chapter XII, and in no nature of small war are they so wholly inapplicable as in the case of conflict with guerilla warriors in a mountainous theatre of operations.

Few armies, ancient or modern, have not been able to point to some page in their history, where the devotion of a few brave men remaining behind after a lost battle has kept the foe at bay for a season, and has saved their comrades from destruction. There is a glamour about these rear-guard exploits scarcely to be found in any other operation of war. But in struggles with guerilla mountaineers there rarely is any scope for them. Campaigning against such antagonists a rear-guard could scarcely sacrifice itself if it wished to, because it takes two to make a fight and the average Pathan has no fancy for the risks involved in closing in upon a body of determined soldiers and in annihilating them. On the contrary, if the rear-guard halts and shows an inclination to battle on to the bitter end where it stands, the hillman promptly slips round its flanks and harries the main body or the baggage, whichever may be most convenient. Just the same result will be brought about should the main body push on regardless of the rear-guard; for the enemy will detect that there is a gap with lightning rapidity, and will get between the rear-guard and what it is trying to cover. A column in retreat should as it were resemble a snake or lizard, which feels any pressure on its tail along the whole length of its body; and the only means of approximating to this is to ensure that constant touch be kept from front to rear—not from rear to front. Of course this applies not only to the column as a whole, but also to the rear-guard itself. The main body of the rear-guard should regulate its pace by that of its outermost detachments.

Moreover, as a general rule, the force which is retiring is doing so for its own convenience. Not only is it usually

Y

more than a match for the enemy in a stand-up fight, but it is so much stronger that, so long as it advances or stands still, the foe shuns all contact with it. Only when it turns to withdraw do the tribesmen pluck up courage to harass the hindmost troops, because they know that these have a difficult task to perform and that, relatively to the strength of the force, they are not numerous. Therefore the whole of the troops, if possible, or at least a considerable portion of them, should be kept well in hand and ready to support the rear-guard if the enemy becomes too bold. To be able to do this rapidly and effectively, a gap must on no account be allowed to occur in the retiring column, otherwise the reinforcements will not be at hand when they may be wanted.

Position of baggage in retreats. Of course the conditions differ considerably according as the retiring force is, or is not, accompanied by its baggage. A column sent out on reconnaissance for the day has clearly a great advantage over a body of troops which is moving with all its impedimenta from one place to another. In the latter case there will almost inevitably be a string of baggage animals, extending over a considerable distance and offering a great extent of flank to the enterprises of a guerilla foe. To lay down what should be the order of march of a column which is retiring accompanied by its transport, the first point to be considered is whether the flanks of the line of march have been secured by picqueting the heights. Supposing the flanks to have been so secured independently of the force itself, a very small advanced guard would head the column, followed by the transport with a small escort, which would move as rapidly as possible ; then would come the main body, but this would regulate its pace by that of the rear guard, not of the baggage, the defence of which would be in the hands of its own escort. On the other hand, if the column has to secure its own flanks by detaching picquets as it moves along, the advanced guard must be of sufficient strength to be able to perform this task. In any case, however, the proper place for the main body—those troops not required for picqueting the flanks, or for actual rear guard duties—is behind the transport, not in front of it. The only exception to this is when the rear guard is obviously capable of beating off any possible attack. The story told on p. 175 of what occurred in the Bara valley, on the occasion when Major Downman and his little force were out all night, illustrates this.

Awkward as is the problem of conducting a retirement through difficult mountainous country, pursued by agile, resolute, guerilla warriors who thoroughly know the ground, it is after all, like every other military operation, a question of adapting manœuvres to the special circumstances of the case. Certain rules must be observed, certain precautions must be taken, a certain amount of skill must be displayed in handling the troops, otherwise the force will suffer serious loss and may even meet with terrible disaster. But the regulars enjoy at least this one great advantage—they know almost for certain that it is when they fall back that the tug of war begins, they know what they have to look for, and they can make preparations accordingly.

Up to the present, hill warfare has been in the main considered in this chapter as taking place in theatres of war where the mountain sides are bare of forest growth. But operations often take place in valleys and on spurs and crests, where the whole country is clothed with undergrowth and trees. At first sight it would appear that when such topographical features present themselves, they must add greatly to the difficulties of the regular army. But in reality this is not necessarily the case. The tribesmen of the Himalayas and other ranges around the outskirts of the Indian empire do not seem to practise the plan of cutting down trees on the hill sides, and launching them on the heads of the soldiery, which the Tyrolese found so effectual. For other reasons bush or forests on the slopes rather favour the troops than otherwise.

Remarks on operations in forest-clad hills.

In the next chapter bush warfare will be considered, and
it must be admitted that it is sometimes hard to draw the
line where hill warfare ends and where bush warfare begins.
Forests, especially if there be undergrowth, undoubtedly help
to cloak the movements of guerillas. Large bodies of mountaineers may be able to move unseen along a pine-clad hillside, where they would have shrapnel bursting about their
ears were there no trees to conceal them. But, on the other
hand, the cover makes it far more difficult for the enemy to
know exactly what the troops are doing, and tribesmen, who
have such a wholesome horror of having their retreat cut by
their antagonists, do not like to be in ignorance on such
points. Moreover trees interfere with sniping—when the
slopes are overgrown it is almost always more difficult to see
the bottom of the valley from the heights, than when they
are bare. Of course much depends upon the nature of the
foliage. Trees of the pine class on steep declivities generally
take the form of a long stem with a tuft on the top, and
afford little cover ; bushes and scrub, on the other hand, grant
almost complete protection from view. The case quoted on
p. 328 of the 1st Sikhs and the Waziris, shows how close hill-
men can lie if there is jungle on the slopes. When the Afridis
made the final onslaught on General Westmacott's rear-guard,
mentioned on p. 317, they crept up to the troops concealed
by undergrowth. It is interesting to note that, on the only
occasion during the Tirah campaign where the tribesmen
adopted the traditional Pathan tactics of a downhill charge
of swordsmen—at Tseri Kandao, the Zakka Khels who
made the attempt had gathered under shelter of a wood,
and it was from the cover of this that they dashed out upon
the troops.

Flankers in
such terrain.
In marching through mountainous country, where the
hills are covered with dense forests, flankers must be stationary. They cannot keep a proper look-out and at the same time
traverse such difficult ground. But in such terrain the

stationary picquets need not be pushed out so far to the
flanks as would be the case were the slopes bare of trees,
and being thus nearer to support they need not be numerically
so strong as on opener ground. The enemy to do much harm
is obliged to get quite close to the column, and, that being
so, very small parties of troops, being less easily observed
than larger detachments, afford a good chance of dealing
drastically with attempted hostile ambuscades. The progress
of a column is always slow in hilly country, but when the
whole district is covered with almost impenetrable undergrowth, its rate of march is dependent upon the rapidity with
which a way can be cut through the thickets ; operations in
such country present rather the features of typical bush
warfare than of hill warfare, and can best be considered under
the former heading.

In the Lushai country it has always been a favourite plan Stockades.
of the enemy to place stockades on the hill sides, flanking
the expected line of advance of the troops. Such works
should if possible be surprised from above, special troops
being detached for the purpose as soon as the existence of
one of them is detected. In those districts of the highlands
around the Indian frontier which are overgrown with forests,
it has generally been found that stockades replace sangars.
The attack of stockades is sometimes an awkward task and
their presence is sure to delay the general advance of a force,
but, in spite of this, it is safe to say that the construction of
defence works by the enemy in almost any form is upon the
whole advantageous to the troops. Defence works offer an
objective ; and even if the defenders suffer no great loss, the
fact of their evacuating fortifications which have been
carefully prepared tells against them. " La morale est pour les
trois quarts, le reste est peu de chose" is especially applicable
in guerilla warfare.

Before concluding this chapter it will not be out of place The first re-
to give a short account of a typical day's combat in the hills, to Saran Sar

illustrating the difficulties that unexpectedly arise, and which affords noteworthy examples of the *contretemps* which may occur in such affairs in spite of the utmost foresight and of the most judicious dispositions. No better example could be found than the first reconnaissance to Saran Sar in Tirah, memorable for the losses sustained by a part of the Northampton Regiment and for the devotion shown by officers and men under most adverse circumstances.

General Westmacott had at his disposal for this reconnaissance the Northamptons, the Dorsets, the 15th Sikhs, the 36th Sikhs, a Sapper company, and two batteries. The object of the operation was to visit and examine a pass over the hills by which a track, much used by the Afridis, led eastwards out of the basin of Maidan. Although it is impossible on so small a scale to portray the intricacies of the terrain, especially where the abrupter slopes meet the comparatively level parts of the valley, the sketch facing p. 344 will give a general idea of the lie of the ground.

To Saran Sar Kotal from camp was about five miles; to the foot of the hills was about three. The force started about 7.30 A.M., the disposition of the troops for the advance being that the Dorsets should move on the left covering that flank, the 36th Sikhs on the right, and the Northamptons in the centre generally along the line of the well marked track. The 15th Sikhs and sappers were to remain in reserve with the batteries, one of which was brought into action on the rounded hill, marked A in the sketch, the other a little further back.

It will be observed that a nullah runs along the north side of this hill A, and that this is followed for some distance by the track. Some of the Northamptons advancing up this were fired upon at an early stage; but the resistance was not determined at any point in the centre, and the regiment worked its way steadily up towards the kotal. The 36th for the most part followed in support, as it was soon seen that no opposition would be met with on the right. On the left, however, the Dorsets found themselves confronted by rugged, awkward slopes covered in places with trees; the hill sides here were cut into by deep ravines, and besides making very slow progress the companies worked off rather to their own left and lost touch with the centre—so much so that the left flank of the Northamptons caused General Westmacott considerable anxiety at one time. It was found most difficult to communicate with the Dorsets or to see what they were doing from the centre, and some Northamptons had to be especially detached to watch that side. However, the summit was eventually gained at 11 A.M. practically without loss, and a halt was made for purposes of survey and observation.

As Sir W. Lockhart wished to see the ground himself, the withdrawal did not commence till 2 P.M., which allowed about four hours of daylight to get back to camp—longer than it had taken the troops to reach the kotal. General Westmacott arranged that the Dorsets, who had not advanced far up the slopes, were to keep on their own side—the right flank in retreat. The 36th Sikhs were to guard the left flank and to act in support in the centre. The Northamptons formed the rear guard.

Five companies of the Northamptons on the left were to hold their ground, while the other three, more to the right, withdrew; this movement was carried out successfully without a shot being fired. Then the five began to withdraw and the tactical genius of the tribesmen at once displayed itself. Four of the companies retired without the enemy showing any sign of activity, but as the rearmost one crossed an open space it was suddenly assailed by a flanking volley from a wooded spur to the north. Several casualties occurred and considerable difficulty was found in covering its retirement. General Westmacott at once ordered the 36th Sikhs to reascend and help the Northamptons. After that the retirement to the dip east of the hill A was carried out most successfully and was completed by about 5.30 P.M., the casualties at that hour not being much more heavy than is almost inevitable in such an operation.

The day's fighting seemed to be almost over. The troops were practically at the foot of the slopes. The enemy was evidently in some strength among the woods to the north, but was very unlikely to pursue clear of the hills. It was getting dark, so, all the wounded being reported safe, General Westmacott sent off the batteries and ordered the retirement to continue, the 36th on the left, Dorsets on the right and Northamptons in the centre, each regiment having practically to look after itself, as when night begins to fall any general control or supervision becomes impossible. The 36th Sikhs, who were the last to move off, took the route round the east and south of hill A; but the Northamptons, retiring round its other side, unfortunately descended into the already mentioned nullah, and the Afridis, at once perceiving the error, began to hurry down side gullies to reap the benefit of it.

This nullah is a comparatively shallow depression, but it follows a most intricate and tortuous course, its sides are very steep—precipitous in places—and it is joined on either side by numerous minor ravines of similar character. Offering as it did the shortest road to camp, with an easy track along it convenient for marching by and for conveying wounded along, having, moreover, been traversed by part of the regiment in the morning, it is not unnatural that troops, who were inexperienced in the peculiarities of Indian mountain warfare, should have selected a gully for their line of retreat without picqueting its flanks. The enemy with characteristic cunning waited till the advanced companies had passed on and till the troops on either flank were well on their way towards camp. Then the Afridis suddenly opened fire from the precipitous banks on to the rear companies, and these at once became encumbered with wounded. Desperately situated as they were, they retreated slowly down the nullah, making what reply they could to the hostile musketry but engaged chiefly in carrying along their wounded, of whom the number swelled each moment. Fortunately some companies of the 36th Sikhs and some Dorsets, ordered back in haste, came to the rescue and helped to extricate the Northampton rear-guard. But about 20, including two officers, had been killed, and over 20 had been wounded in the fatal nullah before the regiment got clear of it.

This reconnaissance is singularly instructive as an illustration of hill warfare with stealthy guerillas for foe. In the first place it illustrates the difficulty of control over troops launched into the hills in this class of fighting; the Dorsets were practically lost to the force at a time when their absence might have been most inconvenient. A regiment saturated with Indian frontier tactics would probably have advanced more rapidly and have kept touch with the centre almost instinctively; but what comes natural to a battalion well versed in this peculiar kind of warfare, can only be learnt from experience by infantry which has not enjoyed this advantage, unless a special training has been adopted beforehand on suitable ground. Had the wooded spurs north of the track up to the kotal been thoroughly cleared by the regiment on the flank, the Northamptons might not have suffered so much when the retreat commenced, and the retirement to the vicinity of the fatal nullah would probably have been completed long before dark. The prompt appearance of the 36th Sikhs when the rear guard found itself checked on the summit, shows the value of making the retirement of the main body dependent upon the pace of the troops as the tail of the column. The delay in starting on the return journey was unfortunate as it turned out; but the retirement was virtually completed before dark and, had it not been for the unfortunate route taken by the Northamptons at the last moment, the regiments composing the column, having no transport to protect, would have had little to fear from the Afridis once they were clear of the hill sides.

The dangers of a nullah, unless the crests on either hand are picqueted, are vividly exemplified by what happened to the rearmost detachments of the Northamptons. The troops on the flanks did not safeguard the knolls close in immediately overhanging the depression, which should therefore have been held by the regiment itself when it followed this route. It is doubtful if the growing darkness seriously aggravated the situation—the bad light must have told against the accuracy of the hostile fire; but by daylight the evil plight of the detachments in the nullah would at once have been observed by the other troops. The winding course of the gulley made communication between front and rear most difficult; still the imperative necessity of touch being kept between head and tail of a column in retreat, is demonstrated by the fact that companies of the regiment for a time tramped stolidly on towards camp in ignorance of the tragedy being enacted a few hundred yards in rear, where their comrades were fighting for their lives and fighting for the lives of others unable to defend themselves. Finally, the deft manœuvres of the tribesmen, their astuteness in restraining their fire 'till it was bound to tell, and the instinctive grasp of the tactical situation shown by the promptitude with which these semi-

PLAN XIV.

SARAN SAR

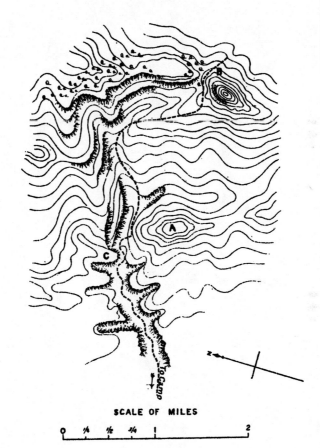

SCALE OF MILES

0   ⅛   ½   ¾   1   2

B......*Saran Sar Kotal*
C.......*Point where Northampton's*
       lost most heavily.

I.D. W.O. 1120⁽ᵗ⁾   Janʸ. 1899.

savages, scattered all over the hill sides, swooped down upon the troops when these fell into a snare, bear signal testimony to the genuinely war-like character of the borderland Pathan.

Before quitting the subject of hill warfare it is necessary Scouts. to say a word on trained scouts. The idea of specialists in any form is distasteful to many ; and it is no doubt in the highest degree desirable that the soldier should be a jack-of-all-trades. But is this possible ?

The idea of trained infantry scouts working on foot in advance of the firing line is one of the novelties of up-to-date regular warfare. Their value has, however, been fully recognized for some years in bush warfare, and seeing that it is almost always arranged in theatres of war thickly overgrown with jungle to organize a special corps of them, it is hardly logical not to accept them in the hills. It is open to question whether the scouts should not form an independent body, rather than detachments of them forming part of each battalion. Of the services of the Gurkha scouts in Tirah there can be no two opinions. Whether the expeditionary force as a whole accounted for many more Orukzais and Afridis than its own list of casualties amounted to, is doubtful ; but the scouts beyond question killed such a number of tribesmen that their own trifling losses seem absolutely absurd in comparison. The fight mentioned on p. 305 must not be taken as a typical example of their methods ; it only shows that when put to it they could bring off a good thing on quite different lines. Ordinarily they acted as skirmishers thrown out on the hill sides ahead of the column. They treated the tribesmen in their own coin, watching them, stalking them, and superior to them to the extent that the man who is determined to get at his opponent is superior to the man who is determined that his opponent shall not get at him. They were up to every trick, they could move as fast as the fleetest of the tribesmen, and they made themselves a terror to the enemy by night and by day.

To hope that the average soldier could be trained to attain so high a state of perfection at such difficult work without the requisite terrain being available for practising over in peace time, would be delusive. It would seem wisest to accept the inevitable, to consider special scouts for hill warfare as a necessary consequence of a mountain frontier, and to leave nothing undone likely to add to their efficiency in future campaigns.

Outposts. The question of outposts will be dealt with under the head of service of security in Chapter XXVI, and need not be considered here.

Conclusion. In this chapter the examples given in support of theories and suggestions put forward have been drawn almost entirely from the campaigns on the Panjab frontier in 1897–98. This is not because many of the difficulties to which regular troops are exposed in such conflicts, and the best mode of overcoming them, have not been demonstrated in other expeditions into the highlands where the Pathan is found, as well as in campaigns in the Caucasus, in Switzerland, and in parts of Spain. It is because no operations of recent years have afforded so vivid a picture of what warfare in the mountains means. In the Ambela Campaign the losses were proportionately far severer than in Tirah. In Waziristan and the Black Mountain the peculiar conditions of hill warfare were admirably illustrated. The guerillas whom the Russians had to deal with in the Caucasus were as daring and adventurous as any class on the Indian border. But the outbreak of 1897–98 is still fresh in our recollection, many of the incidents which occurred in the consequent punitive expeditions were keenly and not always wisely criticized, and there can be no question that the operations in the Afridi country presented difficulties to Sir W. Lockhart's forces, such as no regular troops have been beset with in a mountainous theatre of war within living memory.

That these difficulties were to a certain extent heightened

by the want of experience and training among parts of the
army engaged is fully admitted. The tactics which guerilla
warfare in the hills necessitates, are as distinct from the
operations which the armament of to-day brings forth on the
modern battle-field, as the stealthy cut-throat of the Trans-
Indus highlands is distinct from the Pomeranian grenadier.
To a soldiery accustomed only to drill-book manœuvres practised on gentle undulations, a few of the simple maxims known
to every Gurkha havildar are, when retiring down a mountain side in the gloaming dogged by ferocious clansmen, worth
a whole folio of Prince Kraft. At almost any moment some
portion of the military forces of the British empire may be
called upon to engage in hill warfare, and although the art
of manœuvre in face of an enemy can only be fully acquired
by actual experience, an acquaintance with its theoretical
principles cannot fail to be of some service in the hour of
trial.

CHAPTER XX.

Bush warfare.

Bush warfare presents many characteristics similar to those which are found to arise in operations against hill tribes. In the first place the enemy adheres, as a general rule, rigidly to the guerilla mode of fighting. Then again it is the serious obstacles constantly opposed in the way of the troops by the topographical features of the country which constitute one of the main difficulties of such warfare. Moreover, it is found that in the bush as among the hills, a regular force must be ever on the watch against hostile enterprises directed upon its flanks and rear, whether it be halting or be on the move. Campaigns in such terrain are almost always prolonged, they are rarely marked by brilliant episodes of war, and they are extremely tedious and harassing to a disciplined soldiery. In all these respects bush warfare resembles the hill warfare treated of in the last chapter. But in other respects, the operations of regular troops when they take place in districts covered with undergrowth and jungle, must of necessity differ widely from the mode of fighting adopted when in conflict with mountaineers.

In the first place the adversaries against whom the trained soldiers find themselves pitted in bush warfare are rarely by nature very warlike. They no doubt fight bravely enough at times. They are quick of movement, are cunning, and often display astonishing endurance. But, on the other hand, they have not the love of war for its own sake nor the sporting instincts—if they can be so described—of the hill-man. This comparison is, of course, merely a general one. The Maories in their day were certainly to the full as warlike as most of the hill tribes of highland Burma; but it would be absurd to place the races of West Africa on the same platform as warriors with the Pathans and Gurkhas of the Indian frontier. The savage denizen of the tropical forest is, it must be confessed, rather a poor creature as a fighting man, and this is a fact which necessarily influences the conduct of operations in bush and jungle as a whole to a remarkable extent. Moreover the adversaries usually met with by regular troops in bush warfare are very badly armed—this does not, needless to say, follow as a matter of course, but it is usually found to be the case. Having no breech-loading rifles, and being obliged to let the troops approach fairly close to them before they can fire with any hope of doing harm, their usual plan is to blaze off a sudden ill-aimed volley and then to scuttle away to a place of safety.

In the last chapter "sniping" has several times been referred to. There is none of this in bush warfare. The troops are seldom exposed to the long range fire of individual foemen, and there is in consequence no need for flanking parties thrust out to considerable distances to protect the force from snipers. Any fighting which takes place must indeed almost necessarily be at comparatively speaking close quarters, and thus the disciplined soldiers are given better opportunities of striking home than they are likely to get on rugged hill sides. Moreover it will always be the case that, however well the savage may know his way through his thickets, the movements of columns of regulars in the bush cannot be observed by the enemy as effectively as in a mountain country.

But against all this has to be set the fact that forests and jungles offer great opportunities to the foe for forming ambushes and for carrying out petty but harassing and damaging surprises. In such terrain the range of firearms is of necessity restricted, and in consequence the weapons of precision with which the regulars are supplied lose much of their efficacy. The physical features of the arena of conflict render the maintenance of tactical control in action most difficult for commanders, and in consequence the disciplined force is apt to lose that cohesion and that power of concentrated exertion of its strength, which constitute the sheet anchor of a regular army when operating against savages. In addition to this, the obligation of actually cutting their way through thick undergrowth, which is so frequently imposed upon the troops, renders progress at times slow and most exhausting. Transport often offers especial difficulties, owing to the narrowness of the tracks to be followed, and to animals being prone to all manner of sickness and to destruction by the bite of insects. The enemy, acting it may be assumed on the defensive, has constantly at hand the materials necessary for running up stockades, a form of fortification which is in reality far more efficacious than the sangar of the hills. Lastly, theatres of bush warfare are almost always unhealthy, noisome, fever-stricken tracts of country, where officers and men become enervated by the heat, and where a disciplined army is soon decimated by disease.

The question of scouts.
Bush warfare is essentially an affair of surprises and ambuscades, and experience has shown that corps of scouts—natives of the country—are a great assistance to the disciplined troops, if they can be organized. In the Ashanti campaign of 1874, and again during the unopposed advance to Kumasi in 1895, small corps of this kind, recruited from friendly tribes, were got together and proved simply invaluable. For work of this kind trained European soldiers are of little use, and even disciplined levies are unsatisfactory. Natives of the country can by day creep about the forest paths, stealthy and watchful, bringing back news of danger. By night, working in very small parties, they form an excellent outer line of picquets—experience proves, however, that they dislike moving about alone in the dark, and patrolling in parties is generally a mistake.

Scouting in the bush is an art in itself, an art which can only be learnt by experience and a duty for which all are not fitted. Natives of jungle-grown countries have a natural talent for wood craft, for detecting footmarks and for noting details not observable to the uninitiated eye. The objects of the scouts is to see and not to be seen, to discover in advance where the enemy is gathering his forces, where he is erecting stockades, and where he is cutting clearings. The lithe savage can swarm up trees to obtain a look out—a very necessary precaution at times ; and if blue-jackets have on occasion vied with the aborigines in climbing, it must be admitted that the trained soldier does not shine at such work. Bush warfare is, it must be remembered, a form of guerilla warfare, and therefore it is all important that when the presence of hostile parties has been ascertained, they should be hit hard and should if possible be surprised. That being the case it is essential that the scouts should not be seen, that they should creep about with stealthy footfall, and should use to the full the natural cunning which the lowest classes of humanity are rarely deficient of. A strong and justifiable prejudice exists against special corps of any kind, and as has been already pointed out in considering the question of the so-called scouts in hill warfare, it is certainly desirable that troops in general should be trained to perform every sort of work if possible. But scouting in the bush is exceptional ; it is best left to irregulars enlisted on the spot, and this principle is now very generally accepted when a bush campaign is in contemplation.

The scout who proves so useful in bush warfare differs, it must be remembered, altogether from the scout or skirmisher known to all who took part in the campaign in Tirah, because he is not under ordinary circumstances intended to fight. His weapon is rather given to embolden him and to put him on good terms with himself, than with any idea of his effectively using it against the enemy. Scouts in the bush have for their duty the discovering of the hostile detachments before the troops come in contact with them. Once the foe is detected, they are supposed to stand fast or to fall back after notifying what they have seen, otherwise they are liable to get in the way, and may even run risk of being fired at by friends as well as foes. Of course occasions will sometimes arise when the scouts may attack the enemy on their own account. To lay down that they are never to do so would act as a drag upon them, and it might seriously hamper the freedom of the officers who are undertaking the leadership over a class of levies who are not very easily managed. But such action would be exceptional, and would generally only be justifiable when the scouts are far from support and when the opposing forces are of small account.

Special infantry organization necessary.

Owing to the peculiar conditions of bush fighting, conditions which also sometimes obtain in combats in woods during conflicts between disciplined armies, a special organization of the infantry is very desirable when such operations are about to take place. Companies of fifty to sixty files have been proved to be too large a unit, and it has generally been found that working by sections, or in even smaller groups, is the most satisfactory arrangement to meet the case. The French in Dahomey practically made the section the permanent unit; in that campaign a section meant about twenty men. In Sierra Leone in 1898 companies were divided into sections of ten men. Once committed to action in attack the sections or groups must be independent, and they must look to their own leaders as they advance through the bush. If the troops are acting on the defensive the same difficulty of control does not arise as in attack, the force being almost necessarily in a more compact order of battle; but even so the small unit will generally prove serviceable.

When the conditions usually presented by an engagement in the bush to regular troops acting on the offensive come to be considered, the arguments in favour of a group organization permanent during the operations, will be appreciated.

Companies get involuntarily broken up into parties, which may miss their proper direction and which are very liable to fire into each other. Such combats are most trying to the troops, the leadership is a strain on the nerves of the commanders, and it is only by a system of thorough decentralization and by a plentiful supply of capable subordinate leaders that the men can be kept in hand. Detachments once committed to a fight cannot be extricated, nor can their progress be watched by the commander ; they are constantly falling into ambuscades where they are received by a volley, which at close quarters cannot fail to do some damage. After the volley the adversary evacuates his lair at once and gets away before the men can charge in with the bayonet, unless these are resolutely handled by subaltern officers actually on the spot.

The Ashanti war of 1874 presented all these characteristics to an excep- Sectional tional extent. The theatre of operations beyond the Prah consisted for the organization most part of forest land, the feet of the gigantic trees draped in a dense in Ashanti. undergrowth difficult of passage. Paths were hewn through the bush in the heat of action with sword bayonets. The topographical character of the country was such as to illustrate in every engagement the difficulties and uncertainty that beset disciplined troops when fighting in woods and copses. The normal tactical formation of the Ashantis was a loose skirmishing order, which permitted them to display their aptitude for concealment and for rapid movements through thickets apparently impenetrable, to great advantage. " One point," wrote Sir G. Wolseley in his despatch after the first brush at Essaman, " stands forward prominently from the experience of this day—viz., that for fighting in the African bush a very exceptionally large proportion of officers is required. Owing to the dense cover an officer can only exercise control over the men close to him, and for this kind of work there should be at least one officer to every twenty men."

With a view to decreasing the tactical unit as far as possible, orders were given for each company to be broken up into sections, each section to be permanent during the war as regards command and for administrative purposes. In action three sections were extended, one remained in support from 40 to 80 yards in rear. This sectional organization worked to perfection, and by its means the men were kept well in hand under circumstances of exceptional difficulty. The various groups were allowed a good deal of independence, and they used it to good advantage. At Amoaful the different commands lost all touch of each other, and although the total

ignorance as to the position of neighbouring detachments rendered co-operation most perplexing, the group system prevented any serious disintegration
of the force at any point. On one occasion at Ordahsu a whole company
suddenly opened fire in all directions when there was absolutely nothing
to fire at, misled by the sound of musketry which seemed close by. Officers
were directed to work by compass, and the success that crowned their efforts
in keeping the rank and file under control, showed the value of the especial
organization devised to meet the case.

In the Ashanti war, as also in the bush fighting in the
Waterkloof in 1851–52, in the Maori war, and in most campaigns in thick undergrowth, the loss in officers has been dis-
proportionately heavy. The reason for this is that they have
to be in front and that hostile marksmen are able to pick
them off at close range, and it adds considerably to the difficulties of such warfare. It cannot well be avoided, but it is
a strong argument in favour of having plenty of subordinate
officers. The modern principle of forming the infantry permanently into very small groups should work very well in this
class of warfare, but it has hardly yet been put to the test
of practical experience by well disciplined regular troops
under these conditions.

Tendency of
the enemy to
attack flanks
and rear.
Flanking
parties.

In bush warfare it is generally found that except when
very strongly posted, the enemy instead of opposing the advance of the regular troops by barring the road directly,
endeavours to operate against their flanks and rear. As
troops moving through such country are always accompanied
by large transport columns, and as they must be attended
by stretcher bearers, spare ammunition, and other impedimenta, even when going into action, it is always necessary
to move with flankers on either side of the line of route, and
with a sufficient rear guard. The column moves in fact in the
form of an extended, elastic square.

The flanking parties may be stationary, detached from
the advanced guard as this moves forward ; or they may move
parallel to the column if the country admits of it. If the
rate of march is fairly rapid and if the bush is not very thick,
small groups moving parallel to the column may be the best

arrangement. But if progress is slow the flanking parties will often merely consist of a number of double sentries who remain stationary while the column passes. The procedure to meet the case very much depends upon the nature of the opposition, the enterprise of the enemy, and so forth ; but if there is any chance of a sudden attack, the flanking parties should in any case be strong enough to keep the enemy at bay for the moment without being reinforced. Touch must be carefully preserved, and great care must be taken that no extensive gaps are left through which the enemy might penetrate. There is, however, no need for the flankers to be at any great distance from the central line of the column, as in such terrain the enemy will rarely be able to bring long-range fire to bear. Should the system of stationary flankers be adopted in very thick country, it may be desirable to have a second and even a third line of them, so as to ensure proper observation and to afford support to the groups most exposed. If the enemy be formidable and enterprising, it may become necessary to contract the whole force into a fairly compact square and to advance very slowly.

This elastic square formation was employed largely by Prince Woronzoff in his operations against the Chechens amid the extensive forests on the northern slopes of the Caucasus, to cover the working parties which slowly hewed clearings through the woods. In such fighting the arrangement is advantageous at times, even when the enemy's attacks are merely of a desultory kind. It may be necessary when owing to the thickness of the bush the force is moving very slowly—as must often be the case in certain parts of tropical West Africa. In Dahomey and Ashanti the French and British forces found themselves operating against determined savages in very thick bush, and the enemy at times pressed up in strength close to the columns.
This leads to a kind of square formation being very generally adopted.

During the French operations against King Benanzin the elastic form of square was their normal battle formation and
Its employment in Dahomey.

it was employed with signal success. A formation which could fairly be described as an elastic square, was only taken up when an action actually commenced ; the troops did not march in square, they marched in parallel columns so arranged that by deploying certain bodies a formation approximating to that of square was arrived at. The final operations in the advance on Abomey took place for the most part through country densely overgrown with jungle and bush, often so thick that it was only possible to see a few feet to the front ; it was most difficult for the columns to keep their intervals, their relative positions being often only known to each other by shouts. On coming in actual contact with the enemy, square formation was at once adopted ; but there were often considerable intervals in the paces owing to the difficulty of rapidly taking up this order of battle in such country. It was found that the Dahomeyans gradually gave way before the French advance and did not show much inclination to attack their antagonists in rear ; only a small detachment was therefore generally detailed for the rear face, while sometimes there was no rear face at all, or this was formed by the cavalry.

This elastic form of square offered the great advantage that different faces or portions of faces could if desirable advance against the enemy by rushes without causing confusion—the effect was merely to enlarge the gaps. The enemy trusted to fire, not to shock tactics, so that as long as the gaps did not grow very largely there was no great risk of hostile bodies penetrating through the spaces into the interior of the square ; their movements were not quick enough, nor were their onslaughts pushed with sufficient determination, for that very awkward situation to arise—the enemy getting inside the square in force.

When General Dodds first organized his expedition he formed his column into three groups, each complete in itself. In the earlier actions square formation was not always adopted, although during their progress the force as a rule gradually assumed an approximation to the formation. Later on, when square became the normal order of battle, it was arranged that two groups should form the front and rear faces, while the remaining one formed the two side faces. When the expeditionary force approached the hostile capital it became necessary to march in square, and the column was then re-organized and broken up into four groups instead of three, one to form each side of the square. It was in this formation that the final actions before the capture of Abomey were fought. The square would at times open out, one or more of the groups working off to a flank if circumstances rendered it desirable; but the formation was always resumed again as soon as possible. The principle kept in view throughout was that the square was to be maintained till the action had developed sufficiently to make the enemy show his hand—the normal order of battle was not departed from till it was clear that attacks were not to be anticipated on the flanks or on the rear. The enemy had prepared entrenchments barring the route which the column was following, and it happened from time to time that in the thick bush, where reconnoitring was difficult and hazardous, the square would arrive within close range of these hostile barricades before they were detected.

At the action of Amoaful in the Ashanti war the force was, to start with, formed up roughly as a square of large dimensions. The bush was very thick and, as had indeed been foreseen, the sides lost touch very much in the end of the front face which bore the brunt of the fighting. The rear face during the progress of the action reinforced the front face. But although the square formation gradually dissolved during the course of the fight, it served its purpose in that only small hostile bodies were able to work on to the rear of the front face, through the intervals between it and the troops to the flanks which had originally formed the side faces. That the enemy was inclined to attack the column in rear, *Example of Amoaful.*

was shown by the fighting which took place at the same time at Quarman a few miles further back, where the convoy had been left under escort; the Ashantis moreover closed in between the main column and Quarman.

In this sort of bush fighting against fairly well armed savages who can muster in large numbers, and where the terrain is practically unknown, the elastic square formation seems excellent, at least at the commencement of an action. An advance in line affords no protection to the non-combatant services. An advance in column of route has a restricted front and permits of the enemy delivering a sudden attack from a flank, thereby cutting the column in half; this formation moreover admits of no protection for the convoy which always accompanies a regular army in these campaigns. The bush was not generally as thick in Dahomey as in Ashanti, so that it was far easier in the former country for touch to be kept up between the different sides of the square, and for the commander to keep the movements of the whole under control. But in any case the principle of the square formation is sound in this kind of fighting, because the flanks are always to a certain extent in danger. Even if these are merely protected by stationary flankers while the troops are on the march, there still always is a line of detached posts on either hand which to a certain extent represent the sides of a square, and there is, all round the column, a sort of fighting line which can offer some show of resistance to hostile attack from whatever direction it may come. If the enemy's presence be detected the flankers can be rapidly reinforced, the advanced guard can be deployed, and the rear guard can spread out so as to complete the square.

But, once it has been formed, the square is generally an elastic square, not a rigid square such as regular troops adopt to meet the onslaught of fanatics. The sides, or the front face, or the rear face, can safely advance short distances to attack the enemy, should such a course be desirable—only they must take care not to move more than a very short distance at a time. There should be detachments in support of a firing line, no matter what direction it advances in, which should be ready to extend if necessary and to take its place, so as to prevent the square formation being altogether lost. To ensure, however, that there may be no serious confusion nor complete disruption, it is essential that each of the groups shall know beforehand what its particular function is in the different situations likely to arise.

The baggage and supply train are nearly as great a trouble in bush warfare as they are in the hills. The transport consists generally either of pack animals or carriers—the latter being the more common. As the paths are usually very narrow, only allowing of coolies or animals moving in single file, the columns stretch out to great lengths even if the force be small. In some respects coolies are even more inconvenient than animals as transport, because if scared they throw down their loads and bolt. One result, however, of narrow tracks and of pack or coolie transport is that, as in hill warfare, the fighting portions of columns must be small, otherwise the length of the whole on the march becomes excessive. *Baggage and supply trains.*

As the baggage column must necessarily occupy a lengthy stretch, it is generally best to leave this behind parked under escort and to clear the route for some miles ahead before moving it. Should this course be for any reason impracticable it will generally be best to break up the whole force into detachments, each moving with its share of the baggage, with intervals in between. Up to a certain point the smaller the column is the more compact and manageable it is. *Arrangement of marches in the bush.*

Moving with baggage the advanced guard must travel very slowly, making constant halts to ensure that the carriers or animals keep well closed up, and that the flankers, whether they be stationary or moving, are in their places. If the flankers are stationary they join the rear guard when this comes abreast of them. But after a time it obviously becomes necessary for troops to move up from rear to front as otherwise the advanced guard would be reduced to an unsafe extent by this constant drain. If the flankers are moving parallel to the column this difficulty of course does not arise ; but their advance will often be very tedious and slow as compared to that of the rest of the column, which will almost certainly be following some sort of path. In any case there should be troops in the centre told off beforehand to reinforce the flankers if necessary, who must move outwards at once if any emergency arises. If the enemy is met with, the bulk of the head of the column should halt and the baggage should close up, every effort being made to get the whole column as compact as possible. When a column is thus impeded with baggage, commanders of detachments whether in the advanced guard, in the rear-guard, or on the flanks, should be cautioned against pushing forward at once more than a few yards towards the enemy. Too great eagerness at first may lead to gaps in the different firing lines just when the baggage is probably in some little confusion, and hostile parties may penetrate through these spaces and do damage. It must be remembered that the force is really acting as an escort, and its primary duty is to ensure that the transport under its charge shall be unmolested.

Action of troops when fired upon. On the other hand, it is a broad general tactical rule that in bush warfare troops when suddenly fired into should promptly charge towards the spot whence the fire comes. To stand still is the worst thing they can do. Some difference of opinion exists as to whether a volley should precede the charge, although officers experienced in bush warfare generally favour this procedure because it is often the only way of causing casualties among the enemy. If the troops are armed with magazine rifles, magazine fire for a few seconds to start with would generally seem the wisest plan. But above all things the enemy must not be allowed time to fire a second volley, and to prevent this a prompt bayonet charge is almost always expedient, a charge which, however, must not mean more than a short sharp rush. Supposing the force to be moving in the form of a rough square, the main point to bear in mind is not to rush too far, and if necessary to fall back after the charge, should touch be lost— this is especially necessary when safe-guarding baggage, or when the hostile musketry opens without any warning of the enemy being at hand, and the hostile strength cannot therefore be gauged. Time should always be allowed for the baggage to close up before the troops adopt any aggressive tactics beyond the preliminary charge over 30 or 40 yards, which will ordinarily be the distance of the enemy's ambuscade.

Of course if there be no impedimenta troops can act with much more boldness ; but even so they must try and keep touch with the nearest detachments. Considering what a theatre of war covered with bush and jungle means, and how difficult it is to see what neighbouring groups are doing or where the hostile shots are coming from, it is obvious that warfare of this nature offers extraordinary difficulties. It can only be carried out effectively if subordinate commanders use forethought and judgment, and as long as they keep their parties thoroughly in hand. The experience of wood fighting on the Continent of Europe goes to show that even with the best of regular troops, the men are likely to get out of hand. In bush warfare it is often the case that the force consists of native soldiers of excitable temperament and of limited discipline, and this makes the task of the subordinate commanders all the more difficult.

All this presupposes that the scouts, if there are any, have fallen back on getting touch of the enemy. If the scouts are suddenly fired into it is seldom incumbent upon the nearest troops to support them—never if such a movement would tend to disintegrate the general formation of the advancing force. The scouts should fall back so as to unmask the fire of the troops. Having detected the presence of hostile bodies and warned the force they have performed their task.

It is often the case that very small columns are employed in bush warfare.   It will be remembered that the German column which met with disaster at Owikokero, as mentioned on p. 255, consisted of under fifty mounted men.   Very small columns cannot of course adopt any formation analogous to the square on the march ; they have not the necessary men to spare for flankers.   Therefore when bodies of troops consisting of only a company or two have to penetrate through jungle, they must trust to vigilance and to constant preparedness for all eventualities for safety.   Infantry should march with bayonets fixed, and parties should be told off to charge in any given direction at a moment's notice.   Sir F. Roberts' instructions, quoted further on on p. 368, were designed to meet such cases as this, which were constantly occurring in Burma.

In the last chapter it was pointed out that small wars in some regions combine to a certain extent the characteristics of hill warfare and bush warfare, and some remarks as to the ordinary course to be followed when these conditions present themselves are to be found on pp. 339 to 341.   In such terrain moving flankers become almost impossible, and owing to the topographical features troops are of course liable to be fired down upon from knolls and eminences if the jungle be not too thick.   Even in this sort of terrain, however, the broad principles of bush warfare hold good, in that the enemy generally confines himself to sudden volleys at comparatively speaking close quarters, and that the best mode of meeting such tactics is a quickly delivered charge up to the spot whence the fire proceeded.   It is also worthy of note that in broken ground stationary flankers, as long as they keep still and act with judgment, have a better chance of detecting hostile parties who may be prowling about or lying in ambush, than they would have were they on the level.

The attack of stockades in the jungle is always a some-what awkward operation.   Natives make great use of such defences in their local quarrels, and are generally adepts in their construction—it is interesting to note that the Ghurkhas, now so famed for their offensive tactics on the hill sides, showed remarkable aptitude in the rapid construction of stockades in the days of the Nepaul Wars. Stockades are by no means easy to break into, without the help of guns, so much so indeed that it may become necessary to turn them. The French advancing on Abomey used to march right round the stockades in square, but this plan has the objection that the enemy suffers little or no loss. It seems better to occupy the attention of the defenders by a show of activity in front while parties creep round the flanks to act effectively when the foe attempts to escape. A direct attack is generally met by a volley which will probably do some damage, and after that, while the assailants are clambering over the defences, the enemy slips off into adjacent thickets and is gone before the troops can get a shot. A combined frontal and flank attack is likely to achieve the best results, especially if the turning movement be confined to a few picked shots who await the cheer with which the main body delivers its onslaught.

Of course if the force be small and if its reaching its destination in good time be of paramount importance, it will be best to manœuvre the enemy out of his stockades.

In Sierra Leone in 1898, a small force destroyed twelve stockades in a single march by employing flanking parties to take them in rear. Paths were cut from the main road round to the rear of the stockades by carriers, who had been provided with especial tools for the purpose.

Stockades of course vary in different theatres of war as regards solidity of construction and ingenuity in securing a field of fire. In the Maori war the stockades or pahs were very skilfully constructed, and were often of extremely solid construction. Direct attacks upon them caused serious losses on several occasions; but the fighting assumed its most determined character when the enemy's retreat was completely blocked ; the Maoris, brave as they were, generally fled as soon as they found that there was a risk of being cut off. Fortunately it is not often the case that irregular warriors in the bush recognize the value of having several stockades supporting each other in echelon, each preventing the next to it from being outflanked. But if the enemy is wide awake enough to make such an arrangement, it may be necessary for part of the regular force to make a wide turning movement, so as to manœuvre the defenders out of at least some of their works.

In very thick jungle, where the troops have to cut their way through the bush with hatchets, one of the greatest difficulties which they have to contend with is that the enemy can build fresh stockades as rapidly as the force advances, and that this may in consequence find it impossible to avoid direct attacks on the defences from time to time. In dense thickets the stockades are come upon very suddenly, it is therefore generally advisable for one or more guns, if there are any with the force, to be pushed up well to the front during the advance so that some artillery may come into action at once. If from the nature of the case guns cannot be got along, rockets at very short range may prove effective ; their tubes are always easily carried.

Movement through very thick jungle.　When the bush is so thick that it is necessary to carve a way through it before the army can move, the convoy should always be left behind under escort, in some form of zeriba if possible. The force can then advance without any anxiety concerning it. Having opened the route the troops, or some of them, return to bring the convoy along. It is generally advisable in very dense jungle to hew three parallel paths, those on the flanks for the flanking parties when the column advances, that in the centre for the main body and convoy, which latter should therefore be wider than the others. While the parties are actually at work they must be protected by covering parties with fixed bayonets, ready to act at a moment's notice. Clearings should be made at certain points or existing clearings should be improved, to act as it were as stages on the line of advance.

If a comparatively speaking rapid movement is to be undertaken along a narrow path through dense undergrowth when there has been no time to cut flanking paths, it will inevitably happen sometimes that, owing to swamps and so forth, it is impracticable for the column to be protected by flanking parties. When such conditions obtain, flanking patrols of natives trained to act as scouts and intended to give warning of danger rather than to fight, may be found of considerable use. They should be directed to retire along their own track after firing rather than to close on the central path, otherwise they are very likely to be shot by their own friends—the scout always does run this risk. The natives of Africa with a rifle and with a few rounds of ammunition concealed in his scanty raiment, can creep through the thickest jungle and can traverse any swampy ground where an enemy can go. But when a column depends on this kind of flank protection alone, it must be very much on the alert and it must not put too much trust in a form of side armour which may fail it at any moment.

In bush warfare it is generally indispensable to be well supplied with guides, and to keep a sharp look upon the movements of these. They are very likely to make off if the enemy is suddenly met with or if any confusion occurs. Steps must always be taken to insure that they do not escape and leave the troops in the lurch. A corps of scouts, if these know the country being traversed, may of course entirely do away with the need for guides; but if the scouts are recruited from another district than that which is the immediate scene of operations, they cannot be depended upon. *Guides.*

It is always difficult to promptly follow up a success in this kind of warfare, and this tends to tempt an enterprising foe to try the effect of counter-strokes. It is a remarkable fact, and one which enforces the importance of keeping pressing on, *Difficulty of following up success in the bush and consequence of this.*

that it is in typical bush fighting such as occurred in New Zealand, Ashanti, and Dahomey, where rapid advance is impossible, that irregular warriors generally show a special liking for attempting counter-attacks, even if these be not driven home with much resolution. This tendency is often observable even after some distinct success has been in the first instance gained by the regular troops.

In the final fight at Ordahsu before Kumasi in 1874, when after the village of that name had been captured by a resolute advance, a pause occurred in the action, the Ashantis, after a short lull, developed a most vigorous and determined counter-attack. A fresh regiment was thereupon brought up from the rear to drive the attack home. " Then followed," wrote Sir A. Alison, " one of the finest spectacles I have ever seen in war. Without stop or stay the 42nd rushed on cheering, their pipes playing, their officers to the front ; ambuscade after ambuscade was successfully carried, village after village won in succession, till the whole Ashantis broke and fled down the pathway on their front to Kumasi."

Such an intrepid advance is not always permissible in the bush, even when success is assured and the foe is giving way at all points. The troops in attack may have to feel their way, and the enemy thus gets breathing-time and attributes the failure of the soldiery to follow up their victory to timidity or weakness. It is due to the deliberation which is usually necessary in pursuit through the jungle that the adversary, gaining courage, will often attempt counter-attacks at some inconvenient moment. Such counter-attacks are liable to cause a certain amount of loss and confusion if the troops have been allowed to get at all out of hand and disseminated—it is inevitable, indeed, that in bush fighting individual detachments will from time to time expose their flank to a wary and enterprising foe. For this reason pursuit should as a general rule be steady and deliberate, and, unless the enemy is clearly on the run, the general direction followed by all groups should be the same. If hostile parties attempt to stand they should be charged at once by the troops in contact with them, but these should then allow the general line to come up with them before they proceed further.

The advance as a whole should in fact be deliberate, but on the other hand long pauses are to be avoided. On the outskirts of a clearing it is generally judicious to call a momentary halt so as to secure cohesion, because the enemy is very likely to be found in strength on the far side, and because the open ground had better be crossed by a rush in considerable force—a rush of this kind will disturb the aim of the opposing marksmen and will probably render their volley harmless. As regards clearings, it may be laid down as a rule that columns must never file along one side of an open space unless the bush on the far side has been occupied.

In the remarks made above with regard to attack on stockades, the advisability of sending parties round the flanks has been pointed out. It must however be remembered that in bush warfare special dangers attend division of force. In this sort of country touch between detached bodies of troops can only be maintained within restricted limits. Communication by signal is generally impossible. Detachments, even when within a few hundred yards of each other, are entirely cut off from each other, and do not know each other's rate of progress nor movements. *Danger of dividing force in such country.*

On p. 182 a very remarkable episode which occurred in Achin was quoted to show how in a country overgrown with tropical forests, a force was almost annihilated within a very short distance of support. That similar cases have not occurred oftener is probably due to the fact that the need for keeping forces of regulars compact when campaigning in such a country, is universally recognized; moreover, foemen so warlike and so well armed as the Achinese are not generally met with in bush warfare. Circumstances will no doubt often render it desirable and even necessary to divide up a force which is operating in jungle country and in actual touch with the enemy, into separate columns for some special purpose; but, where such an arrangement is decided upon, each column should be self contained, so that no risk of its being beaten

when unsupported shall be incurred. Great care must, moreover, be observed that separate columns do not fire into each
other ; this is one of the greatest dangers of campaigning in
the bush.

**How to avoid
the enemy's
ambuscades.
Impossibility
of doing so
in some
theatres of
war.** By a happy arrangement of flanking parties or patrols,
and if the force is accompanied by efficient scouts, it may be
possible to avoid ambushes. But in spite of all precautions
the force must be prepared for falling unexpectedly into traps,
and must be ready to act with vigour the moment such an
accident occurs. In campaigning in parts of Kaffirland, in
Cuba, in Dahomey, and in the Philippines it has often been
found impossible to avoid being ambushed from time to time.
No precautions have availed to prevent the unexpected volley
out of the bush which in these theatres of war the enemy
rightly looks upon as his best means of inflicting injury upon
regular troops. In anticipation of such tactics on the part of
the enemy the whole force must be ever on the alert, ready
to assume the offensive in any direction and at a moment's
notice.

**Sir F.
Roberts's
instructions
for dealing
with ambus-
cades in
Burma.** In the instructions issued by Sir F. Roberts in 1886, for
the guidance of the columns operating for the pacification of
Burma, the following passage occurs—" To meet ambuscades,
which usually take the form of a volley followed by flight,
and which in very dense jungle it may be impossible to discover or to guard against by flankers, His Excellency the
Commander-in-Chief would like the following plan to be
tried :—Supposing, for instance, the fire of the enemy to be
delivered from the right, a portion of the force should be
ready to dash along the road for 100 yards or so, or until
some opening in the jungle offers itself. The party should
then turn to the right and sweep round with a view to
intercepting the enemy in his flight. A party in rear should
similarly enter the jungle to their right with the same object.
The centre of the column would protect the baggage or any
wounded men. The different parties must be previously

told off, put under the command of selected leaders, and must act with promptitude and dash. Each party must be kept in compact order, and individual fire must be prohibited except when there is a clear prospect." The Burmese, it must be remembered, could be trusted to take to flight. But more warlike races could not safely be dealt with in quite such uncompromising fashion when the strength of the party forming the ambuscade was unknown; there would be the danger of the enemy falling in overwhelming force upon one of the detached parties, or upon the baggage.

Owing to the normal conditions obtaining in a bush campaign, retreats and retirements are not so marked a feature of the operations as is the case in hill warfare. Retreats in face of the enemy are indeed so rare in jungle fighting that in discussing the subject the lack of examples makes it difficult to deal with it effectively. *Retreats in the bush.*

The warriors whom regular troops have to act against in this kind of terrain seldom seem to pursue with much resolution or vigour, and, should they come up with a retreating body of soldiers, a smart counter-attack would probably bring them to an abrupt halt if it did not throw them into panic flight. Even the Achinese seem to have failed completely in the role of pursuers. Moreover in the bush a retirement can easily be concealed, and a retrograde movement would generally proceed a considerable distance before the enemy was aware of it. Then again the retiring force will generally be moving along a known track while the pursuers may have to work through the thicket. But it must be admitted that a really enterprising foe should be able to make it very unpleasant for a force of soldiers retreating in this kind of country, and this was found to be the case by the German party ambuscaded at Owikokero. Creeping round the flanks and discharging sudden volleys from unexpected points, the savage inhabitants of a tropical forest could greatly retard the movement of the troops, and the same difficulty would be very likely to arise with regard to the wounded as has so often caused anxiety in the hills. Flankers would be very likely to be shot when falling back to join the column, and bringing them in, if wounded, might turn out to be almost impossible.

In case of a harassed retreat it would probably be best to dispense with flankers and simply to march in as compact a formation as possible, certain units being told off to charge on the instant should a volley be fired by the enemy. Baggage, carriers, &c., should be sent on as rapidly as possible escorted by part of the force, and moving by a path these should be able to outstrip pursuers obliged to work their way through the jungle. Troops in retreat when they have to cross a clearing should leave a party to hold the edge of the clearing next the enemy till the rest of the force has got across ; the men left behind should of course rejoin the remainder at a double. The fringe of a clearing, away from the enemy, should generally be held for some little time, and during such pauses a convenient opportunity is afforded for reorganizing the column. Guns would generally move in the middle of the column well protected.

It must be remembered that in bush fighting a very few rifles may impose upon the enemy and may induce him to imagine that he is confronted by a strong body of infantry. For this reason troops on rear-guard should be well spread out, and should be instructed to shift their positions so as to deceive the enemy. When retreating in the bush, ambuscades might be employed with great effect. But the dread which irregular warriors always show of having their retreat cut off, and the uncertainty which must prevail in their ranks as to the exact position of the troops which they are pursuing, are, perhaps, the greatest safeguard which a force of regulars enjoys in a retrograde movement of this kind.

Heavy expenditure of ammunition. In Chapter XXII the essential importance of infantry fire discipline will be referred to, and some of the main points tending towards its maintenance will be touched upon. But it must be remembered that in bush warfare it is very often the case that the " troops " consist, largely or wholly, of hastily enlisted native levies with rudimentary notions of discipline of any kind. To keep the fire of such soldiers under some sort of control in the surprises and uncertainties of jungle fighting is a most difficult matter, and one to which it is impossible to pay too much attention. The Swahili and Waganda levies wasted ammunition to an alarming extent during the suppression of the Uganda mutiny, and it is generally found that such troops cannot be got to husband their rounds.

The maintenance of a rigid fire discipline is one of the chief reasons for adopting the small units for infantry which have been found so satisfactory in the case of regulars. But in the case of levies an organization of this kind is impracticable unless there are numbers of trained officers and non-commissioned officers told off to the various corps. This question of waste of ammunition is a very serious one in the bush warfare which so frequently occurs in parts of Africa, and one for which it is not easy to find a solution.

This question of expenditure of ammunition leads naturally to the question of " searching the bush with volleys," a method which was freely made use of in the advance to Benin in 1897. In that campaign the enemy was scarcely ever actually seen, but the columns were constantly fired into out of the jungle by individuals. It was found that while marching along bush paths, occasional volleys fired into the thickets had the effect of hurrying the enemy's fire. They caused the hostile marksmen to shoot at random and at longer ranges than they had intended to, and this made their fire comparatively harmless. These precautionary volleys were made use of both by the Houssa force and by the naval brigade, and to save ammunition they were delivered generally by a few files, not by whole sections or companies. In spite of this

Searching the bush with volleys.

(10830)   2 A 2

precaution they, however, gave rise to liberal expenditure of ammunition ; but it was probably well expended ammunition, considering the results achieved by the system.

During the operations of 1898 against the insurgents in Sierra Leone, a place called Karina was blockaded by the rebels for some days. A small force moving out to a locality some miles off adopted this system of precautionary volleys in the bush. But it expended so much of its ammunition that it was obliged to return to Karina to replenish. It so happened that the conditions at the moment were such as to render a successful offensive movement very desirable, the failure was therefore somewhat unfortunate.

It is only in very thick jungle and when fighting an enemy who will not stand, that precautionary volleys would be used. The Benis were very ill-supplied with bullets and depended largely upon slugs. It was therefore very important to get them to discharge their muskets at some little distance from the troops, because the slugs were then prevented from doing any harm by the luxuriant foliage ; they were well aware that their arms were of little use firing through zones of thicket, and they only assembled in force at clearings, where they could be satisfactorily tackled. The precautionary volleys really aimed rather at keeping the snipers at a distance than at driving off hostile bodies of appreciable strength.

Firing the bush.
It may be mentioned that in bush warfare the enemy can sometimes bring advancing troops to a standstill by setting the bush on fire. This is of course only possible in the dry season. The tropical jungles of West Africa do not burn readily at any time of the year.

Conclusion.
There is, perhaps, no class of irregular warfare which it is so difficult to discuss tactically as that which takes place in the bush. So much depends upon the thickness of the bush and the general nature of the vegetation that many elements enter into the problem. But it has generally been found that in the dense tropical jungle, where advance is most difficult and where the maintenance of control over troops in action becomes almost an impossibility, the enemy is cowardly and is unsupplied with weapons of precision. Were

the inhabitants of some of the theatres of recent wars in West Africa brave fanatics like the Sudanese, or were they supplied with magazine rifles as were many of the Afridis in 1897, it is not easy to see how operations could be brought to a successful ssue without a deplorable loss of valuable lives.

Happily the warlike instincts of races inhabiting bush-grown territories almost seem to vary in direct proportion to the thickness of the cover. When the country is fairly open they are enterprising and courageous. When its whole face is clothed in almost impenetrable thickets they are timid and unskilled in war. The elastic square formation, which may be indispensable to security when antagonists are formidable, is therefore generally in practice only required in those theatres of war where the terrain does not forbid its employment. On the other hand in districts where flankers are an impossibility, and where the column must feel its way forward depending perhaps entirely on a rabble of scouts for intimation of the enemy's presence, the enemy will, as likely as not, never venture upon anything more audacious than a volley followed by precipitate flight.

CHAPTER XXII.

INFANTRY TACTICS.

Scope of this chapter.

IN previous chapters dealing with attack, with defence, with squares, with hill warfare, &c., the question of infantry tactics in general has necessarily been touched upon under various conditions. But there are still some points with regard to the chief arm of the service which have to be discussed. Fighting formations best adapted in certain phases of hill and jungle warfare have been described, but some explanation of the ormations assumed by infantry under more ordinary conditions in small wars are still necessary, and the reasons for assuming them have to be explained. The very important question of fire discipline has moreover up to the present been scarcely touched upon.

Object of normal infantry fighting formation.

The fighting formation of infantry in the present day under ordinary circumstances would generally be a firing line in extended order with supports some distance in rear, and reserves some distance in rear, and a general reserve still further back. The principle of sending scouts ahead of the firing line has moreover been introduced in the British service after experiences in South Africa. The above arrangement is the product of the battle conditions arising from modern arms of precision. The long range and the rapid fire of rifles and of guns demand a formation presenting little target to the enemy, and the extended firing line is a result partly of this and partly of the necessity for freedom for the individual soldier to use his weapon with good effect ; the supports and reserves are intended to fill up the gaps in the firing line caused by casualties and to give solidity and impetus to the final charge at the supreme moment of the fight.

But a fighting formation suitable in operations against well armed opponents is not always applicable to the conditions of the case in small wars. In combats against irregular warriors the losses from hostile fire are not as a rule very severe. The scathing, irresistible stream of bullets which in modern warfare has compelled the compact battle array of a former epoch to give place to-day to a loose elastic formation, is seldom met with. This being so, the main reason for the existence of supports and reserves does not hold good. On the other hand when determined onslaughts of masses of reckless fighting men armed with spears and swords are to be expected, a scattered fighting line has not the firmness and rigidity needed to meet the shock, and when this is the case, the old shoulder to shoulder formation in two ranks is resorted to.

A feature in fact of the usual infantry formation which is generally especially noticeable in irregular warfare is that there is so little depth. There is seldom need for it in infantry formations in small wars. The reason for this absence of depth is, that on the occasions when a scattered firing line is applicable strong bodies in rear to feed it during the course of action are unnecessary because losses are slight, and that on occasions when serried formation is essential there is no need or reason for depth inasmuch as the enemy's onslaught breaks itself against the fighting line. This absence of depth is generally a distinct feature of attacks in warfare of this nature. Owing to the circumstances strong reserves are not generally needed—the object of reserves is to fill up the gaps in the firing line, but gaps do not occur fighting against foemen who, even when their weapons are not antiquated, have not the ability to properly utilize the firearms which they have in their possession. Troops in the fore-front of the fray are not sacrificed wholesale as in regular warfare. Moreover experience shows that the enemy, in firing at the fighting line, often causes considerable loss to troops in rear, if the advance is made with large supports and reserves.

This was very noticeable in the action of Khushab in Persia in 1857 where Sir J. Outram drew up his force for attack in two lines; nearly all the loss occurred in the second line owing to the misdirected fire of the Persian army. The great object to be kept in view is to develop to the full the fire effect of the modern rifle, and to push all men that can safely be spared from the reserves into the firing line.

Proportion of supports and reserves can generally be reduced in the attack. Experience has shown that attacks can generally be pushed home by the firing line which opens the engagement. Some reserves and supports are of course desirable, but it is generally found that these are used up rather in extending the fighting line than in feeding it. The troops push on in groups with rapid rushes, halting to fire occasionally and to gather breath for a fresh effort. The losses are insignificant, except when the firing line is brought to a halt by something unforeseen under close fire of the enemy, or when it happens to be necessary to cross a zone of open ground under concentrated fire from a sheltered enemy, as at Dargai. Irregular warriors seldom stand to receive a bayonet charge. Only a small percentage of such opponents will meet disciplined troops hand to hand, although their inferiority in the use of the *arme blanche* is generally far less marked than it is in the use of fire-arms. In attack, therefore, the object to be sought for seems to be not so much depth of formation with a view to feeding the firing line as the assault progresses, as extension, coupled with sufficient rigidity in the firing line to make it secure against a sudden counter-stroke. Practically, instead of firing line, supports, and reserves well apart—three distinct categories—only two categories seem to be required, viz., firing line with supports close up, and reserves. Scouts in front of the firing line will, speaking generally, be out of place; they would be rather in the way than otherwise, except of course in bush warfare where, as pointed out on pp. 350 to 352, they are so often a special feature.

In hill warfare it has very generally been found best in attack for an extended skirmishing line to be followed by groups of supports only a few yards in rear of it, while other groups in reserve should be only a short distance in rear of the supports. Thus a battalion might put six companies in the fighting line; each company would extend three sections, and have its other section advancing in rear of these, from 25 to 75 yards back; the two companies in reserve would follow 100 to 200 yards behind the general line of supports. As the enemy's firing line is approached the whole gradually closes up, so that the charge, if delivered at all, is delivered roughly in line. The companies in rear are, however, often pushed off to the flanks, so as to make enveloping attacks. In any case it is always necessary to fix bayonets as the crest of the hill is approached, and the supports should then get very close up. There is always a chance of a charge of swordsmen at the last moment in attacking heights held by tribesmen; and if the enemy bolts the right thing to do is to rush up and get the heaviest possible fire to bear on the fugitives before they get under cover, so the supports should be handy to join in. When the crest is reached it is better for the firing line to lie down for a moment. Hostile detachments will often be in some position within range which may bring a damaging fire to bear upon the troops when they show on the skyline.

Considerable difference, however, manifests itself in different armies as regards the general method of carrying out infantry attacks in irregular warfare. It is impossible not to be struck, when reading between the lines in accounts of battles fought by British infantry on the one hand and by French infantry on the other, by the fact that the latter are more deliberate in their movements, that the troops are kept more thoroughly in hand, and that stricter fire discipline is maintained than with us. In some respects the more dashing the attack is the better, for the moral effect is greater. But on the contrary, the less the men are kept in hand in their advance, the worse is the fire discipline and the less the enemy suffers. In combat against such opponents as are generally met with in these campaigns, the object is not merely to drive them off from their ground, the object is to inflict heavy loss on them as well, and unregulated firing is not calculated to deal destruction in the hostile ranks. It may be laid down as a broad rule that fire should be reserved as long as possible, and until it is likely to be really effective. Nothing can be more unfortunate than to alarm the enemy too soon by musketry which at long ranges cannot cause many casualties. In the usual British form of attack there is emulation between individuals, between groups, sections, companies, and even battalions, and the enemy cannot face it. But the enemy also cannot face the more orderly advance of the French, and their deliberate volleys have done great execution. The magazine rifle has been introduced since the days of Tonkin, and volleys are no doubt now rather out of date ; but the great point to bear in mind is that the troops must do execution if their success is to be of any real use. When it comes to a bayonet charge it will not be found that a steady and systematic advance up to that moment militates against its being delivered with all possible dash.

Reserving fire in attack.   In an earlier chapter it has been shown that a premature employment of artillery fire may have most unfortunate results in this kind of warfare—it may drive the enemy away. The same principle applies to a certain extent to musketry. If the infantry begin sweeping the place where the enemy is with a hail of bullets long before they get near him, he will as likely as not take himself off at once. In nine cases out of ten the less firing there is the better during an advance, till the range is close enough to allow the men a chance of making good shooting. The men are always keen to fire and this tendency should be sternly checked unless the infantry is evidently going to be determinedly opposed. This is a very important point, and the principle should be inculcated upon subordinate commanders that fire is to be reserved.

But attacks in small wars are not by any means always delivered in scattered formations, and it is interesting to note that orders of battle, very akin to the time-honoured thin red line, were adopted at Tel-el-Kebir and the Atbara against opponents very differently armed on the two occasions. Formation at Tel-el-Kebir.

Sir G. Wolseley's intention at Tel-el-Kebir was that the assault should be delivered in the same formation as the night march was carried out in, although discretion was left to the divisional commanders. In the Highland brigade, the battalions were formed into two lines, each consisting of two companies of the right and two of the left half battalion and the brigade was formed up in line of battalions at deploying intervals; the march and attack were carried out in this formation; but before the assault the half battalion double columns had closed in upon each other to such an extent, that it was practically delivered in two nearly continuous lines. The leading brigade of the other division advanced in columns of half battalions at deploying intervals; but it was deployed into line as it approached the entrenchments, and, the Highland brigade having delivered their assault before it had got close to the enemy, it assumed the attack formation. In this case the Highland brigade attacked in line formation, because (as had been hoped) it got close to the enemy's entrenchments before fire was opened.

The Atbara zeriba was stormed by three brigades, one British and two Egyptian, each of four battalions. The formation was as follows:—The British Brigade, under General Gatacre, on the left, was formed up with the Cameron Highlanders in front deployed into line, the Lincolns, Seaforths, and Warwicks 100 yards in rear in column of companies; the idea was that Nos. 2, 3, 6, and 7 companies of the Camerons were to overpower the enemy with their fire, while 1, 4, 5, and 8 companies pulled away the zeriba so as Attack on the Atbara zeriba

to form large gaps through which the other three battalions
would pass and deploy inside. Egyptian battalions had only
six companies each ; each Egyptian brigade was drawn up
with three battalions for attack and one in reserve ; the
centre brigade had three companies of each attacking battalion in line with the other three in column behind, while
the left brigade had four companies of each battalion in line
and two companies in reserve behind.

When the attack was ordered the brigades advanced, the
fighting line thus consisting of 29 companies in line, to within
300 yards of the zeriba ; then after independent firing for
some minutes, they rushed forward on the advance being
sounded a second time. The Egyptian brigades maintained
their formation till well within the defences. The Camerons,
on the other hand, breaking through the zeriba all along
their line, continued advancing. Only the Seaforths, being in
the centre, succeeded in deploying in rear of them, there
being no room except for two companies of the Lincolns ;
and the two Highland battalions became to a certain extent
intermingled in advancing across the successive lines of
intrenchments inside the zeriba. The first obstacle proving,
in fact, easier to surmount than had been expected, the plan
of the one battalion in line making gaps through it, and
then letting the battalions in rear pass through at intervals.
was not carried out in the end. In this case the attack was
delivered in line in broad daylight on formidable defence works.
It was foreseen that, although the enemy was armed to a
considerable extent with breech-loading rifles, the fire would
not be so accurate (especially after a heavy bombardment)
as to render this compact formation unjustifiable, and the
order of battle ensured that the shock would be tremendous
even against opponents whose *forte* was hand to hand fighting.

If we compare the formations adopted at Tel-el-Kebir
and the Atbara to those usual in hill or jungle warfare, it is
seen at once how extraordinarily tactics vary in different

kinds of small wars. In bush campaigns the infantry work
in small groups in loose formation, each group ready to dash
forward independently for a short distance at a moment's
notice ; no great rushes in serried ranks to the sound of pipes
and drum take place as at the Atbara, cohesion is often
maintained only by sound and not by sight. In hill warfare
ranks are only closed up actually at the moment of the charge,
or just before it when there is sometimes a chance of a sudden
rush down hill of fanatical swordsmen. But the principle of
reserving fire seems to hold good in all cases, whether the
troops come up against the hostile position in line or in
scattered groups ; the fundamental principle of attack formations in small wars is to get close up to the enemy by whatever method is best suited to the circumstances of the case,
ignoring the hostile fire if necessary altogether.

It is remarkable how often it occurs that, even when a
normal battle formation of infantry is adopted, supports and
reserves are drawn into the firing line at a comparatively
early stage of the fight so as to develop the fire. This occurred
at the sudden Afghan onslaught at Ahmed Khel—when,
however, the infantry were standing on the defensive, not
attacking. The tendency of the enemy to endeavour to outflank the regular force often leads to this ; the troops are compelled to extend their front to meet the hostile manœuvre.

Tendency to draw supports and reserves forward to extend the firing line.

In the action on the Gara heights near Dakka in Afghanistan in 1880,
the infantry advanced to the attack with 300 rifles in the fighting line, 200
in support and 200 in reserve. During the attack the right, finding itself
outflanked by the enemy, extended in that direction. This left a gap in the
centre, but the gap was at once filled by the supports.

The supports and even the reserves are often used up in
this fashion. It is not the purpose for which they are intended
in regular warfare ; but the system works remarkably well.

It is a striking fact that so skilled and experienced a
leader as General Skobelef should have been strongly opposed
to anything like dispersed formations in Asiatic warfare.

General Skobelef's peculiar views.

" We shall conquer," he wrote in his instructions prior to the attack on Yangi Kala already referred to on p. 178, " by means of close mobile and pliable formations, by careful, well-aimed volley firing, and by the bayonet which is in the hands of men who by discipline and soldier-like feeling have been made into a united body—the column is always terrifying." And again, " The main principle of Asiatic tactics is to preserve close formations." These maxims are not quoted as conclusive— on the contrary, they appear to have been enunciated under a mistaken estimate of the Tekke powers of counter-attack and of the fighting qualities of the Turkoman horse. But they are none the less interesting and instructive as the views of a great leader who thoroughly understood the art of war and who never failed in what he undertook.

The company frequently made the unit. There is generally a marked tendency in small wars to make the company the unit, although this is less observable in the British than in the French, Russian, and United States armies. General Skobelef laid particular stress on this point. Considering the battalion too large a unit in Dahomey, General Dodds' force from the beginning worked practically entirely by companies, and later on worked entirely by sections ; this was, however, a case of bush warfare. Although French, Russian, and Italian companies on distant campaigns seldom amount to the war strength of 250, which is the supposed establishment, they muster stronger than a British company even at its full strength ; a company in the Turkoman and Tonkin campaigns was generally about 150 strong. When only small forces are engaged, the fighting unit is also necessarily small. The Russians have for years accepted the company as the unit in their Central Asian campaigns, and they always calculate the strength of a force detailed for a small war by the number of companies, not by the number of battalions. Although the importance of this company system is most clearly established when infantry is acting on the offensive, owing to the elasticity which it allows in that each

company forms its own supports and even reserves, it is also
at times a convenient arrangement when on the defensive.
In the chapter on bush warfare the special procedure in this
respect in Ashanti has been dealt with.

There is one very important point to be noted as regards Attacks should usually be carried out at a deliberate pace.
infantry attacks in small wars—a point which is sometimes
neglected in the British service. When the enemy is evidently
determined and means to put up a good fight the advance
should, as a general rule, be conducted deliberately. Of course
where it is a case of cutting the retreat of an assemblage of
irregular warriors, or where some zone swept by effective
fire has to be crossed, the movement cannot take place at too
rapid a pace. But nothing has so great an effect upon undisciplined forces holding a position as a steady advance
against them, except of course threats against their line of
retreat.

It moreover is usually the case in these campaigns that
owing to the terrain, the heat, and so forth, rapid movements are very trying to regular soldiers, and officers must
never forget that they have less to carry than their men.
The health of the men has to be considered, and the risk
which they run of chills if over heated by a prolonged
movement at a rapid pace. In regular warfare advance must
be carried out by rushes very exhausting to the foot soldier
because of the enemy's accurate and effective fire, and on
this account the tendency of infantry training is for attacks
to be carried out as fast as the men can go. But in small
wars there is not always the same need for this, because the
enemy's fire is not likely to be very deadly. It may be
suggested that this slow deliberate sort of advance will have
just the effect which heavy firing would have at an early
stage, that it will drive the defenders away before the troops
can get to close range. This does not however necessarily
follow. If the troops come on slowly and deliberately,
irregular warriors will be inclined to hang on to their position

till the assailants get fairly close, and then a rush may carry them right in before the enemy can get away. It is the last two or three hundred yards which are critical, and, if the assailants can get up as close as this with enough left in them for a dash at the end, they may manage to do a good deal of execution even if the defenders bolt the moment the charge begins.

Once irregulars break and run the ordinary infantry-man has not the slightest chance of catching them; but if he is not out of breath and exhausted by rapid advance he may do great execution with his rifle, and it must never be forgotten that in small wars it is not capturing positions but thinning the hostile ranks which brings operations to a triumphant close. This question of pace really requires a good deal of judgment on the part of commanders, especially if the advance be made up hill. If the troops are hurried they straggle, their fire becomes totally ineffective, and if suddenly rushed by fanatics they may not be able to meet them with a firm and steady front—this actually occurred at Barara Tangi in Waziristan.

The failure of the attack on Laing's Nek, which went so near succeeding, has been a good deal attributed to the fact that the advance, led by mounted officers, was made too rapidly. The men of the 58th Regiment were hurried up the steep declivity which they had to breast, and the consequence was that they arrived near the top out of breath, exhausted, and incapable of making a final effort. In those days, however, the Boers were very skilful marksmen, which made it highly desirable to cross any ground under their fire at a rapid pace.

In the Tirah campaign and during other operations on the Indian frontier in 1897, although the tribesmen were armed partly with breech-loading rifles and even had some magazine rifles, their aim was not generally found very deadly. They made good shooting enough when they were in ambush or were following up retirements and had got to close range, but when being attacked their fire was generally wild and ineffective, causing few casualties, so that a steady advance did not expose the infantry to serious loss.

Infantry crossing especially dangerous zones.

There is one point with regard to infantry attack which has not been referred to before, but which deserves a special mention here. This is the problem of how best to get across a stretch of open ground swept by the concentrated and well aimed fire of hostile bodies posted some distance away. Lieut.-Colonel Martin in " Mountain and Savage Warfare " says on this subject : " When exposed ground has to be crossed, the men should be sent across rapidly and in small numbers—a second unit being pushed out before the first has reached its cover. It is fatal to allow the enemy to concentrate his fire on one spot on reaching which each unit will be shot down. It is often possible to dribble men across a dangerous zone in twos and threes, and it is remarkable what a number of men can by this means be rapidly concentrated at some point where cover is available." Now the plan here advocated will work excellently as a general rule, but it may not work always.

If the enemy be armed with matchlocks, if the zone be short, and if the fire be not very heavy, the driblet system is admirably suited for the purpose. The hostile marksmen will be in doubt what to aim at, and if they fire at one spot the assailants who do not happen to be on that spot get across before the defenders can load again. But when the foe is supplied with modern weapons and is numerous, and when the exposed zone extends over some distance—conditions which prevailed at Dargai—the driblet system is fatal. In the first place small parties will turn back if they find those in front of them shot down, they will lack that feeling of confidence and enthusiasm which will carry a swarm of good troops across the most bullet swept spot, and they will not face the dangers that they see before them. In the second place the enemy will in any case be able to wipe out each driblet in succession before it can reach its cover. For such a case as Dargai, one which, it is true, will very rarely occur in irregular warfare of any kind, the only plan seems to be that adopted by Colonel Mathias, to rush the greatest body of men that can be got together across the zone of danger, and to chance the losses. The enemy no doubt gets a big target. Losses will be severe. Failure to reach the far side will be disastrous. But on the other hand the opposing warriors feel that they are being collared, they suffer in morale, are apt to lose their heads, and end by firing wildly ; it is almost certain that a considerable proportion of the stormers will reach the far side in safety, which is, after all, the primary object to be achieved. The driblet plan will be the right one to adopt in probably four cases out of five but the fifth time it will be wrong.

These dangerous zones may occur in bush warfare as well as in hill warfare. In campaigns in the jungle clearings are often swept by heavy musketry. But in such cases the problem is not so much how the patch of ground is to be crossed with the idea of getting cover on the far side, as how to charge across the open and drive the foe from the fringe of the thickets on the far side. The enemy is not securely posted at some little distance, but on the contrary is close at hand and can only maintain his fire at the risk of being bayoneted. The dangerous zone in bush warfare can generally be effectively coped with by a bold charge in force across the clearing, and the chances are that this procedure will lead to the enemy flying through the jungle precipitately after firing off their weapons. The driblet system is generally entirely out of place, except when it is a question of crossing an exposed stretch of ground with a view to assembling in some sheltered spot beyond it before proceeding further.

Compact formations desirable on the defensive. It is necessary now to say a few words as to infantry tactics on the defensive. The defensive is an attitude so seldom adopted in small wars, and then only under such peculiar circumstances, that, when it is adopted, abnormal formations will probably be expedient owing to the existence of peculiar conditions. Regular troops as a rule only allow themselves to be attacked if the enemy be in very superior force, or if his method of fighting inclines to shock tactics. In either case it is desirable to present to his onslaught a

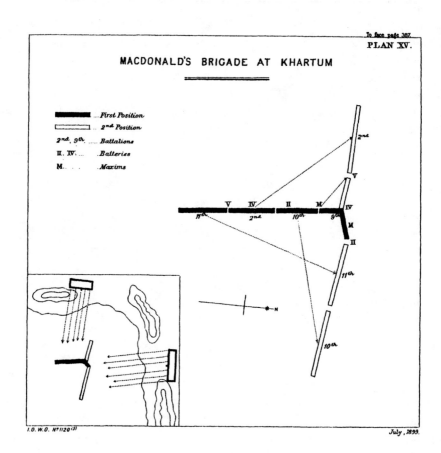

MACDONALD'S BRIGADE AT KHARTUM

First Position
2nd Position
2nd, 9th .... Battalions
II. IV. .... Batteries
M .... Maxims

I.O. W.O. Nº 1120 ⁽³⁾

July, 1899.

compacter formation than the scattered firing line which is so
suitable in attack. In square such as was used in Zululand
and the Sudan, the infantry are of course formed up in two-
deep line. The danger of attempting to meet a determined
attack of savages in great force by a scattered firing line was
shown conclusively at the disastrous fight at Isandlwhana.
In motion the old-fashioned line formation is difficult to
maintain, and in attack it interferes with fire; but standing on
the defensive these objections to its adoption disappear.
Against a two-deep line of good troops on fairly open ground
ghazi rushes, the charges of Sudanese fanatics, and the reckless
onslaught of Zulu swarms, avail the enemy little. The fact
of the troops being in a rigid formation under perfect control,
ensures the maintenance of that fire discipline which is at
the root of success when the conditions are critical. The
compactness of the formation gives the troops confidence
when facing a savage charge, and ensures that the line will not
falter.

No better example of the value of the two-deep line formation of former days when infantry is exposed to the resolute
attack of masses, could be found than the case of Colonel
Macdonald's brigade at the battle of Khartum.

Macdonald's brigade at the battle of Khartum.

When the guns had, as narrated on p. 234, precipitated the advance of
the western mass of Dervishes, the force was drawn up as shown in the
sketch opposite. Four out of the six companies of each battalion were in
line and two in reserve, except in the case of the 9th which had five companies in line. The western force attacked with reckless courage; but the
steady infantry volleys and accurate artillery fire mowed the fanatics down,
brought them to a standstill, and eventually compelled the survivors to
seek safety in flight.

Before the overthrow of the western force had been accomplished,
however, the second and northern hostile host was already on the move.
Colonel Macdonald had ordered off the 11th to deploy on the right of the
9th, facing the new enemy while the fight still raged with the western mass,
and number II battery came into action simultaneously between the 9th
and 11th. Then the 10th were moved across to the new alignment, and
the half battalion of the 9th was wheeled forward. The other batteries
and Maxims conformed. Finally the 2nd, which by its fire had completed the discomfiture of the first assailants, was advanced and extended

the new front on the left of the 9th. The battalions as they deployed into their new positions put all their companies into line, so as to develop to the utmost the fire against the second mass of Dervishes, which was more formidable even than the first and which advanced with extraordinary determination.

Colonel Macdonald timed his changes of front to the instant, his battalions moved with barrack-yard precision, and it was demonstrated beyond possibility of dispute that as long as their commander is prepared for every eventuality good troops have, even when armed only with single loading rifles, little to fear from the onslaught of a fanatical horde on fairly open ground.

Infantry opposed to irregular cavalry.

It is generally acknowledged that in regular warfare infantry has nothing to fear from cavalry, unless it be taken by surprise and except when it is in retreat. If this is the case in campaigns where the infantry are liable to attack from highly-trained, well-mounted and admirably-handled bodies of horse, it almost follows as a matter of course that the same holds good in small wars where the hostile cavalry is in every respect, except at times individual swordsmanship, far inferior to what may be met with on a European battle-field. Adepts at scouting, excellent horsemen, highly skilled in wielding their sabres and their lances as are the horsemen met with in Central Asia, in Tartary, and in other theatres of minor campaigns, as cavalry on the battle-field they are not formidable. The great masses of horse brought into the field at Isly, in many of the fights of the war of 1859 of the Moors against Spain, and in Tunis, gave little trouble to the regular infantry. It may on occasion be desirable for the infantry to form rallying squares when attacked by such horsemen. If there is risk of the baggage being molested, it may even be necessary to form squares all round it. But steady infantry is safe unless surprised, and if good fire discipline be maintained in the ranks, it should inflict ruinous loss upon the enemy's cavaliers.

Great importance of thorough fire discipline.

Fire discipline has already been mentioned incidentally in this and other chapters. Its importance is supreme. No amount of dash and intrepidity in attack compensates for its deficiency. On the defensive its maintenance during all

stages of the fight is the surest road to victory and to the
compassing of the decisive overthrow and collapse of the
assailant. Good fire discipline is the final test of infantry
efficiency on the battle-field, and it is the principal point to
be attended to from the moment that the infantry is launched
into the fight till the day is decided. Modern armament is a
mighty power, but it is a power which must be kept under
control or its effectiveness will suffer. It must never be forgotten that in almost all cases in small wars the great object
to be kept in view on the battle-field is to inflict the heaviest
possible loss upon the enemy. A civilized army may be
compelled to admit itself beaten as a result of the skilful
combinations of a great commander, but the speediest method
terrifying irregular warriors into submission is to thin their
ranks. This will not be effected by wild unrestrained fire of
excited men, unless the aim be steady and unless the sights
be properly set, there will be noise and little else.

In some small wars the want of fire discipline among the
infantry has been very marked. In the campaign of 1859
the Spanish troops appear to have been little if at all superior
to the Moors in this respect ; to this can largely be attributed
the numerous battles which it became necessary to fight before
the forces of the Sultan were finally overthrown. Vigorously
handled and determined infantry may be able to carry the
day without it in attack, but the losses inflicted upon the foe
will not be serious. The battle will be won because the enemy
gives way before the assailants, not because the hostile ranks
are decimated by the bullet. On the defensive the absence of
well regulated fire control when acting against opponents
who trust to sudden rushes in great force, is sure to have unfortunate results and it may even lead to disaster.

The battle of Khartum is the first example of combat on   Magazine rifle
open terrain between infantry armed with magazine rifles in the case of
standing on the defensive, and irregular warriors attacking fanatical
in mass, and it seems to prove that the new weapon settles rushes.

for good and all any little chance of victory that the enemy may have had before its introduction. Whether in consequence of this it will be in the future practicable to substitute for the rigid square formation adopted at Ulundi and the earlier British campaigns in the Sudan, a more elastic one admitting of gaps and of the units having a greater independence, remains to be seen. But it seems impossible for hostile warriors to approach infantry supplied with such arms across any stretch of ground offering a reasonably good field of fire, except at night. The Dervishes never got near the British infantry, their phalanxes being mowed down and having ceased to exist while they were still some hundred of yards off; but they approached to within short range of Colonel Macdonald's brigade before its steady volleys laid them low. The superiority of the new infantry weapon over the old under these particular conditions, was shown conclusively by the contrast between what occurred in front of the British portion of Sir H. Kitchener's army, and what occurred in front of the Egyptian troops. There can be no question that the superiority of the regular troops campaigning against this class of antagonist has been enormously increased by the change in infantry armament.

The question of volleys and of independent fire.   In the most recent developments of the tactics which are considered adapted to the conditions of regular warfare, volley firing has been relegated to the background. Volleys are not in conformity with that great development of musketry in action which the experiences of operations in South Africa and in the Far East have proved to be indispensable. But it is open to question whether in small wars volley firing should not still be made free use of. It must be remembered that infantry detailed for campaigns of this class is not always armed with magazine rifles of small bore, and that it does not always consist of troops of high pretensions who are inured to fire discipline by careful training. Rules suitable for highly trained regulars supplied with the most modern weapons, do not necessarily apply to infantry of a lower type who are armed with older rfles and are from their nature inclined to get out of hand on small provocation. For such troops as campaigns in East and West Africa are generally carried out by, volleys do not seem to be at all out of date, and their employment may be the only means of preserving fire discipline at all and of preventing a waste of ammunition which, unless it is checked, may lead to awkward results.

It used to be considered that volley firing by sections would, if well regulated and directed, be found effective at a range of 800 yards against a small section, 1,000 yards against a large section, and so on, and assuming such targets to present themselves, volley fire would of course be as effective against irregular warriors as it would be against disciplined troops. But it cannot be too strongly insisted upon that in attack, when fighting against opponents whom it is difficult to bring to battle, fire should generally be reserved as long as possible. Under the conditions ordinarily existing in small wars, effective fire at 800 yards range, whether it be independent fire or be volley fire, does not pave the way for decisive victory; it leads merely to an abandonment of his position by the foe. Officers have not merely to enforce fire discipline among their men, but must enforce it upon themselves. There is a great temptation to open fire during the pauses which necessarily take place in an attack, and the men naturally like to use their rifles. But all ranks must bear in mind that as a rule, the great object to be achieved, is to get up close to the enemy and to fire effectively on the fugitives when they quit their cover. It is interesting to note that at the attack on the Atbara zeriba, independent fire—not volley fire—was employed almost entirely by both British and Egyptian infantry; but there was little musketry till the front line was quite close to the defences; once inside the zeriba, control of fire became of course most difficult, and it seems certain that some of the losses among the troops were caused by bullets intended for the enemy.

On broken ground and in hill warfare, where the enemy
is well concealed and where the only target presented is a man
showing now and then for a moment, it will almost always be
better to employ a few picked marksmen firing independently,
than to let all the men fire freely. This plan has been largely
adopted of late years in hill warfare, and it holds
good whether the troops are acting on the offensive or on the
defensive. General Egerton says in his "Hill Warfare on the
Indian Frontier ":—"Much ammunition is wasted in volley
firing in hill warfare. It is seldom that an opportunity occurs
of firing at a formed body of the enemy in the open, when
volley firing would properly be resorted to ; but, as a rule, the
target is against individuals or small bodies ensconced amongst
rocks or behind sangars, and against such, independent firing
(controlled) is far more effective and economical. When
volleys are fired the enemy watch for the smoke and duck
under cover, but they cannot avoid independent fire in this
way." Should volleys be employed in such a case they
might be delivered by sections or groups alternately, so as
to maintain practically a constant fusillade. The enemy
would not of course see the smoke from magazine rifles, but,
except with the idea of steadying the men there is little advantage with the modern rifle in substituting volleys for
carefully regulated independent fire.

The condi-
tions which
in regular
warfare make
unrestrained
fire at times
almost com-
pulsory, do
not exist in
small wars.

It should generally be far easier to maintain thorough
control over infantry fire in warfare of this character than in
contests with disciplined and civilized troops. It must
be remembered that in regular warfare losses are suffered
from hostile fire which are unknown in minor campaigns.
Infantry moving to the attack, no matter what formation
they may be in, over anything approaching to open ground
are struck down by scores. The tension is so great that
after a time it becomes practically impossible to maintain
fire discipline. " Of all the incidents of a modern fight,"
writes Colonel Maurice, " that of which it is hardest to give

any conception is the intense absorption in the mere fact of firing, which almost like a catalepsy takes possession of a man." The soldiers must be allowed to fire freely to keep them occupied. They must be kept on the move. Confidence must be maintained at all hazards. A thorough fire discipline in the early stages of the fight is excellent, but as the crisis approaches its maintenance becomes well nigh impossible, and this is the direct outcome of modern armament upon the modern battle-field.

In small wars, however, the conditions are not analogous. The loss caused by the small-arm fire of irregular warriors is very slight, even at close range. There is no excuse for not maintaining a well-regulated fire discipline, and there is every reason for the musketry being under thorough control, as it is essential that the shooting shall be accurate. Unless the shooting is accurate, the enemy suffers little loss and is not really defeated even if he retires. The men ought not to get excited, because the proportion of casualties is so small as to be almost insignificant. In attack, in fact, there is seldom any reason for very rapid or magazine fire except at the closest quarters.

When infantry is acting on the defensive it is impossible to exaggerate the importance of its fire being kept absolutely under control. The adoption of a defensive attitude will generally, although not by any means always, mean that the regular force is at least temporarily at a disadvantage. It will often be very necessary to carefully husband the available ammunition ; but in any case it is well to reserve fire till the range is so short as to ensure its being thoroughly effective. Of course a case like the battle of Khartum is exceptional— regular troops armed with magazine rifles will rarely find foemen approaching them for many hundred yards across the open, in phalanxes several ranks deep and affording a target not easy to miss. Under such exceptional conditions very long range musketry is likely to inflict heavy loss upon

Fire discipline on the defensive.

the enemy ; here it is not a question of reserving fire, for the assailants are not likely to think better of their intention to attack and therefore to withdraw almost undamaged, it is rather a case of pouring in fire from the moment that it can tell, so as to destroy a foe roused up to fanatical frenzy. When it is a case of an enemy making a formidable attack in great force over a comparatively short stretch of open ground, there can be little question that steady controlled fire should be maintained up to the last possible moment before magazine fire is resorted to.

When levies or troops of inferior calibre are rushed by swarms of fanatics it is most difficult to maintain fire discipline, and this has frequently led to disaster. This was Baker Pasha's experience at Trinkitat. The disaster at Gumburu, in Somaliland, was caused apparently by the ammunition running out, and it is reasonable to assume that this was partly due to insufficient fire discipline. At Major Gough's successful fight at Darotaleh a few days later ammunition nearly ran short which placed the little force in a position of considerable danger. It is often best for troops of this kind armed with single loading rifles to adhere entirely to volleys.

Advantage of reserving fire for close quarters.

Reserving fire till the range is such as to ensure its being effective is equally desirable in attack and in defence, and this point has been several times referred to already. To ensure this in regular warfare is most difficult, on account of the losses which are suffered even when at some distance, and of the strain which this produces in the ranks. In small wars, however, when acting on the offensive, it must never be forgotten that under ordinary circumstances the great object is to let the enemy get to fairly close quarters. To drive savages off by long distance fire is a mistake, decisive victories are not gained by such methods and to a fight irregular warriors on these lines is to play at war, not to make war. It is a fundamental principle of tactics when operating against such foes that the troops must get at their adversaries and give them a lesson which they will not forget. Similarly when standing on the defensive it is often better to reserve fire. Nothing can be more unfortunate than the premature checking of an attack by irregulars who would probably with better management approach close enough to get a good lesson. The object is to tempt them to come on till they are within effective range, because savages when they are repulsed by long range fire do not consider themselves beaten and in reality are not beaten, not having suffered such losses as to take all fight out of them.

It is worth noting that the French infantry in Tonkin and in Dahomey depended almost entirely on volley firing as long as the enemy showed a bold front; in pursuit, on the other hand, independent firing was sometimes resorted to. The excellent fire discipline contributed very largely to the almost uniform success enjoyed in these campaigns. At Kailua, the final fight in Tonkin referred to in Chapter XIV, the admirable fire discipline was the most prominent and remarkable feature of the battle; it was the main cause of the defeat of the Chinese when in great force and flushed with success. In the attack on the village of Nam in front of Bacninh, on which occasion some of the infantry used up an immense amount of ammunition, it was found that volley firing was far more efficacious than independent fire and that it made less smoke—this latter point has now of course lost its significance. In attack a few skirmishers used to be sent on ahead to open the fight, who, of course, made use of independent fire; but as the action developed they gave way to sections advancing by rushes and firing volleys. General Skobelef in his Turkoman campaign insisted upon the importance of volleys and deprecated independent fire under ordinary conditions. In the official account of the French expedition to Antananarivo in 1895 there is constant reference to the steady volley fire of the infantry; magazine fire

Foreign methods.

seems scarcely ever to have been resorted to. Abroad, as
in " Combined Training," the utmost stress is always laid
upon keeping fire absolutely under control, and it remains to
be seen whether foreign troops will adhere to volley firing in
the future when campaigning against irregulars or savages.

Remarks on
the expendi-
ture of
ammunition.
Experience proves that the expenditure of ammunition is
not heavy in irregular warfare, because conflicts are rarely of
long duration. This is, however, compensated for by the fact
that owing to the difficulties of transport which are normal
to such operations, it is more difficult to replace the rounds
expended. Statistics show that a few rounds a man
generally represents the amount in each fight. At the
actions in Ulundi, Ginghilovo and Ahmed Khel, all of them
fights where the enemy showed daring and resolution in
attack, the expenditure was not over 10 rounds a man. At
Charasia the 72nd fired 30 rounds a man, being heavily
engaged for some hours. Although individual sections and
companies sometimes run short, the experiences of the many
campaigns carried out of recent years by European troops
against all sorts of irregular opponents, tend to show that the
supply of ammunition is not as a rule a subject of much
anxiety, and that the replenishment of ammunition actually
on the battle-field is not a question likely to often cause much
difficulty. Still the cases in Somaliland referred to on an
earlier page must not be forgotten ; both at Gumburu and
Darotaleh the fighting lasted for several hours.

The Russian infantry during General Lomakin's disastrous attack on Denghil Tepe fired 246,000 rounds, or considerably over 100 rounds per man actually engaged. In the
bush fighting in Ashanti the amount of ammunition used
up was altogether abnormal. At El Teb the troops most
committed fired about 50 rounds a man, and the same proportion represents what was expended by the broken square
at Tamai. At Kirbekan two companies sent in the first instance to storm the high ridge, and which were unable to

achieve this, fired away all their ammunition except four rounds a man. At the attack on Nam, near Bacninh, already mentioned on p. 395, the sections most heavily engaged fired the enormous total of 240 rounds a man. At the remarkable engagement at Achupa in Dahomey, which was referred to earlier in this volume on p. 260, 25,000 rounds were fired by about 300 men in two hours and a half, or about 80 rounds a man ; in this case the magazine rifle was employed. On the only occasion that French troops were pressed in 1895 in Madagascar, when two companies forming the rear guard of the flying column near Antananarivo were attacked by very superior numbers, the ammunition nearly gave out. Upon the whole, however, there does not seem to be much reason to fear that the amount of ammunition carried upon the soldier will often prove insufficient, especially with the small bore rifles now in vogue. Still in those campaigns, where small detached bodies of infantry are often fighting hard for many hours, it is of immense advantage for each man to carry an abundant supply of rounds. Bringing up reserve ammunition on mules is by no means an easy matter under fire from skilful marksmen in concealed positions. On one occasion in 1897 over 6,000 rounds were lost by the mules being shot during a retirement, the troops being too hard pressed to save the boxes. When a replenishment seems desirable the opportunity should be carefully chosen, at a moment for instance when the operation will not draw a heavy fire. If particular units run short, it will sometimes be best to send them up a fresh supply by hand, parties from other units being detailed to carry it in haversacs or to employ their own pouches temporarily.

The experiences gained during the night attacks on the Malakand posts go to show that on such occasions the defenders are apt to fire away a great deal of ammunition, and the same was found to be the case during some of the Boer night attacks in latter part of the South African war. It

Expenditure of ammunition during night attacks.

must be remembered that in the case of Malakand the garrison consisted entirely of native troops, that the casualties among the British officers were exceptionally heavy, and that therefore the maintenance of fire control was most difficult. Although there was a considerable reserve supply the heavy expenditure gave rise to some anxiety, and a squadron of Lancers, hurried up as reinforcement from the plains, managed to carry 10,000 rounds in their holsters and haversacs. Some regiments fired about 50 rounds a man in a single night, and it is obvious that a fusilade of this kind, on several nights in succession, created a serious drain on available resources. But the hostile efforts were very determined, firing was often at close range, and it is by no means certain that British infantry would have expended less under like conditions.

The bayonet of great value, although theoretically the superiority of the regulars should be more marked as regards musketry than in hand to hand fighting. In small wars of the old musket days, it was not unusual to find the enemy in possession of fire arms effective up to longer range than those of the regular troops and as efficient in their use. It was so in the first Afghan war, and it was so in the Spanish Campaign of 1859 against the Moors. But in the present day it is safe to assume that the enemy from the nature of his weapons, want of training and so forth, is almost invariably far inferior to the trained infantry as regards the efficacy of musketry. Exceptions might occur in the case of a rebellion, and in the peculiar conditions of the Boer war of 1881 the enemy certainly had the advantage; moreover, recent experiences on the Indian frontier have prepared us for the gradual introduction of small arms of precision among semi-civilized races and savages, a fact which, as was pointed out in the introductory chapter, will have to be taken into account in the small wars of the future. Still, as a rule, the superiority of the regular infantry is undisputed. The point is referred to because it would at first sight seem natural that under such circumstances any resort to the bayonet must be a mistake. But all experience shows that this is quite a fallacy, and before closing this chapter it is desirable to draw attention to the immense value of what is the secondary Great effect of bayonet weapon of the infantry soldier. Spanish troops in Morocco, charges. French troops in Algeria, in Tunis, in Tonkin, and in Dahomey, Russian troops in Caucasia and in Central Asia, and British troops in all parts of the world, have proved the value of the bayonet against irregular warriors over and over again. The bravest of them turn and flee before a bayonet charge. The foemen whom the trained soldier meets in these campaigns are often supplied with spears and swords in the use of which they have been practiced from their childhood, and these weapons are generally of excellent quality, such as they are. In hand to hand fighting the regular infantry seem to throw away all the advantages which they derive from their very superior armament. Still the fact remains that the bayonet charge scarcely ever fails and that the enemy will not even face it as a rule. A few Ghazis may sell their lives dearly, a group here and there brought to bay may fight on to the bitter end, but such isolated efforts are of no avail. Apart from fanatics and from exceptionally brave savages like the Zulus, irregular warriors, be they Pathan hill-men or Somalis or Boxers or Boers, have no stomach for the infantryman's cold steel. This is a very important point to bear in mind. It often happens that small parties of infantry, suddenly exposed to a heavy fire from superior forces of irregular warriors, find themselves in gravest peril ; at such a moment a resolute bayonet charge may save the situation and may win escape from a serious dilemma.

When the enemy acts as assailant the affair is sometimes On the defensive not quite so one-sided. The Ghazis at Bareilly rushed right the bayonet on to the bayonets. Some of the more reckless of the Mah- is less certain. dists would charge down and prove that in a melée they could be dangerous. Fanatics and savages will in the excitement of attack, fearlessly throw themselves upon the lines of steel if the bullets permit them to get to such close quarters, and in the scrimmage they may cause deplorable loss with their swords and spears. Magazine fire, or steady volleys from single-loaders, should, however, render it almost impossible for them to get so near unless they can creep close up under cover before they deliver their onslaught, and it can safely be said that for regular troops to have to actually use the bayonet when acting on the defensive, is unusual.

There is always the chance, however, that a disciplined force acting on the defensive may have its general front pierced at some point by the assailants. When this happens the bayonet comes at once into play. The very fact of the regulars not being the attacking side as a general rule involves their being drawn up in an order of battle intended to meet hostile onslaughts from any side—the troops will be in square, or in a zeriba, or they will be acting as garrison of a work or a system of works. Should, under such conditions, the enemy by any chance penetrate within the lines, the infantry are very likely to fire into each other if musketry be relied upon to retrieve the situation. The best method of ejecting the intruders in a case of this kind will almost always be a counter-attack with the bayonet.

It was mainly with the bayonet that the interior of the square at Abu Klea was cleared of the fanatics who had got inside of it.

On the first night of the attacks on the Malakand positions in 1897, the enemy penetrated into the bazaar at one point, but they were promptly turned out by a company of the 24th Punjab Infantry at the point of the bayonet. At another point the lines were also forced, but the tribesmen here also were driven out ; a handful of officers and men went at them, and after two unsuccessful bayonet charges, finally expelled the hostile party by a third charge. For such work as this there can be no question that cold steel is best, whether by day or at night.

CHAPTER XXII.

CAVALRY AND MOUNTED TROOPS GENERALLY.

THE nature of the mounted troops employed in small wars Variety in
differs greatly in various campaigns. Sometimes they con- mounted
sist of, or include, picked European cavalry, at other times employed.
they consist of Cossacks mounted on mere ponies, at other
times they consist of colonial mounted rifle corps, at other
times again only mounted infantry are employed. The
tactics employed necessarily differ somewhat according to the
arms carried by the troops, to the character of their horses,
and to the training to which they have been subjected.

But before dealing with some of the special peculiarities Necessity
in the tactics of mounted troops in operations of this class, generally of
it will not be out of place to point out the imperative im- force of
portance of a respectable force of cavalry or other mounted troops in
troops being detailed to form part of the expeditionary force these
in most theatres of irregular war. For scouting duties, and campaigns.
for service as an advanced screen concealing and covering
the movements of the army, the need of mounted troops
in regular warfare is fully acknowledged by all, but there is
in some quarters a tendency to doubt the efficacy of cavalry
upon the modern battle-field. This question is of course
quite outside the scope of this work, but it will be as well to
say at once that in small wars it is only in exceptional terrain that cavalry has not a distinct and important place in
action. In campaigns against irregular warriors shock
tactics are by no means out of date. Cavalry charges remain efficacious in all phases of such struggles as long as
the ground permits of their taking place. It is notorious that
cavalry has performed its greatest exploits rather in virtue of

its moral influence than of its capacity for inflicting grievous loss, and it is in small wars that moral influence is an exceptionally potent force. Even in hill warfare, where at first sight the cavalry soldier would appear to be out of place, mounted troops are of great value from the fact that mountaineers have an extraordinary terror of a class of troops which is necessarily rather a novelty to them.

The necessity for cavalry or mounted troops in pursuits has been already referred to in dealing with that subject. Infantry are helpless owing to the rapidity with which the adversaries retreat, and the incalculable value of horse has been displayed in most theatres of irregular warfare. The lack of cavalry was much felt in the Indian Mutiny during the early stages. The smallness of the active cavalry detachment which accompanied Sir H. Stewart across the desert from Korti to Metemma was a source of much inconvenience. The want of mounted troops in the French expeditionary force which co-operated with the British in the China war of 1860, was most prejudicial on several occasions. The Italians had no cavalry at Adowa, and to the want of mounted scouts may largely be attributed their ignorance of the position and strength of the enemy until the last moment. Experience has proved that the regular army is in small wars often almost helpless without plenty of mounted troops.

The Boer war of 1881 is the most remarkable example of this. The small British force took the field with only an insignificant mounted detachment. The Boers proved themselves then, as they proved themselves in the later and greater war, to be the beau-ideal of mounted infantry. Their ponies were inured to hardships and hard work and were trained to stand when their riders dismounted and left them. They themselves were good shots, and, what is almost more important, good judges of distance. Against a force such as this infantry could do little and artillery could do less. The Boers in taking up a position at Laing's Nek

with the idea of defending it to the last, played their adversaries' game and incurred a great risk, although it was
justified by the event. At the Ingogo fight, on the other
hand, they employed exactly the tactics best suited to a
force constituted as theirs was if operating against infantry
and artillery, and they reaped the full benefit of the want of
mounted troops on the British side ; owing to this absence of
mounted troops in the camps of their opponents, they were
able to strike without the slightest fear of suffering a serious
reverse. Regular troops have seldom in a small war been
placed in a more ignominious position than Sir G. Colley's
little army. Had the British force included a few squadrons
of cavalry the Boers could not have manœuvred with the
freedom they did outside their entrenchments at Laing's Nek,
and it is very doubtful if they would have attempted to hold
those entrenchments at all had they found a cloud of troopers
sweeping round their flank. The presence of cavalry in such
conditions would have completely altered the situation.

Mounted troops have always proved invaluable in South
Africa, where the nature of the theatres of war generally
favours their action. Infantry have never been able to catch
the Kaffirs except when these retire into some stronghold like
the Waterkloof or Sekukuni's Mountain. In the wars against
the Red Indians in the Western States the same has been
found to be the case. It is indeed only in thick bush or in
exceptionally rugged mountains that this arm of the service
seems to be out of place when campaigning against irregular
warriors.

For raids such as the French instituted in Algeria, such Need of
as the United States troops carried out so successfully troops for
against the Red Indians, and such as the Russians frequently raids.
employ in the steppes, mounted troops are indispensable.
In such cases, and in dealing with guerillas operating over a
great extent of country like the rebels in Rhodesia, the need
for mounted troops arises from the necessity of mobility, and

therefore mounted infantry will serve the purpose. But in action against determined opponents who do not confine themselves to guerilla operations but who accept battle, the shock tactics of cavalry are requisite if the mounted force is not to play an altogether secondary rôle in the fight.

Importance of cavalry shock action. While mounted rifles and mounted infantry are, speaking generally, only supposed to fight dismounted, cavalry fights both mounted and dismounted. The tendency has been of late years in some armies, and especially so in the British service, to give to cavalry shock action a very secondary place in tactics and to make the rifle the main arm of the cavalry trooper. Difference of opinion exists whether in this respect the reformers in preparing the arm for the exigencies of regular warfare have not moved too fast, but it may in any case safely be laid down that in campaigns against irregular warriors the time-honoured principles of cavalry tactics still hold good. Indeed the fundamental principle which, except in certain special cases, governs the proper conduct of all small wars affords strong evidence in favour of cavalry shock action on the battle-field. A bold initiative for the plan of campaign, and resolute attack when the enemy is met with, point the way to triumph. The action of cavalry on horse-back is necessarily never defensive. It is the special characteristic of the arm that, apart from dismounted work, it always attacks—cavalry in fact incarnates the spirit which should animate the operations and which does animate them when in proper hands. The moral effect of a charge of trained and disciplined horse upon a mob of irregular warriors is tremendous. It is like the bayonet charge of infantry, only that it generally admits of no escape and that it is much more easy to bring about.

Small wars offer the cavalry leader magnificent opportunities on a minor scale. On favourable ground there is scarcely a limit to what his command can effect if handled with boldness and skill. The achievements of cavalry in the

Indian Mutiny were brilliant in the extreme. In that campaign, where the offensive was adopted almost as a matter of course, the mounted troops were in their element; the very fact that the rebels were organized after a fashion and fought somewhat in the European manner, favoured the employment of the arm—there were formations to break, hostile squadrons to be swept away and guns to be captured. In Algeria the French cavalry seldom failed to make its presence felt, and did grand service. For work like this cavalry is far superior to mounted rifles or mounted infantry in any form.

In considering the tactics of cavalry and of mounted troops generally, it will be convenient to deal with mounted action first. The great risk that cavalry runs in this sort of warfare is that it may fall into an ambush on ground where it cannot act with effect. In all theatres of war there is the danger of coming unexpectedly upon concealed obstacles or upon impracticable ground. The remarkable charge at Ramnugger which routed the Sikhs, ended in the cavalry getting into deep ground and suffering very heavily before it could be withdrawn from action. Such incidents are not uncommon in regular warfare, and they are frequent in conflicts with uncivilized races. Sometimes, as in the action at the crossing of the Swat River in the Chitral campaign in 1895, the approach of cavalry will dislodge irregular warriors from ground where they are in reality perfectly safe from the mounted men; but this cannot of course be depended upon, and experience shows that cavalry pushed too far in unfavourable ground may get into very serious difficulties if it falls into an ambuscade or comes unexpectedly under fire of hostile bodies under cover. One or two examples of this are worth quoting.

Risk of falling into ambushes or getting into ground where cavalry cannot act.

The affair of Mukur, during General Nott's advance from Kandahar to Ghazni in 1842 is a good instance. A small cavalry force came upon some Afghans in the open, cut them up, and pursued the fugitives to the hills. Here the enemy showed up in force, and the troopers fell back. Hostile horsemen thereupon pressed forward and, becoming more and more threatening a part of the cavalry was sent to attack them over rough ground. This suddenly found itself exposed to very heavy fire from Afghans concealed on the flank. Retreating in haste it was immediately charged, and being outnumbered and at a great disadvantage it had to seek refuge in flight.

At the battle of Castellijos in Morocco in 1859, two Spanish squadrons, carried away by the excitement of a charge, dashed right into the enemy's position up a narrow valley. In withdrawing they suffered very heavily without having apparently achieved any substantial success.

Cavalry able to act effectively on broken ground where it would be useless in regular warfare.

At the same time it cannot be too strongly insisted upon that, opposed to irregular warriors, it is not generally a *sine qua non* that the ground which mounted troops are to operate over must be such as cavalry can charge over. The best known cases where cavalry have got into serious difficulties owing to unexpected obstacles have mostly occurred in regular warfare, where this arm of the service must almost of necessity act at a high rate of speed. Instances can be quoted where troops and squadrons have gone headlong over precipices to their destruction. But such disasters only befall the troopers when they are acting in formed bodies with the reckless dash which is traditional with the cavalry soldier. There is an idea very generally entertained in other branches of the service, and it is one which is to a certain extent encouraged by writers on tactics, that cavalry is of little use in broken, rugged country. That this is by no means the case in operations against undisciplined forces was shown in the campaigns of 1895 and 1897 in the valleys of the Swat and Panjkora Rivers. Some of the most effective work performed on horseback by the mounted troops during the operations against the Mamund clan was carried out at a deliberate trot in awkward, rocky ground, where a gallop would often have been wholly impracticable and would always have been dangerous. Savages, Asiatics, and adversaries of that character have a great dread of the mounted man, and they are apt to lose their nerve on his approach, even when the ground is unfavourable to him and when he can go little faster than they can. It is quite different in regular warfare, where cavalry can effect little against infantry except by surprise, and where in broken intersected terrain it would be sacrificed if it attempted to approach foot soldiers.

It is, however, only right to point out that the mounted troops which performed such signal service during the advance towards Chitral and during the operations of the Malakand field force, enjoyed the advantage of great experience in irregular warfare. Because regiments like the Guides and the 11th Bengal Lancers were able to play an important tactical rôle in theatres of war so awkward to traverse by mounted men as Swat and Bajaour, it does not follow that corps trained on more favourable ground and accustomed only to ordinary cavalry manœuvres, would do as well under the same conditions. Still, although the services of less practised corps might not be so valuable, they would yet be far from useless, and it seems to be definitely settled that in irregular warfare the trooper has a well established place, on a rugged battle-field cut up by nullahs and full of pit-falls as well as upon ground more congenial to his ordinary mode of fighting.

One of the greatest difficulties which in these campaigns cavalry has to contend with when delivering a charge is the dispersed straggling formation in which the enemy so generally fights. In regular warfare the main object of the charge is to throw the adversary into just such confusion as constitutes normal battle order of Pathans, Sudanese, Somalis and their like. Loose crowds of this description can be ridden through without their fighting efficiency being much affected, although the moral effect cannot fail to be considerable. One of the reasons that the memorable charge of the 21st Lancers at the battle of Khartum was so effective was that the hostile force ridden through was massed thickly together. Sudanese throw themselves down to avoid the troopers' sabres, and jumping up, ham-string the horses. At El Teb a great throng

Irregular hostile formations militate against effective cavalry charges.

of the Mahdists was charged through several times by the cavalry brigade, but from the want of lances—this question of lances will be referred to later—no very serious loss was inflicted upon them. On the other hand at the fight of Khushk-i-Nakhud two native squadrons charged a considerable gathering of Afghans, mostly footmen, on open ground and killed no less than 163 of them, thus showing that even under the unfavourable circumstances of charging through dispersed gatherings of irregular warriors cavalry can sometimes strike a heavy blow.

In pursuit the results are of course more satisfactory. The enemy is demoralised, and individuals are less adroit in avoiding the sabre and the lance. Even here, however, the tendency of such antagonists to disperse in all directions, defeats to a certain extent the object which the cavalry have in view. In campaigns where the enemy fights in formed bodies, such as the Indian Mutiny and the Egyptian War of 1882, cavalry in pursuit have of course a well defined rôle to perform in breaking up any semblance of formation which the fugitives may try to maintain—in operations such as these, where the hostile troops adopt the form of modern tactics without enjoying the confidence and cohesion of a modern army, cavalry is indeed seen almost at its best. Operating against forces of this nature the Hussar and Lancer find exceptional opportunities for distinction. In the Indian Mutiny the cavalry even broke rebel squares, and by its determined efforts and restless energy it assumed in the open field an extraordinary importance.

Cavalry and horse artillery.

Small wars seldom lend themselves to a happy co-operation between cavalry and horse artillery. The terrain does not as a rule admit of guns manœuvring at a high rate of speed. When the ground is suitable, however, this combination has a great opening for decisive action owing to the freedom with which the artillery can work. The Indian Mutiny afforded some splendid examples in those phases of the campaign where the enemy, acting in formed units, was brought to bay in the open field. It is, however, unnecessary to discuss the form which such tactics take, because they are described and illustrated in most works on the military art, and are practised on the manœuvre ground.

The opponents met with in irregular operations can often boast of mounted forces deserving of respect. In some cases the hostile cavalry is formed in squadrons and works effectively as an organized body, in others it merely represents a mass of horsemen ready to follow a few acknowledged chieftains. Good cavalry, boldly handled, has not much to fear in either case. Still it is generally of great importance, where the enemy's mounted forces are really worthy of consideration, that the troopers should be kept thoroughly in hand and should work in compact formation, because it is in their discipline and cohesion rather than in any superiority of armament that their advantage over the hostile horsemen lies. Cavalry acting against hostile mounted troops.

It was a saying of Napoleon's that two Mamelukes could defeat three French horsemen, that 100 French horse could hold their own against an equal force of Mamelukes, that 300 French would defeat the same number, and that 1,000 French would defeat 1,500 Mamelukes. For the Mamelukes were better armed, better mounted and individually more skilful than Napoleon's troopers; but as the size of the respective forces grew, tactics, order, and the power of manœuvring grew more and more decisive, gradually turning the scale in favour of the trained and disciplined cavalry. The horsemen met with by the French in Algeria and by the British in many Indian campaigns have been individually most formidable ; they have been well mounted, have been generally very well armed apart from firearms, have been dexterous swordsmen, and have been experts in the handling of the lance. It is moreover worthy of note that when mounted irregular foemen are inclined to assume the initiative they will often act Importance of discipline and cohesion in such work.

with great boldness. Owing to the hardy constitution and
good condition of their horses, they can in addition to this
lay claim to considerable, and sometimes to quite remarkable,
mobility. In many respects they are in fact really formidable,
and the only point in which, speaking generally, they are
found to fail is in the power of using concentrated force at
the bidding of their leaders in the right direction. That being
so, it is essential that this one point, in which the trained
cavalry holds them at so great a disadvantage, should be
profited by to the full.

To enumerate instances where small bodies of regular
cavalry have overthrown far superior numbers of irregular
horsemen would be tedious. As long as the trained troopers
are handled with skill and vigour, and as long as they reap to
the full the advantage which they hold in virtue of their
superior discipline, they will seldom fail to win success even
when the odds are enormously against them. It is not, however, always so, as the following example shows :—

> In 1864, a French squadron suddenly found itself in presence of a body
> of about 1,000 hostile Arabs at a place called Ain-el-Khata in the undefined
> territory known as Southern Algeria. The small French force at once
> boldly charged the formidable lost. The Arabs let it come on and dash
> right in among them, but they then surrounded their bold assailants and
> cut them down.

Still, considering the number of cases where small bodies
of regular cavalry have utterly defeated and dispersed masses
of brave, well-armed and well-mounted horsemen, and the
very few instances of failure except from bad management,
it may almost be accepted as a principle that the regulars
should not shirk an encounter even with very superior forces
of hostile horsemen on suitable ground.

Difficulty of
meeting a
reckless
charge of
fanatical
horsemen.

A wild charge of fanatical horsemen is not always easy to
meet satisfactorily, and it is essential that the cavalry subjected to such an onslaught should be ready to act in a decisive direction and at a moment's notice. The theory of

tactics when cavalry fights cavalry is to attack the enemy in flank, and regular squadrons always endeavour to work on this principle. Irregular cavalry is not so dexterously handled, nor is it sufficiently under control to enable it to carry out evolutions directed by its leaders at a critical moment. Charging in dispersed order, as such horsemen do, an onslaught on their flank is no doubt in some respects less effective than a similar manœuvre directed against a force of regular cavalry would be, because they are in confusion as a matter of course, while the great object of regular cavalry is to avoid being thrown into confusion. Still a flank attack of this kind on a swarm of irregular horsemen is very likely to put them to flight, inasmuch as they have not the manœuvring powers to meet it and they have not the pace to escape it. In theory indeed, some part of a force of cavalry taken at a disadvantage by a sudden onslaught of a swarm of irregular horse ought always to be able to deliver a flank attack on the enemy, even supposing that the bulk of it is obliged to retire for the moment. Experience nevertheless shows that such manœuvres are not always possible at a critical juncture. Thus at the commencement of the fight at Ahmed Khel some native cavalry on the left flank of the British line were thrown into serious confusion by a mass of Afghan horsemen who swooped down from the hills upon them very suddenly, and caught them in difficulties.

Moors, Tartars, and some of the Asiatics of the Steppes fire from horseback, and the Cossacks adopted the plan of firing mounted in the days when their guerilla tactics made them so formidable. In the later stages of the South African war of 1899–1902 the Boers did the same with some success. This mode of fighting on the part of irregular horsemen gives regular cavalry a great chance of operating against them with deadly effect. At the battle of Isly the Moorish horse charged in enormous masses of successive lines close up to the French infantry and then discharged volleys, the lines in rear fired

Enemy's horse inclined to use firearms from the saddle.

in the air, numbers of the French being hit by spent balls; but no impression was made and the hostile cavalry soon began to give way under the steady infantry fire. Thereupon Marshal Bugeaud sent out his squadrons and these really completed the victory, capturing the hostile artillery and camp. On two occasions small cavalry detachments charging at an opportune moment overthrew large masses of Tartar horse in the China war of 1860, the efforts of the Tartars to beat off the attack by firing from horseback proving quite ineffective. Horsemen who trust to their firearms as a principal weapon when in the saddle, are of little use in a cavalry combat, and cannot therefore be proceeded against too energetically.

Cavalry if rushed to keep away from the infantry. A very important point in campaigns where the enemy is addicted to sudden rushes, is for the cavalry to keep well away from the infantry; otherwise the mounted troops may be borne back on the infantry in one of the hostile onslaughts, may mask its fire, and may perhaps throw it into confusion. At the attack of the Arabs on General McNeill at Tofrek in 1885, the vedettes galloping in caused considerable disorder on one side of the zeriba. It should always be clearly understood that when the force is opposed to this class of enemy, the cavalry must if possible withdraw to a flank if obliged to fall back.

Cavalry dealing with horsemen who fight on foot. It used to be thought—and in earlier editions of this work the view was maintained—that cavalry opposed to mounted rifles or mounted infantry would certainly be able to act with great effect against the horses which mounted troops must leave under charge of horse holders when they fight dismounted. It must be confessed, however, that the South African war of 1899–1902 affords little evidence in support of this theory. The Boers were no doubt exceptionally skilful and well-armed fighters. But they were mounted rifles who fought dismounted, and the result of months of warfare in which some of the finest cavalry in the world was pitted against them, was that they,

irregulars as they were and to all intents and purposes untrained in the art of war, compelled that cavalry to transform
itself into mounted rifles. In the later stages of the war some
crack regiments of Dragoons and Hussars and Lancers abandoned the *arme blanche* altogether as a useless encumbrance—
it is not suggested that such action was right, but it is necessary to record the fact. It is impossible to disregard the teachings of that war when the question of cavalry versus mounted
rifles is considered, even if the lessons are not accepted as
final.

The Boers were, of course, a very different class of foe
from most of the irregulars against whom civilized armies have
to operate. Antagonists of this kind rarely possess the grit
displayed by our opponents in South Africa, and they are not
as a rule armed with Mausers. The old theory that cavalry
ought to overthrow mounted infantry on anything like level
terms, would probably be found still to hold good in action
when campaigning against an enemy armed with inferior
weapons who is mounted but who fights on foot. The business
of the cavalry is of course to go for their antagonists' horses
if it can possibly be managed, these offer a fine opportunity
to a quick-eyed squadron leader, and if they can be captured,
or even if they can be stampeded, the enemy is in a very
awkward position. Supposing the circumstances to be
favourable, it should often be possible to occupy the attention of the hostile horsemen with dismounted fire, while a
troop or detachment works round their flank and makes a dash
for their horses. But antagonists who depend upon scrambling
on to horses, or mules, or camels during the battle if the
day goes against them, and who when they have mounted
have no arms to defend themselves with, have an instinctive
terror of the cavalry soldier when he looks like business,
and they are always very anxious about the safety of their
mounts, so much so that capturing or stampeding these requires
deft and sudden movements.

Although it is, of course, outside the scope of this work to treat of arms and equipment except incidentally, the desirability of cavalry being armed with lances in such warfare has been too frequently and too clearly demonstrated of recent years for the subject not to be referred to here. The lance has obvious objections in regular warfare, owing to its inconvenience when the trooper fights on foot. But in campaigns against savages or guerillas or against troops of very inferior class it is a splendid weapon. Asiatics know this well. In pursuit of an enemy who scatters in all directions, who lies down so that only the most expert swordsman can get at him effectively, who becomes panic stricken in the moment of defeat, the lance is simply invaluable. This was well shown at Ulundi. After the experiences of his charges at El Teb, Sir H. Stewart armed his Hussars with Arab spears. At Kambula the mounted rifles in their pursuit armed themselves with Zulu assegais. Just as in small wars it is often necessary to resort to old shoulder-to-shoulder formations for infantry, so it is also necessary to give to shock action of cavalry a great prominence in such campaigns, and to depend largely upon the lance, however inconvenient it may be when the cavalry takes to dismounted work.

Before dealing with the question of the dismounted action of cavalry and of mounted troops it is only right to notice that the views expressed in an earlier paragraph as to the desirability of cavalry acting with great boldness in warfare of this nature, had an opponent of undoubted authority in the person of General Skobelef. His instructions to his cavalry in the Turkoman campaign throughout breathed the spirit of caution. " As long as the enemy's cavalry is unshaken and is not in an unfavourable position, *e.g.*, with an obstacle in rear, in a hollow, &c., our cavalry must not enter on a combat with it. Pursuit of a retreating Turkoman cavalry is useless, as it only breaks up the tactical formations—our one strong point and sheet anchor." Such were his orders, and they sound strange enough, for, in a word, General Skobelef taught his cavalry to be afraid of the Turkoman horse. It must, however, be remembered that the Russian cavalry operating beyond the Caspian was ill adapted for shock tactics, and that with mounted troops of a different class at his disposal the general might have held other views. Such a leader's recorded opinions are always entitled to respectful attention even when not accepted as necessarily sound.

It is necessary now to refer to what in small wars is for cavalry a secondary rôle—dismounted action. It is of course practically the only tactical rôle of mounted rifles or mounted infantry. *Dismounted action of cavalry.*

Should mounted troops, unsupported by infantry, come upon a hostile gathering on ground where charging is impracticable, they have no option except to dismount and to act on foot. On ground where there is a good field of view there is no objection to cavalry doing this ; but it is most dangerous when there is any fear of a sudden rush of determined foemen directed either against the dismounted troopers or the horse-holders, and under these conditions mounted rifles always have an awkward task. At the action of Hashin, near Suakin, in 1885, some cavalry were dismounted in country partly overgrown with bush ; they were unexpectedly attacked in force by the Arabs and suffered some loss in escaping. In the case of cavalry it would very rarely be judicious to dismount the whole of the available men except the horse-holders, supposing the ground to be such that the enemy may manage to creep up close ; there ought to be a party of men on horseback ready to charge and to cover the mounting of the remainder should these or the horse-holders be rushed.

When mounted troops are acting dismounted there is always this risk that the horse-holders may be attacked if the enemy be enterprising. The more broken the ground the greater chance is there of a hostile counter-stroke of this nature succeeding, because it may be possible for parties of the *Risk to horse-holders and horses.*

enemy to approach unperceived from different sides. In any case the horses are apt to get frightened in the event of a sudden scare and to become unmanageable. Clustered together as they are they present a good target and a number of them may be shot before the dismounted men can get back to them—as happened at Owikokero. It is needless to say that under such conditions a careful look-out must be kept. In the affair of " Petrusvitch's Garden," related later on on p. 421, the horse-holders were seriously threatened ; and the following example from the operations near Inyat Kali, in 1897, will be of interest in this connection :—

A determined attack had been made by the tribesmen on the camp at night, and as soon as day broke a squadron of cavalry started in pursuit of the assailants who were overtaken and charged with great effect. The squadron then dismounted and opened fire, the tribesmen having got on to impossible ground. The enemy thereupon turned and made a bold dash for the led horses. One man was wounded and two horses were killed, and the troopers rushed back to their horses ; but in the confusion four of these broke away and galloped off, and altogether six men were left dismounted. These six were taken up in front of other troopers, and after the squadron had got out of range the loose horses were re-captured. The tribesmen, as soon as they saw the cavalry in the saddle again, fled to the hills.

This tends to show that in cases where the irregulars with whom the cavalry is dealing have a special dread of mounted troops, dismounted action should not be resorted to too readily, and that in any case a proportion of the men should remain mounted and unencumbered with led horses because of the moral effect which they will produce.

Combination of mounted and dismounted work suitable in certain conditions. The art of combining mounted and dismounted work when the enemy is not very daring is a most valuable one to possess on the part of a cavalry leader, especially when acting on the defensive. The art has been brought to great perfection in some of the Indian regiments. The system is to work in small groups, the men composing some groups being on foot, those composing others remaining on horseback. Spread out in this fashion a comparatively small force of cavalry will cover a great extent of ground. An unenterprising foe dare not close with the dismounted men for fear of those in rear who are on the watch, ready to charge ; and small mounted groups can generally manage to find cover from the not very damaging hostile fire till they are required to act. Of course such an arrangement is adapted only to somewhat broken ground where a charge on a great scale could not be carried out. The great principle to observe is that of constant co-operation between the mounted and dismounted groups.

The most awkward part of such operations is the retirement, should this for any reason become necessary. While the dismounted men are getting into the saddle there is no fire to hold the enemy in check, and hostile parties profiting by the ground may push forward and bring a damaging musketry to bear alike upon the groups which are mounted and on those which are mounting. Those which have been on foot would as a rule retire first, covered by the others ; the withdrawal when all are mounted would be carried out in extended line and at a rapid pace. Should the enemy be very aggressive it may be necessary to threaten a charge, or even to deliver a charge, so as to gain time to get away.

It may on occasion become necessary for cavalry, engaged in covering a considerable stretch of broken ground by means of the combination between mounted and dismounted tactics described above, to carry out a slow, deliberate retirement in face of the enemy as a part of some general operation. A retreat of this kind demands no little skill and judgment on the part of all concerned. In principle it should be conducted on the lines of an infantry withdrawal, part of the troops always covering the retirement of the remainder by fire, and the groups passing alternately through each other's intervals. But the enemy will probably be pressing on the rear, and it is always a critical moment when those men who are dismounted and in close contact with the pursuers have to scramble into the saddle and ride off. If possible there should be always some mounted parties ready to charge at a moment's notice so as to extricate the rearmost detachment, and to recover wounded men should the hostile fire take effect. Cavalry sent out on foraging duty, or detailed to cover other troops engaged in foraging, is often called upon to work out movements of this character, movements which may prove very trying owing to the easy target which the horses offer to the enemy.

Higgling sort of work this may seem to be, and out of keeping with the traditions of an arm accustomed on the battle-fields of last century to shine in more dazzling episodes. But small wars often present such peculiar conditions as regards the fighting methods of the foe and the broken character of the scene of combat, that cavalry may find no opportunities for shock action on an extensive scale. In many of the minor campaigns which take place in various quarters of the globe, troopers who are unskilled in these irregular manœuvres do not justify their presence with the expeditionary force. Nor do regiments which excel in such petty warfare seem to lose their capacity for reverting in a moment to those time honoured manœuvres by which bodies of horse have so often won renown in struggles of a higher class.

Dismounted action the only possible action of cavalry in very broken ground.

In spite of the experiences in the Mamund country to which special reference was made on p. 406, it will often be the case that, when the terrain is greatly cut up and broken, cavalry cannot act at all otherwise than dismounted. Charging may be out of the question. Even operations such as have been sketched in the preceding paragraphs may be impracticable. The cavalry is then compelled to fight entirely on foot—it may indeed be obliged to act mainly on the defensive, especially should it be unsupported by infantry; but even at purely dismounted work troopers can, of course, perform valuable services. Occasions must constantly arise in the ever changing conditions of irregular warfare where cavalry, unable to act on horseback, can by its fire afford very appreciable assistance to hard pressed infantry especially now that it is armed with the magazine carbine.

As an example of this may be cited the behaviour of the small force of cavalry at the action of Umbumedi, in Dahomey. The mounted troops were forming the rear of the square in which the French were advancing through the bush. The Dahomeyans, while offering a stubborn resistance in front, worked round the flank and on to the rear. Part of the cavalry thereupon dismounted and kept the enemy at bay till some infantry by means of a counter-attack put an end to an offensive movement which for a few moments gave ground for anxiety.

Near Ben Metir in Tunis in 1885 a reconnaissance sent out came under a heavy fire from the Kroumirs concealed in the wooded ground. Nearly the whole of the cavalry dismounted to assist the French firing line, and a prolonged musketry action ensued at the end of which the Chasseurs d'Afrique, the squadrons engaged, had nearly exhausted their ammunition. But the opportune arrival of infantry reinforcements enabled the French to attack and drive the enemy off.

Dismounted action by a detachment of cavalry posted on a flank may be highly efficacious in a hot action, and this is especially the case when the enemy collects in masses intent upon attacking or holding in check the main body of the regular troops. The smallness of the forces engaged in most fights of this class often admits of the detachment's fire sweeping the whole front. The mobility of the cavalry and its independence of the other arms enables it to take up a satisfactory position, from which it can in security bring a heavy carbine fire to bear on a well defined target. At Tamai in 1884, while the disordered square was gradually retiring before the Arab onset, a squadron of cavalry was rapidly brought up so as to take the enemy in flank, and it greatly assisted the hard pressed infantry by its fire, playing an important part in the action without incurring any appreciable loss. The charge of the 21st Lancers at Khartum did not completely break up the formidable body of Arabs attacked, so a proportion of the troopers were dismounted and completed the job by their fire, which illustrates what a difference

Valuable where judiciously used against hostile masses otherwise engaged.

there is between cavalry tactics in small wars and in regular warfare ; cavalry can rarely charge unbroken infantry, but, for it to charge through a great body of infantry and then to finish this off with dismounted fire is an operation almost unheard of on the modern battle-field.

Dismounted
action in
general.

We now have to consider dismounted work by mounted troops in general when there is no question of shock action or of alternating between fighting on foot and fighting on horseback.

Mounted
troops when
dismounted
sometimes
able to pose
as a large
force and so
deceive the
enemy.

Small bodies of mounted troops acting dismounted will often get openings for performing most valuable service in posing as larger forces. Their mobility lends itself to the employment of this very effective ruse. The plan was, as already mentioned on p. 176, tried with most satisfactory results at the attack on Wedza's stronghold. In the later stages of the South African war the Boers proved themselves adepts at this sort of bluff, and made full use of their mobility. It was almost impossible to tell whether they were in strong force or not. A few shots would be fired. Then, if the troops were rushed into attack, if often turned out that the enemy was present in considerable numbers. But if, on the other hand, elaborate arrangements were made for outflanking the enemy and time was lost, it generally transpired that there were only a few snipers about.

After Sir R. Buller had withdrawn from Gubat to Abu Klea in 1885, the enemy became more aggressive. One evening large hostile bodies occupied a hill commanding Abu Klea and inconveniently near the wells. From this position the Madhists were driven in the following morning, chiefly owing to the action of Major Wardrop and a few troopers who, appearing successively at different points, made the hostile leaders believe that they were threatened by large bodies of troops from the rear.

Mounted
troops
attacking,
dismounted.

In campaigns against undisciplined forces opportunities will often occur for mounted troops to actually attack on foot. Occasions for such action rarely present themselves in regular warfare because opposed to infantry even in small bodies, armed with weapons of precision, the horses are likely to suffer very severely unless they can be satisfactorily got under cover, and because in the nature of things the chances are that the opposing troops will be in superior force. But in small wars these dangers do not arise as a rule, or at least do not present themselves to at all the same extent, and some interesting examples of attacks of this nature are to be found in the records of these campaigns.

Near the Shuturgurdan Pass during the advance to Kabul in 1879, a party of native cavalry coming unexpectedly on a gathering of Afghans in broken and hilly ground, ousted them from their position by the attack of a portion of their number dismounted.

The affair of " Petrusvitch's Garden," near Denghil Tepe in 1880, is an admirable illustration of this sort of work and of its dangers. The enclosure was held by the Tekkes in some force. At dawn the whole of the cavalry and some guns moved in this direction under General Petrusvitch in obedience to orders to that effect. When at about 180 yards from the enclosure the general ordered his men to dismount and to attack, the horse-holders retiring some distance, while a mounted troop remained in reserve. The dismounted men cleared the enemy out with the bayonet (the cavalry had bayonets), but General Petrusvitch was mortally wounded at their head and there was some confusion in consequence The Tekkes now issued out round their flank and threatened the horse-holders, but a portion of the reserve troops dismounted and, assisted by the guns, repulsed this offensive movement. Very severe fighting continued about the enclosure for some time, but the cavalry managed to hold their own till infantry reinforcements, which had been urgently asked for, hurried up and secured what had been won.

Wedza's stronghold was captured by detachments of the 7th Hussars. But the skilful operations previous to the final assault which have been already detailed on p. 176, had the effect of reducing the resistance at the last to a minimum.

There is of course no reason whatever why mounted troops on foot should not attack if occasion for it arises, as long as the horses are secure ; it was constantly done during the late South African war. The great difficulty is that, as the troopers advance, they get more and more separated from their mounts. Horse-holders are always left, but these, hampered with reins and so forth, have no means of properly defending their charges. If there be any chance of a sudden rush on the part of the enemy, whether mounted or on foot, it will always be dangerous for the troopers to go far from their horses.

Mounted
rifles and
mounted
infantry as
compared to
cavalry.

In any sort of warfare mounted rifles and mounted infantry are inferior to cavalry, provided, of course, that the cavalry has been thoroughly trained to fight on foot as well as to fight on horseback. But in small wars this inferiority will generally be especially marked, because mounted troops are likely to get such fine opportunities for shock action, and the only excuse for employing the inferior class of troops is generally to be found in the fact that they may happen to be on the spot. In the British service mounted infantry is cheaper to maintain in peace time than cavalry, and it is sometimes convenient to keep up small forces of it on foreign stations in preference to breaking up regiments of cavalry. Mounted rifles and mounted infantry are very generally mounted on cobs or ponies which are preferable to horses for dismounted work, are more suitable in very rough country, and require less forage ; but there is nothing to prevent cavalry troopers being mounted on cobs or ponies for a special campaign. When it comes to charging, or to pursuing a flying enemy, it is, of course, better to have horses than smaller animals. But even when mounted on cobs or ponies, cavalry are necessarily more valuable than troops without lances or swords who are similarly mounted, because the former can fight both mounted and dismounted. The horse of the mounted rifleman or mounted infantryman is merely a means of transporting him rapidly from place to place with a view to his fighting as an infantry soldier when he gets to his destination. While in the saddle, he is just as useless for fighting purposes as the gun is when it is limbered up and in movement.

But between the cavalry trooper proper and the mounted infantryman proper there are really several intermediate grades. The Russian dragoon is a cavalry soldier trained especially to fight on foot and provided with a rifle and bayonet. Some irregular corps raised in the colonies have had swords, although destined in the main for fighting dismounted. As already mentioned the irregular mounted troops who were unsupplied with side arms at Kambula used assegais with great effect. During the operations in Rhodesia the mounted infantry on one occasion charged with fixed bayonets. The fact is that although the function of mounted rifles or mounted infantry is to fight on foot, small wars produce such strange situations and afford such scope for boldness and dash that it is well for them to be prepared to fight on horseback on occasion. Were mounted infantry ever to be employed in the heart of the hill country north of the Panjab they would probably be quite as useful on horseback as on foot without ever attempting to charge home, simply owing to the moral effect which cavalry has been proved to exert among these tribesmen and to the recollections of what the cavalry did in the Swat valley in 1897.

The instructions contained in " Cavalry Training " as to dismounted service are in general applicable to small wars, but there are certain special points to note. In operations of this class the mounted troops are likely to be working in small bodies and isolated, and they will often be in very bad ground. If there is a sudden rush of the enemy in great force the situation of the dismounted men may become very awkward. There is always the tendency on the part of the enemy to work round the flanks and to try to cut the dismounted men off from their horses, or to cut the detachment as a whole off from the rest of the force. Great vigilance is in fact required, and in terrain where there is not a clear view it is generally unwise to get the dismounted men far from their horses. It is here assumed that the mounted troops are only armed with the rifle or carbine, and that they cannot therefore keep ready a small body to charge the enemy supposing the situation suddenly to become critical.

Final remarks on dismounted work.

The general rule as to reserving fire till it can tell, for fear of frightening the enemy prematurely and preventing a fight, of course holds good just as much with mounted troops acting dismounted, as it does with infantry. If attacking, the great point to bear in mind should be that the main object is to inflict loss and that this can be best effected either by getting part of the force round the flank so as to bring fire to bear when the opponents take to flight, or else by bringing up the mounts as the dismounted men advance, so that they can get promptly into the saddle and follow up.

Need of dash when on foot.   It cannot be too much insisted upon that for this kind of work the men must have dash while on foot as well as while on horseback; the Boers in this respect were nothing short of a revelation, they were busy with their rifles almost the instant they were off their horses. Half the tactical mobility possessed by mounted troops is thrown away in a fight, if this important principle has not been inculcated into all ranks, and if it has not constantly been put in practice on the manœuvre ground. This, of course, applies just as much in the case of regular as of irregular warfare, but the importance of the point was especially brought to notice in the guerilla stages of the South African war, and it is therefore only right to draw attention to it here.

CHAPTER XXIII.

CAMEL CORPS.

CAMEL corps have many of the properties of mounted in- Camel corps fantry. Troops on camels differ, however, from mounted a form of mounted infantry in the very important particular that they have infantry. little mobility in actual action—they cannot be manœuvred with the freedom of mounted troops on the battle-field. For, besides being slow in moving from one part of the ground to another relatively to other mounted troops, the difficulty and delay involved in mounting and dismounting prevents their being able to fight effectively unless they have had a little time to prepare for action.

The object of camel corps is rather to enable troops to Object to move long distances through the theatre of war than to be able to traverse long transfer them from point to point when in close contact with distances. the enemy. Their mobility is strategical rather than tactical. The French have made satisfactory use of camel corps in Senegal. Abd el Kader depended very largely upon camels in making the rapid movements which were the feature of his guerilla warfare against the conquerors of Algeria. The Turkomans and Kirghiz have carried out very effective raids against the Russians and against tribes friendly to Russia, on camels. But in all these cases the camels have generally been left in some safe place before actual fighting took place, and in the main the camel corps, whether on the side of the regular army or on that of the enemy, have been designed with a view to strategical and not to tactical mobility. This was well shown in the march of Sir H. Stewart's force from Korti to Metemma, where the principle was to

form a zeriba in which the riding camels were left with the
baggage, and to go out and fight on foot.

The celerity of the movements of irregular warriors has
been commented on frequently in earlier chapters. Camels
cannot keep up with them in pursuit and cannot evade them
in retreat. In action against such adversaries camels are in
fact somewhat out of place, their security is a source of
anxiety unless they are protected by the position of other
troops engaged. The camels will of course often be perfectly
safe on the battle-field when the camel corps is merely part of a
mixed force ; but the idea of a camel corps as a rule is for it
to work more or less independently or, as has been very
general in the Egyptian army, with the cavalry. It should
be noted that during Sir H. Rose's Central Indian campaign in
1858 a small camel corps was organized and performed excellent service in conjunction with the other troops.

At Kalpi this corps acted most effectively at a critical juncture. The
rebels had skilfully concealed their strength. For a time they only pretended
to threaten the British left, but then they suddenly developed a strong attack
against Sir H. Rose's right. The infantry were being forced back by stress
of numbers and even the guns were in danger, when the camel corps was
rapidly transferred thither from another part of the field. The men dismounted, charged, and completely changed the situation, the rebels being
in the end defeated with heavy loss.

That camel corps are not very well adapted for working
with cavalry on the battle-field was shown at the battle of
Khartum, what occurred suggests that it is not desirable to
expose a force which possesses so little tactical mobility to
the danger of combat with very superior bodies of fanatics
capable of very rapid movement.

At Khartum the camel corps, while operating on one flank with part of
the cavalry and a battery, had to bear the brunt of a resolute advance
of a mass of Dervishes. The slow movements of the camels placed the
whole force in some jeopardy. Two guns were temporarily lost, many
casualties occurred, and had it not been for the enemy coming under fire
of the gunboats the affair might have had a serious ending.

Lord Wolseley's instructions to the camel corps in the Nile Expedition of 1884–85 laid great stress on the point that troops so organized were helpless if attacked when on the move. It was laid down that the men were never to be taken mounted over ground where there appeared to be any likelihood of an attack being made on them—it must be remembered that, during the march across the desert, practically the whole force consisted of camel corps except for the small cavalry force which proved so valuable for scouting purposes. These conditions were essentially different from those of the Central Indian campaign, where the camel corps could rely upon the active support of all arms of the service. In no case in the campaign on the Nile in 1884–85 were the camel troops exposed to an attack when mounted. A sudden onslaught can best be met by the men dismounting and forming a square round the camels as far as circumstances permit, but the essential principle of camel corps tactics is that they must not be placed in such a position, because, if they are, there is grave risk of disaster. It should be noted that very small parties cannot form a square possessing any defensive strength round their camels; in the case of a small detachment being assailed the camels must be used as a parapet, the men inside—a plan which the Turkomans used very successfully on one occasion, shortly before General Lomakin started for Denghil Tepe in 1879. This incident gives a remarkable illustration of camelry operations and deserves to be narrated.

Their helplessness when mounted. How to act if suddenly attacked.

A large number of camels had been collected around Burnak near Krasnovodsk on the Caspian Sea for the impending expedition, and were scattered over the plains, very insufficiently guarded by Kirghiz and a few irregular horsemen. There was a detachment of infantry at Burnak.

One morning a force of Tekkes suddenly appeared, seized a large number of the camels and drove them off. The garrison of Burnak promptly turned out to recover the spoil. The enemy had, however, got a good start, and the Russian infantry, toiling on foot after the marauders, suffered greatly from thirst and soon began to tail off. The chase was becoming hopeless

The affair of Burnak as illustrating camel operations.

when, with ready resource, the officer in command collected some of the camels which were browsing in the vicinity and mounted his men on them, and then the pursuit was resumed and pushed with vigour.

The troops came up with the freebooters towards evening and found them drawn up on a hill, and within a laager formed of the camels which they had captured. Made to lie down in the form of an oval, the camels provided an effective rampart behind which the enemy was in comparative security. This improvised fortress the weary Russians were obliged to attack, and the assault on it completely failed. During the night reinforcements arrived from Krasnovodsk, but when day broke it was found that the Turkomans had, under cover of darkness, withdrawn with most of their booty and had disappeared.

This little affair is of singular interest in connection with the question of camel corps. One side formed itself into a camel corps on the spur of the moment for a rapid march. The other made a zeriba of camels and stood an assault in it.

Camel corps only suitable in certain theatres of war.

Camels are only suitable in certain theatres of war and therefore the question of camel corps does not often arise. Their extraordinary capacity for dispensing with water enables them to be used when horses would break down altogether, and there is no other method of pushing troops unaccompanied by transport rapidly across long stretches of desert. Camels moreover thrive on scrub and bushes which other animals will not eat. But on the other hand they cannot travel over rough country on account of their feet, and they are quite helpless on slippery ground. Camel corps are in fact of use only under given conditions. The small camel corps which exists as part of the Egyptian army, and which played an effective part in most of the engagements fought by the Khedive's troops against the followers of the Khalifa, serves as a model for such forces.

CHAPTER XXIV.

ARTILLERY TACTICS.

IN an earlier chapter it was pointed out how, what is known Artillery
preparation. as artillery preparation, is often entirely out of place in such battles as occur in small wars, but that this depends very much upon the circumstances of the particular case. If the enemy be strong or be posted in a formidable position it may be desirable for the guns to make an impression before the infantry can safely attack. In almost all actions which occur in warfare of this nature the principle of pushing the guns well to the front, however, holds good, even if they do not necessarily at once come into action. Whether it be in the preliminary phases of the fight, or during the period when the attack is being fully developed, or at the crisis of the battle, artillery can be and should be as a general rule handled with a boldness not always permissible in combats between regular armies. Artillery preparation presents in fact somewhat different characteristics from the prolonged concentrated fire of masses of guns which used to be understood by that expression in military phraseology.

The moral effect of artillery is very great against irregular enemies. The high esteem in which Asiatics hold guns was referred to in Chapter XII, and if the adversary be so posted or be of such strength as to demand respect, the utilization of this moral effect may be very desirable. But material effect is still more desirable, and if the enemy does not happen to be formidable it is essential that, if the guns are to be used at all, they shall inflict loss.

Bearing this in mind it may be taken as a broad principle Guns to push
up to close
range. governing artillery tactics in campaigns against irregular warriors, that throughout an engagement guns should be used at as close quarters as possible, so that their full value may be got out of them and so that they can push up into the enemy's position and bring shell fire to bear as soon as this has been evacuated. Of course close range is not always the most effective range—in hill warfare plunging fire will frequently be more destructive; but where casualties in the hostile ranks will be increased by pushing the artillery well up to the front, forward tactics will almost always be expedient. The enemy's fire in such warfare is rarely really dangerous, even at comparatively speaking close quarters. Exceptions to this of course occur, as in the case of the Boers. In Tirah the Afridi fire was often fairly effective as long as the enemy could fire from points of temporary security. But in the majority of cases guns have not very much to fear from the firearms of the adversary in small wars, and they can therefore be manœuvred with a boldness which in regular warfare would only be justified on very special occasions and to achieve very special objects. In the normal conditions which prevail in struggles against uncivilized foes or guerillas, the guns can safely advance to ranges at which they would inevitably be silenced by regular infantry unless this had been previously shaken by artillery preparation or by other means. Of course difficulties of terrain often greatly limit the choice of positions; but except for this and for the fact that artillery when in motion is out of action, it might almost be laid down as a broad rule that the proper place for the guns is little in rear of the infantry firing line, whenever plunging fire is not required. The nearer they get to their work the better. If they are required to prepare the way for the infantry they should, as far as circumstances permit, be in action at the point where the infantry has come to a standstill, and this is the principle upon which, when the regular forces are acting on the offensive, the artillery usually does act if in efficient hands.

Examples.   The Indian Mutiny affords some notable instances of these forward artillery tactics. Out of numerous striking examples may be quoted the cases of the Sekunderbagh and Shah Nujeef at Lucknow. Before the infantry could attack the Sekunderbagh, the guns were dragged up to within 100 yards of its loop-holed walls, and they had to be fought for some time in the open at this close range before the breaches were practicable and before the infantry could get at the rebels. After the Sekunderbagh had been stormed, it became necessary to capture the equally formidable Shah Nujeef. The guns of the Naval Brigade were dragged up by the sailors and 93rd to within 20 yards of the massive walls of the building. "Captain Peel," as Sir C. Campbell wrote in his despatch, "behaved very much as if he had been laying the *Shannon* alongside the enemy's frigate." The mosque long resisted all efforts of the assailants, and it was night before it was in British hands ; early next morning, however, signals and the bugle call from the roof of the great edifice told the expectant garrison of the Residency lines that all was going well and that their weary vigil was to be exchanged for action. The bringing of the guns up to the very walls of the Sekunderbagh and the Shah Nujeef is a splendid example of forward artillery tactics.

At Amoaful the guns had to be pushed up into the firing line in the bush to break down the enemy's resistance on several occasions, and they caused great slaughter among the Ashantis at this very close range. At Ordahsu one gun with the infantry, advancing a short distance at a time, gradually worked right up to the village. It was very nearly silenced, it is true ; but it did its work.

At the attack upon Konoma in the Naga hills in 1880, after the capture by storm of the first hostile work, the two guns with the force moved into it and opened fire from it upon another fort only 50 yards off, breaching it. Three assaults on this failed. The retreat of the storming party after the last failure was effectually covered by the guns, which fired over the stormers' heads as they lay down. Their fire promptly cleared the walls, which had been reoccupied by the Nagas when the guns were masked by the infantry.

A French column which was moving to the relief of Tuyen-Kwang in Tonkin in 1885 made an attack upon the Chinese works at Hoa Moe. The defenders fought with great determination, and one of the redoubts held out after the others were captured. Two mountain guns were promptly brought up within 50 yards to batter down the parapet of this, and they very soon effected their object.

These episodes have been cited as good illustrations of the principle of pushing artillery to the front in this sort of warfare. Bold initiative and seizure of every opportunity of getting to close quarters with the enemy, are the surest means of making the guns tell. The enemy generally does not understand daring and resolute tactics whether on the part of infantry, of cavalry, or of artillery, and they demoralise him.

Battles may be won by long range bombardments in the sense
that the adversary quits his position, but they are not so won
in the sense that the adversary is crushed, cowed, and con-
vinced that unless he lays down his arms he will be utterly
destroyed. Owing to the configuration of the ground or to
some special reason, it may sometimes be necessary that the
guns should open fire at ranges of 2,500 and even 3,000 yards.
But such procedure must be looked upon as exceptional and
one only to be adopted under unusual circumstances.

Chief risk
run by guns
pushed well
to the front.

It must be remembered that in these campaigns the guns
if they push well to the front, rarely run any risk of being
actually silenced. Experience proves that there is little chance
of the casualties among the gun detachments being so heavy
as to put the pieces out of action. The chief danger that they
incur is that of falling into an ambush or of being rushed on
ground where they cannot act effectively; for protection
against this they look to the infantry with which they are
working. Artillery has no more title to immunity from losses
than have cavalry or infantry, and it cannot be used too boldly
as long as it is supported by other troops, a principle which
happily is very generally recognized in the British service.
To show, however, that difference of opinion on this point
exists among military men, the action of Sahamafi in the
French campaign against the Malagasys in 1885 may be cited.
In this affair a battery of artillery was pushed up to within 550
yards of a palisaded earthwork. It suffered considerable
losses, for which the admiral in command of the attack was
somewhat harshly criticised. In the end the hostile position
proved too strong to be stormed and the French force was
withdrawn. The incident is mentioned as showing that a
tendency exists to blame the exposure of guns, even when the
issue of a fight is more than doubtful. In such theatres of
operations as small wars usually take place in, guns are somewhat of an encumbrance to a force except on the battle-field,
therefore when they get a chance of striking hard even serious
losses must be accepted as the fortune of war.

Although the importance of massing artillery in action Massing of guns unusual and generally unnecessary. is not now considered so great as it was a few years ago, the principle of concentration of fire is still under most conditions an axiom of modern tactics, and it is, to a certain extent, the basis of the normal action of the arm on the battle-field. In small wars this massing of guns will seldom be applicable. Large numbers of guns are unusual in the combats which occur. The very fact that artillery preparation at long range should be the exception and not the rule, militates against the concentration of the artillery at any particular point of the battle-field, inasmuch as the space is sure to be limited when the guns are drawn up at short ranges. But, on the other hand, concentration of fire may be very desirable, even if that concentration be carried out by isolated sections or guns. If there is any point where the enemy is offering a sturdy resistance or which will clearly be difficult to carry by storm, a convergent artillery fire may have a very decisive effect.

Supposing the enemy to have guns, it may sometimes be desirable to crush these as a preliminary, and a concentrated shell fire will soon achieve this object. At the Atbara the hostile guns were completely silenced before the assault, the Dervish gunners being found dead round their pieces. The Chinese guns in Tonkin were often treated in this fashion, although their fire generally seems to have been ineffective. But in dealing with hostile artillery it must never be forgotten that the end to be kept in view is its capture, and that, although a heavy fire of shells will almost certainly silence it, the result may be that the enemy finding it overmatched will manage to withdraw it.

The primary duty of artillery in warfare of this nature is Question of dispersion of guns in attack. to ensure that it is at hand at the critical moment and well to the front. Difficulties of terrain in some cases, and the fact that the guns are so often portable guns and not guns moved by horse traction in others, render very rapid movements impossible at times. Still the artillery should generally

(10830)   2 E

be able to move as fast as the infantry. If the guns are kept concentrated at one spot, none of them may be able to get to the point where they are really wanted at the proper moment, and for this reason it will generally be best to keep them to a certain extent dispersed. In regular warfare this would be quite wrong, the breaking up of batteries being rightly held to be unsound, under ordinary conditions, on the modern battle-field. But in combats against adversaries whose gun fire and musketry are not much to be feared, the necessity for keeping the battery intact as a fighting unit is not so great. The accepted system of fire discipline makes it desirable that the battery should not be split up if it can be avoided, but this system is designed to meet conditions which seldom present themselves in small wars. Speaking generally there is not the same necessity for rapid ranging when coming into action against irregular warriors, as there is when the battery has to be prepared for accurate and perhaps concentrated hostile fire the moment that it shows itself.

Of course if the battery can be kept intact, so much the better—should there be several batteries on the battle-field the requisite dispersion will rarely necessitate half batteries or sections working independently, or lead to the tactical unit being broken up. But as a rule the available guns are not numerous. It is when the force is accompanied by only one or at most two batteries that the necessity arises for detaching groups of two and three guns to various parts of the field, even at the cost of loss of accuracy and rapidity of fire. On very open ground where field or horse artillery can move about rapidly, there is little chance of the infantry at any point being unable to get guns to help them on emergency, or of shell fire failing at some moment when the enemy offers a good target. But on broken ground, or when only portable guns are available, there must be no question of gun fire failing wherever it may suddenly be required. On this account the splitting up of batteries into sections may be not only judicious but may be absolutely indispensable. Experienced mountain artillery officers in India are perfectly well aware of this, and they deprecate the tendency on the part of commanders to stick to text book theory when dealing with conditions to which the theory does not apply.

Plenty of examples have of course occurred in small wars where the massing of several batteries for purposes of concentrated fire has been most effective. At the attack on the Sempagha Pass leading into Tirah the two brigade divisions of mountain artillery were for a considerable time kept intact, and their fire was most effective in clearing the successive lines of sangars. At the battle of the Atbara—one of those cases, so rare in warfare of this nature, where a regular artillery preparation was necessary—the guns poured a concentrated fire upon the Dervish zeriba, doing great damage to the defences and to the hostile personnel. At Tel-el-Kebir the British guns were massed in the original order of attack in the centre, acting as a pivot on which the infantry divisions on either flank might rely in case of reverse; but concentration gave way to dispersion on that occasion, as soon as the infantry poured into the Egyptian lines; there was no massing of fire.

The principle of dispersion of guns applies just the same Dispersion of on the defensive as it does in attack. From the point of view guns on the defensive. of the other arms there is rarely any justification for collecting the guns at any particular spot, even admitting that fire discipline suffers if batteries are split up. The main object to keep in view is that there should be one or two guns ready to meet the enemy wherever he may endeavour to push his attack home. The tendency of irregular warriors when acting on the offensive being generally to envelope their antagonist, a dispersion of the artillery becomes almost inevitable. The position of guns in squares has already been referred to in the chapter dealing especially with that formation, and it has been shown that in practice they have often

(10830) 2 E 2

been put singly at the corners, although there are objections to this plan. In laagers and zeribas it is of course necessary to disperse the guns so as to ensure artillery fire in all directions. Defensive actions are so often fought by regular troops in broken or bush grown terrain in this kind of warfare, and the field of fire is so frequently restricted, that the splitting up of batteries can seldom be avoided.

Value of guns on the defensive against fanatical rushes.

The effect created by artillery is tremendous when troops are called upon to receive the attack of warriors like Sudanese, or Zulus, or ghazis who approach in masses, provided always that there be a satisfactory field of fire. Of this the first phase of the battle of Khartum afforded signal proof, disastrous havoc being caused in the Dervish ranks long before they came within effective range even of the magazine rifles. It is very seldom the case that as long as they are in groups, guns cannot defend their own front unless the field of fire is very restricted. During the determined Afghan attack at Ahmed Khel the efforts of the swordsmen to rush the guns only led to their being mowed down pitilessly at the most effective range. At Tamai a battery was in the open between the two squares at the critical juncture, but it beat off the Arab rush against it and stood its ground. On the other hand, a single gun, or even a section, may be unable to defend its own front if unsupported by rifle fire.

When a force is acting on the defensive, the support of artillery is invaluable to the other arms at a critical moment— for instance when the infantry are in difficulties owing to a sudden hostile attack. On such occasions the moral effect of the shells bursting and of the noise of the discharges, may create an influence out of all proportion to the actual number of the enemy struck down. Thus after General Lomakin's unsuccessful attempt to storm Denghil Tepe, the guns effectually checked the Turkomans who were pursuing the shattered assaulting columns as they withdrew in disorder. What the artillery has most to fear at such times is that its own flank may be turned ; at Maiwand two horse artillery guns were lost owing to the infantry on their flanks being rolled up by the ghazi rush. As long as the flanks are secure the front should be secure if the guns are not in a hopelessly unfavourable position. It should be noted, however, that this does not altogether hold good at night, when it may be desirable to post infantry groups in the intervals between the guns.

In the defence of isolated posts guns are of course invaluable. General Skobelef in forming the advanced depôts on the line his troops were to follow towards Denghil Tepe, told off several guns to each, the infantry garrisons being very small. During the defence of the improvised fort at Potchefstrom in 1881, the guns did much to keep the Boer at a respectful distance, and many similar cases could be quoted. In such fortified positions artillery can very largely take the place of infantry ; and as only the guns themselves, with their detachments and ammunition are required, permanent arrangements for their transport can often be dispensed with.

Although the question of artillery material and organization is really outside the scope of this work, there are certain points affecting this subject which arise in small wars and which deserve a passing notice. The first of these is that in Asiatic warfare mud villages have been found by experience to resist shell fire very effectually. The walls do not splinter, and the tiny rooms which are the leading characteristics of the dwellings, absorb the explosion of the projectile and cramp its effect. This is an important fact to bear in mind, because a heavy bombardment prior to an attack on such a village may not have demoralized its defenders as much as the noise and expenditure of ammunition would have seemed to imply. This clearly points to either guns or howitzers of large calibre, firing heavy shells with large bursting charges, being best suited for such work ; but the exigencies of this class of

Comparative powerlessness of guns against mud villages.

warfare in other respects generally forbid the use of such ordnance.

High explosives. The unsatisfactory effects obtained from artillery against mud villages suggests the use of shells with high explosives, and it will probably be found that these will give good results if they can be adapted to the class of gun suited to such campaigns. The melinite shells used by the French against the Hovas demoralized them and gave every satisfaction during the campaign ; but as in that conflict the enemy was always ready for flight on the first possible excuse, it would not be wise to attach too much importance to experiences gained in operations so very one sided. The high explosive shells used by the howitzer battery in the bombardment of Omdurman caused rare havoc in the metropolis of Mahdism ; but ordnance of this ponderous kind is not well adapted to conditions of irregular warfare. It remains to be seen what effect this nature of projectile, when fired from field and mountain guns, will have upon hill-men sheltered in sangars or ensconced among crags on mountain crests.

Guns must be light and generally portable. Owing to difficulties of terrain, it is almost invariably the case that lightness of artillery material is imperative. It is becoming more and more recognized that in the majority of cases draught artillery is out of place. On the plains of India or of the Pehio basin, on the steppe land by the Sir Daria or along the foot of the Kopet Dagh in the land of the Tekkes, on the rolling downs of Zululand, and in many parts of Morocco and Algeria, horse and field artillery can manœuvre as freely as in Belgium or Lorraine. But in most theatres of small wars it cannot act. On the sands of Egypt in 1882, mountain guns were found to possess mobility fully equal to that of field artillery. In Tonkin draught artillery was constantly found to be a great encumbrance. Sir F. Roberts, on his march from Kabul to Kandahar, took only mountain guns. In Madagascar, Dahomey, Tirah, and most theatres of recent operations portable artillery alone could satisfactorily be used. An army which, owing to national conditions, is liable to be called upon at almost any moment to take part in irregular warfare, and which does not comprise in its normal peace organisation a proportion of mountain batteries ready at short notice for the field, lacks an important item in that aggregate of services which constitute a force genuinely adapted for conducting a campaign against savages, or hill men, or guerillas operating in broken ground. It must be remembered that the guns of portable artillery can never be very powerful—their lightness renders it impossible ; but they can go where the infantry can go, and that is, as a general rule, the chief aim of this arm in irregular warfare.

Inasmuch as the leading principle governing artillery tactics in these campaigns is for the guns to push up to close range, and as, when regular troops have stood on the defensive in Morocco and Algeria, in the Sudan, in China, in Afghanistan and elsewhere, experience has proved that the guns must be prepared to check attacks at very close quarters, a supply of case shot used generally to be very desirable before the introduction of quick-firers ; with the modern gun, however, it is doubtful if any need remains for including them in a battery's equipment. It is remarkable what very frequent examples have occurred in small wars of late years of the use of this form of projectile. The three batteries supporting Colonel Macdonald's brigade when it was attacked at the battle of Khartum, fired an immense number of rounds—one battery used up sixty-nine during the day. Case shot is held to be quite out of date in regular warfare ; the tactics of the present day demand that artillery shall work at what would half a century ago have been considered an absurd range. But in small wars guns, whether in attack or defence, will always be liable to find themselves in action at short and even at close range, and they should be equipped accordingly.

Question of case shot.

CHAPTER XXV.

MACHINE GUNS.

THE place of machine guns in tactics is now fairly well established. In the British service, at least, they are regarded as an adjunct of infantry and of cavalry. It is generally recognized that the plan of forming them into batteries in charge of artillery personnel is a mistake for regular warfare, and the same thing really holds good in small wars.

It is indeed only comparatively recently that machine guns have proved a success in any kind of warfare. The older forms, approximating to the mitrailleuse upon which the French in 1870 placed so mistaken a value, are not suitable as a rule. In the terrain usually met with the weapon, unless light and portable, is quite out of place. Moreover, till within the last few years, no dependence could be placed on machine guns at a critical moment. They jammed at Ulundi, they jammed at Dogali, they jammed at Abu Klea and Tofrek, in some cases with most unfortunate results. A weapon which fails just when it is most wanted is a distinct danger. It may do good work when all goes smoothly, winning thereby a confidence to which it is not entitled and causing it to be depended on to secure a vital point of which it is incapable ; but if it proves a broken reed in some moment of supreme crisis later on, its presence with the force may have done incalculable harm.

On the other hand Maxims, which can be easily handled and moved, have done excellent service in East Africa, in Matabililand, and in the campaigns on the North West frontier of India. There can be no doubt that machine guns of an easily portable and thoroughly trustworthy class may be most valuable in small wars, and they will probably be freely used in such operations in future, especially when the enemy is inclined to attack in mass. In hill warfare these weapons scarcely get a proper chance, as they are not very well suited for picking off individuals, and as it is dangerous to thrust them too far to the front with the small parties which are so much used in operations of this class. In bush warfare also the want of a fair target is unfavourable to them, and when the shooting is at short range the personnel is likely to be put *hors de combat,* as it offers such a good target—this happened at Owikokero. An open field of fire, and a well defined object to aim at, are almost more necessary to machine guns than to artillery.

During General Hunter's reconnaissance of the Atbara zeriba four days before the attack on it was delivered, the enemy's horsemen moved out in great strength and endeavoured to surround the force. The fire of the four machine guns, however, proved extraordinarily effective, and kept the foe from charging home. They fired 4,000 rounds.

On the defensive, machine guns can hardly fail to be valuable. In laagers, zeribas, and detached posts of all kinds they are always likely to be of service, and they may to a certain extent take the place of guns for such work. During the operations in Rhodesia in 1896 they were found very useful as a protection to the small laagers left behind by the columns when they moved out for a fight. Two of them did tremendous execution in Chakdara Fort during the siege of that post in 1897. It is interesting to note that at the fight on the Shangani river in Matabililand after the attempt to capture the King had failed, the troops, although they were in a bad position, could not move to a better one for a while, simply because the machine guns would have been thrown out of action during the change of position. Against rushes of Zulus, ghazis, or other fanatics the effect of such weapons is tremendous as long as their fire is well maintained. In the excitement of the moment the best infantry may fire unsteadily; but machine guns can be absolutely trusted to commit destructive havoc in the hostile throng provided that their mechanism does not go out of order.

Their value on the defensive.

CHAPTER XXVI.

THE SERVICE OF SECURITY.

Importance of the service of security. IN warfare against irregular forces the service of security is a subject of paramount importance. Owing to the lines on which such foes conduct their operations, it follows almost as a matter of course that the safeguarding of the troops from the surprises and ambuscades to which they are so greatly exposed, whether they be on the move or at rest, is a matter to which exceptional care and attention must be devoted. The theatre of war is often little known, its broken intersected character usually favours the hostile plan of causing petty annoyance to the troops, information is untrustworthy, and in consequence the regular soldiers must ever be on the alert and must constantly be prepared for the unexpected. At the halt an effective system of outposts is essential. On the move precautions must be taken lest the troops fall into some snare or be thrown into confusion by the sudden attack of an enemy who disappears as soon as they recover from their surprise. All this forms a very important branch of military art in operations of this class.

The service of security always divides itself into two great branches. When the force is halted, outposts have to be arranged for. When it is on the march the protection of the column must be assured by means of mobile detachments—patrols, advanced and rear guards, and so forth. And the former being upon the whole the more important and the more difficult to arrange, will be treated of first.

Outposts. Hour at which the The first point to refer to in considering the question of outposts is the hour at which irregular warriors like to make their attacks. It is somewhat singular that, as experience proves, foemen of this class generally have a marked disinclination for night attacks. Some observations will be included in Chapter XXVII on the best methods of repelling nocturnal assaults when they are attempted, but it may be taken as a general feature of small wars that the enemy is much less disposed to undertake such enterprises than might be supposed from the conditions of the case. Operations in the dark would seem naturally to favour forces which so rarely possess an armament comparable to that with which the regular troops are supplied. By night arms of precision lose much of their value, and there is therefore often a chance for irregular warriors with their swords and spears to rush in to close quarters and in the *melée* to gain the upper hand by force of numbers. History nevertheless shows that the opponents with whom the trained and disciplined soldier has to deal in small wars rarely display much keenness for such undertakings.

Examining the records of the numerous campaigns of the last few decades it is surprising how seldom regular night attacks have been attempted by the enemy. In the Persian campaign of 1857, a resolute attack was made upon Sir J. Outram's force the night before the action at Khushab. A desperate onslaught was made by the tribesmen one night on the celebrated Crag Picquet in the Ambela campaign. A few cases occurred in Algeria and Tunis. The Red Indians made some effective night attacks on the United States troops. The Maoris made one on Sentry Hill; and during the operations against the Mohmunds and Swatis in 1897 the tribesmen showed a disposition to undertake nocturnal attacks upon the British forts and camps which is rarely evinced by the Pathans in hill warfare—it is noticeable that this should have occurred in territory adjacent to Ambela. In the early days of the Tonkin war, when the Black Flags were still to the fore, these made some desperate night attacks upon the

French. During General Skobelef's siege of Denghil Tepe the Tekkes made some most determined sorties under cover of darkness against the Russian trenches. The remarkable night attacks of the Boers upon British camps and columns in 1901–02, to which especial reference will be made further on, are fresh in the memory of us all. But these cases are the exceptions, and it is a noteworthy fact that, except in the case of the Boer operations, there is scarcely an example to be found of such an enterprise on the part of the enemy succeeding. Not many instances can indeed be quoted of such night attacks even causing serious danger.

The Kaffir wars, the Russian campaigns in the Caucasus and Central Asia, the Indian Mutiny and the Chinese war furnish scarcely a single illustration. There were no cases in the Spanish war of 1859 against Morocco. Ashanti, Dahomey, and Achin afford no instances, and Burma scarcely any. In the last Afghan war the enemy attempted only two night attacks, each of them on isolated posts—Fort Battye and Dubrai ; they succeeded in the latter, but these were very minor episodes of the campaign; in 1841, on the other hand, a determined night attack was made on one of the gates of Kandahar. The Mahdists made no such attempts in the Sudan, although the Khalifa appears to have contemplated attacking Sir H. Kitchener under cover of the darkness, as already related on p. 56. In the Zulu war the onslaught upon the little garrison of Rorke's Drift was carried on for many hours into the night, but the fight had been initiated in the afternoon, and except on this one occasion the Zulus made no night attacks in force.

This disinclination of the enemy for assaults in the dark is merely pointed out here as a fact proved by experience. It is not, of course, suggested that because of it precautions should be relaxed at night—quite sufficient instances of nocturnal enterprises by irregular warriors have occurred to render any want of vigilance inexcusable. It must be understood moreover that it is only actual night attacks which are unusual, not attacks at dawn. Attacks at daybreak are of very frequent occurrence in these campaigns.

It should be noted that the small size of the force as a whole, or of its various detachments and columns supposing it to be broken up into fractions, greatly assists the enemy in making his preparations for a night attack. In regular warfare one side can generally only approach the other at night along its front, or to a certain extent on its flanks. But in small wars the camp or bivouac of the troops seldom occupies a large space and it can be approached from all sides. The consequence of this is that a very effective reconaissance can be made by the enemy in the early hours of the night, aided by the lights of the fires and by the noise of the men and animals. Weak points can be thus detected, the vigilance being exercised by the outposts can be gauged, and plans can be perfected for taking advantage of any favouring circumstances. *Comparatively small size of force helps enemy in preparing for night attacks.*

This was well illustrated in the closing guerilla stages of the late South African war. Isolated columns roamed about a theatre of war which generally presented few intricate topographical features. After being on the move all day they would often only reach the bivouac towards evening, or sometimes not till after dark. Then, having come to a halt, the force would gather itself into a comparatively speaking restricted space and would start the necessary cooking and camp duties. A dull roar audible afar off in the stillness denoted its presence. Its position was clearly defined and unmistakeable, and its limits and any defences hastily constructed were easily detected in the bright starlight of a sub-tropical climate.

The Boers turned this situation fully to account, and it is a remarkable fact that those admirably executed night attacks of theirs were only initiated when the campaign had ceased to possess any resemblance to regular warfare. Their success in some of their bold undertakings was little short of astonishing. *The Boer night attacks.*

But, while giving them all credit for the skill with which the operations were conducted, and for the dash, resource and foresight with which they were carried out, it must be pointed out that their success was almost invariably the consequence of inefficiency in the service of security on our side. Sometimes the most ordinary precautions were neglected. Sometimes the outposts generally, or individuals forming part of them, failed to exercise vigilance which the conditions of the case imperatively demanded. The troops consisted largely of detachments and bodies of men untrained to war and fortified with only a vague knowledge of the responsibilities which it imposes alike on the commander and on the private. Circumstances undoubtedly favoured the Boers; but the art of war consists in the main of taking advantage of circumstances, and by the way in which the Boers did this and seized their opportunities, they afforded illustrations of the manner in which night attacks should be carried out and of how they should be provided against, for which few campaigns, regular or irregular, afford any parallel.

Attacks at dawn very frequent.

Whatever may be the case as regards night attacks, it may be accepted as a broad rule that early morning is a specially favourite hour for savages, Asiatics, and irregular opponents of that class in general, to deliver their assault upon regular troops. The reason for this seems to be that, even when such warriors have a perhaps, superstitious dread, of fighting actually in the dark, they are able to creep up mute and unobserved so as to get close to the outposts. They can gather close to the camp ready to rush forward on the given signal at the first signs of break of day; they hope—there is rarely any justification for the hope—to find the regular forces at that time asleep and unprepared. Antagonists of a higher type again such as insurgents in civilized countries, prefer attacking at dawn to attacking actually at night, because it is easier to carry out the operation when there is some little light. They fully realise the advantage of getting to fairly close quarters under cover of the night.

Many examples of such early morning attacks could be given—they are so frequent indeed that in most small wars the regular troops stand to their arms shortly before dawn as a matter of course. A few days after the disembarkation of the French expeditionary force in Algeria, in 1830, the forces of the Dey made a most determined attack upon the invaders' camps at daybreak. The first attack upon the Crag Picquet in the Ambela campaign was made at dawn, the important point being temporarily captured by the enemy; it was retaken shortly afterwards. After the capture of Khiva in 1874 by the Russians, the Turkomans, during some operations to the south, delivered a desperate assault on the Russian camp just before daybreak, the footmen were brought up almost to the bayonets seated behind the mounted men and the enemy was only driven off after a severe conflict. The Zulus attacked early in the morning, although by daylight, at Ginghilhovo; they also surprised a detachment on the Intombi river at dawn and nearly destroyed it. On the other hand, it is very noteworthy that the mutineers at Delhi made only one of their many attacks on the ridge at dawn; they knew that they would find the British force ready for them at that hour, so many of their leaders being perfectly well acquainted with the routine of regular troops on active service. The abortive attempt to break into the Sherpur cantonment at Kabul after the British force had been blockaded there for some days in 1879, was made at daybreak. The Dahomeyans twice made attacks upon the French at this hour, at Kotonou in 1891 and at Dogba in 1892 when General Dodds first advanced. In 1882 the Egyptian army advanced in force to attack the British position near Kassassin early in the morning. Sir H. Stewart's force advancing from Abu Klea to the Nile was not molested during its night march, but immediately after daybreak the enemy began to gather and fighting commenced. The Matabili attacked the British laager on the Shangani river in the grey of the morning.

The Hovas attempted a daybreak surprise at Tsaratsora on the French advanced troops in 1895—it was almost the only occasion on which they showed any enterprise or on which their leaders showed the slightest military skill during the campaign. Dawn is in fact the time at which a hostile assault is especially to be anticipated in these wars, and preparations should be made accordingly. Even if the whole force does not stand to arms the whole of the outposts should do so if there is the slightest reason to suppose that any hostile forces are in the vicinity.

Annoyance by marauders and small hostile parties at night very common.

Although night attacks are unusual, marauders and small hostile parties are fond of causing annoyance, and their methods call for vigilance on the part of the outposts. In most small wars these irritating acts on the part of the enemy cause a great deal of inconvenience and frequently give rise to scares and confusion. Sniping has of late years become a very serious matter in Indian warfare, causing appreciable losses owing to so many of the tribesmen being armed with efficient rifles. These enterprises on the part of individuals are no menace to the force as a whole, but they are very harassing to the troops and they interfere with the repose which is necessary to keep the men in good condition for the fatigues of active service. There is no certain means of preventing them, no assured specific against the evil; but much can be done by vigilant sentries who keep cool and use their rifles with effect, and small ambuscades have proved at times a sovereign remedy. This question is referred to again later on.

Principle of outposts.

The general idea with which outposts are pushed forward to protect an army is the same in every class of warfare. A fraction of the force is detailed to act as a screen to the bulk of the force, enabling this to rest and to temporarily abandon fighting formation even when in proximity to the enemy. The detachments forming the outposts are so arranged and are of such strengths as to be able to offer sufficient resistance to a hostile attack, should one be attempted, for the whole of the force to get under arms and play its part. The detachments on outpost duty remain on the alert and more or less ready to act at a moment's notice. This is the principle, whether the troops they are safeguarding are engaged in operations against disciplined and regular forces or are opposed to semi-civilized adversaries, guerillas or savages. But the fundamental system of the organization of an outpost service differs very materially in the case of small wars from what is generally considered right and proper in great campaigns. Most treatises on the military art include chapters on how to arrange the outposts on the lines sanctioned by the custom and experience of regular warfare, and the principles governing their arrangement are laid down authoritatively in " Combined Training." But much which is accepted on the subject as beyond dispute in the case of modern operations of war, is quite inapplicable to small wars.

A very little consideration suffices to show that considerable modification of the elaborate system of picquets and supports required in great campaigns is permissible in irregular warfare. When engaged in hostilities against trained troops with modern arms, it is clearly essential that these should be kept at a considerable distance from the bivouacs of the main body. The outposts are pushed out a long way so as to form a cordon some miles outside of the area on which the remainder of the enemy is drawn up, and form a screen facing towards the side where the hostile enemy is known to be. The organization of the outposts is designed with the view that, while the most advanced detachments hold their ground as best they can till supported, other portions, withdrawn further from first contact with the approaching enemy, hurry to the assistance of the advanced detachments; this gives the bulk of the army time to prepare and in consequence of this the outposts must necessarily have a considerable depth. Inasmuch as an army almost always covers its communications in regular warfare and is so disposed as only to run risk of contact with the enemy to its front and partly to its flanks, the outposts are only pushed forward in the shape of a fan which covers a small arc of a circle, or at the most a semicircle.

But in most small wars the duties of outposts are entirely different from this, even when the campaign is against well armed guerillas such as the Boers were in 1901–02. The purpose for which they exist and the method on which they are arranged are different. And in practice, the conditions governing their organization, rarely have much analogy to those which call for the system customary in campaigns between disciplined armies.

Liability to attack from any side.

In small wars forces of relatively insignificant numerical strength move forward into the enemy's country, they are not in a position to prevent their opponents from approaching them in flank and rear, and when at the halt they are often liable to attack from every side. They must, therefore, as security against surprise and molestation, push out a ring of outposts all round them, which absorbs a large number of men. On the other hand the outposts need have no great depth, because in the event of attack a small army can be very rapidly drawn up for battle, and because on that account a long warning of impending advance on the part of the enemy is not so necessary as is usually required in regular warfare. Moreover, inasmuch as it is seldom the case that the adversary is supplied with weapons likely to do much damage at long range, they need not be kept at so great a distance from the main body as would be thought necessary in a modern campaign—it is true, however, that nowadays when we find warriors like the Afridis armed with Lee-Metfords, this must be taken as in some cases referring rather to artillery than to small arm fire. Instead of groups and detachments extending far out ahead of the army on one side, as is the case in the normal outpost system of regular warfare, outposts in small wars usually consist rather of a narrow ring all round the army and at no very great distance from it.

It may be assumed that, in the matter of the drain in men which the outposts create, the relatively small depth called for in small wars counterbalances that necessity of extending them all round the force, a necessity which does not arise in great campaigns. In respect to the normal proportion which the strength of the outposts bears to the strength of the army, the question of outposts does not, therefore, perhaps differ greatly in regular and irregular warfare.

The test of actual experience in operations all over the globe, against opponents most diverse in their methods of fighting, goes to show that outposts, at least by day, need generally only consist of a chain of sentries, found by picquets which need not generally be strong unless the ground be intersected or overgrown with scrub. Supports are seldom required, reserves scarcely ever. The distance of the chain of sentries, or of vedettes when these are used, from the main body need not generally be great. Fighting a well-armed antagonist like the Boers it is, of course, necessary in daylight for the outposts to be some distance off so as to give ample warning of the enemy's approach, and under such conditions it may be desirable for the picquets to be strong enough to hold their own till supported. As is pointed out in "Combined Training," everything depends upon the nature of the enemy, the character of the country, and the strength and composition of the force. The procedure necessarily varies greatly by day from that suitable at night, and in hill warfare a special procedure must frequently be adopted.

Outposts generally close in, and not intended to offer serious resistance.

One point of difference between the system of outposts in regular and in irregular warfare, is that while in the former special units are detailed for the service of security, in the latter each infantry unit in the force generally finds the sentries and picquets to protect its own front. The reason for this is that in small wars the army at any point is generally small, and the outposts are seldom very far out. It would obviously be most inconvenient to encircle the bivouac of

Units to be protected generally find their own outposts.

a brigade with a ring of sentries and picquets all found by one battalion, the picquets being probably only a very short distance from the defensive line. No absolute rule of course exists on this point—in hill warfare it is sometimes found best to detail all the picquets from one or two units, no matter where their posts may be with reference to their own and other corps. But the supply of food and all questions of relief are simplified if each regiment finds its own picquets, and there is moreover less danger of the outposts being fired into from the bivouac at night because each corps knows exactly where its picquets and sentries are posted.

Arrangement of outposts, however, varies according to the nature of the enemy.

Before proceeding further it will be well to point out that, looking at the warriors usually opposed to regular troops in these wars from the point of view of what outposts are best suited to act as a buffer against them, they practically may be divided into two distinct and very different classes :—those who in consequence of their courage or their numbers may be expected to deliver actual attacks upon the troops when these are halted, and those who will merely seek to annoy the force by firing into the bivouacs, by cutting off stragglers, and by any similar device which their ingenuity suggests to them. Of course the antagonists met with in small wars sometimes partake of the characteristics of both classes—the tribesmen with whom Sir B. Blood had to deal in 1897 for instance. In the Malakand campaign the hillmen did not shrink from attempting bold night attacks upon fortified camps, although they were also constantly on the prowl in the darkness by night, sniping, stalking sentries, and worrying the soldiery and followers.

It stands to reason that the service of security must be conducted on different lines according as the enemy belongs to one or the other of these two classes. Foes like the Dervishes or Zulus cannot be kept at a distance by a weakly ring of picquets which merely mask the fire of the troops in case of attack. On the other hand Pathans well supplied with modern firearms or guerillas like the Boers must not be allowed to approach a bivouac close enough to fire into it with telling effect. Picquets several hundred yards from any support would be soon effaced by a rush of fanatics in force. Picquets close in afford no protection whatever against the sniper. There is in fact quite as much difference between the two systems of outposts adopted to meet these two sets of circumstances as there is between either of them and the method employed in ordinary modern warfare. Again, the antagonists whom regular troops are confronted with in small wars, are sometimes supplied with fairly effective artillery, fight in formed units, and incline to the tactics of the European battle-field; obviously neither the form of outposts adapted to the circumstances of the Zulu war, nor the very different form which was called for by the Afridi guerilla methods in Tirah, would afford a satisfactory shield to the troops in a campaign like that against Arabi Pasha in the Wadi Tumilat.

There is one characteristic of irregular warriors which must necessarily greatly influence the organization of a system of outposts designed to frustrate their enterprises—the great rapidity with which they generally move. This point is of especial importance when the campaign is being carried on against antagonists coming under the first heading detailed above, viz., those who boldly attack the troops in masses and who try to overwhelm them by shock tactics. Infantry sentries if advanced far from the main body when the operations are being carried out in enclosed country, against Zulus, Sudanese and warriors of that class cannot get back in case of a sudden rush, and they are of course quite powerless to withstand it. Even vedettes can scarcely get in, as was shown at Tofrek where the spearmen charged through the bush almost at the same pace as the cavalry did, who were retreating before them towards the zeriba. Moreover, in these cases the outposts as they rush back for safety mask the fire of the main body, just as skirmishers do when pushed

Extent to which the rapid movements of irregular warriors influence outposts.

out in advance of a square. So much is this the case that it becomes a question whether infantry outposts are not in the daytime a mistake when fighting against such reckless and agile opponents, in close country. In open country they are scarcely required, and in any case vedettes serve the purpose far better if sufficient cavalry be available.

The system of outposts adopted during the daytime by the force which crossed the desert to Metemma in 1885 is worthy of study; it may be taken as typical of what is required in fairly open country where the enemy belongs to the recklessly charging class. No fixed rules were laid down, but the same general principle was observed throughout. The system adopted by night is detailed on p. 462; in the daytime the arrangements were generally as follows :—

> The force depended very much upon vedettes; the terrain was generally open, which enabled the approach of an enemy to be readily descried; the cavalry force being very small, camel men sometimes assisted. The system usually adopted was that of keeping two men together, who were pushed out from 500 to 1,500 yards according to circumstances; one man could ride back and report if anything unusual occurred. There was no need for picquets as the small column could always fall in for action very rapidly, and the vedettes could be trusted to give sufficient warning.

Difficulties of outposts in jungle and bush and in the hills. As in the Bayuda desert so also generally in fairly open ground, the arrangement of outposts by day seldom gives grounds for much anxiety. It is in the jungle and the bush or in broken ground that regular forces must when at the halt be especially on the look out against surprise. A camp or bivouac of trained soldiery when it is steeped in repose, appeals irresistibly to the militant instincts of the savage and the cut-throat, and it is in rough broken country overgrown with scrub and trees, that such adversaries have the best chance of approaching close, unobserved. Irregular warriors when they think fit move almost noiselessly, and there is great risk of the camp being exposed to a sudden onslaught unless a sharp look-out is kept by the sentries. Operating

in such terrain the regular troops are very unfavourably
situated supposing the enemy to be brave and determined,
and the outposts require to be very vigilant in the performance
of their duty of safe-guarding the force.

The attack on the Tofrek zeriba near Suakin in 1885 illustrates the diffi- Tofrek.
culty of outpost duties under such circumstances. The bush all round the
clearing where the zeriba was being formed, was high and thick. Vedettes
were pushed out into this about half a mile, but they could see little. Nearly
all round the clear space where the parties were at work were small infantry
picquets, about 150 yards to the front. When the Mahdists attacked,
they advanced so rapidly that they came on at the heels of the vedettes
as these galloped in. The infantry picquets had practically no warning
and they had to rush back on the main body as best they could, proving
of no use whatever. The outposts were in fact of very little service, the
enemy had got to close quarters before their warning could be acted upon,
and they moreover masked the fire of the troops to a certain extent.

In such a case as this no system of outposts that could
be devised would give perfect security of the force while defences are being constructed. Picquets cannot check a
fanatical rush ; it is not very clear indeed what purpose they
fulfil, as they in any case mask the fire. The troops must be
ready to protect themselves as soon as the vedettes give notice
of impending attack. Tofrek no doubt represents a somewhat extreme case, since experience shows that races living
in theatres of war overgrown with jungle are not generally
addicted to resolute onslaughts upon well-armed troops.
The operations in Burma, Sierra Leone, Achin, and among
the kloofs of Kaffirland, afford no examples of the enemy
attacking with such ferocity, and it is usually found in
districts where the field of view is much restricted that
the enemy confines his efforts to more desultory attempts
directed against sentries or stragglers. In hill warfare
and bush warfare alike, the arrangements for the service of
security have often to be of a special kind, differing altogether
from what is ordinarily suitable on more open ground.

In regular warfare where outposts consist of picquets, Picquets by
supports, and reserves, it is very generally accepted as a day.

tactical rule that by day the line of the picquets roughly represents the line of defence which the army will take up. The idea is that sentries and picquets fall back on this in case of attack, that reserves close up on it, and that the army moves up to it from the rear. But in small wars, where supports and reserves very rarely form part of the outposts, the question arises what action the picquets are to adopt if the enemy approaches. The very fact that picquets will generally form a mere ring of small detached posts all round the army, seems to point to the desirability of their being very close in if they are to fall back, or to their being strong enough to be self contained and able to hold their own for a considerable time if they are to remain where they are. In open country picquets, far out, are rarely required by day. But in hilly country they sometimes cannot well be dispensed with, otherwise the approach of an enemy would not be observed in time.

Objections to the plan of outposts falling back at once on the main body.

Circumstances may sometimes render it necessary by day for outposts to fall back on the approach of the enemy, This would indeed always be the case with vedettes, or where the hostile tactics take the form of determined onslaughts. It may happen that they are obliged to retreat in face of a hostile attack in force which has not been anticipated, when they have originally been sent out rather to keep marauders at a distance. But it must always be remembered that, if the outposts are pushed out on the understanding that they are to fall back on the main body if attacked in force, the spirit of their instructions militates against their offering a determined resistance even to small hostile detachments. Moreover the very fact of their retreat tends to precipitate the hostile attack, owing to the great encouragement which it gives to the enemy. At the action of Nukumaru in the Maori war the enemy crept up close to the sentries in the high fern and flax and overpowered the picquets by a sudden rush; the picquets were reinforced, but they could not stay the enemy's advance on one side till the guns and cavalry were brought into play, and considerable confusion resulted, attended by some loss. If it is intended that in case of attack the troops shall move out and fight on the line taken up by the picquets, it is essential that preparations should be made with this in view.

In hill warfare a ring of picquets at some considerable distance from the camp or bivouac is almost a necessity. The army will generally be halted in a valley or on level ground commanded by neighbouring hill tops, and unless these hill tops are occupied by parties strong enough to keep at a distance the bands of marauders who attempt to approach and fire down upon the force, serious losses may result. It is just as necessary that the hills should be crowned while the troops are at a halt as it is while they are on the move. The improved armament of Pathan tribesmen of late years has rendered this desultory musketry of theirs most dangerous to troops and transport in their bivouacs, and the increased range of the weapons in their hands has made the pushing out of picquets to considerable distances compulsory. The great disinclination of the enemy to attack well posted parties in the hills makes the position of such picquets fairly secure. But, in the hills as elsewhere, it must always be clearly understood beforehand, exactly what course picquets are to pursue if they are assailed. They must know whether they are to hold their ground until help arrives, or whether they are to fall back. Owing to the difficulty of retreating before an antagonist who can move with such rapidity and whose valour so greatly increases should success crown his efforts at the start, it is obvious that isolated picquets must almost always stop where they are, and that they must therefore be strong enough to hold their own. Picquets of this kind consisting of from a section to a company, can be pushed out a long way from the bivouac, and, if the ground be reasonably favourable and be taken proper advantage of,

Picquets in hill warfare by day.

they will almost entirely secure the troops against sniping and annoyance during the day.

If the enemy is inclined to adopt bold offensive tactics, it will often be very doubtful what course to pursue. If the picquets are close in, the camp is sure to be sniped even if the tribesmen attempt nothing worse. On the other hand if the picquets are pushed too far to the front, it will be impossible to reinforce them quickly enough. As long as the picquets are entrenched and have a satisfactory field of fire enabling them to use their rifles to good purpose, they may be able to hold their own without support, even against a fanatical rush. It is fortunately not generally the case that hill-men have much stomach for a bold offensive by daylight, and outlying picquets can generally be placed a good distance from the force which they are protecting.

Outposts in the bush by day. In bush warfare against ill-armed savages who adhere to guerilla tactics, the question of outposts presents considerable difficulties. Then difficulties are greater by day than by night, because in the darkness the sudden volleys which savages deliver on creeping up within range are very likely to prove harmless, while by day such volleys may do appreciable damage. In terrain of this nature there is rarely any object in thrusting out picquets and sentries to any considerable distance from the bivouac. The enemy cannot open fire except at short range, and, inasmuch as the hostile enterprises will most likely be confined to attempts of isolated parties to slip through the chain of outposts so as to bring this short range fire to bear, it is obviously important that the spaces between sentries and between picquets should be small.

When there are timid antagonists to deal with, quite small picquets will generally suffice. Very often all that is really required under such circumstances is a chain of double sentries, the picquets in rear merely fulfilling the object of supplying the reliefs. Patrolling affords security very effectively in the bush ; if employed freely the strength of the stationary outposts can safely be reduced, and in any case either the picquets or else special patrol parties should occasionally move out some distance in different directions to search the thickets. The enemy will be much less likely to attempt approaching the force if he fears that he may unexpectedly meet with small parties of troops. Of course great care must be taken that the sentries do not fire upon patrols ; when returning towards the line of outposts these should signify their movements by calling out. This of course assumes that, as sometimes occurs, the force is halted actually in thick jungle. Generally speaking a bivouac would be arranged with a clearing round it. In that case the line of outposts would more or less coincide with the far side of the clearing, supposing the belt to be so narrow as to admit of the enemy firing into the troops from the fringe.

In thick bush sentries and picquets should not move about unless specially detailed to do so ; they should keep absolutely still and listen. It is often best for the sentries to kneel or sit down, and they should carefully conceal themselves. Sentries should be double. Savages can crawl through the thickets almost noiselessly ; but if the air be very still and if, as is often the case in the tropics, there is no sound of animal life, their approach may be detected in spite of this. Any talking on the outposts should be strictly forbidden, and their existence should be as far as possible kept concealed from the hostile parties which may be working their way through the undergrowth. If the enemy observes the sentries and picquets without being observed, the result is very likely to be a sudden volley which may cause casualties in the outposts. If, on the other hand, the enemy, creeping forward towards where the sounds of the bivouac announce the troops to be, is unexpectedly fired upon by the outposts the situation is reversed.

In country overgrown with bush or scrub it is essential that even the smallest parties should always post look-out men, for fear of surprise. This is so obvious that it would seem almost unnecessary to touch upon the point, were it not for

Need of even small parties always keeping a look-out in enclosed country.

the numerous instances which have occurred in small wars
of negligence in this respect leading to loss.

Near the Gate Pah during the Maori war, a party sent to destroy some
Indian corn, having no guard and taking no precautions, and being suddenly
attacked by the Maoris, suffered very heavily ; the men were scattered and
quite unprepared. In Achin in 1874 a Dutch picquet, in rear of their position
while a fight was actually going on in front, was surprised in broad daylight ;
it was only saved from destruction by the timely arrival of reinforcements.
On a historic occasion in the Zulu war a mounted party reconnoitring
halted on open ground close to tall grass ; no outlook was kept and it was
surprised with most unfortunate consequences. At the Matabili attack
on the Imbembesi laager, which was situated on an open space with extensive
bush some distance off, a picquet of two troopers had dismounted close to the
thickets ; the two men not being on the alert when the enemy delivered
their onslaught, were surprised, but one of them managed to get away.

Regular troops to a certain extent at a disadvantage in outpost work in small wars.
The fact is that at outpost work in irregular warfare regular
troops are scarcely a match for their adversaries, and their inferiority is especially noticeable when the operations are taking
place in the hills or the bush. The enemies met with in these
wars may not be very formidable in the open against disciplined bodies, but at creeping and crawling about, at
lying low for hours waiting till a sentry they have stalked grows
drowsy, they are more than a match for the most highly-trained
European soldier. The greater be the confidence of the force, the
more certainly will it be victorious on the battle-field, and the
bolder be the scheme of operations, the greater as a rule will be
the chance of decisive success—it is the fundamental principle
of conducting such campaigns. But when it comes to the
minor details which concern the service of security, irregular
warriors must be treated with respect. Here the trained
soldier has to cope with a cunning and wary foe. The teachings
of the barrack square do not tend to place him on the same
level as his opponent in craft and instinctive watchfulness,
he has the advantage in arms but in nothing else. Sentries
must keep their wits about them and must keep their eyes and
ears open. Picquets must be prepared for sudden emer-
gencies, and must act with coolness and self-reliance—it may

be laid down as an invariable rule that arms are never to be piled. The system of outposts differs very materially in small wars from that accepted in modern tactics as the correct one, but the duties are to the full as important and as difficult to carry out in the former case as they are in the latter.

So far, outposts have been considered chiefly from the point of view of their organization by day. The question of out- posts at night must always be a difficult one, and the service of security is almost invariably more exacting in the dark than by daylight. It was stated at the commencement of this chapter that irregular warriors do not show that taste for nocturnal attacks on disciplined troops which it might be supposed they would. But some system of outposts by night is absolutely indispensable in small wars, and to decide what is the system best suited to the circumstances is often a matter on which there may be considerable diversity of opinion. Even if there be little fear of a hostile onslaught in force, it is essential for the well-being of the troops that they shall not be disturbed by marauders. Armies engaged in these irregular operations are moreover generally accompanied by numbers of non-combatant camp followers who have to be protected from harm. Experience proves that, should the enemy pluck up courage and deliver a night attack, there may be very serious confusion, and that there may be considerable danger should the force not have time to occupy its alarm posts before the rush.

The arrangements of outposts by night of course differs considerably according to the nature of the terrain and to the character of the enemy. It is in hill warfare that the security of the troops during the dark hours is especially a source of anxiety owing to the sniping in which mountaineers so generally indulge. But in bush warfare an efficient outpost service at night is also most difficult to devise, unless the force to be protected is camped in an extensive clearing. Even on open ground the stealth and activity of irregular warriors

General remarks on outposts at night.

makes them individually very formidable in the dark when they get to close quarters.

On open ground the arrangement generally adopted is that the army surrounds itself with a ring of small picquets close in, with sentries pushed out a very short distance to the front to give warning of the enemy's approach. If attacked in force the sentries and picquets rush in within the line of defence. This assumes that the plan of a " perimeter camp " is not put in force. In a perimeter camp the combatant part of the force forms a ring all round the impedimenta, horses and so forth, and sleeps there. But if there be a defensive perimeter to the camp—a breastwork or fence of any kind—the sentries would be inside of this even if the troops do not sleep in the perimeter. The object of the picquets is not merely to provide sentries, but also to ensure that a few men shall instantly line the perimeter if the enemy should deliver an attack. The system of outposts adopted at night by the Desert Column in 1885 may be taken as typical of the arrangement which experience has proved to be the best in open country. It was as follows :—

By night the force was generally in some form of a zeriba. The picquets were either in the zeriba or immediately outside of it. Each picquet—the zeriba being usually roughly in form of a square, there was one as a rule to each side, making four altogether—found two or three double sentries. These were posted from 100 to 400 yards to the front, but as a rule not much over 200 yards. A picquet would thus find four or six sentries at a time. Visiting patrols were sent out from the picquet, an officer or non-commissioned officer going out every hour, or oftener if there were any grounds for alarm. It was understood that in case of an attack the sentries fired their rifles and then rushed in on their picquets.

The position occupied at Gubat consisted of a zeriba on the Nile, and of a little fortified village on higher ground about one-third of a mile off from the river. At first a chain of outposts—picquets and sentries—in the form of a horse shoe was tried, including the whole position. But this was found to take up too many men, so later on each position had its own outposts. The plan adopted by the Guards' Camel Regiment who held the little village was very economical of men. There were eight groups out, each of three men, one on sentry and the other two asleep alongside of him ; the officers and non-commissioned officers on outpost duty slept just outside the village.

An arrangement like this seems upon the whole the best suited to these conditions, and it is certainly preferable to a system of picquets far out which are very likely to be overwhelmed. Still, when the outposts are so very close in, there is little time for the force to get under arms in case of a hostile onslaught. At Tellinouet in Algeria the French were very nearly rushed one night, the Arabs being upon the zeriba ere the troops could man the defences ; General Bugeaud himself, bursting out of his tent in scanty apparel and a night-cap, restored order and discipline then soon prevailed, the enemy being beaten off by charges with the bayonet. In the Matabili war of 1894 the plan generally adopted was to have several small picquets making a ring round the laagers ; each picquet found one double sentry, and about 10 such picquets generally sufficed. In the Zulu war, and in the Sudan when zeribas have been formed, the sentries have often been placed actually inside the enclosure at night.

Reference has been made in certain paragraphs to the Boer night attacks in the later stages of the South African war. Outposts at night in the South African War. The best security against them was found to be the perimeter camp, with outposts a little way to the front if there were any koppies or suitable undulations available to put them on. If no such rising ground existed the picquets and sentries were placed either in or very little in advance of the perimeter. The difficulty about this arrangement was that when columns came to consist entirely, or nearly entirely, of mounted troops, there were not men enough available to form a satisfactory perimeter round the extensive area which the horses and transport took up

Owing to the nature of the terrain it was generally possible to place the bivouac in a position where rising ground, close at hand, offered itself for the posting of picquets—the undulations often created a sort of horseshoe in which the bivouac could nestle, which was very favourable for the distribution of outposts in fair proximity to the force. In the closing days of the South African War the enemy was very short of ammunition, and at no time did the Boers attempt sniping at night to any appreciable extent. The compact perimeter camp with its mass of animals and its outposts not far from its outskirts, presented an admirable target to the sniper ; other adversaries as well armed might have made themselves a great nuisance. The clear atmosphere and bright starlight was, however, a great assistance to sentries, who were almost generally doubled. The Boers generally left those columns where vigilance was displayed and where proper precautions were taken, severely alone. In an army containing so large a proportion of irregular troops as that which finally conquered the Boers, outpost duties are certain to be from time to time neglected, and to this is to be mainly attributed the success which so often attended the hostile night attacks.

Distant picquets at night.

Dispensing with outlying picquets has the great advantage that there is no fear of the outposts being fired into by the main body in case of a scare, the danger of which is well illustrated by what occurred on the occasion of a false alarm at Fort Newdigate in the Zulu war.

The ordinary arrangements for security at night were that the camp was surrounded by groups of infantry with supports in rear, small parties of natives being stationed between these groups. At 9 P.M. on the 6th June, the natives forming one of these parties thought they saw a Zulu creeping towards them. They promptly fired three shots, which was the recognized signal that the camp was attacked. The groups on either side of the party ran in on their supports, the officer in charge of which, after firing two volleys, retired with his men into one of the unfinished forts. The troops at once struck tents and manned the wagon laager. The "close" was sounded to bring in the outposts. Then fire was opened from all faces by infantry, and two rounds were also fired by the artillery. Orders were soon issued to cease firing, but five men of the outposts had been wounded by the fire of their friends in withdrawing, when apparently there was no enemy at all.

Objectionable as they are, outlying picquets must often be absolutely indispensable by night—as will be seen further on they have been latterly employed to a very large extent in hill warfare. It will sometimes be the case that certain lines of approach have to be especially watched and that the only means of doing so is to send out a party to act as an outlying picquet a long way from camp. If the enemy is determined and enterprising it will generally be necessary to establish some kind of fortified post for this, because the picquet must be prepared to hold its own against all comers unsupported. Picquets retreating at night towards the camp or bivouac they are supposed to be protecting, are very likely to get a warm reception from their own side. As long as they remain stationary the troops in rear, if previously warned of their exact position, ought not to fire into them; but this cannot possibly be guaranteed once they quit the spot assigned to them.

The great point to remember in detailing a party for an isolated duty such as this, is that it must be capable of offering a stout resistance to any attack to which it may be exposed. It is not a question of how many sentries the picquet has to find —that is a mere question of detail—it is a question of thrusting out a small force far to the front to spend the night isolated and without support. It should be noted that outlying picquets would generally not be relieved till after daylight; movements in the dark are so dangerous that the plan of relieving them at dawn does not answer. It is interesting to note that the Boers depended for protection very largely upon picquets posted on routes and tracks a long way from their laager. They recognized that a force coming to attack them by night must inevitably follow a route till it got close to their position, and their picquets were sometimes several miles from the bivouac of the commando.

It is always desirable to keep up communication between the outlying picquets and the main body in case of any unforeseen move on the part of the latter. The importance of this is illustrated by the following episode :—

One night during the operations in Rhodesia, news reached a camp that there was a party of Matabili some miles off, so a party of 50 hussars was hastily despatched to try and catch them. There was a picquet over some water close by which was not informed. This fired on the hussars, without however doing any damage. The officer in charge of the picquet was found fault with, not for opening fire, but for failing to do any execution.

Ambuscades as outposts.

General Bugeaud recommended small parties under an officer sent out far to the front by night to act as ambuscades and he employed them with some success ; the enemy coming unexpectedly upon them is apt to think he is in contact with the main body, and retires. General Lewal strongly advocates this system in his " Études de Guerre " ; he recommends that the party should not fire but should use the bayonet. The idea is a good one, and, as will be seen further on, it is largely put in force in Indian hill warfare. The enemy, having reconnoitred the camp by day, creeps up intending to surprise it or to molest the sentries, but is suddenly attacked himself when he least anticipates it. In Algeria and Tunis the French occasionally made very happy use of this method of protection, and the Russians have also tried it successfully in Central Asia. Good native troops are very well suited for such work, as they have natural cunning and they delight in stratagems. Indian troops recruited in the hills are particularly good at the game. The great object of outposts at night in these wars is not so much to give warning of impending attack, which is the exception, as to prevent the main body from being worried and disturbed, which is the rule.

General Yusuf's system peculiar.

It is interesting to note that the very able and experienced General Yusuf, who saw probably more service in Algeria than any of the great French leaders reared in that theatre of prolonged warfare, used to push his outposts out far further at night than by day. This is exactly the opposite of the normal practice on ordinary ground. Placed 150 yards from the faces of the square by day they were sometimes sent out as far as 1,000 yards by night. Small parties so far from support of course run risk of annihilation if the enemy comes on in force and really means mischief; but the terrain in Algeria was often such that an enemy coming to attack had to follow certain routes, and picquets a long way out were therefore a great convenience. The arrangement is mentioned as that adopted by a past master of the art of irregular warfare, but its merits seem to be open to question. It is only fair to mention that the Kabyles rarely delivered regular attacks in the darkness, although parties of them sometimes approached the encampments.

The arrangement of outposts by night in bush warfare should be much the same as that described on p. 458 as suitable for such terrain by daylight. Picquets and sentries must, however, be very close in. It is absolutely necessary that a clearing should be made round the force, and if this be 50 yards wide or more, the picquets and sentries should be close to the perimeter of the bivouac—there is no object in pushing them out beyond. A force benighted in thick jungle should keep as still as possible and should have a ring of double sentries close in all round it. *Outposts by night in bush warfare.*

In such country the lighting of fires at night is very objectionable when the enemy can creep up near to the bivouac; a volley aimed at random towards the light is very likely to cause casualties, even if the hostile weapons are only charged with slugs. Isolated picquets sent out for some special purpose should never light fires, or at least should never lie down by fires which they have lit. A neat form of ambuscade has been occasionally used with effect in the bush; a fire is lighted and the party moves off a few yards and watches; hostile marauders crawl up near to the fire, but when they discharge a volley at it under the impression that troops are lying round it, these fall upon them with the bayonet; it is capital if it comes off.

The necessity for out-lying picquets by day in hill warfare when the enemy is armed with modern rifles has been already explained. Till recently it was the practice to withdraw *Outposts by night in hill warfare.*

these picquets from the heights towards nightfall, and to rely upon the close-in system of outposts round the immediate precincts of the camp or bivouac, which is usual in small wars when the terrain is open. But experience has led to a great change being introduced in this respect of late years. The process by which the new system was arrived at is so well explained in Captain Peach's " Handbook of Tactics—Savage Warfare," that the passage deserves to be quoted.

" It is not to be supposed that the full system . . . was reached at once. On the contrary, at first, the practice of picqueting distant heights from which the camp was fired into, was regarded with suspicion. Much more so the idea of leaving the picquets out at night.

" But the losses inflicted in camp by the long range fire of the tribesmen were so severe, that it was found absolutely necessary to deny to the enemy these commanding positions and to occupy them ourselves. Accordingly the distance of day picquets was gradually extended, but the nuisance was, as might be expected, much greater by night than by day. Gradually it was seen that picquets well placed and protected by sangars, easily held their own against all attacks, and that indeed the chief losses occurred in the withdrawing and taking up of the positions.

" It was therefore decided to leave them out all night in spite of the fact that they could neither retire nor be reinforced till daylight. That they would be attacked was only to be expected, and at first the enemy charged in some cases right up to their breastwork, but in no single case did they ever succeed in overpowering a picquet, or indeed in doing any material damage to any one of them, however isolated or distant.

" The relief to the camp was very great, as the enemy used to occupy the position of the day picquets immediately on their withdrawal, and even opened fire on the retiring picquets themselves. As the picquets had to be. retired early in the afternoon owing to the danger of moving in and out of camp in the dark, there were always some hours of daylight in which the whole camp could be overlooked and all our movements observed, and the best positions noted on which to fire after dark. Many of the above evils were manifestly at once removed by the system of night picquets.

" The picquets thus drew a good deal of the enemy's attention that had previously been bestowed on the camp. But it was not to be expected that the system could put a complete stop to all night firing into camp, nor did it ; but it lessened it greatly, and moreover the mere presence of the pic-quets was calculated to raise the apprehensions of the tribesmen, who in-variably disliked having any of our troops behind them. Finally it will be readily understood that the fire from the lower ground often went over the camp, instead of into it as formerly."

This explains the reason for the system of outlying picquets which played so conspicuous a part in the outpost arrangement by night in Tirah. When a column marched into camp, the heights were in the first instance crowned by picquets from the advanced guard; these were relieved if possible by detachments from the main body when this reached the ground, and the new picquets held their ground all night, their posts being rendered as defensible as possible. The picquets may have to be as much as 1,500 yards from the perimeter of the camp, if the enemy is supplied with long range weapons ; they must be well posted, and should if possible occupy commanding positions not overlooked at close range by spurs and crests further out. The sangars should if possible be shoulder high, with large stones here and there round the top to make their outline irregular ; the enemy is apt to creep up very close, and the sentries' heads are distinctly visible if the sky-line of breastworks was not broken. As a general rule the sentries and picquet are close together, if possible within one single sangar. If there are buildings or villages near the camp it is almost always desirable to place picquets in them, otherwise the enemy will occupy them and fire on the troops, and even small hostile parties who shelter themselves in such favourable places for defence may not be easy to turn out.

In addition to the distant outlying picquets, it is often very desirable to have some picquets on lower ground and within 300 to 500 yards of the perimeter of the encampment. But these should not take up their positions till after dark, as a rule, so that the enemy may not know where they are. The stealthy tribesmen like to creep in through the intervals between the outlying picquets on the heights, and to open a desultory fire from points within the ring of outposts ; but if they come suddenly upon an inlying picquet they are liable to receive an unpleasant surprise. Nothing so much disturbs the plans of these skulking marauders as the idea that detached parties of troops may turn up in unexpected places. It must be understood, however, that picquets of this kind are only applicable when the enemy adheres entirely to guerilla tactics ; having no sangars to rely upon and not having the advantage of command which, as has already been mentioned in Chapter XIX, influences hill-men to so singular an extent, they run great risk of being overwhelmed in case of a determined night attack.

The system of distant picquets at night not always adopted in hill warfare.

It is interesting to note that while the system above described was very generally employed in Tirah, the Malakand field force, the operations of which were going on almost simultaneously, adhered to the old system of depending mainly upon picquets close to or actually within the perimeter of the encampment; Sir B. Blood's plan of making neighbouring villagers responsible for any worry at night (mentioned further on on p. 474), tended to relieve his bivouacs from sniping. The tribesmen of the Swat, Bajaour and Mohmund countries were not nearly so well armed as the Afridis ; but, on the other hand, they showed an unusual inclination for resolute night attacks during which the position of picquets far from support might have been very precarious. Operating against many of the Pathan tribes, or against the mountaineers of Sikkim and other hill districts of the Indian borderland, there might be no need for the system of outposts adopted in Tirah. It was the excellent armament of the Afridis and Orukzais, their skill as marksmen and their cunning and military insight, which compelled the expeditionary force to leave out picquets on the hill tops far from support ; adversaries with less formidable weapons and who were worse shots would not require such precautions to be taken against them at night.

In the absence of distant picquets, the system of sentries and picquets close in, or even actually within the lines, should be adopted in hill warfare just as in open country. There are many mountain races scattered over the globe, the Berbers of the Riff country for instance, the Kurds and some of the tribes of Indo-China, with whom regular troops may have to fight. It should be clearly understood that the arrangement of outposts would in most cases be rather that adopted by the Malakand field force, than that which circumstances rendered necessary in Tirah. All hill-men are inclined to snipe into the troops at night, but their fire is generally a nuisance rather than a danger. The great difficulty involved in employing far off picquets by day only, lies in the operations of withdrawing them in the evening and of their re-occupying the posts which have been abandoned over-night on the following morning; there is always risk of loss on both occasions.

Were troops to be engaged in operations against hill-men as well armed and as skilled in the use of rifles as the Afridis, but who also did not hesitate to attempt night attacks in force such as the Swat tribes led by the Mad Mullah tried against the defences of Malakand, it would be a very difficult question to decide whether or not to employ distant picquets. These picquets, unless they are very strong and are posted in well constructed defences, would be in great jeopardy. On the other hand, were there no picquets thrown out a good way from the camp, the troops and transport would certainly suffer very severely from the snipers. In a campaign against such antagonists, the outpost system at night would in fact become a very difficult problem, and it is not certain what would be the best arrangement to adopt. It must be remembered that in a case like this the plan of sending out stalking parties to harass the marauders and snipers who approached the encampment might not be practicable, and that thus, what is perhaps the most effective method of frustrating hostile designs, might be lost to the force.

It is most important that snipers should not be fired at from the camp. Shots aimed at random at the flashes are most unlikely to take effect, and reply to their fire only

Remarks on dealing with snipers at night.

impresses the enemy with the idea that their efforts to cause
anxiety and annoyance have been successful. If ignored
there is always a chance that the hostile marksmen may take
their departure. Unless they are cautioned sentries are very
much inclined to reply to this sniping, and this only encourages
the marauders to persist.

The best method of dealing with the nuisance is to dis-
patch small parties out to stalk the snipers, or else to arrange
ambushes for them such as were mentioned on p. 469. These
stalking parties do not shoot, they trust to the cold steel.
The Gurkha scouts in Tirah revelled in enterprises of this
nature and were most successful in surprising the Afridi
sportsmen. The European soldier is not at his best at this
sort of work, but Gurkhas and Pathans are great adepts at
hoisting nocturnal prowlers with their own petard. Lord
Roberts relates how in the Ambela campaign the tribesmen
used to call out to the Gurkhas and Pathans when on outpost duty, " We do not want you ! Where are the Sikhs and
Europeans ; they are better sport." When the adversary
falls back on this essentially guerilla mode of fighting, he is
very careful of himself ; if he thinks he is being stalked
he will probably sneak off, hoping for a better and safer
opportunity.

Whenever there is a chance of this annoying and sometimes deadly fire into camp at night, care should be taken
that, as far as possible, the position of head-quarters and
similar points of importance be not made obvious to the
enemy by daylight. It is surprising how readily guerillas
detect and note such matters, and what accurate fire they
sometimes deliver at night when they can creep up to
effective range.

Sentries at
night.

Sentry duty on active service is always an anxious and
unpleasant task at night, and is even more so in small wars than
in regular campaigns between disciplined armies. The kind
of performance which the sentry goes through in peace time

is utterly opposed to what he will have to do campaigning against irregular warriors—it is the worst conceivable training for the soldier, although the spectacular effect is good. It is not the custom for regular troops to undertake cutting up of isolated sentries and to prowl about at night in small parties, little would be gained by such manœuvres; but guerillas and Asiatics and savages practice such tactics largely, and are often extremely clever at them. For this reason single sentries are almost always a mistake in irregular warfare at night; double and even treble sentries are a much better arrangement. General Yusuf, in Algeria, used to have posts of four men under a corporal, all required to be on the alert. Sentries should rarely move about. They should stand still or even sit, and should be off the skyline and so placed as not to afford a good target to the enemy. It is always an important point that they should have an easy line of retreat to their picquet. They should, moreover, be close to their picquet; it will rarely be advisable or necessary for them to be more than 50 yards off, and if they can see what is required they should be quite close to it.

Owing to the tendency of sentries to fire at nothing, and to thus cause alarm, some officers go so far as to recommend withdrawing their ammunition. This would hardly seem to be a wise course to adopt, but it must, nevertheless, be impressed on them strongly that they are never to fire without good cause, and only when they feel that they have a reasonable chance of hitting something.

In this kind of warfare it is generally most important Posting of that picquets should be concealed and should shun the sky- picquets at line. A picquet should if possible be to a certain extent an ambuscade. In South Africa it was often arranged that picquets should be on the reverse slope so that an approaching enemy would to them appear on the sky line; this had the advantage that any defences thrown up by the picquet were not observed beforehand by the Boers. There is of course no need for a clear view to the front from a picquet, nor is there much reason for an extensive field of fire.

Defensive
arrangements
in front of
outposts at
night.

Some sort of breastwork in front of picquets, and even of sentries, is often very desirable for fear of their being rushed at night. Sangars can only be arranged if the necessary stones exist. Abbatis will sometimes serve the purpose. The most trifling obstacle may prove to be of use, cover from view being in itself a matter of considerable importance. It is at times a good plan to light a fire some 50 yards or so in front of a post, so as to light up the ground which the enemy must cross ; the light must be far enough out not to expose the post. In hill warfare it is a good plan if the ground fall sharply in front of a post, to collect some large stones ready to roll down if hostile parties try to approach. Wire entanglements are of course admissible if there is time to construct them. In Algeria a system of laying down firearms in advance of the outposts with tight cord stretched across, and attached to, the triggers was tried with success, the discharge giving the alarm. The plans of attaching tins which rattle to a strand of wire was made plentiful use of in South Africa.

Sir B. Blood's
plan of using
villagers as
outposts.

It is deserving of mention that in the frontier campaign of 1897, Sir B. Blood made considerable use of the villagers near camp for outpost work. By threatening to burn their villages—a threat which was carried out once or twice—they were not only deterred from marauding at night themselves, but they also prevented others from marauding. The effect of this system is demonstrated by the fact that in six months there was only one casualty due to sniping, and only one follower was cut up. This plan of using the inhabitants of the country in this fashion might be utilized in other theatres of war.

Service of
security on
the march.

The service of security when on the march necessarily differs considerably in small wars from what is customary for

purposes of protection in great campaigns. In small wars
it generally consists merely of small parties detached as
advanced guard, rear guard, and to either flank. In regular
warfare it is only necessary to push out a detachment in one
direction—that where the enemy is known to be ; but the
detachment will often represent a considerable fraction of the
whole force. It has already been pointed out that in irregular
warfare a force has generally to be prepared for attack from
any side, and it must act accordingly. Buonaparte's army of
experienced campaigners marching from Aboukir to Alexandria was at first completely non-plussed by the tactics of
the Bedouins and Mamelukes hanging about the flanks,
till they learnt that flanking parties were indispensable in
such operations. Charette on more than one occasion fell
upon the flank of the Republican columns on the march in
La Vendée, throwing them into complete confusion. Irregular warriors and guerillas are far more inclined to operate
against the flanks and rear than the front of troops on the
march, therefore the rear guard and the flanking parties
assume a special importance, and the ordinary rules laid
down for the march of an army are scarcely applicable.

The tendency of the enemy in these campaigns, even in
the heat of action, to avoid decisive collision with the front of
the regular troops but to work against their flanks and rear,
has been enlarged upon in former chapters. In Algeria, in,
Morocco, on the Indian frontier, in Ashanti, in Afghanistan
and in Somaliland, this characteristic hostile method of making
war has displayed itself constantly. The Boers adopted the
same tactics as soon as they escaped from the spell thrown over
them by the guns and paraphernalia with which they entered
upon their great contest. It is a favourite and effective plan
when the enemy desires to harass and delay columns of regular
troops on the march. While refraining from engaging the advanced guard he will watch for a favourable opportunity to
attack the advancing force in flanks and rear, and unless

Effect of hostile tendency to operate against flanks and rear.

precautions are taken much confusion may ensue even when the foe does not push his attacks home. Therefore the vedettes and flankers must be pushed as far out as possible consistent with reasonable safety, so that they may give early warning of impending attack and may give notice at once if there be any sign of the enemy. The great speed at which irregular warriors advance must always be kept in mind.

A column on the march is, of course, very badly situated to withstand a flank attack. Its train in small wars is always large relatively to the strength of the force. The route is generally indifferent, and straggling is most difficult to avoid. In a great modern campaign the cavalry screen in front of the advancing army ensures it against unexpected demonstrations against the flanks of its columns. But in small wars an effective cavalry screen is very often out of the question.

Service of security when marching in square.

The square formation dealt with at length in Chapter XVII, to a certain extent obviates the need of advanced guards, flanking parties, or rear guards. Still even in this order of march it is usual to move with a cordon of vedettes all round the force. Baker Pasha and Sir G. Graham in their advances from Trinkitat in 1884 adopted this plan; the objection to vedettes and still more to skirmishers is, as has been explained in Chapter XVII, that they may mask the fire of the square.

Flanking parties and rear guards.

It is in hill and bush warfare that this safeguarding of the flanks and rear is especially necessary—the question of how best to assure this in such terrain has, however, been already dealt with fully in Chapters XIX and XX. On more open ground the army on the march will look especially to its cavalry and mounted infantry or, where such troops exist to its camel corps, to give timely warning of any danger. The more open the country is, the easier it is as a general rule to keep the column compact, and flanking parties and patrols can both move out further and travel faster. In such country the risk of attacks on the flank and rear are much less serious than in a more intersected and broken terrain.

When there are ravines or hills near the line of march, it is indispensable that these should be reconnoitred before the transport passes them and that they should be watched during the time that this is in their vicinity. If, owing to circumstances, flanking parties cannot march parallel to the column, it becomes necessary to send out detachments from the advance guard to hold points from which the flanks can be protected. The detachments so sent out join the rear guard as the force moves past them as in hill warfare; to meet the drain the advance guard must be strengthened sufficiently to ensure that it shall remain able to perform its duties efficiently up to the completion of the march.

Nothing can be more discreditable than for a force of adequate strength, moving in moderately easy country, to be surprised on the march. No amount of precautions will ensure that it shall not be attacked. Flanking parties and rear guards cannot be expected to stem a really formidable hostile advance. But they should at least be able to give sufficient warning of what is impending, to give the bulk of the force time to form up so as to repel the enemy.

In case of a convoy, *i.e.*, a column of non-combatants Convoys. guarded by a comparatively speaking small escort, the main rule to observe is to keep the protecting troops in parties, and to make these parties of sufficient strength to afford every probability that they will be able to make head against such attacks as, from the circumstances of the case, the enemy may be able to deliver. It may be necessary to scatter part of the escort along the column to maintain order and to prevent gaps from occurring; but the rest of the troops should on no account be allowed to straggle. Flankers must generally be detached, and all the ordinary precautions usual on the line of march must be taken. Commanding points should be occupied while the convoy passes them and held till it is clear of them. Artillery in a convoy is very useful because it will often scare away hostile parties who might give a great deal of trouble;

the object of the escort to a convoy is to get its convoy to its destination in safety, and, that being the case, long range rifle or shell fire is fully justified. It may be assumed that a convoy will not be despatched with a weak escort through any district where the enemy is likely to appear in strength, and that the duty of the escort will not go beyond repulsing the onslaughts of small marauding parties.

Importance of keeping columns on the march well closed up.　　Owing to the great rapidity and suddenness with which irregular warriors deliver their assaults, it is most necessary that the force on the march should be kept well closed up. A long straggling column is an invitation to the enemy to attempt a surprise. Its flanks cannot be properly guarded, nor can a proper look-out be maintained. At Shellala in Algeria in 1881 the head of a French column was defeating the Arabs and putting them to flight, at the same time that marauders were delivering their attacks upon its convoy far in rear with such effect that the whole column was obliged to return to Greyville for supplies. It was fortunate at Ahmed Khel that the Afghans attacked the troops leading the advance and not the transport in rear, which formed a long and somewhat straggling column and which might have suffered very severely. General Philippovitch in Bosnia in 1878 always moved with strong detachments on his flanks to repel the guerilla attacks of the people of the country, foreseeing that his column was sure to extend over a great distance. The very rapid movements of the nomad Boers made the protection of the flanks of long columns on the march a service of considerable difficulty in 1901–02. Important as it ever is to avoid undue intervals on the march and to keep the force compact, it is especially so in irregular warfare where raids against the flanks are always probable. The possibility of adequately safeguarding the column against hostile enterprises by flanking detachments will generally depend entirely upon this.

Duties of the advanced guard.　　Tactical works rightly attach great importance to the composition of advanced guards and to the explanation of their duties. An advanced guard is generally in great campaigns supposed to fight, it acts as a spring to break the first shock of contact with the enemy. In small wars, on the contrary, the duty of the advanced guard is rather that of observation, its purpose is to protect the column from ambuscades and surprises. On obtaining touch of hostile bodies, it warns the main body and then retires upon it should the hostile gathering be on a large scale. The great principle of campaigning against irregular warriors is to keep the army concentrated till it is about to strike ; owing to the inevitable exposure of its flanks, there will generally be serious risk of the advance guard being cut off from the main body if thrust out a long distance to the front, and there is rarely much object in pushing it very far ahead. Even on the rare occasions when the enemy can put guns in the field, their fire is not formidable ; the question of giving the main body time to form up out of range of the enemy does not therefore arise to the same extent as in regular warfare. There is not the danger that the force on the march will suddenly be enfiladed by judiciously-placed guns, which is always present in regular warfare unless there is an efficient advanced guard and unless this be well to the front. In irregular warfare the advance guard is rather a feeler than a buffer.

The service of security is a subject of great importance Conclusion. in all classes of warfare, and it is impossible to pay too much attention to ensuring its efficiency in campaigns such as this volume deals with. It is worthy of note that the more desultory the operations of irregular warriors are, the more difficult as a rule is it for regular forces to carry out this service satisfactorily. In campaigns like those against the Sikhs, like the Zulu war, and like the prolonged struggle against the forces of Mahdism, no very heavy strain has generally been thrown upon the detachments pushed out to guard the regular forces by day or by night, whether they were on the march or at the halt. It is in guerilla warfare, whether it be in the Indian hills or in the African bush, whether the theatre of war be Cuba or the Caucasian forests, whether the adversary be the mounted and well armed Boer or the prowling West African savage, that disciplined troops learn by bitter experience the dangers of any inefficiency in the service of security, of any errors of judgment on the part of individuals, or of any carelessness in performance of outposts and similar duties.

CHAPTER XXVII.

NIGHT OPERATIONS.

THE ever-increasing power and precision of artillery and of small arms have of recent years attracted a great deal of attention to night attacks and to night operations generally. It is obvious that the advance of science as regards weapons makes it desirable to deliver attacks under cover of darkness upon opponents who enjoy the advantage of possessing modern arms of precision, provided always that the operation can be carried out without the troops falling into confusion or being overtaken by panic. But the qualification that it is essential that there should be no confusion or risk of panic is an all important one. *Reason why night attacks find so much favour in the present day.*

"Night attacks upon good troops are seldom successful," wrote the Duke of Wellington, appreciating the difficulty of carrying them out owing to the danger of the assaulting columns becoming disordered, and to the impossibility of controlling the operation beyond a certain point. Against bad troops this objection to nocturnal attacks is not in certain respects so great; they are more likely to be dismayed by the onset and to collapse before a more efficient force, even supposing that this has lost its formation. But on the other hand there is not much reason for undertaking such enterprises when the struggle is against a rabble. Usually the object of a night attack is to drive the enemy from his position without incurring the losses which are inevitable in advancing against well armed and efficient troops by day. Undisciplined forces so rarely get full value out of their weapons that their fire is not of much account, and there is in consequence seldom any temptation to incur the perils almost *General question of their advisability in small wars.*

(10830)   2 H inseparable from assaults undertaken under cover of the darkness. Speaking generally, irregular warriors have not arms of great precision, and if they do possess them they do not employ them to good purpose. On the other hand, the risk of confusion is almost as great in attacking savages in the dark as in attacking picked troops. The consequence is that night attacks are seldom deliberately undertaken, and the reason for it is obvious enough.

Upon the whole the drawbacks decidedly outweigh the advantages.
It may happen on occasions that Uzbegs, or Afghans, or Kaffirs, or Red Indians, may take up a position so strong, or may occupy a post so well fitted for obstinate defence, that an assault by day promises little chance of success or that it exposes the troops to losses which their commander is not prepared to risk. Under such circumstances he may elect to make his attack under cover of darkness. Still such cases are rare. At night the Zulu with his assegai or the Pathan with his knife can fully hold his own against the trained soldier with his bayonet. Hand to hand struggles with such foemen are therefore to be avoided unless it can be assured that they will be carried out with the steadiness which an organized body thoroughly under control alone is capable of. Troops purposely engaging in night combats against irregular foes as a rule deliberately abandon their advantage in weapons and, what is almost worse, they may at the same time abandon the cohesion which is the sheet anchor of a disciplined body of soldiers. To engage in nocturnal operations involving the chance of a *melée* in the dark is seldom advisable in irregular warfare. In regular warfare there may be abundant justification for night attacks, but in most small wars there is none.

But this is assuming that the enemy is indifferently armed. It does not of course at all follow that the enemy is worse armed than the regular troops, and supposing that the weapons in the hands of the adversary are modern rifles the argument against night attacks must be based mainly on the difficulty of carrying out military operations in the dark.

When the regular troops are operating against adversaries like the Boers, or against opponents such as would sometimes be met with during a rebellion in a civilized country, the enemy may, even in a small war, be so well armed as to suggest nocturnal attacks on him. Small war is an elastic expression covering a great diversity of conditions. But when the enemy is civilized and well armed, one of the best excuses which can be alleged in justification of nocturnal enterprises in irregular warfare, will generally be found not to apply. It has already been pointed out earlier in this volume that irregular warriors are apt to disregard the necessity of having outposts at night, and on this account a night attack upon such opponents may prove a complete surprise. But the guerillas met with in civil warfare are fully alive to the need of keeping a look-out at all times. Such foemen are not easily caught napping, and they are generally almost as difficult to surprise by a night attack as are regular troops.

The danger of confusion in delivering a night attack is extreme, and confusion at such a moment may lead to a deplorable disaster. The attacking columns may fire into each other. Part of the force told off for the undertaking may lose its way, and may not arrive at the scene of action at all. One body may reach the hostile position prematurely and may have to bear the whole brunt of the battle unaided. If it is difficult for the commander of an attacking force, which is split up into separate detachments, to control the operation by day, it obviously must be far more difficult for him to maintain control at night. Even when the assault is started with a body of troops well in hand, it is by no means easy to keep it in hand in the dark, to detect where a check is occurring, or to prevent dissemination when the encounter is at its height. Then there is also the risk of sudden panic. Napier vividly describes the effect upon some stormers of Badajoz of the sudden cry of " A mine," when there was no mine. The soldier likes to know what he is about, where he

Risk of confusion and panic.

is going to, where his officer is and where the enemy is. The storming of Kars by the Russians in 1877, and the battle of Tel-el-Kebir, which latter, however, did not involve night fighting, have shown that arrangements for an attack can be carried out by night, and that the attack can sometimes be made at night without confusion or misunderstanding. But they do not prove that there is no danger in such operations, nor do they prove that enterprises of this character should be undertaken except under very special circumstances.

The difficulty of controlling troops at night in case of alarm was well shown a night or two after the French army landed at Sidi Feruch in Algeria. About 2 A.M. a loose horse in front of the line startled a sentry, who fired and gave the alarm. The battalions close by seized their muskets and fired wildly into the darkness, and the blaze of musketry soon extended along the whole line ; it lasted for more than a quarter of an hour. Four men were killed and ten wounded in this panic about nothing.

In this case, of course, the French were not attacking, but the principle is the same. Examples of confusion occurring in night attacks made by regular troops in small wars are difficult to find, for the very good reason that such operations are seldom undertaken. It is recognized that they are generally out of place, except on a very small scale and with detachments so restricted in strength that they cannot well fall into disorder. General Reynier's brilliant night attack upon the Turks in 1799 with a considerable force—" Une des plus belles opérations de guerre qu'il soit possible de faire," as Napoleon characterized it—is one of the very few instances of a successful nocturnal attack under these conditions upon an enemy of inferior organization and discipline. Against the remarkable success which attended General Hunter's attack on Gun Hill and that of the Rifle Brigade on Surprise Hill during the defence of Ladysmith, can be set many failures in the same war. Advocates of night attacks like the Russian General Dragomirof base their arguments upon the overwhelming

effect of the fire of modern troops upon an attacking force—
upon conditions which do not exist in most small wars.

At Nui Bop in Tonkin General Négrier attempted a night attack upon
the Chinese position with one of his battalions. But this, getting into difficulties in the broken ground, no actual assault took place ; one company.
however, got close to the hostile lines and separated from the remainder.
It was attacked vigorously by the Chinese at dawn, and its position was for
a time highly critical ; but it stood its ground against very superior numbers
till reinforcements arrived.

The objections to night attacks on a small scale are far Objections
less serious than when the operation is intended as a great less serious in
operation of war like General Reynier's attack referred to attacks on a
above, and Lord Cornwallis's storming of Tippoo's lines scale. very small
before Seringapatam in 1792. The smaller the force is the
less fear is there of mistakes and disorder. " Not only the
risk, but the difficulty of execution as well," says Clausewitz,
" confines night enterprises to small bodies." This perhaps
is too arbitrary a dictum, but it will be found correct if it is
accepted merely as a broad general rule. There is no great
difficulty in moving a small body of troops about in the dark.
Their leader can make his voice heard, can exercise close
superintendence over the whole of his command, and if the
project fails no very great harm will perhaps be done.

It will very rarely be the case that the plan should admit Division of
of the force being split up into detachments moving separately. force at night
An operation of this kind is a delicate one to execute under any a mistake.
circumstances, and any complications are to be deprecated.
Even supposing the different detachments deliver their assault
simultaneously there must be great risk of their firing into each
other by mistake, which will give the alarm to the enemy
even if they do not do each other grave injury. The Boers,
it is true, managed to deliver attacks upon bivouacs at night
from all sides, which shows that it is not impossible to get
several detachments to deliver an assault simultaneously in
the dark; but the operation is so difficult that it will

generally be better not to make the attempt, and to deliver night attacks, when they have to be delivered, on only one side and by a single force.

When a project of this nature is determined upon the most careful preparations must be made. It is impossible to overrate the importance of the orders being detailed, and of the exact course of action to be taken under all circumstances being clearly laid down. A mistake may lead to most serious disaster. Some trifling blunder may be fatal to success. The night assault upon the Kabul Gate of Ghazni in 1839 nearly failed, owing to the retreat being sounded under the impression that the engineers had not succeeded in blowing in the gateway. It is essential that the obstacles likely to be encountered should have been ascertained by previous reconnaissance, otherwise the troops may lose their way. It has been already stated that irregular warriors do not generally anticipate night attacks and that they rarely have an efficient outpost system to guard against them. But this cannot be assumed as a matter of course. The crafty Arabs in Algeria used to leave their fires burning at night when they expected a French attack, and to draw off ; then they would form an ambuscade and would fall upon the assailants as these returned disappointed to their bivouac.

Precautions should be taken that the troops shall recognize each other. In a Spanish guerilla attack upon the French in the Peninsular War their leader made them wear their white shirts over their other clothes. Operating against African savages the white helmet is an excellent distinction, but it is no distinct mark when the troops are fighting Asiatics with their white turbans. These are matters of minor detail perhaps, but nocturnal attacks are risky undertakings and demand the most careful forethought if they are to succeed. Moonlight nights are of course unsuitable, and great care must be taken to prevent the glint of bayonets or of other metal from giving the enemy warning of what is impending.

The general plan of attack and all the details of it which affect subordinate officers should be made known to them; this is far more necessary in the case of nocturnal operations than in the case of attacks by daylight.

Finally it cannot be too much insisted upon that the bayonet is the proper weapon for night attacks. It is diffi-cult enough to preserve fire control by day, but by night even the steadiest troops will fire wildly. The opponents with whom regular forces have to deal can rarely stand a bayonet charge of disciplined troops working together. It must always be remembered that by night the moral effect of the initiative increases enormously; if good troops are so liable to panic in the dark, there can be no question that irregular warriors are apt to be scared and to lose all self-control under like conditions. A handful of trained soldiers well led and acting in concert at night, may terrify a host of Asiatics or savages and may achieve a notable triumph without firing a shot or getting home with the bayonet. It must not be forgotten that by eschewing fire there is far less chance of injuring friends—the danger of this is very great unless a most rigid fire discipline be maintained. Troops belonging to the same side ought not to bayonet each other, they will see their mistake when they come to close quarters ; but they will shoot each other for a certainty if the least disorder occurs in the attack, or if in their excitement they fire wildly. Volleys may sometimes be permissible, but independent firing never— the objection to this latter is of course increased by the intro-duction of the magazine rifle. *The bayonet the weapon for night attacks.*

The following two examples show the efficacy of night attacks on a small scale in warfare of this nature. *Examples of successful night attacks on a small scale.*

During the hostilities in Mexico in 1862, the enemy one night occupied some heights above the town of Orizaba, held by the French. A company was promptly sent to deal with the intruders. This pushed the enemy back for a time, but eventually, when the opposition became too strong, its advance was checked, whereupon the commander ordered the men not to fire so as to conceal his weakness. After waiting for some time another company arrived, and the French then charged and drove off the Mexicans. The French, who numbered only 140 all told, placed no less than 250 of the enemy *hors de combat* and they took 200 prisoners.

Morosi's Mountain in Basutoland stands at an elbow of the Orange River with three almost precipitous sides. When the night attack was made on it in 1879, it was strongly fortified on the remaining side. Morosi's men were good shots, and the place was most formidable for a small force to assault which was weak in artillery. It had been decided to make the venture about midnight. A fissure had been discovered on one of the perpendicular sides, and by this a storming party with ladders managed to reach the top, the enemy in the breastworks on the open side being in the meantime kept occupied by artillery fire till the last moment. The result was a complete surprise, the storming party reached the top of the cleft before the Basutos could assemble in large numbers to oppose it, and the formidable stronghold, which had baffled two previous attacks, was captured with very little loss.

It should be noted that in both these cases the ground was fairly well known. This was also the case at Gun Hill and Surprise Hill. It makes a great difference if the position to be attacked has been under observation for some time, or has been carefully reconnoitred beforehand.

Night marches. When especially advantageous.

Although it may be said that upon the whole night attacks are seldom advisable in small wars, the same rule does not hold good with regard to night marches, even when the enemy is close at hand. Night marches, made almost in the presence of the enemy with a view to attack at early dawn, have on many occasions in recent campaigns led to brilliant successes. It was indeed pointed out in Chapter XII that the early morning is generally the best time to deliver an assault, and this almost necessarily involves a previous movement under cover of darkness. Most of the good captures of Boers made in the closing days of the late South African war, before the institution of the drives, were brought about by attacks in the early morning following on night marches sometimes of great length. The veld presented few serious difficulties to columns following a track at night. The darkness in that region is seldom so great that a path cannot be seen and obstacles avoided. There have been

few campaigns where night operations have played so great
a part, even if actual night attacks were seldom attempted
by our side.

One of the great dangers of a night march in proximity Risk of move-
to the enemy is that, even if the hostile outpost and patrol ment being detected by
arrangements are defective, the movement may de disclosed some accident.
by some accident for which the troops are no wise responsible.
Colonel Maurice, referring to the case of Tel-el-Kebir, makes the
following observations: " It has happened in the past that
some night attacks have failed in consequence of the attacking
troops meeting on their route cattle, geese, or other animals,
which have aroused the defenders, or roused inhabitants who
have given warning to the enemy. By a curiously bad logical
deduction a conclusion has been sometimes drawn from this
fact that therefore all night attacks are chiefly a matter of
chance. An examination of the circumstances and of the orders
for the night march upon Tel-el-Kebir will show that an
altogether different conclusion may be drawn, viz., that the
possibility of meeting dogs, cattle, geese, &c., is an element that
has to be taken into account by a commander in arranging his
plans for a night march. It was almost as certain that on
the night of the 12th September the infantry and cavalry
who moved to the north of the canal along the desert would
not meet with cattle, geese, or dogs as that they would not
meet with whales. It was absolutely certain that the Indian
Brigade which moved through the wady to the south of the
canal would meet with animals of all sorts before reaching
the lines ; therefore the hour of the march of the Indian
brigade was fixed accordingly." A commander would not
however always be so well acquainted with the ground about
to be traversed as was the case on this occasion. Horses insist
on neighing. In the countries where small wars are carried out
there is generally some vexatious form of bird which emits
weird noises when startled out of its repose. There is in fact
nearly always a certain element of chance in a night

march intended to bring a force into position to attack at dawn.

Enemy keeps a bad look-out at night.   The enemy seldom keeps any look-out at .night except quite close in to the bivouac or to the locality occupied, and would not,.as a rule, lie in wait for the troops on the march unless news of the contemplated movement had somehow leaked out.   The Boers, as was pointed out on p. 465, used to have picquets a long way out from their laager, but it was not their practice to form ambuscades at night.   Some cases, no doubt, have occurred of attacks by irregular warriors— upon marching columns being made at night the Persian attack upon Sir J. Outram's force the night before the fight at Khushab, and the disastrous episode of the attempted relief of Arrah from Dinapore, referred to on p. 215, may be cited as examples.   But the experience of many campaigns tends to show that, except in guerilla warfare in a civilized country, irregular adversaries hesitate to interfere with regular troops during a night march and are not generally prepared for such a move.   They do not seem to anticipate nocturnal operations even when the opposing forces are in close proximity.   At any rate they generally do not interfere with the march.

The case of Sir H. Stewart's advance from Abu Klea towards the Nile is a remarkable example of this.   The Mahdists must have foreseen that such an advance was certain to take place, either by day or by night.   Owing to the column passing through a considerable patch of bush in the dark, it got into great confusion when not far from Metemma where the enemy was collected in force.   As the march was very slow it is almost certain that the Arabs must have become aware of it while it was in progress.   But no attempt was made to meet it till dawn.   Then crowds of Mahdists came swarming up from the river to oppose the British advance.   An attack upon the column when disordered in the bush would have had most disastrous consequences, and it is strange that fanatics, who attacked with such desperation by daylight, should have made no attempt to molest the troops at night when they could have depended upon getting to close quarters. But, as has been pointed out earlier in the chapter, opponents of this nature seem to shirk night attacks, and to dread making them.

Another notable instance of this in a campaign against an enemy very different from the savage followers of the Mahdi, is afforded by Sir G. Colley's safe withdrawal from the scene of his defeat at the Ingogo. When evening closed in on the engagement, the enemy was grouped practically all round the British force. Nevertheless Sir G. Colley succeeded during the night in withdrawing unopposed out of the dangerous position in which they found themselves, not only his infantry but also his guns. The Boers, when morning broke found only the killed and wounded left, and they were not a little disconcerted to find their opponents gone. They did not commit such blunders two decades later.

When General Oughterlony was advancing on Katmandu in 1816, all the passes generally used over the first range of hills above the Terai were held by the Gurkhas, and reconnaissances showed the defences to be most formidable. A route was however discovered which the enemy had neglected, by which the hostile positions could be turned. This route passed through a deep, narrow ravine for some miles, and it offered extraordinary difficulties to a march in the darkness. But one brigade starting after dark one night advanced by it, and reached the crest of the hill unopposed about dawn after an arduous march through most difficult country. The Gurkhas were taken completely aback by this remarkable exploit, and they abandoned all their first positions.

The withdrawal of the picquets from the Guru Mountain under cover of darkness during the Ambela campaign is a good example of a retrograde movement of a part of a force in the darkness, unobserved by a particularly vigilant enemy.

Sir R. Buller's retirement from Abu Klea, already referred to on p. 245, is a notable instance of a force of regulars withdrawing by night from a position in presence of the enemy without their movement being discovered.

In close presence of an enemy who does not appreciate the need of a proper system of outposts, and who does not recognise that skilfully carried out night marches on the part of the regular forces may entirely alter the strategical and tactical situation, movements under cover of the darkness may achieve most decisive results. But it must never be forgotten that they are exhausting to the troops and transport, and that there is great risk of serious confusion occurring even with the best arrangements if the terrain be unfavourable —some instances of this occurred on a small scale during the Indian frontier campaigns of 1897. In the bush such movements are frequently quite impracticable, and they will always prove difficult to execute ; night marches if attempted in a theatre of war of this nature must be carried out with great

Risk of confusion on the march.

deliberation, the head of the column halting every few minutes to ensure that the column may remain compact. The practice which to a certain extent prevails in the East of marching by night in very hot weather has almost as many opponents as it has advocates, and a succession of such night marches tends to demoralise a force. Nocturnal movements are upon the whole adapted rather for isolated undertakings than for constant practice. But under certain conditions and when fighting guerillas they may be unavoidable. They were absolutely unavoidable in the later stages of the South African war and it was mainly by constant night work that the nomad Boer commandos were gradually hunted down and stamped out. Many examples could of course be given of columns falling into confusion in the darkness, but the following are perhaps particularly noteworthy :—

Early in 1864, during the operations in Bhutan, it was found necessary by the garrison of Dewangniri to evacuate the post by night. The arrangements for retreat seem to have been well enough thought out, but the main column somehow lost its way, and a panic ensued. The guns had to be abandoned and the force reached its destination in a state of demoralization.

The confusion into which this column fell during its night march from Abu Klea to Metemma upset Sir H. Stewart's plan of reaching the Nile at daylight, and it was in consequence the cause of serious loss to the force.

During the night march towards Adowa, two of the Italian brigades which were intended to advance by separate routes, got intermingled and some delay was caused. The *contretemps* does not, however, appear to have contributed much to bring about the disaster of the following day.

The case of Nicholson's Neck naturally comes to mind. On that occasion the ground was no doubt difficult, but it was typical of what may ordinarily be expected in irregular warfare.

Importance of the troops being well disciplined.

There is one point which must not be overlooked when considering night marches in small wars. It is very often the case that the troops employed are not of the highest class as regards training and discipline. Under no conditions does the difference between good troops, and troops which cannot be classed as better than indifferent, become more apparent than on·a night march. In South Africa there was often a considerable difference even between one regular battalion and another on the march in the darkness, and irregular troops and levies are always very difficult to keep in hand at night. Few officers who took part in those nights of marching on the veld in 1901–02, will not remember instances of matches being lighted, of gaps in the column, of men straggling and being left behind, of *contretemps* arising from lack of discipline, which were only such as might be expected in an army made up so largely of irregular corps, but which were none the less dangerous on that account. In weighing the pros and cons before attempting some nocturnal operation in wars of this class, the discipline and steadiness of the troops to be employed must be taken into account.

Instructions with regard to night marches are to be found in various military works and need not be given here ; the necessity for previous reconnaissance of route, for guides, for especial precautions at points where part of the column might get off the line, &c., of course holds good just as much in irregular warfare as in other campaigns. Looking at such operations from the point of view of small wars, the main thing to be said in their favour is that in such campaigns columns on the march are seldom attacked at night, and that night movements are particularly likely to surprise and perplex the enemy. On the other hand, they generally involve especial risk of confusion in the force owing to the difficulty of moving through roadless country, and for the same reason they are especially likely to exhaust the powers of man and beast. To actually deliver an attack upon irregular warriors in the dark will seldom be advisable, because, even if the want of discipline and cohesion in the hostile ranks gives promise that their resistance in a nocturnal combat will not be very obstinate, the regular troops by fighting in the dark sacrifice their superiority in weapons. In a word, night operations in irregular warfare are not to be lightly entered upon, although circumstances will sometimes justify and even compel their adoption, and although many examples can be quoted where they have been crowned with brilliant success.

General conclusion as to night operations.

That night attacks by irregular warriors are upon the
whole unusual, has been pointed out in a former chapter, but
numerous instances were at the same time given of enterprises
of this nature being attempted by the enemy in many parts
of the world, and it is always necessary to be well prepared for
them. The first safe-guard against any hostile assaults in
the dark is of course to be found in an efficient system of
outposts. But the advantages of having these close in to the
force under normal conditions were noted in the chapter on
the service of security, and it will often be the case that
the time between the first alarm being given and the actual
onslaught of the foe upon the encampment, is a matter of
only a few moments.

When the picquets are in close proximity to the bivouac
or camp it is essential, if the enemy be at hand, that the
troops should have their arms beside them, that guns should
be in action, that some of the horses should be saddled up, and
that the force should be in a position to assume fighting formation at a moment's notice. It is usual indeed for the bulk of
the combatant portions of the force to sleep on the perimeter
of the camp. All ranks must be ready to spring into their
places at once without confusion. It is very important
that no firing should take place when the alarm is given
except by order of officers, otherwise the picquets may be
shot down, ammunition may be wasted, and the noise is sure
to add to the excitement and bustle of a moment when good
order is essential. It would rarely be the case that a force
so situated has not some form of defence work round it, even
if this be of a very slight character; but, whether such arrangements exist or not, the troops should bivouac at their fighting
posts. In South Africa one of the great difficulties during a
night attack was found to be the prevention of a stampede
of the horses, of which there were generally large numbers in
the bivouac; horses are especially likely to take fright at
night when firing suddenly breaks out, and a considerable

portion of the fighting force may have to remain with them
to be ready for eventualities.

When there is any chance of a night attack, it is of great Lighting up
the ground.
advantage to have some means of lighting up the ground to
the front of the troops. Star shell are excellent, but their
illuminating power is transient, and the artillery must husband
its small supply of a form of ammunition which is not designed for man-killing purposes. If it be possible to arrange
bonfires a little way to the front, to be lighted in case of
attack, these may prove invaluable ; but care must be taken
not to ignite them in case of a mere false alarm as their glare
will enable the enemy to fire into the encampment from a
distance and to do damage. It must be remembered that
lighting up the battle-field will benefit that side which has the
advantage in the matter of armament, therefore fires, even
supposing they are within the defenders' lines, may aid them
more than they aid the enemy should an actual assault be
delivered.

This was the case at Rorke's Drift. The glare of the burning buildings enabled the hard-pressed defenders to use their rifles with most telling
effect upon the swarms of Zulus surging around the epaulments.

After the first two nights of the tribal attacks on the Malakand post in
1897, bonfires were arranged for, to be ignited in case of assault. They
were placed some distance to the front of the line of defence and proved
most efficacious.

It is a good plan if night attacks be at all probable, to Artillery and
machine guns
in case of
night attacks.
train guns and machine guns by daylight upon points where
the enemy may be expected to mass, or from which assault is
to be anticipated. This was done at the defence of Chakdara in 1897 with excellent results. Experiments have
shown that rifles on fixed rests can be similarly trained. It
is also advisable, although artillery officers do not always
like the arrangement, to fill the intervals between the guns
if these be in battery on the perimeter of the encampment
with a few infantry men. Cases have occurred where the

enemy has crept in between the guns by night. This would of course not be necessary if there were some satisfactory form of breastwork in front of the guns.

The question of reserves.

In anticipation of a night attack in this class of warfare, it is generally very important to have a considerable proportion of the whole force told off to act as a reserve—more so than by daylight. In the darkness the blow falls so suddenly, and there is such a probability of isolated strokes being delivered by the enemy on different points, that it is better to sacrifice a certain amount of fire along the whole front, than to run the slightest risk of the confusion and danger which must arise if the line be penetrated by a rush at one spot and if troops be not available to at once fill up the gap. Whether there should be only a central reserve, or whether there should be local reserves, or whether there should be both, depends to a certain extent upon circumstances. With a small compact force one central reserve under the immediate orders of the commander may be the best arrangement. If the encampment covers any extensive area it will almost always be better to have several local reserves. In all positions certain points are especially exposed or especially important, and detachments in reserve should generally be placed near these.

Need of strict fire discipline.

The importance of maintaining a strict fire discipline in case of a night attack or night alarm can hardly be over-rated. The case of Sidi Feruch, quoted on p. 484, illustrates the tendency of even well disciplined troops to open a wild fire at night. In the chapter on Infantry Tactics the heavy expenditure of rifle ammunition during the succession of night attacks on the Malakand post, and the danger which arose at one time of ammunition actually falling short, have been referred to. There is of course generally less likelihood of ammunition failing a force in a defensive position than when it is attacking, because the available supply will, as a rule, be larger. But it is most important that the enemy should suffer heavy loss for his temerity in attempting a nocturnal assault, and to bring this about the musketry must be under control. Hostile enterprises of this nature are undesirable, and if irregular warriors are once beaten off with great slaughter there is a reasonable probability that they will not make such an attempt again. Should there be any outlying picquets, careful supervision will be necessary to prevent the troops from firing in their direction, however thoroughly they may have been previously instructed as regards the positions of the imperilled detachments.

It was laid down in Chapter XXI that, should the enemy force his way into a position held by regular troops, the best and safest method of expelling the intruders is a bayonet charge, and it has been indicated in an earlier paragraph of this chapter that when troops deliver night attacks upon irregular antagonists the bayonet is the proper weapon to use. Should any fractions of the hostile force which deliver a nocturnal assault upon disciplined troops in one of these campaigns, gain a footing within the position, there is nothing like the bayonet. In the confusion which will occur in such a case any firing may be most disastrous. The signal success which attended the use of cold steel under these trying circumstances on the occasion of the first night attack on the Malakand position in 1897 has been already referred to on p. 400. It may be accepted as a rule that this will invariably be the right way of dealing with savage opponents who have got within the lines in the darkness. Once the intruders are expelled it might be best to complete their discomfiture by musketry fire, but that would of course depend very much on the circumstances at the moment.

Bayonet to be used if the enemy penetrates into the lines.

It is quite impossible to lay down rules with regard to counter-attacks in case of a nocturnal assault by irregular warriors. Offensive returns of this kind when attempted on a small scale have the disadvantage that the troops making them are apt to be fired into by their own side ; confusion and

Counter-attacks in case of a night attack by the enemy.

doubt is an almost inevitable consequence of any sudden movement in the dark. On the other hand, if the enemy establishes himself close to the defensive line and renders the position really critical, the only thing to be done will often be to drive him off with a bayonet charge. But in any case it will generally be advisable to prepare for a vigorous counter-attack at the first break of dawn, when there is a great probability that the assailants will be beginning to make off. After the second night attack on the Malakand defences, a determined advance made by part of the 24th Panjab Infantry as soon as it was light enough to make the movement, proved most effective ; the enemy was hunted for a long distance over the hills and suffered such heavy loss that the tribesmen drew off before dawn on succeeding nights, dreading a repetition of it.

Conclusion.

Reference to this incident forms a satisfactory close to this volume. It is an example of the advantages of the offensive when dealing with irregular warriors. The fundamental principle of carrying out operations against antagonists of this class is to assume the initiative whenever it is possible to do so, and to maintain it as long as it is practicable to maintain it. The endeavour of the preceding pages has been to give this principle prominence even when dealing with defensive formations. The commander who takes the field against guerillas, or savages, or hill-men must make up his mind to strike hard, to move rapidly in spite of the impedimenta which encumber him, to pursue relentlessly after a victory has been won and to seize the first possible moment for a counter-stroke should he meet with reverse.

INDEX.

2 ɪ 2

Amsal. Attack on, without artillery preparation at battle of Wad Ras, 155. Flight of Moors when, was captured, 190.

Angoni Zulus. Operations against, 141.

Anglo-Egyptian. Advance on Red Sea littoral at one time always insured a hostile gathering, 40. Value of efficient intelligence department shown by successful, advance from Wady Halfa to Omdurman, 50. Khalifa not prepared for rapid advance of, forces to Omdurman, 89. Happy results for. army of bombardment of Omdurman, 154. Chance of decisive victory obtained by army by reconnaissance before Atbara, 235.

Annam. French campaign in, of 1861, 38. Experience of French in, 38.

Antananarivo. Duchesne eventually made short work of Hovas. before, 45. Transport column with army detailed to capture, 60. Distance from coast to, 116. Final advance to, as a flying column, 120. At attack on, turning force turned two captured guns upon enemy, 157. Attack on Amboluminas position during final advance on, 167. Official account of expedition to, dwells on effect of volleys, 395. Ammunition nearly gave out when rear guard was severely pressed near, 397.

Arab, Arabs, of the Barbary States, 32. Effect of the, razzias in Algeria, 129. Stout resistance of, at Kirbekan, 167. Attack of, upon baggage at Tokar, 204. Barbarossa drew, out of their camp at Millel by a feint, 230. Proverb as to stratagem and war, 232. Successful ambuscade of, by French at Muzaia, 233. Failure of an attempt by French to surprise, 242. Deception of the, by General Philebert, 245. Skill of the, of Algeria at forays, 245. The, ambuscaded at Takdempt, 251. French cavalry ambuscaded by, 253. The, at Shekan, 254. Rear face of a square broken by, the day before Shekan, 262. The, attack at Tofrek, 283. 21st Lancers did not completely break up, mass by their charge, 419. The, reached the zeriba at Tellinouet before the troops could man the defences, 463. The, in Algeria, used to leave fires burning and slip off before an expected night attack by French, 486. The, must have been aware that Sir H. Stewart was making his night march towards the Nile, 490.

Arabi. Troops of, 30. Difference of forces of, from Zulus and Matabili, 30. First heard of move from Alexandria and Ismailia when in Ceylon, 55. Had Sir G. Wolseley not made a direct attack on Tel-el-Kebir, would have avoided an engagement, 92.

Arcot. An example of effect of boldness and vigour, 78.

Argandhab. Cavalry sent to make a wide detour beyond, at Kandahar, 173.

Arhanga Pass. Transport out at night on the, 314. Action of Lance-corporal Simpson on baggage guard in the, 319, 320. Afridis caught in a ravine near the, 323.

Armament. When regulars operate against enemy of inferior, this constitutes a small war, 22. Tactics mainly a question of, 23. Effect of improved, of enemy on small wars, 24. Of enemy to be considered, 29. Excellence of, overburdens regulars with non-combatant services, 85. Advantage in, gives regulars upper hand in battle, 90. How improvement in, of hill-men has affected the distance to which flanking picquets are sent out, 297, 298.

Arms. Relative progress of, of regulars and of enemy, 23. Of enemy sometimes efficient, 23. Of enemy often not well known, 43. Enemy when defeated conceals, 159.

Arnold, Major. Victory of, at Bida, 269.

Arogee. Battle of, as an example of enemy being unintentionally drawn out of position by hope of plunder, 233. Hill-men may be trapped as the Abyssinians were at, 324.

Arrah, The relief of, by Major Eyre, 82. Attempt to relieve, from Dinapore, 215.

2 K

frequent frontal attempts on enemy's position served to attract his attention entirely to that point, 236.

Kailua. Action of, as an example of active defence, 203. French fire discipline at, 395.

Kali Nuddi. Action of, as example of cavalry falling on enemy in retreat, 170.

Kalpi. Important influence exercised by camel corps at, 426.

Kalumpit. Unexpected presence of guns with Filipinos at, 48.

Kambula. A defensive battle, 76. Zlobani mountain some miles east of, 183. The battle of, as a typical example of a successful feint, 229, 230. Mounted rifles at, armed themselves with assegais in pursuit, 414.

Kandahar. Advance of Ayoub Khan on, 48. Sir F. Roberts's supply train on march to, 60. Marri country flanked route to, 61. Investment of, by Ayoub Khan, 74. In Afghan wars both Kabul and, always aimed at, 108. In Sir F. Roberts's march to, communications absolutely abandoned, 121. Capture of enemy's guns at, 155. Containing force at, 163. Major White's action at, 172. After battle of, enemy concealed arms and pretended to be peaceful, 209. Reconnaissance the day before battle of, had effect of keeping Afghans in their position, 235. Night attack in 1841 on one of the gates of, 444.

Kaptrgala. Disaster to, infantry, 333.

Karina. Heavy expenditure of ammunition owing to precautionary volleys near, 372.

Karmana. Reconnaissance up the, defile in the Chamkani country, 333.

Kars. The storming of, at night by the Russians, 484.

Kassala. Capture of, by Italians an excellent example of surprise at dawn, 240.

Kassassin. Vital importance of securing, lock, 67. Attack of Egyptians on British at, 106. Attack of Egyptian army on British lines, at, early in the morning, 447.

Katmandu. Remarkable night march of a brigade round Gurkha flank during General Oughterlony's advance on, 491.

Kaye. Account of an ambuscade under Dennie near Jellalabad by, 250.

Kelly, Col. Advance of, from Gilgit to Chitral, 94. Advance of, for relief of Chitral as example of manœuvring enemy out of position, 94. Had the column of, failed to reach Chitral doubtful if force from south would have been in time, 112. Example of unintentional feint during march of, force to Chitral, 233, 234.

Ketchwayo. Armies of, 28. Although, impis were well organized, invasion of Zululand at three points prevented him from invading Natal, 111.

Khaibar. Number of troops on, line in 1880, 117. Consequence of failing to crown the heights in 1841 during the retirement through the, 293. General Pollock's forcing of the entrance of the, as an example of seizing the heights in forcing a defile, 294. Temporary loss of two guns owing to McCaskill's brigade being benighted in the, 316.

Khalifa. Mustered more men for his last stand at Omdurman than the intelligence department expected, 50. Contemplated night attack before Omdurman, 56. Not prepared for Sir H. Kitchener's rapid advance, 89. Bombardment caused, army to quit Omdurman, 154. Reconnaissance before Atbara had effect of encouraging forces of, to hold their ground, 235. The, appears to have contemplated attacking Sir H. Kitchener at night, 444.

Khan Band. Forcing of the, defile as an example of unpreparedness of enemy for flank attack, 162.

Khanki Valley. The, with reference to the actions at Dargai, 303.

Khartum. Relief of, objective of Nile Expedition, 42. Critical situation at, obliged column to cross the desert, 69. Result of fall of, 69. Not difficulty of getting troops themselves up to, in time but of supplying them which caused failure of relief expedition, 70.

Castellijos, 251. Skill of, at ambuscades, 253. Movements of against flanks and rear of Spaniards at Wad Ras, 257. Small results of Moorish horse against infantry in campaign of, against Spain, 388. The, as well armed as the Spanish, 398. The, fire from horseback, 411.

Moral effect. Importance of, 37. Napoleon on, in war, 72. Advancing in several columns has great, 109. Of capturing banners, 158. In small wars, of almost more importance than material gain, 158. Of attacking in several columns, 177. Of artillery fire, 429.

Morocco. Spanish invasion of, in 1859, 21. In Spanish campaign against, enemy used to disappear after everv fight, 88. Spanish forces drawn into purposeless engagements in, 101. Effect of exposure of communications during Spanish invasion of. 117. Value of bayonet found by Spanish troops in, 399. On the defensive in, troops must bo ready for attacks at close quarters, 439. No cases of hostile night attacks in Spanish war against, 444. Tendency of enemy to work against flanks and rear shown in, 475.

Morosi's mountain. The night attack upon, 488.

Mount Prospect. Hostile demonstrations against communications of Sir G. Colley's force at, 117.

" Mountain and Savage Warfare." Quotation from, as to strength of picquets in hill warfare, 297. Quotation from, as to crossing dangerous zones, 385.

Mountain artillery. Mobility of, sometimes overlooked when attacking in hill warfare, 307. Has little effect on Pathan villages, 308. On sands of Egypt the, possessed mobility equal to field artillery, 438. See also **Artillery.**

Mountain guns. See **Mountain artillery.**

Mounted infantry, rifles. Value of, at beginning of a retreat, 217. Value of, for feints, 232. Use of, for surprises by day, 241. Compared to cavalry, 422. The distinction between, and cavalry, 422, 423. Charged with fixed bayonets in Rhodesia, 423. Value of, in hills north of the Panjab, 423. Tactics of, 423. Similarity of camel corps to, 425.

Mounted men, troops. On the prairie and steppes guerilla warfare confined to, 127. Need of, for guerilla warfare on the prairies, 127. If live stock is to be raided, an essential, 136. Chiefly used in Rhodesia, 138. Nature of, varies in different campaigns, 401. Cavalry acting against, of the enemy, 410, 411. Tendency of hostile, to fire from horseback, 411. See also **Cavalry.**

Mpseni. Operations of 1898 in, country, 141.

Mukur. Action of, as an example of cavalry falling into ambush, 405.

Multan. Suruj Kund near, 162.

Mutiny, The. In, enemy made first move, 71. Rebels for a time secured initiative in, 74. Examples of overawing the enemy by dash and audacity taken from the, 81, 82. Remarkable for readiness with which enemy accepted battle, 104. During, Delhi and Lucknow formed two distinct gathering points of rebels, 108. Assistance afforded by artillery to infantry in, 154. Signal services of horse artillery and cavalry in, in flank attacks, 170. Successes always followed up in, 171. Cavalry operations against hostile flanks and rear in, 174. In, guns handled with great boldness, 174. Want of cavalry for pursuit in early days of, 208. Great results achieved in, largely due to extraordinary efforts to make each victory as complete as possible, 209. Happy combination of horse artillery and cavalry in pursuit in the, 211. Want of cavalry much felt in early stages of the, 402. Achievements of cavalry in the, owing to the enemy being organized, 405.

Printed in the United States
65313LVS00002B/532-543

9 780803 263666